WHEN THE KITE BUILDS...
WHY and HOW we restored Red Kites across Britain

Dr Mike Pienkowski
(Chairman of the Red Kite Project Team from its establishment to 1995)

"When the Kite builds, look to lesser linen"
A Winters Tale, Act 4 Scene 3. William Shakespeare

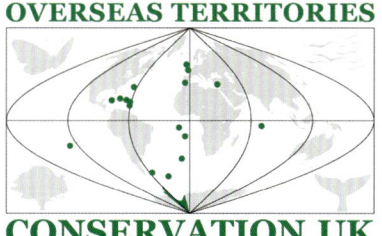

Published 2023 by UK Overseas Territories Conservation Forum
102 Broadway, Peterborough PE1 4DG, UK
https://www.ukotcf.org.uk

Visit our bookshop
www.ukotcf.org.uk/kite-book/

A proportion of the income from each book sold goes towards UKOTCF's charitable conservation activities.

Copyright © Dr Michael W. Pienkowski (2023)
Copyright © of the photographs and illustrations remains with the photographers and illustrators

All rights reserved. No part of this publication may be reproduced, stored in a retrieval system or transmitted, in any form or by any means electronic, mechanical, photocopying, recording or otherwise, without the prior permission of the publishers.

First published 2023.

British-Library-in-Publication Data
A catalogue record for this book is available from the British Library.

ISBN 978-1-911097-05-1

Layout by NatureBureau

Printed and bound in the UK by Gomer Press Ltd

Front cover: Red Kite of the English re-established population turns hard left after spotting prey [Dr Mike Pienkowski]
Back cover: Kite chick in basket being lowered from nest in Spain [MP]; **Author puts kite chick into box for flying to UK** [Dr Eric Bignal]; **Fully grown young kites just before release; Kite flies free from rearing cage** [MP]

Contents

viii	**Acknowledgements**
xii	**Foreword**
1	**1. Introduction**
1	The programme and why
5	Birds of prey and the British heritage
7	Positive initiatives – are they worthwhile?
9	Why projects happen
10	**2. History**
10	The Middle Ages
11	Tudor and Stewart times
12	1600–1900: a history of persecution
13	The 20th century
14	Towards 2000
16	**3. Reaching a decision**
16	Questioning the most effective way to conserve kites; proposals for reintroduction
18	Approval to pursue and establishment of a project team
22	Precedents: what could we learn?
32	Was the Red Kite a suitable candidate for re-introduction?
34	Resources
37	**4. Identifying the true world distribution**
37	Discovering the true state of the world distribution of Red Kites
43	The Red Kite's prospects before the reintroduction project
47	Possible sources of kites
52	Finding sources of birds after the trial year: sources of birds for the rest of the initial programme
57	Summary of sources of birds during the experimental project

58 5. Identifying the right places
58 Requirements for success and selecting suitable areas for rearing and release
60 Timing of local information release
61 Site selection for rearing and release areas

68 6. Collecting and importing the nestlings
69 Collection of kite chicks from Sweden
71 Wales
72 Continuing the supply
72 Sweden
73 Wales
73 Spain

88 7. Rearing the kites
88 Previous experience and aviary design
89 Rearing and release sites
91 Rearing kite chicks at the release site
94 Marking

97 8. Release, behaviour in the wild and initial survival
102 Behaviour in the wild
104 Dispersal in England in 1989
106 Release and dispersal in Scotland in 1989
107 Summary of the first year
108 Releases in 1990
110 Survival
110 Rehabilitation
110 Effects of the kites on Game
112 Dispersal overall

116 9. Kites breeding in the wild
119 Age of first breeding

123	What the analysis of first-year breeding performance tells us more generally
125	Build-up of breeding numbers
126	Differences in performance at the Scottish and English sites
133	Breeding dispersal
135	Population growth
135	What was happening in Wales?

137   10. Education & public awareness

137	Opportunities and expectations
146	Poisoning

149   11. From experimental success to operational delivery

149	The challenge of the Government's destruction of the Nature Conservancy Council
157	Management of the Experimental Red Kite Project
158	Progress by 1994–5
159	Operational phase
170	Update on Wales and the first English and Scottish sites
182	The English Midlands reintroduction 1995–1998
188	The Central Scotland reintroduction 1996–2001
190	The Yorkshire reintroduction 1999–2003
190	The Dumfries & Galloway (SW Scotland) reintroduction 2001–2005
190	The Northumbria (NE England) reintroduction 2004–2006
190	Aberdeen reintroductions 2007–2009
191	Republic of Ireland 2006–2011
192	Northern Ireland 2008–2010
194	Lake District 2010–2012
195	Review

196   12. What are the outcomes?

202	Outcome: re-establishment of the Red Kite
206	Outcome: reduced persecution of birds of prey

213 Outcome: the attitudes to ecosystem restoration

219 Outcome: facilitating appropriate reintroductions and recovery programmes more generally for other species of wildlife – the lessons from the Kite programme

236 Outcome: public attitudes and perceptions

241 References

250 Annexes

250 Annex 1: Chronology

255 Annex 2: Extracts from the note for the file, prepared by the Wales kite leaders, following the [Wales] Kite Meeting of 13 March 1987

257 Annex 3: NCC's Ornithology Note no. 5. Current work in ornithology: the reintroduction of the White-tailed Eagle

261 Annex 4: Extracts from Ornithology Note: Conservation of the Barn Owl *Tyto alba* in the United Kingdom

266 Annex 5: The options and consequences of manipulating Red Kite broods in Wales

269 Annex 6: Some of the points we made to landowners and their staff, when arranging rearing/release sites, in relation to kite/gamebird interactions

272 About the author

Dedication

This book is dedicated to the huge number of people who have helped this restoration of Red Kites across Britain, and now Ireland too - not just those contributing to the experimental project, but also those building on that work. Most of these people worked wholly or partly in an amateur capacity. I hope that the others will not mind my singling out of these volunteers, my wife Ann, a biologist too but also a teacher, who has supported at all stages throughout; without her, the book would not have happened.

Acknowledgements

The Experimental Reintroduction of Red Kites to England and Scotland was a joint programme between the Nature Conservancy Council (NCC) and the Royal Society for the Protection of Birds (RSPB). NCC, UK's then statutory nature conservation body, took the operational lead in England and RSPB, a non-governmental organisation, in Scotland. A large number of people and organisations helped achieve the success of the project. For reasons of site-security, it was not possible to acknowledge publicly in early publications the help of all of them. Many thanks to all for their invaluable support and assistance, and apologies to any I have inadvertently omitted from the lists.

In most cases, I have tried to give names fairly formally here in the Acknowledgements, but more simply in the main text, except where quoting a document makes changes difficult. This style does not necessarily match normal documentation at the time.

Officers responsible for the project were Dr Mike Pienkowski (NCC Head of Ornithology Branch, Chief Scientist Directorate) and Richard Porter (RSPB Headquarters, Sandy). The Project Team included initially myself (as Chairman), Richard, Dr Leo Batten (who had responsibility for both licensing and species protection legislation for birds, NCC), Roy Dennis (RSPB Highland Office), Dr Ian Newton (Institute of Terrestrial Ecology & NCC Advisory Committee on Birds, with great birds of prey experience), Peter Walters Davies & the late Peter E Davis (both Wales Kite Committee and with long field experience of kites), and the late Mrs Sandy Collinge (who managed the financial and administrative matters for NCC's Chief Scientist Directorate). This group became the Red Kite Project Team, which I had the honour of chairing throughout its existence from 1987 until early 1995.

These initial members of the Project Team were joined in April 1988 by Sarah Garnett (NCC South England Region) and Graham Elliott (RSPB HQ) with, in October 1988, Dr Lawrence Jones-Walters and Ted Green (NCC South England Region), taking over from Sarah; then, in January 1989, by the late Dr Jeff Watson of NW Scotland Region (also an experienced raptor researcher). Subsequent joinings to the Team included, in November 1989, Dr Ian Evans (NCC Kite Project Officer), Dr Nick Fox (leading the kite rescue rearing in Wales), Jonathan Spencer (NCC South England Region), and Dr Ken Smith (RSPB HQ) with, in October 1990, Roger Lovegrove (RSPB Wales).

After NCC reorganisation (see Chapter 11), additional participants in December 1991 included Dr Tim Stowe (RSPB new Regional Officer for Northern Scotland), Dr Ron Summers (RSPB Scotland) and Duncan Orr-Ewing (RSPB Scotland); with, in December 1992, Dr Colin Galbraith (Joint Nature Conservation Committee, JNCC), Nicola Crockford (RSPB), Steve Parr (Countryside Council for Wales, CCW), Dr Greg Mudge and Dr Nigel Buxton (both Scottish Natural Heritage, SNH), and Phil Grice (English Nature, EN); and, in the final year of operation of the Project Team as releases ended and we reviewed matters in April 1994, Lorcan O'Toole (RSPB Scotland) and Dr Mark Avery (RSPB HQ), with David Henshilwood (replacing Jonathan Spencer as EN local officer) joining for the last meeting of the Team, in November 1994.

I would like to express my thanks also, for high level support to: the late Dr Derek Ratcliffe (NCC's Chief Scientist and my then boss) and the late Professor Peter R. Evans (Chairman of NCC's Advisory Committee on Birds and University of Durham, where he had been my former boss when I had been a senior researcher and teacher there).

Without an international willingness to supply kites, to help secure the long-term security of the species, there would have been no project. For the supply of birds and necessary licences, we are grateful to Mats Eriksson and the Swedish National Environment Protection Board; Magnus Sylven and WWF (Sweden) [WWF originally stood for World Wildlife Fund but, in some countries, it was confusingly renamed World Wide Fund for Nature; the initials remained constant, but not to be confused with the World Wrestling Federation!]; Skanes Ornitologiska Forening; Rune Frisen & Christer Borgh, Naturvardsverket SNV; Johnny Karlssson; Welsh kite workers; the Spanish Instituto Nacional para la Conservacion de la Naturaleza (ICONA), particularly Dr Borja Heredia and Dr Luis Mariano Gonzalez; Snr Jose Ignacio Elorrieta, Director General, Servicio de Medio Ambiente, Pamplona, Navarra, and his staff, especially Alfonso Senosiain; and Diputacion General de Aragon (Departamento de Agricultura, Ganaderia y Montes), and Junta de Castilla Leon Servicio Territorial de Medio Ambiente y Ordenacion del Territorio de Segovia Salamanca, as well as Grupo de Rehabilitacion de la Fauna Autoctona (GREFA) and Buitrago Raptor Rehabilitation Centre. I would like to thank also Michel Terrasse and his fellow kite workers in France, who were very willing to supply kites but whose generous offer we did not take up, for logistic reasons (see Chapter 4.)

We needed to get the birds to UK, one of the most administratively and logistically complex parts of the operation to set up. For transportation, we thank Station Commander and personnel at Royal Air Force Kinloss, especially 201 Squadron, and the British Airways Assisting Nature Conservation Programme and its Co-ordinator Rod Hall MBE, with the crew of flight BA459 and all the supporting staff and successors on later flights, as well as Dr Hugh Somerville, Head of the Environment, British Airways. For help in respect of licences, regulations and meeting the requirements of these, we thank I. Muchmore and C.J. Froud (Department of the Environment), Miss J.A. Collins, Dr Death, Mrs J. Kelly, Mrs Lui, Mrs Sue Mulvey (Ministry of Agriculture, Fisheries and Food, MAFF), Mr J. MacVicar and Nick Wilson (Department of Agriculture and Fisheries for Scotland, DAFS), MAFF and DAFS veterinary inspectors, the staff of the Animal Quarantine Station (AQS) Heathrow, staff of HM Customs and Excise, and British Airways' staff and agents at both Madrid and Heathrow.

Without secure rearing and release sites, nothing would be possible. For help (in addition to that provided by NCC or RSPB personnel listed above or below) in finding potential sites (whether they were used in the end or not) and in arranging or providing permission for those that were used, we are deeply indebted to: the Crown Estates Commissioners and their personnel, particularly Deputy Commissioner Lt. Col. Bob Osborne and Head of Agriculture & Forestry Mr Jeff Stumbke; Mr B. O. Pryor, Strutt and Parker; land-owners at the Black Isle and the Chilterns at and near the release areas; and a large number of individuals (including landowners, farmers, gamekeepers, foresters, factors and naturalists), organisations and sporting estates, who contributed by helping to protect kites and granting us access to private land in order to monitor the kites. This is a crucial part of the project since it builds up a picture of the movements and behaviour of the birds and helps us determine which factors are important for their survival. The whole team thanks all the volunteers who helped with monitoring work.

I would like to express thanks in particular to the late Sir Paul Getty and the late Mr Christopher Gibbs for permission to use The Wormsley Estate as the first English release site, and Viscount Richard Parker (now Earl of Macclesfield) for permission to use the adjacent Portobello Farm for the second set of rearing and release cages. At these estates, the team thank, for much help, Ed Deane, John & Polly Hedges, and Gavin & Angela Jones; and, for volunteer help in building the cages, Roger and Ursula Castle, Allan Lucas, Gerald Marsh and Peter Stevens. Peter became local kite monitor and helped with this book; I was saddened to hear of his death while the book was in proof.

Many colleagues among NCC staff and contractees (in addition to those named above) gave major help. These included Nigel Adams, Dr Eric Bignal, Dr Roger Bray, Peter Clement, Michael Cox, Tony Cross, Alison Garton, John Halliday, Wendy Hebden, Sam Mariner,

Simon Melville, Jenny Mitchell, Chris Monk, David Morgan, Steve Moore, Martin Nugent, Dr Tim Reed, Dr Peter Schofield, David Stroud, Dr Peter Tilbrook and other staff, especially at Foxhold House and Northminster House – and also those who joined the successor bodies and helped, including Gill Kane, the late Karen Mossman, David Smith, Jonathan Smith, Nigel Snell and Sue Wenlock.

Further colleagues amongst RSPB staff contributing strongly included the late Simon Aspinall, Dr Len Campbell, Colin Crooke, Dee Doody, Brian Etheridge, the late Richard Evans, Dr Rhys Green, Andy Knight, Kate Rhodes, Norman Sills and Iolo Williams.

Others outside these organisations provided greatly appreciated assistance: Kevin Baker and colleagues at the Ringing Office, British Trust for Ornithology; Lorraine Bambridge; Sue Bignal; Austin Brady; Michael Colston; Mr N.E. de Ban & Associates; Mr Dundas; Forest Enterprise; Jimmy Gordon; Pete Haws; John Hedges; Mr J.B. Henerson (ADAS); Charles Hill; Johnny Karlsson; Dr Robert Kenwood; Dr James Kirkwood (Institute of Zoology) and others who provided veterinary support; Sir Michael Leighton; Charlie Macdonald; Mike Ounsted (Wildfowl & Wetland Trust); Dr David Parkin and colleagues (Nottingham University, for undertaking genetic studies); Andy Parsons; Nigel & Janet Phillips; Ann Pienkowski; Richard Plumbridge; Dave Pullan; John Smith; Charlotte Spicer; David Stoodley; Dr Alan and Helen Stormont; Mike Thompson; Ian Walker; Roy Walker; the Welsh Kite Trust; Bob & Jane White; David White; Pete Whittle; Ed and Nick; and the bird recorders for several counties and regions.

I would like to thank all those who have contributed information; most of them have been acknowledged individually in the text. Others include: Frederic Bouvet, Chalabi Bouzid, Henrik Dissing, Dr Philippe Dubois, Dr Jean Francois, Gernant Magnin, Lars Norgaard, Ros Ottaway, Alison Stattersfield and Dr Niklaus Zbinden.

The core of this book is about the Experimental Project, which developed the approach, trialled techniques and established successfully self-sustaining populations. After this, as new release areas were established, I do not have first-hand knowledge and so my additional acknowledgements will be far less complete. However, as well as thanking those of the above who continued to help, I would like to recognise the later contributions of everyone concerned in all the later releases. As I do not have the full lists, I have included mention of those of whom I am aware in the relevant sections of Chapter 11. However, we started contact with our colleagues in Germany during the experimental project, although the political situation in Europe at that time did not allow us to activate this source then. They were able to provide the kite nestlings for the fourth release site, in Central Scotland. Therefore, I would like to thank those involved in that release (in addition to continuing support from some of those mentioned above): Sachsen-Anhalt Lande; Vogelschutzwarte Steckby; British Airports Authority Glasgow; HM Customs & Excise Glasgow; Martin Luther University, Halle; Avis; Parks Car and Van Hire; Duncan Orr-Ewing; Ron Summers; Dave Dick; Chris Rollie; and Mike Trubridge. Members of the Highland and Central Raptor Study Groups, and members of the public also provided sightings which were vital in locating some nests and some of the released birds that dispersed.

This book is in essence from a personal viewpoint, although I have attempted to ensure that all the factual points are supported by the record. Particularly after I handed over responsibility for the project in 1995, there were many aspects in which others were much more closely involved. I have drawn from the information they provided in reports and discussions, where appropriate.

I would like to thank my colleagues in the project team for the various reports and other documents I have drawn from, and to several of them for comments on drafts of parts of this book, and to my wife Ann for checking all the later drafts. Ann also gave very many days of help in processing the scans of photographic slides (the medium in use in the years of the experimental project and for years afterwards). Those who have experienced only the convenience of modern digital photography may not be aware that the colours of slide film fade over the years at rates erratic between colours and individual slides – not something that the manufacturers stressed! I am indebted to Ann for rescuing those that could be.

I thank my old fellow pupils at Bemrose Grammar School in Derby, Alan Roe, John Middleton and Stuart Pimm. We re-met fairly recently. At the request of Professor Pimm, I recorded a lecture "Kite-flying for beginners: The Reintroduction of the Red Kite to England and Scotland, 30+ years on – Conservation informed by Science". This was for Duke University, USA, while it was teaching online during the Covid-19 pandemic. After that, my old friends strongly encouraged me to resume writing this book.

As I was writing the book, it was important to re-visit Wormsley. I am grateful to Mr Mark Getty for permission to do this and, for much help from the Wormsley team, including Alexander Getty, Sarah Kate Edwards, Alistair Cane, Joe Wasylowski and their colleagues.

It is said that a lawyer who represents himself has a fool for a client. Although I do a lot of editing myself, any author needs a sub-editor. I am grateful to Paul Goriup at NatureBureau for putting me back in touch with Jonathan Spencer, with experience of this type of work, following his retirement from Forest Enterprise England. Jonathan had been closely involved in part of the Experimental Red Kite project, and in later years took a leading role in re-establishment of other species, notably the White-tailed Eagles in the Isle of Wight. His old links with the project in no way moderated his professionalism, and we have had strong debates on commas and other matters. However, it was a luxury to have someone with direct experience of the work as a sub-editor, with Jonathan able also to remind me of a few details of the work. The book is greatly improved by his efforts. I thank also my daughter, Clare Ballard, who read a late draft from the viewpoint of someone not greatly involved in birds (despite my efforts) as well as using some of her professional skills as sub-editor and proof-reader.

I am grateful to those who have made available their photographs, including Dr Eric Bignal [EB], Dr M. Budden [MB], Tony Cross [TC], Robert Cruickshanks (Ootmahoosewindae) [RC], Ian Evans [IE], Darren Hardy [DH], John Love [JL], Ann Pienkowski [AP], the late Pete Stevens [PS] and Gerry Whitlow [GW], by staff photographers from the project partner organisations working for the project, including C.H. Gomersall of RSPB [CG] and Steve Moore of NCC [SM], and flickr/Tambako The Jaguar. My own photographs are credited as MP and uncredited ones were taken on behalf of the project team by unspecified members, including persons using others' cameras. I thank Philip Snow (www.snowartandbooks.co.uk) for permission to reproduce the superb Red Kite studies kindly commissioned by my then colleagues at JNCC and presented to me on my departure from that body. Thanks also to those who helped source photographs, including Ian Ballard and Dr Tony Mitchell-Jones. I am grateful to those (acknowledged in captions) who allowed reproduction of previously published material, particularly: my then colleagues in the project; the British Trust for Ornithology for material from the Atlases (which were joint projects of the BTO, BirdWatch Ireland (and previously the Irish Wildbird Conservancy) and the Scottish Ornithologists' Club), the BTO/JNCC/RSPB Breeding Bird Survey, other surveys (including a compilation by NBN) and *Bird Study*; BirdWatch Ireland; the editors and publishers of *British Birds*, the British Ornithologists' Union and Wiley for *Ibis,* Bloomsbury Publishing Plc and Oxford University Press. For help in arranging these permissions, I am grateful to Prof. Juliet Vickery and Mike Toms (BTO), Niall Hatch (BirdWatch Ireland), Stephen Menzie (*British Birds*), Angela Langford (BOU), Janany Sudarshan and Mary O'Connell (Wiley), and Claire Weatherhead (Bloomsbury).

I would like to thank Peter Creed and Daniela Siska of NatureBureau for design and organising printing, the Council of the UK Overseas Territories Conservation Forum for approving publication, and their Executive Director, Catherine Wensink, for much help in this. I am very grateful to Lord (John) Randall for his generous Foreword.

Foreword

We live in an era when sadly, all too often we are subjected to stories of how nature is being negatively affected both here in the UK and internationally. We increasingly hear of the imminent extinction of species through a loss of habitat or other man-made causes. Numbers of formerly relatively common species have declined alarmingly and new generations are growing up missing out on so many of the joys of the wild environment that people of my age took for granted, the purring of a Turtle Dove or the nocturnal snuffling of a Hedgehog.

Regrettably the United Kingdom currently has the distinctly unenviable record of being one of the world's most nature-depleted countries. It therefore makes a very reassuring change to read the account of a really successful conservation project that has made a thoroughly positive impact on restoring the population of a species that was on the brink of extinction in the United Kingdom. Not all is gloom and doom and humans, despite causing so much devastation, can help nature with a helping hand to heal.

Reintroductions have increasingly become a tool in nature conservation but they can be controversial and certainly need an immense amount of detailed research. One of the key considerations is of course whether a species might naturally return to previous haunts. This could be because of habitat improvement or because of population expansion elsewhere or indeed because of the lack of persecution. The return of Avocets to East Anglia has been followed in recent years by the arrival of southern heron species such as Little and Great White Egrets. Spoonbills are now breeding in the UK with no need for reintroductions. Even within the UK we have seen a notable range expansion of Pine Martens. However other species would not become re-established without human intervention. Both the Chequered Skipper and Large Blue butterflies are two notable cases in point.

The population of Red Kites in the United Kingdom in the sixties and seventies was in a very precarious state indeed. Despite some conservation measures, the prognosis for the survival of the species was not a good one. Like Dr Pienkowski, I and other birdwatchers of our generation needed to make a pilgrimage to a few closely guarded sites in central Wales to have a chance of encountering and watching these magnificent birds of prey. Although we young birders knew that in Elizabethan London they were supposed to be common scavengers, that gave us scant consolation and the relict population did indeed look doomed.

If someone would have told me then that forty years later I would be seeing them on a daily basis over my garden in suburban Uxbridge, I would have laughed aloud at such an incredible suggestion. Amazingly that is exactly what has happened. It is no longer an ornithological fantasy.

This is the story of one of the most celebrated and indeed visible success stories of wildlife conservation in recent times.

It is a tribute to Mike Pienkowski and the huge cast list of dedicated persons that so many people now not only recognise these impressive birds but have also grown to love them. The Red Kite is now such a regular and highly visible feature of many areas of the United Kingdom as a result of the hard work of all the people involved in the scheme.

This modern day miracle of the kites' reintroduction did not happen easily. Far from it in fact. This was real pioneering stuff which has encouraged many other inspiring reintroductions. In fact the success of the Red Kite project has inspired many ambitious plans but as yet nothing has quite reached the amazing success of the return of kites to parts of the UK that had not been graced by these magnificent raptors for centuries.

This was only possible because of the efforts of many, not just in the UK but from those countries in Europe that allowed some of their precious birds to be used in the project to repopulate our islands. Their efforts have now been rewarded in kind as Red Kites are now being sent from the UK population back to Spain to augment falling numbers there: a real international cooperation conservation success story.

This project succeeded because of the incredible team work of professional ecologists, both in the government agency, which at that time was the Nature Conservancy Council, and many non-governmental organisations, principally the RSPB but also together with other conservation and research bodies. The demise of the NCC is worthy of a chapter in itself if not a book and it is interesting to speculate what effect that has had more generally on nature conservation in subsequent years. There was also an army of volunteers who worked alongside businesses and corporations such as the British Airways Assisting Nature Conservation programme. The armed services in the form of the Royal Air Force worked together with landowners and their gamekeepers, as well as conservationists and authorities across Europe. Together their collaborative work brought about this remarkable transformation of the status of this bird. It ranks alongside many of those equally well-known and worthy stories of bringing a species back from near extinction, such as the Arabian Oryx or the Ne-Ne.

Such was the dedication of all those involved that many, including professionals, worked in their own spare time. That patience and teamwork made things happen.

I have no doubt that many other raptors benefited from the reintroduction as it brought increasing awareness of the dangers of illegal persecution and poisoning. A spotlight was shone on some of those illegal practices as a result of the project and as the author notes, Common Buzzard numbers have also benefited hugely as well as other species such as the Raven.

Red Kites are now truly one of the UK's most recognisable birds, featured in numerous street names and their image commonly used for commercial purposes by businesses where the birds are now ubiquitous.

This book is a tribute to the hard work of the dedicated men and women who brought the species back from the brink.

John Randall – Rt. Hon. the Lord Randall of Uxbridge PC, former ornithological tour leader and director of department store, Member of Parliament for Uxbridge 1997–2015, Government Deputy Chief Whip and Treasurer of Her Majesty's Household in the Coalition Government 2010–2013, Special Envoy on Modern Slavery to the Mayor of London 2016, Special Adviser on the environment to the Prime Minister 2017–2019, member of the House of Lords 2018–, Council member or trustee of the RSPB, the Human Trafficking Foundation and the UK Overseas Territories Conservation Forum.

1. Introduction

The programme and why
There is something special about Red Kites *Milvus milvus*. Even I – who had undertaken most of my research fieldwork on coastal ecology and shorebirds, with their spectacular migrations and exotically varied breeding strategies – have to admit this. Kites have relatively small bodies for their enormous wing area. This combination gives them their buoyancy and manoeuvrability in flight, much of it achieved barely moving their wings, but steering by twisting their characteristic V-notched tails as they fly apparently effortlessly over the countryside. This buoyancy, manoeuvrability and ability to wind-hover led to their name being used also, from the 1660s for toy kites, a light frame covered with paper or cloth, which can be made to hover in the air like a bird. (The actual origin of human-made kites, whatever they were then called, was earlier, probably in China, SE Asia or the Pacific Islands.)

People are essentially unaware of how slight they are, taken in by their apparent size. This has led to incorrect perceptions of impacts on other species and misguided calls for their destruction. In fact, these medium-sized birds of prey feed chiefly on carrion but also small live mammals, birds and invertebrates, particularly earthworms. They soar frequently and for long periods but, when flying rapidly or in tight spaces, wingbeats are deep and flowing, rather like large terns. Their ability to hover is less intensive than Kestrels *Falco tinnunculus*. When moving on the ground or perch, they tend to hop or use a shuffling and bouncing walk. They tend to be a solitary raptor of open deciduous woodland, but nesting pairs can be close. In winter, parties may gather at food concentrations (Cramp & Simmons 1980). Their commonest call is a shrill mew, like several other birds of prey, high pitched and often quickly repeated. This is probably the origin of the birds' name, from Old English *cyta*, probably imitative of its cry; the name was applied initially also to other birds of prey.

The Red Kites' ruddy variegated plumage, combined with their aerobatics, make them one of the most striking and attractive birds of prey to watch. However, up to the end of 1989, viewing them required a special trip to central Wales, an attractive location in itself – but should the rest of the country not see them back in their natural distribution throughout the country? This would also give the kites the best chance of long-term survival.

I had intended to write this book nearly 30 years ago. I had set up the Experimental (that word is important – see Chapter 3) Red Kite Reintroduction Programme (in conjunction with colleagues at RSPB and elsewhere) and chaired its steering committee for several years. I was about to hand it over as a working project at a time when we had established its success. However, there was a communication mix up with my then publisher. By the time that was sorted out, I was over-committed to other conservation projects. It will be a much better book with the writing completed now than it would have been then. At that time, we were sure that we were running what would be a successful programme; now we know the outcomes more fully...now we can truthfully say "When the Kite builds, look to lesser linen"!

Red Kites formerly bred over many areas of Britain. In the Middle Ages, they were the subject of some of the first bird protection legislation in Britain, because of their importance as scavengers in keeping the streets of London and other cities reasonably clean. Changing attitudes, particularly in the 18th and 19th centuries, brought persecution which reduced the species, formerly widespread throughout Britain, possibly to fewer than 10 pairs in central Wales by early in the 20th century (Chapter 2).

The return of these magnificent birds throughout much of England, Scotland and now Ireland, as well as reinforcing the previously tiny Welsh population, depended ultimately on our experimental programme. This was run jointly by the Nature Conservancy Council (NCC, the forerunner to the present statutory nature conservation bodies in England, Scotland and Wales, and the Joint Nature Conservation Committee, JNCC), and the Royal Society for the Protection of Birds (RSPB). This proved to be one of the most strikingly successful conservation projects in recent years – although it had to overcome several challenging stages which severely endangered it. The *Independent* newspaper of 20th September 2004 remarked: "The reintroduction of the species to England and Scotland has been a great success story of modern conservation."

In 2020, Natural England (2020) issued a press release to celebrate 30 years since the start of the Red Kite reintroduction project. (It was actually 31 years since we imported and released the first kites, but few organisations – especially governmental ones, with continual re-organisations, staff turnover and the abolition of most librarian posts – are sharp on corporate memory.) Their Chairman, Tony Juniper, said "Thanks to this pioneering reintroduction programme in the Chilterns, increased legal protection and collaboration amongst partners, the Red Kite stands out as a true conservation success story. The flagship Red Kite reintroduction project paved the way for further species reintroductions, helping to reverse the historic deterioration of our natural environment and our precious species that inhabit it."

Jeff Knott, RSPB operations director for Central and Eastern England said: "The Red Kite introduction project has been a fantastic example of conservation in action and is the result of really effective partnership working, which we're proud to be part of. It's been amazing to see a species once persecuted to near extinction in this country, brought back and welcomed by local communities, with local economies reaping the dividends of the return of this iconic species. In the 1980s, anyone wanting to see a Red Kite had to make a special pilgrimage to a handful of sites. Today it is a daily sight for millions of people. In a few short decades we have taken a species from the brink of extinction, to the UK being

Sequential photos of an individual kite using its tail to steer while its wings are almost still. Flapping flight is enormously expensive in energy. With its huge wingspan, relatively light weight and twisting tail, a kite can save great energy by being a superbly effective glider. [MP]

Kites using a thermal (a bubble or column of warm rising air) to gain height: the birds hold their wings almost still to save energy and steer to stay in the tight thermal by twisting their tails. [MP]

home to almost 10% of the entire world population. It might be the biggest species success story in UK conservation history!"

Danny Heptinstall, Senior International Biodiversity Adviser at the JNCC, said: "Thirty years ago the reintroduction of a lost species was a radical act. Thanks to pioneering projects like the Chiltern Red Kites, it is now a standard tool in the nature conservation toolkit. In 1990, the UK had only a few dozen Red Kites; 30 years later there are over 10,000. JNCC is delighted to have played its part in this ground-breaking conservation success story and look forward to the continuing success of the project and others like it."

Why did we do it? How was it done? Why was it successful? Is this approach appropriate for other species or should resources for conservation be deployed in other ways? These are some of the questions which I want to address in this book. In doing so, I need to combine some scientific information on the Red Kites and their environment, the process by which scientific information and other matters are fed into decision making, and how the decisions were put into action. I add a little leavening by personal accounts of some of the diverse experiences involved.

I need also to put the work in the context of the time. We had desk-top computers, and primitive laptops (and very bulky by today's standards) were coming in. GPS and satellite tracking were a long way in the future. I recall, when trying to equip each of my Ornithology Branch team with computers to enhance productivity, my then boss said, "Surely you don't need one on every desk?" I managed to achieve it in the end by buying, using funding from the projects they would help, budget machines – none of which reached the capital purchase limit (which most personal computers then exceeded). I discovered that there was a running joke in the finance team that I was trying to buy a super-computer in units of under £1000 each!

Communications were another matter. Inter-organisation emails were not in general use, and the World-Wide Web had not been invented. Nor had mobile phones as we now know them. Mail was physical post, so responses from overseas took weeks. If a scientific paper was not in our library or possessed personally by one of the team, we had to secure it via postal Inter-Library Loans: to borrow a copy or get a photocopy sent from another library. What mobile telephones existed were rare business machines. NCC HQ had one, which I booked out for some of my visits to the kite-rearing site. It was the size of a large briefcase, and actually had a handset, like an old-fashioned landline, sitting on top. The size and weight (as well as the costs) of these machines meant that no-one would carry one around other than in a car. In fact, most were built into cars (one of the leading mobile phone companies in UK still has the word "carphone" in its corporate name). During our project, these machines came down in weight and size, but reductions in purchase and operating costs had to wait until the companies decided that they should market them as personal fashion items, rather than business machines. I was amused to find many carbon copies, as I checked through lots of documents while writing this book (I mean the real thing, not cc in an email), and there were notes from me to the Project Officer asking him to phone (from one of the famous red public call boxes or the nearby local NCC office), as I could not call him, there being no phone where he lived. A different world indeed!

Although this book draws heavily on the experiences of others, it is nevertheless a personal account. This means that I can express some views, for example as to why some things worked and others did not, but it does mean that the account is inevitably weighted more towards the aspects of the work in which I was personally involved. This was, at least, wide-ranging: I led for NCC in all the key preliminary discussions in the mid-1980s and chaired the Project Team from its establishment, for over 7 years, until early 1995. I also had management responsibility for the reintroduction to England. I have tried to illustrate the state of knowledge at various stages by quoting from some project or other contemporaneous documents in several places. Most of these are previously unpublished internal project documents, but some are the results of analyses that we undertook at the end of the experimental project in 1995, in order to advise on any following work. Some of these have since been published as separate scientific papers (to which I refer), and I draw in elements here in order to keep the story complete (though with less detail in such cases).

Having been involved in many years of producing documents by committee, I know that writings by a single author are generally far more readable! I hope that this book will not prove to be an exception. However, the fact that this book has been brought together by one person should in no way hide the reality that success of the reintroduction depended heavily on many individuals and organisations. Indeed, for many years rather more people than kites were involved in the exercise! This co-operative approach, involving contributions from several countries, illustrates the need to avoid a parochial or nationalistic approach to conservation, but instead to address issues at an appropriate scale, which is international for many bird species. This was, indeed, recognised by the European Communities' (EC) Council of Ministers Directive 79/409 on the Conservation of Wild Birds, and other international agreements to which UK Government is – or was – a party (and often one of the drafters). The project also highlights the fact that, although the NCC and RSPB led the initiative, ultimate success depended heavily upon the support and cooperation of landowners, game-keepers, farmers and volunteers. We are greatly indebted to all these people for the encouraging progress.

This international project was a long-term programme. It aimed to safeguard the long-term future of Red Kites in the most effective way: by enabling them to establish viable populations throughout their former range. The Red Kite was of high conservation priority in the 1980s and later, because it was one of only three species occurring in Britain which was endangered on a world scale.

Birds of prey and the British heritage

When, as a school-boy, I started bird-watching, birds of prey of almost any species were not a common sight. This was in the early 1960s in Derbyshire, in the Midlands of England. My school friends and I cycled or hitch-hiked around the countryside – or used rural train and bus services, such environmentally sound systems still just existing then.

We pored over our copies of "Peterson" (Peterson *et al.* 1974) to brush up our identification skills, and soon progressed to taking part in British Trust for Ornithology (BTO) projects, such as the Nest Record Scheme, the Common Birds Census and later the Ringing Scheme and the *Atlas of Breeding Birds* (Sharrock 1976). We also organised our own projects. (In those days, "twitching" was a brief stage people passed through, rather than the mass-participation sport of today.) One such project was the survey of an old local gravel pit by the school natural history society. The Bemrose School Natural History Society was entirely run by pupils, and its work led to the eventual protection of "our" gravel pit as a local nature reserve. It also introduced a great many boys (sadly, secondary schools in Derby at the time were single-sex) to natural history. I suspect that, with modern regulations on safety and so on, no such pupil-run society could operate nowadays – but I hope that I am wrong. How on earth are young people supposed to learn responsibility for themselves and others and assess risks without experience in such activities? We never had any of the fellow students in our care injured.

Two of the very few bird of prey species surviving as reasonably common in the English Midlands in the 1960s: female Kestrel (top) [MP] saves energy, compared with still-air hover, by using the wind to hover stationary to the ground while hunting – one of its old names is 'wind-hover'; and (below) Tawny Owl [RC] lands with small mammal after successful hunt.

I describe this background to illustrate the point that we were serious and committed birdwatchers. However, the only birds of prey we regularly saw were Kestrels. In the twilight, Tawny *Strix aluco* and Barn Owls *Tyto alba* could be added if we were lucky.

Apart from this, we were restricted to very rare glimpses of Sparrowhawks *Accipiter nisus*. This generally involved a nearly 2-hour bus-ride, followed by an hour's walk to a particular nature reserve (and the reverse after a couple of hours of birdwatching), with a chance of catching a glimpse of these rarities. When we trekked up to the Peak District, we might get lucky and see a Merlin *Falco columbarius* or a Short-eared Owl *Asio flammeus* on the moors. On really special occasions, we

Merlin, one of the then rare birds of prey of which we were lucky to catch an occasional glimpse when visiting the Peak District of Derbyshire [MP]

might devise ways of visiting special places in East Anglia to see a Marsh Harrier *Circus aeruginosus* ... or "secret" locations in central Wales in the hope of glimpsing a Red Kite.

Our perception was that this was "normal". To us, most birds of prey were rare and found only in special localities. Like many other people, we began to question this as we ventured further afield. In my case, organising undergraduate research expeditions to study migrant waders (shorebirds) in Iceland and overland to Morocco gave an impression of a rather different situation even as we drove across the territory of our nearest European neighbours, an impression heightened by further experience. Why was this?

The start of our birdwatching occurred during and just after the massive decline in many birds of prey caused by the introduction of persistent and highly toxic organo-chlorine agricultural chemicals. The story of the discovery of the impact of these on birds of prey and, through this, the potential effects on the wider environment is one of the classic pieces of applied ecological studies. Newton (2015) provides an excellent summary of the key role played by Dr Derek Ratcliffe (later NCC's Chief Scientist). This was world-wide, not something that was unique to Britain. For example, Rachel Carson's (1962) *Silent Spring* provided a popular and influential account from a North American perspective

Rather more characteristically British was the persecution of birds of prey as competitors with game-shooting interests. Whilst such persecution had occurred in many countries, especially in Europe, the thoroughness of the Victorians in Britain to these campaigns of extermination was remarkable (Chapter 2). These attitudes persisted in many parts of the country well into the last and into this century – with interruptions only during the two

Peregrine Falcon *Falco peregrinus*, famous as the fastest animal on Earth, suffered greatly from organo-chlorine pesticides – and one which provided the key in both Europe and North America to identifying the problem [MP]

world wars when both keepers and sporting gentlemen were largely otherwise engaged (*e.g.* Newton 1979, Cramp & Simmons 1980). Fortunately, we now live in rather more enlightened times, with support for the conservation of raptors coming from many landowners and gamekeepers.

Intensification of farming and consequent simplification of habitat structure has been linked to loss of raptors across a range of European countryside types (*e.g.* Donázar *et al.* 1997, Watson 1991).

For several years, raptors remained for me fascinating birds and the subjects of exciting studies particularly by people such as Derek Ratcliffe, Ian Newton, Jeff Watson *etc*. However, my own research – first as an amateur while at school, then while taking a biology degree at the University of East Anglia – on shorebirds, wildfowl and coastal ecology did not lead to much involvement. I continued on shorebirds and wildfowl for my PhD (Durham University, out-posted to Lindisfarne, Northumberland), several short research contracts for various bodies, and in post-doctoral posts at Durham University. Raptors impinged as predators of shorebirds, and their appearances caused spectacular flights by wader flocks – usually it seemed at the critical moment when we were preparing to catch a flock for ringing or colour-marking. We did notice, however, that such incidents seemed to occur more frequently on the continent than in Britain!

Positive initiatives – are they worthwhile?

In late 1984, I moved from a senior research post at the University of Durham to become Head of Ornithology at the Nature Conservancy Council, as a member of the Chief Scientist Directorate. This post was responsible for providing ornithological advice to NCC staff and Council, Government and others, and identifying, designing, commissioning and managing the research work necessary to provide evidence on which to base advice that might be needed. Among the roles I inherited then or shortly after were the chair of the project team reintroducing the White-tailed Eagle *Haliaeetus albicilla*, membership of the Kite Committee in Wales and the management of the Upland Bird Survey (later Moorland Bird Study) and Seabirds at Sea Team, as well as of the major contracts with the British Trust for Ornithology (BTO) and the Wildfowl and Wetland Trust (WWT). Many projects had aspects with a strong raptor involvement.

One of my first tasks in the initial few months in my new role was to review information needs and conservation initiatives. I did this largely by ecosystems.

For marine birds, we had the Seabirds at Sea Team surveying bird (and mammal) distributions at sea, so that we could advise government and the oil industry effectively on minimising any negative effects of oil and gas exploration and production in the North Sea (which was underway) and west of Scotland (*e.g.* Tasker *et al.* 1987; Tasker & Pienkowski 1987). I was able to negotiate the continuance of this, with continued shared funding by the oil industry. (Climate change issues were not really evident then. Oil companies were a source of complementary funding, with a common interest in research to minimise pollution and its adverse consequences.) I was also able to work with that team to commission a repeat census of seabird colonies (Lloyd *et al.* 1991), about 20 years after the previous one, to make a start on national monitoring.

Coastal and wetland birds were monitored within the contracts with WWT and BTO, the latter including also the bird-ringing and nest-recording schemes and monitoring of primarily lowland birds.

Dr Tim Reed, with whom I had worked jointly on wader surveys before I joined NCC, had run the successful Uplands Bird Survey, providing increasingly important data as the threat of habitat destruction appeared and increased for these areas (see Chapter 11). Tim moved on to even greater things in NCC, and I was fortunate to be able to recruit David Stroud, to set up and run the Moorland Bird Study to build on the Upland Bird Survey. David was already an expert on birds and peatlands (and much else), and had been responsible more than anyone else for saving the vital White-fronted Goose *Anser albifrons* habitat of Duich Moss on Islay from unnecessary destruction.

I identified an ecosystem that we seemed to be neglecting: the fairly traditionally managed marginal mixed farmland of the low uplands. The importance was so unrecognised previously that it did not even have a name! We eventually called this "Low Intensity Agricultural Land" (LIAL). We later switched to "High Nature Value Farmland", as "high" is psychologically better than "low"! I had noticed that the late Dr Colin Bibby, Head of Research at RSPB, had been managing some relevant studies on aspects of this in Wales. However, RSPB was not then interested in a contract from NCC to develop this work. So, I was eventually able to set up some work on this in-house, under the leadership of Dr Eric Bignal, previously one of NCC's most experienced Assistant Regional Officers dealing with farmers and others in this sort of landscape in SW Scotland, especially Islay, which became one of our prime study areas, with others in the English Pennines and elsewhere. This study had many interactions with our thinking on raptor conservation.

I had also to review the White-tailed Eagle reintroduction programme, which seemed to be progressing rather slowly (see Chapters 3 & 12).

Several other aspects added to how ideas subsequently evolved.

I had responsibility for developing ways of implementing the 1979 European Communities Directive on the Conservation of Wild Birds, a measure much inspired by UK officials and politicians within what later became the European Union (EU). Much of the activity to date had been concerned with identifying special sites to be designated as Special Protection Areas or SPAs. Some of the most vulnerable species for which protection measures were required were the birds of prey. There was some move to make each nest-site of such rare species an SPA. Government officials had doubts about this approach, largely on the basis of practicability and the large number of sites which would be involved. I and my colleagues, as statutory advisors to Government, were concerned as to the effectiveness of such an approach. How would it help the conservation of these birds? There would be a conflict between the need for confidentiality of nest-site locations (at times of both intense illegal persecution and industrialised illegal egg-collection) and the declaration of the sites as protected. What benefits would accrue, especially as the foraging ranges of the birds would not normally be included? Would this approach be just box-ticking or real conservation? We recognised that the European legislation called for "special protection measures" which could include – but were not restricted to – Special Protection Areas. Could we not do something rather more imaginative to achieve real conservation ends?

We were concerned that, whilst site-safeguard is an essential element of nature conservation, it was not enough in itself. This is especially the case for large, mobile animals which need to range widely to fulfil their needs. When one considers the sort of area that would be required to support a viable population of such wide-ranging animals, the need for conservation measures to become an integral part of other land-uses over large areas becomes apparent. This is especially so in such a densely human-populated nation as UK. For this reason, around this time, we were initiating a study of birds and land-use on Islay (see above), which supports a remarkable number of vulnerable species listed by the European Directive, including several birds of prey. We wanted to know why: could this have applications elsewhere? This was the study which identified the importance to nature conservation of "low-intensity agricultural land". It also led to the European Forum on Nature Conservation and Pastoralism, initially within my Ornithology Branch of NCC, before setting it up as a separate non-governmental organisation (NGO).

The essence of all this was the recognition that, to be successful, nature conservation should not just be a land-use in its own right (as in nature reserves) but should also be a component of other land-uses. In other words, these uses should be environmentally sustainable (a rather novel concept at the time). The health of the wildlife should be a good measure of this and people using the land should see the benefits of conserving wildlife. This has many links with the more recent terminology of "rewilding." We were later to move into other aspects of wider countryside conservation strategies – what became known as landscape ecology – and I was able to recruit a newly qualified PhD, Dr Colin Galbraith, to lead some work on this, specifically the conservation of vulnerable and dispersed bird species. When JNCC was created out of part of NCC (see Chapter 11), I built on this by merging most of NCC's Ornithology Branch into JNCC's Ornithology (later Vertebrate) and Landscape Ecology Branch, headed by Colin.

Back at the start of my period in NCC's Ornithology Branch, a further linked underlying theme was the need for positive initiatives, bringing together cooperative efforts of many people and organisations in support of nature conservation. Although conservationists were at last starting to win some major cases, there were dangers in this. Because the efforts tended to be concentrated on site-defence, there was a danger of always seeming to be negative. There was no suggestion, of course, that the defence of important sites should be abandoned but they needed to be balanced by some positive, preferably cooperative, initiatives. Such collaborative approaches could even put future defensive ones into a more positive context.

These reflections were in my mind as I reviewed the existing work and possible needs for ornithological conservation, as I needed to do during the early part of the tenure of my post at NCC. I was pleased, but not surprised, that such ideas were in the minds of several colleagues, both within NCC and in other bodies. On many aspects, we worked closely with colleagues in RSPB, some of whom were addressing similar concerns.

With this background, the time was right for a project like that on Red Kites. It was not any one person's brainwave – rather an idea whose time had come.

Why projects happen

It is a commonly held belief that major projects happen and succeed because big organisations develop them. In my experience, this is only partly true. They happen because individuals, or more usually small groups of people, take the initiative and make them happen. Successful organisations create a system which enables people to take forward these enthusiasms, provided they are appropriate. This project was fortunate to have a team of enthusiastic people in a range of organisations, and organisations with the sense to allow the freedom to make it happen – although it was a close-run thing at times. We were anxious to run a practical conservation project informed by scientific information. We wanted to monitor it carefully, so that we could learn from experience, both for the benefit of this project and for future work. Whether it worked or not, we wanted to learn why.

We were also well aware that projects do not just happen because the scientific information or justification is present. Logical reasons are not enough. The interactions with people are the key.

To my surprise, there seemed to be very few books on scientifically based conservation projects (as opposed to their outcomes), although there were many excellent ones on the natural history or biology of plants and animals. With so much popular interest in conservation, I wanted to give a flavour of the challenges that we met in undertaking the work.

First, however, we need some background on the Red Kites.

2. History

Red Kites formerly bred over many areas of Britain. By the 20th century, and until our project began, they had become confined to central Wales.

At an early stage of considerations, we reviewed the history and current status of Red Kites, as well as their biology. Some of this is drawn from our report on the project to 1990 (Evans, Pienkowski & Dennis 1990).

How could a bird that was once so common have reached a vulnerable world population of only 13,000 pairs with international action needed to protect its long-term future?

The Middle Ages

Up to about 300 hundred years ago, Red Kites were familiar scavengers in London's streets (and those of other towns) with a perfectly happy relationship with humans, scavenging on refuse, excrement and animal carcasses that littered the streets. With this resource so readily to hand, the Red Kites were common. They effectively performed the equivalent public health and recycling services of present-day refuse and recycling collectors. In many areas in Europe, Africa and Asia, this scavenging role is still undertaken by the much more common and often migratory Black Kite *Milvus migrans*.

Red Kites were the subject of some of the first bird protection legislation in Britain, because of this importance as scavengers in keeping the streets of cities reasonably clean – or at least carrion-free. It was a capital offence to kill one. Most of the Red Kites' diet is carrion. They may take occasional earthworms, beetles and small mammals, but essentially Red Kites are scavengers, opportunists. In Mediaeval Britain they flourished.

They shared this role with other species, especially Ravens *Corvus corax*. This role of the Ravens is vaguely remembered in that a small number of at-times pinioned Ravens is kept at the Tower of London. The legend is that, if there are no Ravens there, the Tower or the monarchy or the nation (stories differ) will fall.

Two of the Ravens, Jubilee (left) and Erin kept at the Tower of London, rest on the back of a bench in the grounds within the Tower. [DH]

A Raven in a more natural situation [MP]

Tudor and Stewart times

Early writers reported that Red Kites "swarmed" in the streets of London during the fifteenth and sixteenth centuries (Nisbet 1959). As a carrion-eater, it was a common city scavenger feeding in flocks at refuse dumps. Consequently, it was regarded as rather lowly; being called a kite, as Lear calls Goneril in Shakespeare (1608), was a gross insult. But there was grudging respect too: William Shakespeare (1623) in *A Winter's Tale*, says *"When the kite builds, look to lesser linen."* Kites often decorate their nests with bits of clothing and other unusual items. Modern examples recorded include strips of coloured plastic, bright underclothing, a pink fluffy slipper, hair-bands, gloves and half a teddy bear.

However, in 1457 James II of Scotland decreed that kites and other predatory birds should be destroyed; it is not entirely clear why. This and later vermin laws signalled the decline of the species throughout Britain (O'Toole *et al.* 1998). In England and Wales, in the mid-1500s, a Parliamentary Act for the Preservation of Grain was passed, and the fortunes of Red

The re-established Red Kites have retained their liking for lesser linen: nest in Chilterns with chick (playing dead in usual defence posture), unhatched egg and assorted colourful human undergarments. [PS]

Kites changed there too. Suddenly kites and many other birds were assumed (in many cases probably wrongly) to be threats to human food supplies. There was a price on their heads: *"For every heron or osprey head four pence, for the head of every woodpecker, magpie, jay, raven or kite one penny, for the head of every bird that is called the kingfisher one penny, …"*

1600–1900: a history of persecution

A new Parliamentary Act signalled the start of 400 years of relentless persecution – wildlife across huge areas of countryside was wiped out. The kites' decline can be attributed largely to its fall from favour with humans. Evidence has been particularly well documented in the church-wardens' accounts of the parish of Tenterden in Kent (Ticehurst 1930). These documents cover the period between 1626 and 1711 and include details of rewards paid for the killing of "vermin". Red Kites are first mentioned in the year 1654–5, from when payments were made for two to three per year until 1675–6. In the following year there began what could be described as an intensive campaign to eradicate all "vermin": within the next ten years, a staggering 380 kites were paid for. In the season 1684–5 alone, one hundred were recorded as being killed. In succeeding years, the numbers killed declined from 35 in 1686–7 to 13 and 2 respectively in 1688–9 and in 1690–1. Thereafter, no more than 12 were included in any one year's accounts, even though there was no evidence of any reduction in the effort to kill predators.

Persecution on this scale was undertaken in other parishes nearby and in many other parts of the country. Other old records give some insight into former kite numbers, their distribution and the scale of historical persecution. For example, "vermin" lists show that 105 Red Kites were killed in the Callander Hills in Perthshire between December 1824 and December 1825. Further north in Inverness-shire, 275 were killed on the Glen Garry estate between 1837 and 1840 (Newton 1979). It has to be noted that some doubts have been cast on the accuracy of such records, as inflated claims may have been made in some cases, to increase income. Nevertheless, even if somewhat exaggerated, the numbers killed were clearly enormous.

The species was recorded as being plentiful in Perthshire and Stirlingshire, especially in the pine woods around Loch Lomond, in the early 19th century. Kites were known to winter in Wigtownshire in the early 1800s and formerly bred in Glen App in Ayrshire. They were recorded as numerous in Moray in 1775, and as breeding at Cawdor Castle, Nairn (in 1832), Ballindalloch, Grantown-on-Spey and Rothiemurchus. Kites were also numerous on the west coast of Scotland, with records from Inverary (where they frequented the herring-curing stations and scavenged the fish cleanings), Killmalie and Glenelg. Records from Gairloch show that, historically, many kites were poisoned in that area.

Despite the intensity of the killing, it was not until the middle of the nineteenth century that the Red Kites had become extinct over large areas of Britain. In London, a Red Kite was last reported, above the rooftops of Piccadilly, in 1859 – the same year as Charles Darwin (1859) published *On the Origin of Species*. By an odd coincidence, the previous year, the two papers outlining the independent discovery, by Charles Darwin and Alfred Russell Wallace, of evolution by natural selection had been first publicly read at the Linnean Society, also in Piccadilly (Darwin & Wallace 1858).

It was during the 19th century that the collection of eggs and skins then became a popular pastime, while killing birds of prey as a part of game-management was also intensive. Consequently, many kites fell victim to gamekeepers, who killed these birds not only for the supposed benefits in game-rearing but also for the direct financial reward for supplying specimens for taxidermy. Hence, the combination of the collecting of eggs and skins, as well as the misguided efforts of game preservation and related human activity, finally eradicated Red Kites from England in the 1880s and from Scotland in 1879 (O'Toole *et al.* 1998). An isolated pair bred in Glen Garry in 1917.

By the end of the 19th century no more than a handful of pairs (some estimated 5) of Red Kites survived in the remote hills of mid-Wales. As well as shooting and poisoning for 'vermin control', kites continued to be persecuted by egg and skin collectors.

The 20th century

Only in the remotest parts of central Wales did about a dozen individuals remain at the beginning of the 20th century, though Davis (1993) indicated that the population may have been slightly higher. There is no dispute however that the population went through a genetic bottleneck in the first half of the 20th century. These were the last survivors of what had been a substantial British population. Indeed, the original British population had probably exceeded our recent estimation of the present world population of 11–13,000 breeding pairs.

Extinction of the species throughout Britain would surely have followed if it were not for the unprecedented action of the British Ornithologists' Club, which organised round-the-clock nest protection schemes (Witherby 1909). Such measures were directed principally against egg-collectors and continued, co-ordinated by the Kite Committee in Wales. This had been supported and coordinated in recent years by the RSPB, NCC and its successor body, the Countryside Council for Wales.

Despite persecution, kites survived in Wales due to protection provided by dedicated volunteers. Thanks to them, the Welsh population was recovering slowly. Nearly a hundred years of protection had allowed Red Kites to hang on in Britain and had allowed the kite population to creep up to 62 breeding pairs by 1990.

However, egg collectors were still remarkably persistent. Eight known nests were robbed in 1990. It is difficult to understand the mentalities of people who collected eggs from such rare birds in the latter part of the twentieth century, and even into the twenty-first. These are not children or people acting on a casual impulse, but skilled observers. They must be aware of the consequences of their actions on these birds which they need to study to locate the nests.

In addition to the efforts of volunteers, professional help was sometimes available. The headquarters of UK's terrestrial special forces, the SAS Regiment, happen to be based in the English/Welsh borders, and it seems that hiding in cover for days waiting for egg-collectors or other vandals is excellent training for certain operational tasks. Indeed, it may be addictive as it is reported that some retired members have volunteered their services for similar duties. Of course, it is quite impossible to secure verification of this!

Even allowing for the activities of illegal egg-collectors, the slow nature of the recovery of Kite numbers and range in Wales has been attributed largely to the low productivity of breeding pairs. This

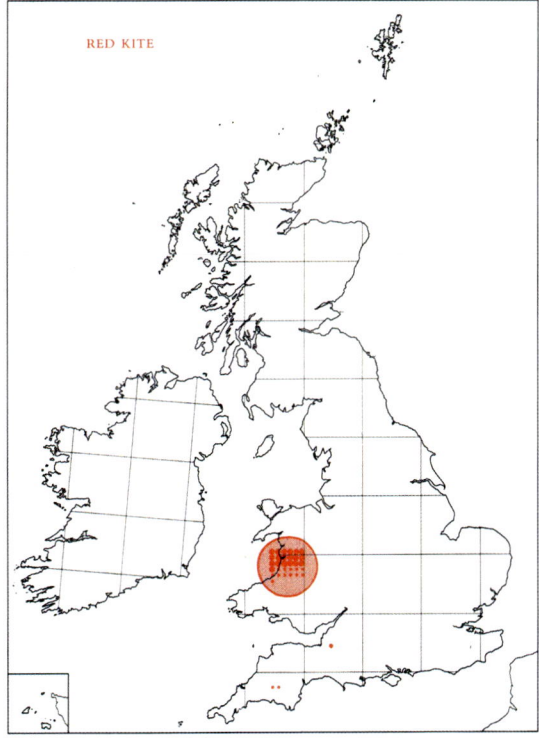

Figure 2.1. The breeding distribution of Red Kites in 1968–72; the published map was slightly stylized to protect the kites, the centre being within the circle but not at the centre of it. Reproduced from *The Atlas of Breeding Birds in Britain and Ireland* (Sharrock 1976), which was a joint project between BTO and the Irish Wildbird Conservancy.

reflects the poor habitat quality in their then Welsh range and the illegal use of poisoned bait by a minority of farmers and gamekeepers. This is intended mainly to control foxes and crows (although it is illegal also for this) but incidentally poisons kites due to their scavenging behaviour. In 1989, at least 11 were poisoned in Wales.

The slow increase may also reflect a rather low genetic diversity, following the restriction by human activity to such a low population size. In 1988, we contracted some work on this, although the results did not come immediately (and were not crucial to the decision as to whether or not to proceed with the project). By comparing blood samples taken from nestlings in Wales, the young that we later brought in from Sweden and Spain, and samples from Germany, May *et al.* (1993) found that 83% of females in the Welsh population were descended from a single female. The other 17% appeared to be descended from a continental female that had arrived in Wales about 20 years before the sampling. (Females only is because the analysis was based on mitochondrial DNA, which is inherited only from the mother, rather than both parents. However, it would be surprising if the situation with males was markedly different.) Genetic variation was thus exceptionally low. As one commentator put it, the Welsh kites were almost as closely related as one normal family.

Towards 2000
After a couple of years of preliminary informal conversations and research, we decided in 1987 to attempt an experimental programme of reintroduction in England and Scotland (Chapter 3), with the aim of establishing two new population centres in England and Scotland to supplement the native Welsh kites. Importations started in 1989. The long-term aim was to ensure the return of the Red Kites to all suitable habitats in the UK. We included also the genetic analysis of the young kites (see above). In summary, why were Red Kites not spreading from Wales? We could identify several possibilities, discussed above:
- Earlier, persistent and highly toxic organo-chlorine agricultural chemicals;
- Illegal killing – still, especially between its Welsh breeding areas and nearby in England;
- Egg collection;
- Genetics (see above);
- Habitat & climate, affecting productivity.

Whatever the reasons, there was clearly a problem.

What was happening to the global Red Kite population? Evans & Pienkowski (1991) reviewed the distribution and numbers of this species across its range (detailed in Chapter 4), following the outline summary map in Cramp & Simmons (1980) – which now seemed to be somewhat optimistic. They found that, in western and northern Europe, the population, although previously fragmented and reduced, appeared to be stable or increasing. However, the situation in the eastern areas was more negative. Britain could therefore potentially make a major contribution to the world conservation of this species.

The survival of the British population in central Wales, and its slow increase in the late 20th century to about 50 nesting pairs, is a tribute to the sustained efforts of farmers and conservationists in that area. However, breeding productivity was low, less than half that in France and Germany. This was probably partly because the area where the kites survived persecution was not particularly rich habitat, especially in respect of food supply in the breeding season.

As summarised in our *Progress Report no 1, November 1989* (Evans & Pienkowski 1989), until 1981 nearly all nesting by UK Red Kites in the 20th century had been confined to an area 70 km by 45 km in central Wales. In the 1980s, there was a slight expansion of range within Wales, possibly related to a reduction in illegal activity there, or possibly the result of some genetic input (see above). However, low breeding productivity remained a problem. Furthermore, spread from this area was probably inhibited by illegal poisoning in surrounding areas.

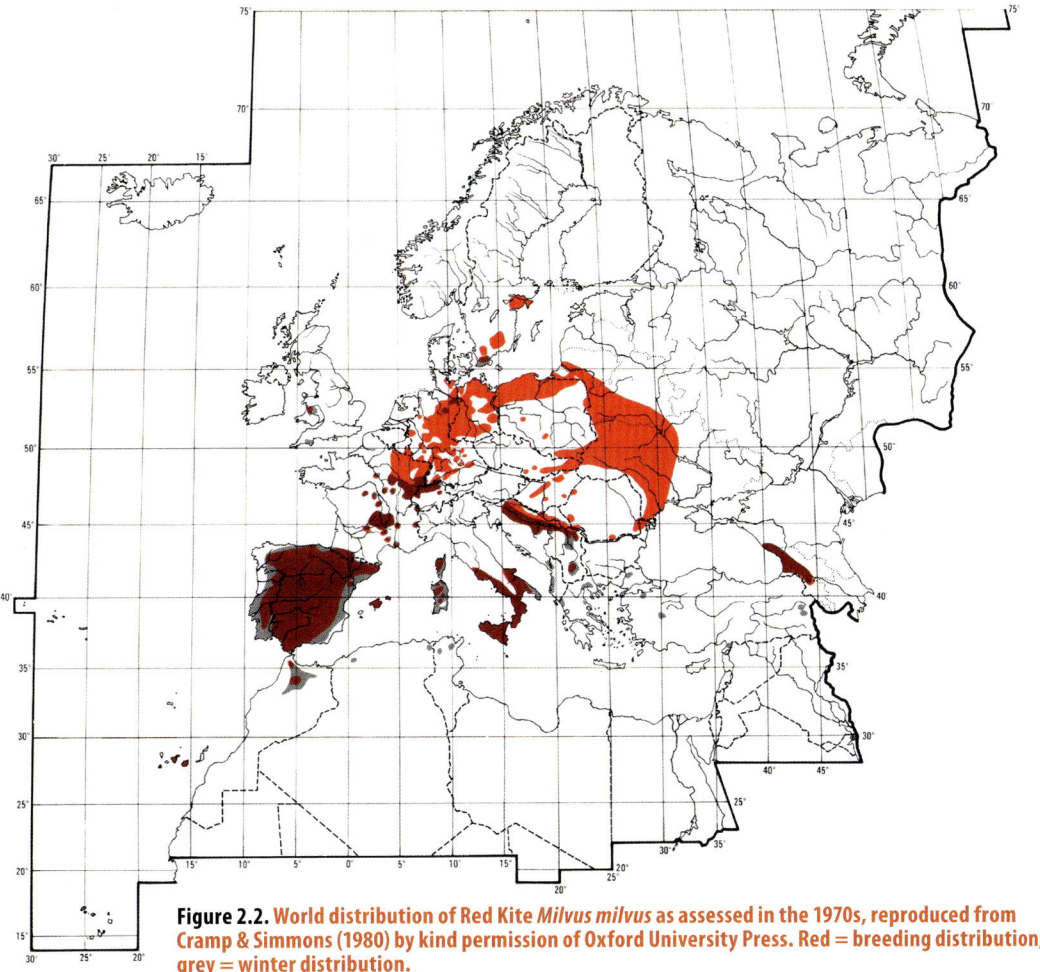

Figure 2.2. World distribution of Red Kite *Milvus milvus* as assessed in the 1970s, reproduced from Cramp & Simmons (1980) by kind permission of Oxford University Press. Red = breeding distribution; grey = winter distribution.

Although the kite population in Wales has survived for many years, populations of birds of prey are extremely vulnerable to sudden, unpredictable changes in the environment. For example, Peregrine Falcons *Falco peregrinus* were wiped out across most of the North American continent (as well as large parts of Europe) before the effects of certain agricultural chemicals were realised (Ratcliffe 1980). A similar impact on the relict kite population would have certainly resulted in their extinction.

Apart from the Welsh birds, Red Kites became extinct in Britain largely as a result of former persecution. Suitable habitat and food still existed in many of their former breeding areas outside Wales. In view of their slight expansion in Wales and the problems of illegal poisoning in intervening areas, as well as the great distances from other breeding areas, kites were unlikely to recolonise these areas naturally. Thus, re-establishing additional populations in these areas, particularly where a higher breeding productivity could be achieved, could safeguard the long-term future of Red Kites in Britain, making it far less dependent on events in any one area. This would also contribute significantly to the international safeguarding of these vulnerable birds.

In the next chapter, I describe how we started to pull this information together to inform policy and reach an agreed decision.

3. Reaching a decision

Questioning the most effective way to conserve kites; proposals for reintroduction

During 1985 and 1986, the status and potential for Red Kites were the subject of occasional discussion between myself, representing NCC, and colleagues in RSPB. We had become involved in the group overseeing joint RSPB/NCC involvement in kite conservation in Wales. We had nothing but admiration for the achievements of kite-workers and farmers in Wales. However, we were aware of the world of increasing financial questioning, under Mrs Thatcher's revolutionary regime. We could hear or predict questions like: Will this level of effort have to continue for ever? What about other species? Is this the top priority for scarce conservation funds?

We did not share the same negative approach ourselves but did wonder whether some initiative might move the Red Kites' status to a much safer level that no longer required such a high level of activity to ensure its wellbeing. If this were the case, not only would we have a much safer – and more widely viewable – population of Red Kites, but also we might be able to redirect some resources to the benefit of other species, without risk to the kites.

Some work in this direction had already been undertaken in Wales, although this was concerned mainly with rescuing eggs from nests usually failing due to human action, and hatching and rearing these with the intention of raising the slow rate of increase in Wales (see Chapter 4).

I explored ideas within my ornithological team at NCC and a few colleagues at RSPB, the main contact there being Richard Porter, Head of Species Conservation, but also Roy Dennis, RSPB's Highland Officer and someone who I had worked with previously when I was a researcher at Durham University. I suspect that Roy had been thinking of a Red Kite reintroduction to Scotland for some years, but there were hurdles which I would need to clear if we decided that it was appropriate to proceed (see Chapter 5). Of course, Roy has gone on to set up or encourage reintroductions of several other species since.

By the summer of 1986, we considered that there was a good enough case to warrant serious consideration. For this, and to allow resources to be deployed, we needed the formal approval of our various organisations. A good deal of work would be necessary to consider all the legal, policy, biological and practical aspects, even if we decided in the end not to proceed. To set the ball rolling we agreed that Richard Porter would write to NCC. Of course, once his letter arrived, it would be passed to me as Head of Ornithology at NCC, to pursue.

Some of the main points formalised in Richard's letter, in August 1986, based on our informal discussions, were:

The Objective would be "to attempt to increase the population of Red Kites in Britain and to ensure a greater geographical spread into areas which have the potential for higher productivity, thus enhancing its chances of future survival."

He noted that the Red Kite formerly bred over many areas of Britain but now only bred in central Wales with a population of about 40 breeding pairs. Although it had been increasing slowly in recent years, its productivity remained low (about 0.5 young per breeding pair). Whilst the reasons for the low productivity were not fully understood, it was the considered opinion that it was due either to genetics or shortage of food, the latter being considered to be the most likely (although not all geneticists would agree). The Red Kite was also a target species for egg-collectors (6–8 clutches taken in previous two years) and costly protection schemes had to be undertaken.

Apart from the Welsh birds, the Red Kite became extinct largely as a result of persecution; suitable habitat and food almost certainly still existed in many of its former nesting areas and a number were free from extensive persecution. Kites were unlikely to recolonise these areas naturally (only slight expansion of range in Wales) and it was considered that there would be no risk of upsetting the genetic constitution of adjacent pairs by the transportation of birds from a different gene pool. It thus met the RSPB (and NCC) criteria for reintroduction within Britain (translocation), and was one of very few species to do so; certainly, the clearest and possibly the only obvious one.

The initial approaches would include:

a) The data that had been collected on the productivity of Welsh kites should be analysed (bird of prey expert Dr Ian Newton had agreed to do this).
b) Selected individual pairs should be studied to determine when and why nests actually fail.
c) RSPB and NCC should enter a joint project to incubate artificially eggs of Red Kites (those which had shown a history of natural failure or robbery in the past). Assuming that the incubation process proved sound (and this might present a problem) then, if the eggs hatched, it would show that the causes of failure were unlikely to be genetic, and thus probably the result of food resource problems; this could in turn determine the need for a supplementary feeding programme. Assuming that eggs hatched and birds grew to fledglings, some should go back to the Welsh population and some go to supply the reintroduction programme, in another area of Britain (to be decided, probably Scotland). It was important that the number of birds going back into the Welsh population were not less than could reasonably have been expected to be produced from those eggs in a wild situation.

The paper went on to suggest timescales, with the possibility of starting reintroductions in 1987 from both artificial incubation of eggs from consistently raided nests in Wales and continental imports. It also addressed other issues such as budgets.

He noted that attitudes of members of conservation NGOs had changed somewhat in recent years, in that habitat manipulation had been acceptable, but eyebrows had been raised when practical help (other than protection) had been suggested for an ailing population. Recently, however, there had been a change in attitudes, perhaps linked with the successful reintroduction of the White-tailed Eagle to Scotland and also with the successful reintroduction programme of birds of prey in the USA.

Some other potential concerns were flagged up, so that they could be taken into account.

Whilst agreeing with much of Richard's letter (unsurprisingly, as it was based on our informal discussions over preceding months), I had some reservations, for example about the best area to use, as will become clear.

This letter allowed us to set some formal consultations in train. However, there were some difficulties here. Normally, new ideas were discussed fairly openly, preferably both outside and within the organisation. In this case, however, we foresaw that the public interest would be considerable. The press and public can be a little impatient for the conclusions, whereas we knew that our enterprise would take many months and probably a year to two to assess as to feasibility. Even more importantly, we knew that the project, if it went ahead, could be jeopardised by premature public interest in the areas of release. This could make difficulties in respect of permissions from landowners. We therefore decided, exceptionally, to keep the considerations as confidential as possible, so as not to raise public expectations while the matter was still under review. This was probably the correct decision at that time. It does not mean that it would necessarily be the best course of action in any comparable issue now or in the future, given the rapidly changing world and increased public awareness of these issues – indeed, in part due to the eventual success of the Red Kite programme.

Confidentiality is rather theoretical if knowledge of the issue is available throughout an organisation. Therefore, even within the organisations, information on the issue was released only on a "need-to-know" basis, with interesting results at times. At a later stage, some senior officers of NCC became upset that they did not know some precise locational details when their staff did. I am indebted to my then boss, the late Dr Derek Ratcliffe, Chief Scientist of NCC, for pointing out that he did not need to know such details, providing me with a useful example for others.

At this stage, we needed to consult internally (as did our colleagues in RSPB) with the various groups with an interest or involvement with Red Kites, including the relevant NCC regions and countries. Although this happened more than a decade before devolution within Great Britain, NCC did recognise the country sensitivities and had separate headquarters and directors for England, Scotland and Wales, as well as coming together for Great Britain. It also divided the whole of Great Britain into regions, primarily so that a local team could get to know local issues and the community. Each region was headed by a Regional Officer, in modern parlance a Regional Director, supported by a Deputy. Reporting to them would be a set of Assistant Regional Officers (probably termed County Officers or similar nowadays), each of whom would lead for an area roughly the size of a county. We depended on these local officers a lot.

Probably the most complex set of discussions involved our Welsh colleagues. There were many discussions over the following months, not surprisingly given the history and dedication to Kites in Wales. These were largely concerned with how to continue conserving the remnant Welsh population, rather than the novel idea of reintroductions elsewhere. This culminated with a high-level meeting with my Director, Chief Scientist Dr Derek Ratcliffe, joining myself and others, with the Head of Science and Policy Branch of NCC Wales HQ hosting the meeting. It included the Regional Officer and two key colleagues who had led the kite work in Wales for many years. In summary, the Wales team welcomed the idea of my convening a high-level meeting with partners to plan overall Red Kite conservation, not least because it would help their own planning. Extracts from the note for the file, prepared by the Wales kite leaders, following the meeting, form Annex 2.

Approval to pursue and establishment of a project team

Consultations with various partners, as well as other investigations (see also issues addressed in other chapters) continued, including considering matters raised in the various discussions.

The next formal stage was for NCC's Advisory Committee on Birds (ACB) to consider the proposal on behalf of the governing Council. The next opportunity for this was in July 1987. Meanwhile, preliminary consideration continued, keeping informed the Chairman of that Committee, Professor Peter Evans.

The paper I prepared (incorporating much from Richard Porter's letter and our discussions before and after) for consideration by the Advisory Committee on Birds in July 1987 gives a useful summary of the position, after preliminary assessment but before commencing the detailed study on feasibility and desirability of a reintroduction project. I reproduce it on pages 19–21, because it set the scene for the whole programme. Readers who do not like such policy documents should skip over it.

In discussion, the main points raised related to: agreement that Wales was not the area most suited to kites and how to identify the best areas; the costs of maintaining protection in Wales, and my explaining that short-term savings were not to be expected but they might result in the longer term; the method of reintroduction and some suggestions of captive breeding, to which Dr Ian Newton was able to point out the high costs of this and lower performance of captive-bred raptors of some other species; and the need for a monitoring scheme. All these were addressed, as noted elsewhere in this book. The Chairman summed

NATURE CONSERVANCY COUNCIL   APB/P3/87
ADVISORY COMMITTEE ON BIRDS

CONSERVATION OF RED KITES
A paper by Dr M W Pienkowski, Senior Ornithologist

This paper is based on discussions with colleagues in ITE, RSPB, the NCC/RSPB Kite Committee (Wales), and NCC.

1 Background

1.1 The red kite formerly bred over many areas of Britain but now breeds only in central Wales, with a population of about 40 breeding pairs. Although it has been increasing slowly in recent years, its productivity is low (about 0.5 young per breeding pair, compared with 2–3 times this value in France and Germany). Whilst the reasons for the low productivity are not fully understood, it is considered that it is due either to genetic factors or to poor feeding conditions (the latter being considered the more likely). The red kite is also a target species for illegal egg-collecting, and costly protection schemes are undertaken. These are co-ordinated largely by RSPB but involve NCC staff time and financial input from NCC grant-aid and WHQ [NCC Wales HQ] funds. WHQ staff are also involved in co-ordinating the monitoring of population and performance, which involves also some CSD [NCC Chief Scientist Directorate] resources. The cost of only non-permanent staff involved in purely protection measures was estimated to total £12,000 for NCC and RSPB in 1986 alone.

1.2 Apart from the Welsh birds, the red kite became extinct in Britain largely as a result of persecution; suitable habitat and food almost certainly still exist in many of its former nesting areas, and a number are free from extensive persecution. In view of the only slight expansion in Wales and the distance from other breeding areas, kites are unlikely to recolonise these areas naturally. The species thus meets both the NCC and the RSPB criteria for reintroduction (see below), and is indeed one of the very few to do so, providing perhaps the clearest example.

The situation in Wales

1.3 Local measures are being investigated to improve the situation of kites in Wales. These include a current experiment which involves the artificial incubation of some of the eggs from nests particularly under threat. This experiment has several aims:
- to increase the output of young kites, by partially hand-rearing chicks hatched artificially, and returning them to the wild.
- to safeguard kite eggs from egg collectors, by removing them from threatened nests for artificial incubation.
- to improve our knowledge of the artificial rearing of kites, as a possible future conservation method.
- to assess the performance of eggs and young chicks when removed from some of the environmental constraints.

1.4 Preliminary results indicate that the performance from the assisted eggs is likely to be better than from the more natural situation, although the sample in this first year is too small for statistical conclusions.

1.5 Other current work on the Welsh birds involves blood analyses. These will allow the assessment of whether the Welsh population is as genetically variable as those in Sweden and East Germany.

1.6 Whilst these investigations of the Welsh birds are helpful in clarifying the biology of the species, a reintroduction proposal would not be dependent on further research on such processes, as it is already clear that the Welsh population is not able to expand sufficiently on any appreciable timescale. The earlier analyses by Dr Newton and others concerning the Welsh birds clearly suggested a link between poor performance and feeding conditions: "the main causes of breeding failure (non-laying, non-hatching of incubated eggs and brood mortality) occur commonly in other raptor-species, in which they have been clearly linked with measured food-shortages (Newton 1979). The kites may also have been short of food, despite their varied diets. The poorest year for breeding (1955) occurred when rabbits disappeared, and other poor years (1961–64) included a very hard winter, when several kinds of prey remained scarce for a year or two. In addition, breeding success throughout the 30 years correlated to some extent with vole numbers, with slightly better production in the peak vole years." (Davis & Newton 1981).

1.7 The long-term security of any species is dependent on maintaining as wide a distribution as possible. The kite appears to have survived in Wales not because this is a particularly favourable habitat (which it seems not to be) but because it was the only area where it was not exterminated. Because the red kite occupies a very small part of its potential range, it is very vulnerable. Apart from natural factors, against which the small population has little capacity for "buffering", the small population size itself attracts collectors. There is, therefore, a continuing need for the costly protection exercise, with no prospect of a spread to recolonise former haunts, and hence reduce the need for protection. Indeed, the recent publication of a book detailing nest-sites with grid-references could exacerbate problems of nest-robbing.

2   Suggestions for reintroduction

2.1 The situation described above has given rise to suggestions that red kites be reintroduced to a more favourable part of their former range in Britain. It is envisaged that a Continental source of birds be used, rather than the Welsh stock, so as to avoid extra demands on that.

2.2 Several aspects need taking into account in the consideration of this proposal:
- the problem that the reintroduction of kites could be taken as a precedent for other, less appropriate, (re)introductions, proposals for which are frequently made;
- the identification of suitable areas for reintroduction;
- the location of a suitable source of birds, and provision of rearing and release facilities and expertise;
- the provision of resources to implement the reintroduction, provide protection, and monitor the operation.

Precedents

2.3 The avoidance of undesirable (re)introductions was one of the main reasons that NCC and RSPB developed guidelines for reintroductions. NCC accepted the report "Wildlife introductions to Great Britain" by the Working Group on Introductions of the UK Committee of IUCN (1979) as the basis of its policy. This defines "reintroduction" as "the deliberate or accidental release of animals or plants of a species or race into an area in which it was indigenous in historical times; or a species or race so released." This definition in fact provides the first requirement to be met:

(1) That there is good historical evidence of former natural occurrence. The report indicates four further criteria:
(2) Whether there is a clear understanding of why the species was lost to this country. In general, only those lost through human agency and unlikely to recolonise naturally should be regarded as suitable candidates for reintroduction.
(3) That there are suitable habitats of sufficient extent and isolation to which the species can be reintroduced.
(4) That the individual plants or animals taken for reintroduction are of a taxon as close as possible to that of the native population.
(5) That their loss does not prejudice the survival of the population from which they were taken.

2.4 Points (1), (2) and (3) act against most of the less well-considered suggestions for (re)introductions, some of which concern species for which there is no good evidence for former presence. Many of the other cases concern species for which habitat loss or damage is one of the most likely causes for the decline, reintroduction therefore being totally inappropriate, at least before the habitat is restored.

2.5 As noted above, the red kite fills the specified criteria. Any eventual publicity, if the proposal is to proceed, should include a carefully worded statement drawing attention to the main points to be fulfilled for reintroductions to be appropriate.

Suitable areas for reintroduction

2.6 Prime criteria for a reintroduction area are outlined below.
(1) There should be little, and preferably no, [illegal] game-keeping because of the danger from poison baits.
(2) The area chosen should not be an isolated patch of good habitat in a predominantly game-keepered or otherwise unsuitable region.
(3) The area should offer a good winter food supply as well as that in summer.
(4) In view of the evidence from the Welsh studies that rainfall is a major adverse factor, drier eastern areas should be preferred.
(5) The ecology of the kites is clearly similar to that of buzzards, so that areas of high density and productivity of buzzards should be suitable.
(6) The potential attitude of the local human population should also be considered, and this is noted further below.

No one area is likely to fulfil all these features, but they should provide a useful guide. Points (1) and (2) are probably most essential, the remainder being desirable.

2.7 An initial suggestion for location was northern Scotland. This has certain advantages in terms of limited human population numbers, but this presents difficulties too. For example, the long-term protection and monitoring of the Welsh kite population has placed severe strains on the available local volunteer manpower, even with the relatively large number of employed wardens to help. There could, therefore, be considerable advantages in attempting a reintroduction in a more populous area, where large numbers of volunteers might be available. One suggestion is the south of England (e.g., Surrey, Kent). An added advantage here would be that the reintroduction of a large bird of prey to an area far more lacking in them than northern Scotland would probably be much more greatly appreciated by the general and bird-watching public, and thereby have other positive spin-offs for nature conservation.

2.8 Over their European range, red kites breed mainly in productive lowlands and as noted earlier, their British restriction to mainly upland areas are probably not because this is optimal but because they were eliminated from elsewhere and may be unable to spread greatly from these poor refuges. Davis and Newton (1981) reported that, when the birds were able to increase to some extent, "they occupied a wider area in central Wales. Evidently, at no stage were they restricted by lack of habitat, and similar landscapes and food-sources are widely available today elsewhere in Wales and in other parts of Britain. On the continent, kites occupy an even wider range of habitat than in Wales, and by analogy, they could be accommodated again in almost every British county."

2.9 In order to assess the potential suitability of regions throughout the country, the geographical distribution of two features is under current investigation. RSPB Species Protection Department are producing a map of the variation in occurrence of poisoned baits. BTO, under their research contract with NCC, are investigating geographic variation in performance of buzzards, based on their survey of this species and the nest record card scheme. Overlaying of these two maps should give an indication of the areas warranting further consideration, as being relatively free from persecution and having an inferred high potential productivity of kites.

Sources of birds and rearing facilities

2.10 Reintroduction of continental birds would probably be as fledglings (as for the sea eagle). Birds could probably be placed in tree cage/platforms where they could be fed artificially until able to fly. Quarantining would be necessary and therefore discussions with MAFF [Ministry of Agriculture, Fisheries and Food] essential in due course. There are considerable areas of expertise in relevant skills, not least the current work in Wales and the previous NCC experience with the sea eagles.

Resources

2.11 Apart from the main aim of reintroducing these impressive birds to a situation from where they can spread progressively to their former range, a secondary aim is to reduce the need for the costly protection exercise in Wales. It must be recognised, however, that this release of resources would not occur in the short-term. Indeed, in view of the period of immaturity in large birds of prey, one should hope for significant breeding success on a timescale of 10–20 years from the start of a programme. (One can compare the sea eagle situation, for which reintroductions ran from 1975 to 1985, which was also the first year of successful breeding – and there is still some way to go before a sound breeding population is established.) However, unless a start is made at some stage, there will never be a chance of success.

2.12 The main resource requirement would be to provide for a person to oversee and co-ordinate the operation, including collection and housing of birds, release, liaison with land-owners and volunteers, monitoring project, etc. It is likely that many of the incidental requirements could be obtained without cost. (This information is provided as background as resource allocations are considered in other fora.)

3   Action requested of the Committee

3.1 The Committee is asked to note this paper; comment if they wish, either in Committee or to Dr Pienkowski; and to approve the principle of reintroduction in this case, given the fulfilling of the five requirements for reintroduction detailed in section 2.3. Further progress would be subject to officers considering the results of the further investigations now in progress and, if appropriate, securing any necessary resources.

*****

Some of the Project Team during their visit to the Black Isle rearing and release area on 24th January 1989

up by saying that the project had the backing of the Committee in principle, that it was an excellent idea and that the Advisory Committee on Birds wished to be kept informed. Dr Ian Newton, a member of the Committee, agreed to serve on any project team, on behalf of the Committee as well as contributing his own expertise.

Comparable internal approval procedures had progressed within RSPB. Accordingly, I was able to invite a small group of people to a meeting at NCC's headquarters at Northminster House, Peterborough on 20th October 1987 to discuss "the possible reintroduction of the red kite". I was joined by Richard Porter and Roy Dennis (RSPB), Dr Ian Newton (Institute of Terrestrial Ecology, and NCC's Advisory Committee on Birds), Peter E Davis and Peter Walters Davies (Wales Kite Committee), and Dr Leo Batten and Mrs Sandy Collinge (NCC). This group became the Red Kite Project Team. The full Team, with varying membership over the years (see Acknowledgements), met ten times until it was wound up in 1995. There were meetings twice in each of the first two years as we set things up, and annually thereafter. In between meetings, I collated a number of update notes to keep all in the Team informed of each other's progress, especially at key times, as well, of course, of the many discussions between smaller sub-groups in person or by phone or mail.

The original meeting had the Advisory Committee on Birds paper in front of it and my note indicated the purpose of the meeting was to explore the practicalities of the proposal. The agenda included: sources of birds, legal requirements, rearing and release, identification of suitable areas, local involvement, protection, monitoring, timetable, funding and other resources, publicity and public relations, any other items, and the next meeting.

To help the reader through this maze, however, in the next chapters, I have separated these by topic, rather than remain in a strictly chronological sequence (for which see Annex 1). (In 1995, as the programme went into operational phase (see Chapter 11) the Project Team was replaced by the UK Red Kite Co-ordination Meeting, initially chaired by my colleague Dr Colin Galbraith with long-serving Dr Ian Evans as Secretary, and included RSPB, SNH, EN, CCW and other specialists.)

Precedents: what could we learn?

In adopting our proposal, NCC's Advisory Committee on Birds had effectively mandated us to take various actions. Amongst these was reviewing the context of reintroductions.

There have been various attempts and many more proposals for reintroductions or other releases of birds. Some cases could have been damaging. Conversely, we wanted to make sure that we could learn as much as possible from previous experience, even though this was rather scattered. We also needed to make sure that we did not set any unintended or unhelpful precedents – a factor very important both for a governmental conservation body and for a large national voluntary society and charity.

These issues were important also in other contexts, and we published several information leaflets prepared by NCC's Ornithology Branch in 1989. These are used below to review the situation in the late 1980s, in which we made these considerations. Initially, we considered the issue in general and then reviewing some specific examples.

Pros and cons of reintroduction projects generally

This section draws heavily on text from *NCC Ornithology* [Branch] *Note no. 14* (Pienkowski 1989), some of which was also re-used in Evans & Pienkowski (1991).

Many proposals have been made at various times for releases of diverse birds, and some projects, not then subject to control under the Wildlife and Countryside Act, were actually in progress at the time we started the Red Kite project. Conservation bodies were – and are – concerned about such proposals, as some may actually be harmful to wild populations, despite the good intentions of the persons undertaking the projects.

IUCN (1987) used the term 'translocation' to define the movement of 'living organisms from one area with free release to another.' This includes introductions, reintroductions and restocking. An introduction is the release of either captive-born or free-ranging wild-born animals into an area outside their original range. Such releases often disrupt natural populations, and the NCC [and its successors], voluntary conservation organisations and international conservation bodies all discourage these. Reintroduction (a term widely accepted despite its doubtful etymology) is a translocation that releases animals of any origin into an area within their original geographic range. Restocking is a sub-set of this, usually relating to releases in an area in which some of the original population remains.

Reintroduction schemes are potentially valuable conservation techniques for several reasons:

1. They can restore important elements lost from the wildlife resource.
2. This is particularly valuable in the case of populations of relatively small size and/or distribution. The best way of enhancing the long-term prospects of survival of such populations is by extending their range. Populations of birds of prey are extremely vulnerable to sudden unpredictable changes in the environment. For example, Peregrines were wiped out across most of the North American continent (as well as large parts of Europe) before the effects of certain agricultural chemicals were realised (*e.g.* Newton 1979).
3. Re-established populations can act as 'flagships' to encourage land-use and other practices which favour conservation of habitats, but which are difficult to popularise solely in their own right.
4. Such exercises provide important cases of positive conservation measures. These counter the negative image into which conservation bodies tend to be forced when undertaking the crucial role of resisting habitat damage.
5. For similar reasons, such operations tend to draw in partners, and the relationships built up may help in more difficult situations.
6. Such projects tend to draw in tremendous popular support and publicity for conservation and the participating bodies. The public knowledge of the White-tailed Eagle programme is amazingly widespread amongst people with only a passing interest in nature conservation.

There are, however, counter-points. Enthusiasm on the part of individuals or groups with a less rigorous approach tends to generate a plethora of proposals for reintroduction or release schemes. As well as the resource problem, ensuring that such projects are properly managed and monitored, there are more fundamental difficulties. Responsible conservation organisations would not sanction introductions, *i.e.*, the release of non-native species (as opposed to reintroductions). Ecological text-books fully illustrate the potential folly of this. Examples include the devastating effects on the bird fauna of New Zealand by the human introduction of land mammals (which did not previously exist there), the similar effects of humans bringing rats to many offshore islands and, more recently, the accidental release of North American Ruddy Ducks *Oxyura jamaicensis* in UK threatening the native White-headed Ducks *Oxyura leucocephala* of Spain.

Even for reintroduction and releases, conditions may have become unsuitable. At best, this may mean wasted effort; at worst, releases could severely damage populations still present. In between is a continuum of problems including unreasonable pressures on source populations and poor survival of released birds.

There are also some wider, almost philosophical, potential disadvantages. In some senses, a reintroduction is a last resort: an admission of previous failure to conserve a species or its habitat *in situ*. Prevention would have been better than a partial cure. What about the rest of the flora, fauna and natural processes? Reintroductions obviously focus on large charismatic species – although the enthusiasm such exercises generate may gather support for the less conspicuous elements of nature too. There is also a danger even in success: the erroneous idea may generate that there is always a 'technological' fix to the problems that humans cause to natural systems.

If we are going to proceed with a reintroduction – or, indeed, any nature-management approach – I would advocate what I would term an 'elegant' solution wherever possible. That is the impact may be major, but it should be time-limited, so that natural processes take over from most or all human intervention as early as possible. This is for both scientific conservation reasons and for resource (human time and money) reasons. This time-limit should not normally be set in advance (even though the bean-counters so dominant in modern funding systems would prefer this), because our knowledge is unlikely to be adequate to estimate this in advance. Instead, an information-based progress-review process should be designed in from the outset by the project managers.

Long (1981) estimated that approximately half of known cases of bird reintroductions, translocations and introductions failed. This is not surprising in view of the casual way that many seem to have been attempted. Even under the Wildlife and Countryside Act 1981, only a small proportion of potential schemes required licensing.

In Britain, there have been a variety of reintroduction exercises, but the lack of documentation and monitoring makes it difficult to review and assess these. Capercaillies became extinct in Scotland in 1785 and, after several attempts, were reintroduced successfully, although they are currently subject to a serious decline. Goshawks were reintroduced "unofficially" mainly in the 1970s. Most would consider this as successful, but the nature of the exercise makes any assessment difficult, and there appears to be conflict with other species in some areas.

It was to overcome some of these problems that the UK Committee for International Nature Conservation set up a working group on introductions (see above). The recommendations of this report were adopted by both the NCC and the RSPB, and remain in place, as a set of criteria to test for suitability of proposed programmes, noted earlier in this chapter.

We can now look at a couple of examples, as things stood as we reviewed the situation in 1987. As part of our public-awareness campaign on the pros and cons of reintroductions, we made these publicly available over the next couple of years as *NCC Ornithology Notes*, used to respond to enquiries and to be picked up as sources by several newspapers, magazines and broadcasters. I refer to a couple of contrasting ones below.

Reintroduction of the White-tailed Eagle to Britain

Not surprisingly, I start with the White-tailed Eagle, as this NCC-led project provided much of the experience at the time. As noted earlier, one of my tasks was to review the progress of this and consider what else would be needed to complete this. (I will comment on this review in this chapter below and in Chapter 12.)

This was a very successful programme, run by a team from NCC, RSPB, ITE (Institute of Terrestrial Ecology) and SWT (Scottish Wildlife Trust), albeit probably taking much longer than all had hoped. The case fits all 6 criteria above and is achieving its targets. The state of progress as we started the kite reintroduction is outlined in Annex 3, extracted from NCC's *Ornithology Note no. 5* (Pienkowski & Love 1989).

What did we learn?

The experience of our White-tailed Eagle project gave us great benefits for the Red Kite work, mainly in terms of how to do things, and also identified some points where we might improve, some of these also feeding back to improve the eagle programme (see Chapter 12).

One aspect that we wished to investigate was the rate of progress. Although the sea-eagle project was working, it was working very slowly, and productivity actually depended on a very small number of individuals (see Fig, 3.1, which extends a little later than the time of our *Ornithology Note*).

The remoteness of the area did not help. Even knowing the number of pairs attempting nesting was difficult to determine. Around this time, and while we were undertaking the review of the sea-eagle project, John Love heard from a helicopter pilot working in the area that he thought that it might be possible to survey by helicopter as he had seen eagles and thought that the disturbance by his machine may have been the cause for the birds to fly and become visible. As other methods were not working well, we thought that this might be worth trying – although helicopter time is extremely expensive. I managed to secure some funding to pay for a couple of days of this. We had been very careful in selecting timing for this activity, because we did not want to cause desertions by these birds at such a low population level. Therefore, basing matters on John's information, we timed our trip to be when most birds would be rearing young, which is generally a time less prone to be affected by disturbance than incubation.

Adult White-tailed Eagle on rearing cage at Rum National Nature Reserve [JL]. Other photos from this project are in Chapter 12 and Annex 3.

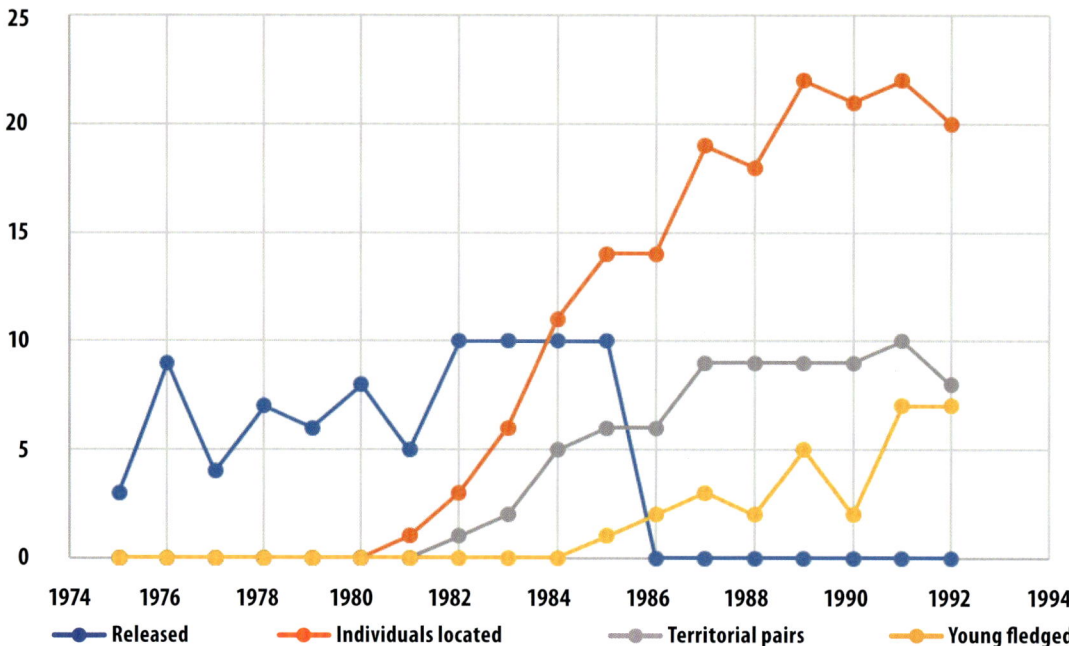

Figure 3.1. Numbers released and performance of White-tailed Eagles in Scotland 1975–1992

We assembled our team at Inverness, one of the bases of the charter helicopter company. As is normal in helicopters, the pilot was in the right-hand seat and I found myself in the front left-hand seat armed with Ordnance Survey maps and a route we planned carefully around the most likely areas, covering as much as we could in the 2 days available. In the two rear seats, as observers to the right and the left, were John Love and one of our most experienced observers from our Seabirds at Sea Team, Andy Webb. Our pilot was new to this base, having recently transferred from the main base in Aberdeen where he had been working in support of the North Sea oil industry. He was very able, and keen to try out this new survey technique.

After the first part of our route across to the west coast of Scotland and flying the initial part of the survey area, we needed to top up our fuel. His company had provided drums of fuel as a supply positioned on the west coast of Scotland. The instructions he had received were not exactly precise. They were in relation to a hotel near a particular village. Checking on the map, I found three hotels near the village and we reviewed them. The first our pilot declined because it was on too steep a slope on which to land. Even I thought the second was too surrounded by dense woodland with no appropriate landing position, and the pilot agreed. I said that the third appeared to be a more open country but warned him that the map showed two electricity power lines crossing nearby, at which he said that he could see not two, but three, and his colleagues appeared to have placed the fuel dump in the triangle formed by these three crossing! He skilfully dropped the helicopter vertically clear of all danger into the triangle, beside the fuel barrels.

The helicopter was equipped with a pump, run off its battery, in order to transfer fuel into its tanks. We connected this up and started pumping. However, I asked with some alarm whether the electrical connecting clip was supposed to spark as it worked. Fortunately, the helicopter ran on jet fuel, rather than anything more likely to catch fire for such a reason – but the situation was somewhat disturbing. So we thought we had better phone the mechanic at its base. This was a little before the time that mobile phones came into common use and, on the ground, the helicopter's radio was out of range. So we set off along the road to find a then familiar red phone-box. We made contact with his mechanic, who explained that, as he

Above: 'Our' helicopter landed with one of the 3 threatening sets of power cables visible above, and our improvised siphoning technique to refuel. Below: Safely anchoring the helicopter in the low evening light and, in the morning, almost ready to go after our overnight stop on the Hebridean island of Lewis and Harris. [MP]

always worked from base with properly powered pumps, he had no idea how the helicopter's own pump worked. Having walked this far, our pilot decided that we should fuel ourselves and we called at the tiny local shop to ask if they could supply us with some sandwiches. The young lady there said that they did not do sandwiches, and so our pilot said he really hoped she could as he had landed his helicopter just down the road. She disappeared into the back of the building and reappeared a few minutes later with some sandwiches to sell to us. As we walked away, our friendly pilot said, "it always seems to work."

Back at the helicopter, we devised a new technique. An old vehicle had been left as a farm-cart nearby and, between us, we managed to push it up alongside the helicopter. At even greater effort, we managed to lift the large fuel drum on to the cart. This gave us enough height to siphon the fuel into the helicopter's tank using the pipe temporarily disconnected from the pump.

Back in the air, a new challenge appeared. Air traffic control at Stornoway warned that an RAF Tornado fighter-bomber was practising low-level approaches in the area. We heard the air traffic controller ask the pilot if he could indicate where he would be operating, but the military don't like to say that sort of thing. So all air traffic control could do was to ask the Tornado pilot to watch out for a small Squirrel helicopter. Our pilot said that he did not understand why he himself kept looking over his shoulder because, as he said, "Even if I see it, there is nothing I can do about it because it moves too fast." Fortunately, we did not meet at close quarters but caught a glimpse of it in the far distance, over the Outer Hebrides.

We did not know of course whether a helicopter survey technique would work for censusing the eagles – this was a test. We had not seen any despite flying for some time through likely areas. We did, however, know of one nest already. I realised that those of us used to seeing things from the ground would have fairly little idea of where we were when viewed from the air. Indeed, it was taking me a great deal of concentration to keep track of this even with the map. I navigated us past the known nest, and we saw no sign of eagles. Once I was sure that we were well past it, I confessed what I had done and asked the pilot to turnaround to examine that area more closely. As we approached the nest again, an eagle appeared in the air, and my colleagues said perhaps it works, after all. However, looking forwards from a front seat, I'd seen what the others could not yet: the other adult was sitting tight on the nest (which we would not have found by scanning without knowing it was there). The bird we had seen first was in fact the off-duty parent coming to challenge this other creature (the helicopter) invading its airspace.

So, our test – albeit very interesting with some spectacular views – had suggested that this technique would not work reliably for finding nests that we did not know about. We had however the remaining time available already paid for, so that we could keep surveying the rest of our key area and pick up any information we could.

Our next stage involved crossing the Minch to the hotel that our pilot had booked for us on Lewis in the Western Isles. Before that, we had to land and don bright orange survival suits for a sea-crossing in a single-engined helicopter. Our pilot climbed to great height, pointing out that, should anything go wrong, he wanted time as we descended to get at least one emergency message out.

Safely across the Minch, we arrived over the hotel and landed on its lawn, with the surrounding saplings bending substantially in our down-draught. A group of amazed people emerged from the hotel. Our pilot asked me to go to speak with them as he closed down – reminding me to always go round the front of a helicopter with engines running to avoid the tail rotor slicing me up. Still orange suited, I went across to the hotel and said that I believed we had a reservation, to which they replied: "Yes, but nobody told us you would be arriving like that."

Views from the helicopter: Sea-eagles' habitat in western Scotland is very patchy, from rich shorelines to barren uplands. [MP]

Looking north, from the helicopter, over Ardnamurchan Lighthouse and Point, the westernmost point of the British mainland, towards Rum (left) and Eigg (right), with Skye beyond. [MP]

The next day, we continued our survey, crossing back to the mainland and then across to Inverness, without recording further eagles. So, we had, rather expensively but with a great deal of fun, completed the test ... and rejected the technique.

The other main problem in trying to work out why the rate of increase of White-tailed Eagles was so slow was that the low numbers themselves meant that formal quantitative analysis was virtually impossible. To get any clue, urgently required for both the eagle work and the proposed kite project, we needed to use less formal evidence. One clue was that at least some of the failures of previously successful pairs were probably due to adverse weather. We really started to query whether treating the places where a species last hung on as being the best habitat might be seriously flawed. This would affect our choice for kites and our recommendations for future eagle releases.

Barn Owl

By contrast, I should also give an example of a case in which the guidelines led to a negative conclusion. Barn Owls had been declining in Britain and had given rise to popular concern. Some of this was usefully directed at conservation efforts and re-establishment of habitat. However, there was also a fashion for the releasing of captive-bred birds of various, and often unknown, genetic origins. One estimate is that up to 3000 Barn Owls were being released each year. These were often into areas where there were wild birds, raising the possibility of competition. Release into areas where Barn Owls were still present or nearby also raises the question as to why the natural population had not increased or spread. There were then no existing powers under the Wildlife and Countryside Act 1981 to limit releases. Analysis of ringing returns by the British Trust for Ornithology (partly under contract to the Nature Conservancy Council and later its successor bodies) showed a much higher mortality rate among released individuals than in wild Barn Owls: over 90% of released individuals died within about 10 months of release. Because of this unacceptable performance, the Barn Owl release schemes could well have fallen foul of the Abandonment of Animals Act 1960. In any event, birds in captivity should not be released to the wild without adequate monitoring and support.

Most releases of Barn Owls had not been shown to fulfil the criteria given earlier in this chapter. Specifically, numbers 2, 3 and 4 had not been demonstrated, and considerable doubt surrounded these, as well as 5 in some cases. The habitat for Barn Owls was clearly the priority for action, and release schemes were an inappropriate approach until this was rectified and might be unnecessary afterwards. NCC was opposed to the release of Barn Owls.

In addition to other problems, Barn Owls were not a priority for action, being a very widespread species across the world. This one had a regular roost on a Strangler Fig, growing through a solution hole "chimney" down to a cave in the limestone in the UK Overseas Territory of the Turks & Caicos Islands in the West Indies. [MP]

Again, this was set out in an NCC *Ornithology Note*. Annex 4 is an extract from an updated version (Percival *et al*.1992), released by JNCC after the government had accepted our recommendation to legislate to prevent Barn Owl releases (and after the government-imposed reorganisation of the statutory conservation bodies in 1992 – Chapter 11).

This *Note* explained that only 15% of adults and 10% of juveniles released survived to the end of their first year (compared with 71% and 21% in wild birds). In most instances they were simply being released to an early death. There are several reasons why this was happening: many were released into unsuitable habitat, and almost all were coming into an environment of which they had no experience. The problem of releasing captive-bred Barn Owls into the wild was not simply allowing them to come to a rapid demise. The introduction of different genes into the population may not have been a healthy process for the conservation of the local wild birds. Birds are generally closely adapted to their local conditions. The viability of wild genetic stock could have been reduced if they interbred with introductions from other regions or in some cases other countries. Introductions of disease to local birds could also have been a potential problem. These released birds could also have competed with the wild birds in areas where resources (*e.g.* food supply, nest sites) are limited, again harming rather than benefiting local wild populations.

Other experience

We did, of course, benefit from the experience of other schemes, especially overseas. As one of several examples, I quote from a file note from my colleague Dr Tim Reed. Tim headed NCC's Ornithology Branch after my promotion to Assistant Chief Scientist, the Branch falling within the set of branches in my division:

GRIFFON VULTURE REINTRODUCTION AT CASSAGNES, CEVENNES NATIONAL PARK

19 September 1990: The visit to the Griffon Vulture Reintroduction Programme at Cassagnes
Griffon Vultures used to breed in the area but were shot out as a function of sheep protection, and lack of carrion. The last vultures bred in 1930. With the depopulation of the area and the change in practices, coupled with the establishment of the National Park, it was thought that it was possible that part of the Cévennes, the Causse Méjean would meet the conditions for reintroduction under the IUCN programme. Between 1970 and 1980, a total of 60 vultures were brought into the area and came from a variety of sources: from captive breeding, from those which were injured, and from zoos. The first of the captive-bred ones were kept in a series of enclosures and the first bred in 1978. These then bred further and in 1981 the first 6 couples of vultures were released. Between 1981 and 1986, 60 vultures were freed but, of these, 20 failed to survive due to hunger, electric power cables and other sources of trouble.

The first birds stayed around the release area. Slowly they began to move into adjacent gorges, taking up and settling at nest sites. In the first 5 years after their release, at the convergence of the Tarn and the Jonte, they began to move up to 10 kilometres either way, using previous nest sites and starting to settle in. At the same time as the released vultures were being followed, using radio-tracking, birds started to come in from the adjacent Pyrenees, both Griffons and Egyptians. The result of this has been possibly to increase the success of the programme. In 1982, the first year after release, 3 pairs set up nests. In 1983 and 1984 there were more nesting attempts and, by 1985, there were 12 pairs which laid 9 eggs and reared 5 chicks. Eight of these pairs came from the release birds and 4 from those who came in under the guise of the protection that was afforded to the release birds. Evidently, the immigrant birds were of the right age, that is 5–6 years, to begin breeding.

Given that the National Park is both a landscape and a farming exercise, and also a conservation exercise, the success of the Griffon obviously depends on the ability of the farmers to produce excess sheep. With a farming premium of 1800 French francs per sheep, there is great encouragement to keep sheep on high ground. One should note here that there is an additional premium from the French Government for hill farmers on top of the 1800 French francs that come from the EEC (twice the level of support given to the Scots and Welsh). Under these conditions, it is not surprising that there is now a good agricultural source of carrion in addition to the carrion that one would normally find. The fact that the farmers are encouraged to bring in dead stock to supplement the carrion increases the food supply initially to the birds.

Although, over the last 4 years, the numbers have doubled and breeding success has gone up, the Programme still continues to establish a very large population (quite what large means is undefined as yet), so that they are resilient to change and can be fully established within perhaps the next 10 years. The fact that birds are coming in from the Pyrennees and from possibly towards the Alps, is remarkably encouraging. The success of the nesting is increasing and so all nests appear to have at least one egg per year. There are one or two problems, mainly from disturbance. These come from either climbing on the very steep pinnacles that surround the edge of the cliffs in the Tarn and the Jonte Gorge and from the possibility of poisoning. This cannot be ruled out. However, the relatively low density of people in the Park (600 people in the Causse end of the Park) means that it is fairly obvious who any poisoners are. Also, the fact that something like 30,000 people arrive during the course of the summer to look at the vultures means that the financial returns to the farmers who almost all have one or two sites for hire means that it's financially counter-productive to consider threatening the vultures. If we note that the Programme gives farmers income for dead sheep, then it is obvious that they can only gain from this Programme. Like the Capercaillie programme, the major emphasis has been on the release of animals. One has the feeling that the biology, that is the breeding biology of the species, and the recent success rates are perhaps deemed to be something that would come anyway. On the positive side, the radio-tracking programme works very well, showing that the birds move quite a long way before settling down. As in other raptors, it's the movement of the young that is the most dramatic; moving quite a long way after release. The fact that the nest sites were not being used by eagles or only to a limited extent by ravens does mean that most of the factors that would be needed for successful re-establishment are there.

A fuller account appeared later (Terrasse *et al*. 1994).

A species with previously unsuccessful or marginally successful reintroduction attempts in UK: Capercaillie - male (left) and female [MP]

Evans *et al.* (1999) updated and extended a review of reintroduction or translocation that we had started earlier in the project. Such exercises had been used successfully to restore several bird of prey populations, *e.g.* Mauritius Kestrel *Falco punctatus* (Cade & Jones 1993), Griffon Vulture *Gyps fulvus* (Terrasse *et al.* 1994), Peregrine (Cade 1985), Osprey *Pandion haliaetus* (Poole 1989). However, several past efforts to restore raptors in the UK by translocation had failed, *e.g.* Barn Owl (Taylor 1993), Buzzard *Buteo buteo* (Harvey 1989), Red Kite (Lovegrove 1990), White-tailed Eagle (Dennis 1968, 1969; Sandeman 1965; before the current exercise), emphasising a need for careful planning and monitoring of the releases. The failure to plan or monitor the uncoordinated reintroduction of the Goshawk *Accipiter gentilis* make it impossible to assess adequately and some concerns have been raised about unpredicted adverse consequences (Kenward *et al.* 1981, Gibbons *et al.* 1993). Amongst non-raptors, Capercaillie *Tetrao urogallus* in the 19th century first failed and then succeeded but the status remains fragile (Harvey-Brown 1879, Evans 1995). An attempt with Great Bustard *Otis tarda* failed but follow-up may prove successful if necessary habitat management is carried out adequately (Goriup & Collar 1980).

Was the Red Kite a suitable candidate for reintroduction?

So, what about the Red Kites themselves? How did the species match up to the criteria for reintroduction? Newton (1988, which is drawn on, together with team discussions and other sources in this section) considered in detail the question of reintroductions of raptors and considered that Red Kites are one of the few species of British birds which may fulfil the criteria. Several aspects were reported also by Evans & Pienkowski (1991).

1. **That there is good historical evidence of former natural occurrence.**
   There is clear evidence of recent natural occurrence (see Chapter 2).

2. **Whether there is a clear understanding of why the species was lost to this country. In general, only those lost through human agency and unlikely to recolonise naturally should be regarded as suitable candidates for reintroduction.**
   The factors leading to the loss are well understood (Chapter 2) and have largely been corrected by modern legislation and public attitudes. The continued illegal laying of poison baits does, however, raise some concern in certain areas, including the relict range

in Wales. Due to these and other factors currently limiting the range in Wales, there was no realistic prospect of Red Kites expanding naturally to occupy their former range throughout Britain on any reasonable timescale.

3. **That there are suitable habitats of sufficient extent and isolation to which the species can be reintroduced.**
   In the assessment of the NCC and the RSPB, there were areas of suitable (and more productive) habitat for reintroduction elsewhere in Britain in many of its former breeding haunts, beyond its relict range in Wales. By establishing additional populations in these areas, particularly where a higher productivity could be achieved, contributions could be made to help safeguard the long-term future of the Red Kite both at home and internationally.

4. **That the individual plants or animals taken for reintroduction are of a taxon as close as possible to that of the native population.**
   Until recent human intervention, the range of Red Kites was more continuous, and it is unlikely that there were any significant genetic differences between the Continental and the British stock: they are similarly sized and look the same. There would be further genetic work to check this, and this was subsequently confirmed (Chapter 4).

5. **That their loss does not prejudice the survival of the population from which they were taken.**
   The reintroduced kites would come from parts of Europe where the conservation authorities and ornithologists considered that the removal of young would not prejudice the source populations (Chapter 4).

The criteria allowing reintroductions were therefore fulfilled, but would such an attempt be worthwhile?
In the 1980s, Red Kites were one of only three globally threatened bird species in UK. In the context of Britain, a major benefit would be the making of the population less dependent on events in just one area of central Wales.

Red Kites are restricted to Europe and a few adjacent areas (see Chapter 4). The distribution and numbers of this species in north Africa, eastern Asia and eastern and south-eastern Europe were decreasing. In western and northern Europe, the population, although previously fragmented after declines, appeared to be stable or increasing. Britain could therefore make a major contribution to the world conservation of this species.

If the conservation of Red Kites in Britain were to serve any real benefit to the safeguarding of this globally-threatened species, every effort must be made to enhance and extend its range. However, factors limiting the range in Wales prevented their spread to the suitable habitat that still existed across large parts of its former breeding haunts outside Wales. Establishing additional populations in these areas could make a significant contribution to international Red Kite conservation.

The team noted also that the reintroduction itself could gain widespread support, and help accelerate improved attitudes to birds of prey, thereby potentially aiding the re-spread of other raptors, such as Buzzards. Sympathy for more sustainable land-use and habitat management might also be enhanced.

After more than two years of detailed assessment, in late 1987 the joint NCC/RSPB project team determined that the Red Kite fulfilled all the criteria for reintroduction. It was considered a conservation priority to help spread the population by translocation into its former breeding range. These conclusions were approved by NCC's Advisory Committee on Birds, on behalf of NCC's governing Council.

The Project Team decided to conduct releases in both England and Scotland. NCC and RSPB personnel remained united in that this would continue to be organised and planned as a joint project. Operational matters in each release area would though be managed separately. Bearing in mind the distribution of key personnel and other matters, we agreed that Roy Dennis of RSPB would lead in Scotland, while I would do so in England. Close coordination would be maintained, through the joint project team, between operations in England and Scotland, and related work on the relict populations in Wales. And of course across Europe given the international aspects of the project.

Resources

Decisions to do something are always subject to resources. Before getting back to the science and conservation proper, the essential but labyrinthine subject of resourcing needs to be explored.

We were very keen that as many as possible of the resources needed to run this project would be donated by volunteers or as gifts in kind from sympathetic companies. However, some direct costs would need to be covered, especially to employ a project officer.

In these days of Species Action Plans, Biodiversity Strategies, implementation projects *etc.*, it will come as something of a surprise to many to discover that, at the time, the Government conservation agency, the NCC, had no budget for species conservation or species recovery projects. One of the reasons for this originated a decade earlier.

When the Conservative Party came into power in 1979, the new Prime Minister, Mrs Margaret Thatcher appointed Michael Heseltine as Secretary of State for the Environment. Mr Heseltine was quite enthusiastic on environmental, and other, matters and asked his officials to produce a new Environment Act. According to several sources, rather than consult the practitioners at their own statutory advisory body, the NCC, some officials threw together the assortment of ideas sitting on their shelves. The resulting major legislation, the Wildlife and Countryside Act 1981, had many useful points. It also had some serious flaws, which might have been addressed by more practitioner involvement at an earlier stage. (I am neutral here; I was an academic at the time!)

Bear in mind that, in much of UK, there are few nationally owned nature reserves. Other public land includes the holdings of the Forestry Commission, Ministry of Defence, the Crown Estate and the Highways Agency. The majority of nature reserves and other protected areas (usually Sites of Special Scientific Interest, SSSIs) are managed by agreement with the individuals or companies owning the land. Usually at that time, this involved some form of payment for profits foregone as a result of taking conservation measures (later replaced by more flexible and positive agreements). The 1981 legislation had formalised this for all areas designated as SSSIs, as well as more formal nature reserves. One major problem was that the 1981 Act, once in place, was found to require all the SSSIs to be formally renotified by a very bureaucratic and unfriendly procedure for communicating with the owners and occupiers (which in some cases totalled hundreds of small-holders for each site). NCC officers hated these procedures; they went totally against their normal way of working with partners. It hurt them even more when, as expected, land-owners and occupiers hated them too, and associated this hatred with the NCC and its officers. Eventually (once it became possible to bring in rather better procedures, more resembling previous practice) relations tended to be restored and improved. However, in the interim, this trauma caused all conservation budget lines to become very site-focussed. This was not unrelated, of course, to the close linkage to immediate results which was also an increasing feature of the then-newish government. Many of us were not averse to linking funding to objectives. However, problems arose in biological systems if these objectives were short-term and doctrinal. This completely distorted the personnel resources and financial budget of the agency, with everything being focused at the time on sites rather than species and ecosystems.

How could we address the interesting challenge of funding a species conservation project with no budget-line for species conservation? The NCC was an interestingly constituted body. The two largest blocks of staff were scientists (usually with a university education in biology and research background) and civil-service administrators who had somehow found their way to this curious near-civil-service body. Surprisingly, these groups generally knitted together well into a team – but this was in the days before the invasions of 1980s-style management consultants.

Working in conservation research for several years, I had previously had good contacts with NCC. As a research scientist arriving into this world, I needed the help of the administrators. With a background in animal behaviour (something I found useful again later when dealing with politicians), I found myself noting that the administrators came in two basic groups. One had some similarities to the caricature, in that the usual response to any enquiry was "you can't do that; the rules don't allow it – it's more than my job's worth to help". Even NCC had some of these "jobsworths" (who would usually imagine a rule against something even if none existed) – but fortunately their presence was in moderation. The other type, faced with a similar situation, were more likely to say "Oh, I see what you are trying to do. We can't do it that way, but we could try this…" I am forever grateful that some of the key administrators with whom I worked came from this type. Fortunately, the finance administrator in our Chief Scientist Directorate (in which my Ornithology Branch sat), the late Mrs Sandy Collinge, was one of the latter. She said to me "would you say that this reintroduction is experimental?" I said yes. So she said "obviously, then, it falls into the research budget." This is why all early references to the project are given as "Experimental Reintroduction of the Red Kite." An experimental project qualified for the research budget – and, indeed, in those first years, it certainly was experimental.

During my time as Head of Ornithology at NCC, my Branch initiated at least two successful species conservation programmes. We simply found other financial headings under which we could justifiably place them. When the species recovery budgets eventually became available in the mid-1990s, the kite project was adopted by that grouping as being sufficiently far advanced as to be showing results while the new "experimental" ones got under way.

At the first Project Team meeting on 20th October 1987 at our offices in NCC's HQ in Peterborough, we agreed that the programme should be funded jointly by RSPB and NCC. The RSPB would take the lead in Scotland and NCC in England. I explained that a bid for resources would be programmed into the next financial year in order to appoint a Coordinator for the English area in autumn 1988. If an NCC employee, he or she would probably be based in a local NCC office though supervised from NCC Chief Scientist Directorate in Peterborough. RSPB would seek internal funds for their share. The hope was that the first birds could then be introduced in June 1989.

As for NCC, all RSPB projects have to go through a review panel; and it was felt that the kite project would be rated highly in terms of importance, if less so on urgency. I noted that NCC were also concerned that if priority is given to urgency, the important ones are then never done. Both bodies were anxious to avoid "urgent" work displacing that with greater longer-term importance.

At the Project Team meeting on Thursday 6th October 1988, near the proposed English release site, Richard Porter reported that the RSPB had the money earmarked for the Scottish part of the project, although they would not be considering employing someone in the post as project officer until April 1989. The person would be employed to deal with other matters as well as the kite project. The costs for this would be around £20,000, to include salary (for both roles), costs and PR work. I reported that NCC had arranged funding for the English part of the project. It was envisaged that the NCC Project Officer post would also be about half-time on the Red Kite project; with half time on assisting other NCC conservation projects in the area. Recruitment procedures were taking place.

At the Project Team meeting on 24th January 1989 at NCC's Inverness office, RSPB's initial estimate was that it was likely to cost £15,000 per year in each area and this was on the basis of full-time employment of one person over a 6-month period and part-time employment for the remainder of the year. NCC's estimate was slightly lower.

In the update to the Project Team on 8th April 1989, I was able to report that Dr Ian Evans, who had very relevant experience and had recently completed his PhD, had been appointed as project officer for the English area in this first season. He would be working with Welsh kite workers in April. From May, he would be preparing the English site. Ian stayed with the project, playing a leading role for several years. Dr James Kirkwood (Zoological Society of London) would be able to check the kites in England and assist in the case of problems. In Scotland, a project officer had yet to be appointed. The Project Team Update of 21st May 1989 later reported that, in Scotland, RSPB had appointed Dee Doody as Project Officer. Andy Knight started as Red Kite summer warden in Scotland on 1st May 1990.

4. Identifying the true world distribution and finding sources of birds

Discovering the true state of the world distribution of Red Kites

A basic need at an early stage of the project was a more detailed review of the world status of Red Kites. There were several reasons for this. First, we needed to know whether the project was of real potential value to the survival of Red Kites, and not merely an attractive project just of local value. Second, we needed to know more of the potential sources of birds. Lastly, bearing in mind our reintroduction guidelines, we needed to know that supplying small numbers of birds from such areas would pose no risk to their local kite populations.

This review provided one of the early roles of our newly appointed project officer, Dr Ian Evans, to lead alongside myself on developing our preliminary work. The results were brought together in a paper for the Project Team and were later made available to a wider audience in the journal *British Birds* (Evans & Pienkowski 1991). The following section is based on these papers, with kind permission of the journal.

Historical status as in the 1980s

Red Kites were formerly common throughout Europe. During the nineteenth century, they inhabited the area then covered by Italy, Spain, France, Switzerland, Germany, Denmark, Sweden, Norway, European Russia, the Netherlands (although rather rare) and, outside Europe, parts of north Africa, Siberia and 'the greatest part of Asia' (Morris 1904), although the last is perhaps rather sweeping and wrong, unless possibly referring to Asia Minor (an old name for what is now Turkey). In Britain, they were said to have 'swarmed in the streets of London' in the fifteenth and sixteenth centuries (literature quoted by Nisbet 1959) and were protected by legislation on account of the benefits of its scavenging habit (see Chapter 2).

Later, the geographic range (map in Chapter 2) was described by Walters Davies & Davis (1973) as extending north from Iberia, through southern and eastern France and Germany to southern Sweden. It extended eastwards as far as the western (then) Soviet Union, from the Baltic Republics in the north to the Balkans and the Caucasus in the south. Within this range, the distribution was rather fragmented, since Red Kites were absent from most of southern Poland, Czechoslovakia (the Czech Republic and Slovakia), eastern Switzerland, Austria, Hungary, Denmark, Norway, Belgium, the Netherlands and north-western Germany. Outside Europe, populations survived in parts of north-western Africa and in the Canary and Cape Verde Islands. The northern breeding populations (with the exception of those in Britain) were mainly migratory and wintered in the Mediterranean area. In recent years, however, increasing numbers of individuals had remained in Sweden and Germany throughout the year (see also Cramp & Simmons 1980, whose summary map is reproduced in Chapter 2).

The decline in the abundance of Red Kites during the nineteenth century has been attributed mainly to human persecution. To some extent, this continued despite legal protection. As a consequence, this species was rare over much of its then range, and it was considered vulnerable in world terms. It was one of only three British species on the *World Checklist of Threatened Birds* (Collar & Andrew 1988), the others being White-tailed Eagle and Corncrake. It had been given protection under Annex 1 of the EEC Bird Directive, Schedule 1 of the Wildlife and Countryside Act 1981, and by the Berne and Bonn Conventions. This legal protection (and in some cases physical protection of nest sites) had been beneficial, since it had halted the decline in several countries and encouraged some recovery of range.

In the past, there had been few attempts to census the entire world population of Red Kites. Meyburg & Meyburg (1987) assessed the status of raptor populations in countries bordering the Mediterranean, whilst Génsbøl (1986) covered the Western Palearctic. In a number of areas (*e.g.,* Wales, Sweden, Belgium, Denmark and Corsica), regular monitoring meant that the population status was relatively well known. In many others (mainland France and Germany for example) only rough estimates could be made, whilst in the rest (*e.g.,* Morocco and the USSR [Soviet Union]) quantitative data were wholly lacking.

We sent requests for information to ornithologists in all countries in Europe, North Africa and the Middle East where Red Kites were thought to have bred or wintered in relatively recent years. Contributors were asked to provide recent information on the actual number of breeding pairs in their country, as well as recent and past population trends. (Remember, this was in the late 1980s – correspondence was by physical post; email had been invented in the previous decade but was not widely available for international – or even inter-organisational – communication until the 1990s. Accessing a publication not available in your own library was a challenge involving Inter-Library Loans, whereby your librarian tried to borrow a copy or secure a photocopy from a library which held it.) A literature survey was also undertaken. The results of the review are given below, and breeding aspects summarised in Table 4.1. This can be viewed against the earlier distribution map reproduced from Cramp & Simmons (1980) in Chapter 2.

In order to aid identification of patterns of change, the summary below of the situation in the late 1980s is ordered approximately geographically. Ian and I tried to minimise breaks in the list where the distribution is fairly continuous. In line with this, I start in the northwest, and proceed eastwards across central Europe, southwards to the Mediterranean, and finally westwards to Iberia and the Atlantic islands. The review uses the national definitions current at the time, because that was how the information was collected. Shortly afterwards, a period of restoration of former countries, boundary changes and other re-organisations occurred as (in most cases) a more democratic system came into place in central and eastern Europe. To avoid inadvertent errors, I stay in this summary with the old country names under which data were collected. This definitely does not imply any nostalgia for those times!

NORWAY There had been no breeding records in the 20th century, although apparently there was a very small population in the county of Östfold up to about 1880. The species remained a rare visitor. There had, however, been a marked increase in the number of records in recent years, with three to four annually. These birds were probably from Denmark or Sweden (Geoffrey Acklam *in litt.*).

SWEDEN Since the early 1970s, the population in the south had increased steadily. By 1980, there were 50 pairs, of which 42 were successful and, in 1981, 54 pairs, of which 49 were successful (Sveusson 1982). By 1986, the population had increased three-fold, to 150 pairs (Sylvén 1987), and, by 1989, to over 200 pairs. Productivity was estimated at 1.98 young per successful pair and 1.54 per territorial pair (Magnus Sylvén, Roy Dennis *in litt*, and verbally).

DENMARK The large population of Red Kites was exterminated at the turn of 19th/20th centuries, but breeding was occasionally attempted between 1920 and 1970. During the 1970s, the species returned as a regular breeder. Only 10–15 pairs had become established, breeding annually during 1980–89, mainly in southeast Jutland (Hans Erik Jørgensen *in litt.*). Breeding success ranged from 53–63% of nests in the core area of southeastern Jutland to more than 50% in other areas. An average brood size of 2.1 young from a total of 54 successful nests had been recorded (Jørgensen 1989).

BRITAIN & IRELAND Formerly bred in every county, but during the nineteenth century relentless persecution exterminated this species from England, Scotland and Ireland. Only a small remnant group, possibly as small as approximately 12 individuals, survived in the more remote parts of mid Wales. This population had, as a result of nest protection, increased very slowly up to the then record level of 69 territorial pairs (of which 52 actually nested and 32 fledged young) in 1989, and 62 nesting pairs producing 70 fledged young in 1990 (P. E. Davis *in litt.* and verbally).

Before 1980, almost all the known breeding was confined to an area of about 70 x 45 km in mid Wales (Davis & Newton 1981). Since 1981, the population had expanded slightly outside this area. Recolonisation of former haunts was, however, continually hampered by the illegal use of poison baits and, to some extent, by the destructive practice of egg-collecting.

The productivity during 1951–80 was notoriously poor, with an average of only 0.54 young per territorial pair. This is equivalent to 0.66 young per nesting pair and 1.34 young per successful pair (n=676). During 1964–80, mean clutch and brood sizes of 2.20 and 1.35 respectively were recorded, and only 40% of all nests fledged young (Davis & Newton 1981). Later breeding statistics for 1985–89 indicated that productivity had remained around these levels (P. E. Davis *in litt.*).

FRANCE Thiollay & Terrasse (1984) estimated 2,300–2,900 pairs in 1979–82. No more recent survey had been undertaken for the whole of France. The main breeding areas for Red Kites in 1982 were Lorraine (740–790 pairs), Franche-Comté (700–1,000 pairs), Champagne-Ardenne (480–550 pairs) and Midi-Pyrénées (800–1,000 pairs). Smaller populations were found also in the Massif Central, Auvergne and Burgundy. Recent estimates were 400 pairs in Franche-Comté (*Atlas du Jura* by Joveniaux *et al.* [1993], cited by Dr J. Francois *in litt.*) and 100 pairs in the Haute-Loire, Auvergne (Bernard Joubert *in litt.*). In Champagne-Ardenne, the large population appeared to have decreased in the previous five to seven years; this was thought to be related to habitat loss and increased cultivation. Many winter roosts had also disappeared in this region; this had been attributed to successive cold spells and a decline in refuse dumps. In Champagne, Red Kite productivity of 1.51 young per breeding pair and 1.86 young per successful pair had been recorded from 53 occupied nests in 1971–82 (Christian Riols *in litt.*).

Poisoning, both legal and illegal, was the main form of persecution and could occur on a very large scale. For instance, a plague of voles (Microtinae) had led to a poisoning campaign over 150,000 ha in south-eastern Haute-Marne, one of the best areas for birds of prey in north-eastern France. Also, in the western part of Marne department, raptors were still poisoned, trapped and shot despite legal protection; the Red Kite was the most vulnerable species (Christian Riols *in litt.*).

In a detailed study of the population of the Red Kite on Corsica, Patrimonio (1990) reported a stable population of 100–180 pairs on the island. The use of strychnine baits against foxes *Vulpes vulpes*, however, posed a threat, although the bird was protected by law. Average clutch size was 2.85 eggs per nest; 46% of eggs produced fledged young. Productivity was, on average, 1.94 young per successful pair and 1.27 per breeding pair (n=22).

NETHERLANDS There had been only two recent breeding records. One was in 1976, when a pair was said to have reared two young, but the report was not properly documented. Two nests were discovered in 1977: one was successful, probably leading to the rearing of two young, while the other was destroyed before the eggs hatched (Edward van IJzendoorn *in litt.*; Scharringa 1978). Incidental breeding could not be ruled out in the future, as individual kites were often seen in spring near the eastern and southern borders, presumably having strayed from breeding areas in Germany or Belgium.

BELGIUM Red Kites ceased to breed from around 1921 until 1973 when breeding was confirmed again. Since then, the population had increased from one to ten pairs in 1973–78 to 15–20 pairs in 1979–89 but had remained stable for several years. The main breeding areas, which were comparatively small, were in the east and southeast. Outside these areas, breeding was irregular and scattered. Productivity was good, with 2.32 young per successful pair (n=19) recorded during 1985–88 (René de Liedekerke *in litt.*).

LUXEMBOURG Since the 1940s, numbers had increased steadily to 12–15 pairs, with a maximum of 20 recorded in one year. It was now thought that the population had reached its upper limit, although possibly some expansion might still occur (David Crowther *in litt.*).

WEST GERMANY After a decline in the 1960s, the population recovered in the mid-1970s to early 1980s. During this time, Rheinwald (1982) estimated the population at 2,000 pairs. The present population was estimated at 1,700–2,200 pairs, of which the majority were found in Lower Saxony and Hesse (600–800 pairs each), although Bavaria, Baden-Wurttemberg, Rhineland and Westphalia also held 100–200 pairs each (Alistair Hill *in litt.*). The population was now declining, which Hill associated with changes in rubbish-disposal methods. The substantial reduction in the number of overwintering kites, which were very numerous at tips during that part of the year, had coincided with a reduction in the number of rubbish tips. Increasing numbers of kites were now migrating to wintering areas around the Mediterranean (Alistair Hill *in litt.*).

EAST GERMANY Previous estimates of 1,200–1,400 pairs (Ortlieb 1980) had now been revised to 2,500 pairs in 1986 (Dr Werner Eichstädt *in litt.*). Stubbe & Gedeon (1989) studied a total of 491 pairs in 1988, of which 72% bred. A total of 645 young fledged from 57% of the nests, giving an average productivity of 2.31 young per successful pair and 1.82 per nesting pair. The density of pairs ranged from 0 to 69.2 per 10 km².

POLAND There was currently an estimated population of about 300 pairs, distributed mainly in the west and northwest, the highest concentration probably being in western Pomerania, with about 60 pairs. Red Kites were only scarce breeders in eastern and central Poland and absent in the mountainous southern regions. Numbers had increased considerably since the nineteenth century. Present trends indicated an increase in some western regions, whilst in others numbers remained stable (Dr Tadeusz Stawarczyk *in litt.*).

USSR (including Estonia, Latvia, Lithuania, Russia, Belarus, Ukraine, Moldova, and Caucasus states) The Red Kite was included in the Red Data Book of the USSR, but it lacked an accurate population census. In the Baltic Republics, it was a very rare breeder: in Latvia, only two or three pairs were thought to breed, although this had not been documented recently (Dr Janis Baumanis *in litt.*); in Lithuania, there were only one or two breeding pairs; while, in Estonia, it was only an occasional visitor, with two records in 1980–89. Farther south, in Byelorussia (Belarus), the Red Kite was also rare, breeding in the western and central parts of the region; the exact number of pairs was, however, not known (Vilju Lilleleht i*n litt.*). On the eastern seaboard of the Black Sea, only a few isolated pairs were thought to survive in the Caucasus. In the USSR as a whole, it is estimated that no more than 100 pairs survived, but this estimate was almost certainly the least reliable of those given here.

CZECHOSLOVAKIA (now the Czech Republic and Slovakia) Red Kites had been recolonising western areas (Bohemia and Moravia) since 1975, where they bred in the nineteenth century. The breeding population had now increased to 20–25 pairs in 1989. Southern Moravia was the main breeding area, holding about ten pairs (Dr Karel Šťastný *in litt.*).

SWITZERLAND A survey of Red Kites during the breeding seasons of 1985–87 showed a considerable increase compared with estimates in 1972–76. There was an approximately 40% increase in the number of occupied 10 x 10 km squares, and a corresponding increase in range, especially in the western part of the Swiss Plateau. The breeding population now stood at an estimated 235–300 pairs, an increase of 55–100%. Northern Switzerland remained the principal breeding and wintering area, but Red Kites were also occurring more frequently on the plateau in winter, probably as a result of two new roosts on the southern border of the breeding range, first discovered in the winter of 1987/88 (Mosimann & Juillard 1988).

AUSTRIA After a lack of breeding records in the 1950s and 1960s, Red Kites had returned as regular breeders, probably by immigration from Germany or Switzerland. Numbers were still very small, at only two to four pairs (Hans-Martin Berg *in litt.*).

HUNGARY Last proven breeding was in the early 1970s at Hansag, in the northwest, near the Austrian border. Since then, the species had become extremely rare also on migration (Zoltán Waliczky *in litt.*).

ROMANIA No information since Cramp & Simmons (1980), who referred to about ten pairs, although the population status in the rest of the Balkans suggested that the species no longer bred in this region of Europe.

BULGARIA There was no recent proof of breeding, and the only breeding-season records were in 1894, 1940, 1960, 1962 and 1969. Persecution and the felling of lowland forest were thought to be the causal factors for this absence (John Lawton-Roberts verbally).

YUGOSLAVIA (Slovenia, Croatia, Bosnia-Herzegovina, Serbia, Montenegro, Kosovo, and Northern Macedonia) Red Kites were formerly distributed throughout the north and in Macedonia. There was, however, a marked decline at the turn of the 19th/20th century with the last record of breeding in the Sava Valley in 1968. Recent sightings were near Apatin in northwest Serbia in 1979 and near Pančevo, in the Belgrade area, in April 1980 (Vasič *et al.* 1985).

ITALY This declining breeding population was estimated by Meyburg & Meyburg (1987) to be in the region of 150–300 pairs. The population was mainly confined to southern Italy (Marco Gustin *in litt.*), with no more than ten pairs in Molise region, 16 in Abruzzo and some tens of pairs in Basilicata region (Dr Massimo Pellegrini *in litt.*). The most northerly population was found in Monti della Tolfa in central Italy. The breeding status of this small, geographically isolated group of three or four pairs had been particularly well studied in recent years. Productivity was low, with mean clutch and brood sizes of 1.92 and 1.08 respectively, 0.6 young per breeding pair and 0.77 young per successful pair (Arcà 1989). This compared with 2.5 young per breeding pair in Sicily (Massa 1980).

Persecution (illegal hunting and nest robbery) by man was said to be mainly responsible for the decline in the breeding status of this species, although habitat change was another contributory factor. This decline was not confined just to the mainland. In Sicily, a population of 80–100 pairs was the healthiest in Italy ten years earlier. Since then, numbers had declined to 40 pairs (Iapichino & Massa 1989), and then 25–30 pairs (Bruno Massa *in litt.*). In Sardinia, some ten to 20 pairs remained (Schenk 1981), but the decline continued. In addition to those breeding, many Red Kites from central Europe wintered in the country, with roosts in Sicily of up to 40 individuals (Galea & Massa 1985), and in central Italy of up to 30 in Lazio (Arcà 1989) and 40 in Abruzzo, where rubbish tips were an important food source (Dr Massimo Pellegrini *in litt.*).

ALBANIA No information was available since Cramp & Simmons (1980), but, in view of trends in surrounding areas, it is likely that few, if any, breeding pairs were left.

GREECE Red Kites were formerly not uncommon winter visitors from October to March in north and central Greece (Lambert 1957). Now, they occurred only irregularly during migration and rarely as winter visitors. Extremely few were involved. It was considered unlikely that breeding ever occurred (George I. Handrinos *in litt.*).

MIDDLE EAST There was no recent proof of breeding in Turkey, although a few summer records of individual birds were reported during the late 1970s and 1980s in northern and north-eastern Turkey (R. F. Porter verbally). Red Kites were rare winter immigrants, with a few on passage in Turkey and north-western Iran. Records from Syria, Lebanon, Iraq, and northern Arabia did occur, but rarely (H. Shirihai in prep. [published 1996]).

CYPRUS Red Kites were classified as accidental visitors, only two of the 13 claimed records of which had been accepted (C. J. L. Bennett *in litt.*).

ISRAEL Red Kites were extremely rare winter visitors, mainly with flocks of Black Kites *M. migrans*. In the last 40 years, only seven individuals had been positively identified, mostly during 1978–89. One appeared regularly at Gevulot and one or two in the Hula (or Huleh) Valley in the winters of 1983/84–1988/89. The species was described as a very common migrant and winter visitor, and to some extent breeder, in the latter half of the nineteenth century and the beginning of the 20th century. It is possible, however, that such reports were incorrect (H. Shirihai in prep. [1996]).

EGYPT Red Kites occurred as rare migrants in very small numbers. For example, the numbers counted at Suez in autumn 1981 and spring 1982 were 11 and five respectively (Mullie & Meininger 1985).

ALGERIA There had been no recent proof of breeding, although Red Kites bred in Ksar el Boukhari and Djebel Dekma in the nineteenth century. The species was now a very rare visitor in both summer and winter (Ledant *et al.* 1981).

TUNISIA During the previous 15 years, no breeding pairs of Red Kites had been discovered and only one individual was recorded in summer, in an oak forest in the northeast (Khoumirie) on 2nd June 1975 (Thierry Gaultier *in litt.*). Apart from this summer record, the species regularly wintered in North Africa in small numbers and was reported annually on spring migration at Cap Bon, where fewer than 20 individuals are seen in any one year.

MALTA The species occurred as a rare and irregular passage migrant. During migration counts in 1969–73, only two individuals (both on autumn passage) were seen, on 19th August 1970 and 27th September 1971 (Beaman & Galea 1974). Up to 1989, only about 15 occurrences had been recorded for the islands (Joe Sultana *in litt.*).

SPAIN Cramp & Simmons (1980) cited estimates of 3,000 and 10,000 pairs, but Meyburg & Meyburg (1987) considered that the population was considerably smaller, at about 1,000 pairs. Current estimates of a stable population of 3,000 pairs were, however, more soundly based (Dr Eduardo de Juana *in litt.*). Within this stability, the number of pairs breeding in any year oscillated considerably (*e.g.,* in Navarra: Aldasoro 1985). There were major regional variations. For instance, in Catalonia in the northeast, Red Kites were resident breeders and scarce autumn and spring migrants (Muntaner 1985). The breeding distribution was rather fragmented and present population trends were unconfirmed but thought to be stable. The illegal use of poison, forbidden since 1983, was probably the main reason for the species' absence from large areas of this region, although shooting, electrocution by overhead power-lines and egg-collecting were frequent and must also have been detrimental to the population. Muntaner (1985) considered that the Catalonian population was probably buffered by immigrants from Aragon, where the species was considerably more abundant.

The status on the Balearic Islands was not known precisely. On Mallorca, Red Kites were formerly widespread but, within a few years, had become restricted to a remote mountain region owing to human harassment, and were now seriously threatened. On Menorca, the population was thought to be stable, but its size had not been surveyed; it was considered to be common on the island (Muntaner 1981), and in 1974 R. J. Prytherch & R. Brock (*in litt.*) estimated at least 100 pairs and possibly twice that number.

PORTUGAL The Red Kite had been one of the most persecuted raptors in this country. This had probably been the main cause of the species' marked decline in the previous few decades, although since 1974 the species had been given full legal protection. Other closely related species such as the Black Kite *Milvus migrans* had not been adversely affected, since most raptors were shot in the hunting season, and this affected mainly resident species (Palma 1985). The current size of the breeding population of Red Kites seemed to have stabilised at about 100 pairs according to observations made by CEMPA in 1985–89 (Dr A. M. Teixeira *in litt.*). This compared with population estimates of 100–120 pairs during 1978–84 (Rufino *et al.* 1985).

MOROCCO The Red Kite was one of the raptors on which there was least information. There was, however, no doubt that it still inhabited the forests of the Rif, pre-Rif and western Middle Atlas, albeit in reduced numbers. There had also been several reports of individuals observed in summer in eastern Morocco, the Central Plateau and the central High Atlas (Thévenot et al. 1985). The breeding population was estimated at no more than 20 pairs (Bergier 1987) and was probably declining. Breeding had not been proven in the last ten years (Michel Thévenot *in litt*.). A small number of European Red Kites also overwintered. According to migration counts at Gibraltar, 100–200 were seen making the annual trip during the main passage times of late February to early June and mid–August to mid–October (Bergier 1987). The future of the Red Kite was rather uncertain. Although, like all Moroccan raptors, it was fully protected by law, this was often ignored, and direct killing (trapping, hunting and destruction of nests) still remained one of the principal causes of decline of many raptor species. The use of toxic chemicals was perhaps the most serious threat to the survival of Red Kites, since strychnine was officially used in massive doses in campaigns against carnivorous mammals, while Parathion was used against House/Spanish Sparrows *Passer domesticus/ hispaniolensis* and Starlings *Sturnus vulgaris* (Thévenot *et al*. 1985).

CANARY ISLANDS Lack & Southern (1949), in their survey of Tenerife, observed several Red Kites, mainly in the mountains and sometimes near the coast. By the late 1960s, however, the species had been exterminated in the archipelago (Aurelio Martin *in litt*.).

CAPE VERDE ISLANDS The Red Kites on these islands had been described as a distinct subspecies, *M. m. fasciicauda* Hartert 1914, which resembles the normal Red Kite except that it has a barred tail (C. J. Hazevoet *in litt*.). Bourne (1955) did not record Black Kite, but described how it resembled *fasciicauda*, which he reported to be abundant everywhere, especially in the towns and along the shore. Black Kites had increased considerably and by the 1980s *fasciicauda* was very rare, as a result of factors which had not been fully elucidated. Persecution may have been a factor in the decline of *fasciicauda* in the past, but was not a problem now, since there were very few firearms on the Cape Verde Islands. Nest robbery by children may have been another factor, since it was at the time proving detrimental to both the Buzzard and the Barn Owl (C. J. Hazevoet *in litt*.).

C. J. Hazevoet (*in litt*.), during four prolonged visits in 1986–89, saw only one Red Kite on the island of Santo Antao and occasional individuals showing the rather puzzling characteristics of both Black and Red Kites on the islands of Santiago and Maio. Apart from such birds, only Black Kites were seen. C. J. Hazevoet also received details of birds that were alleged Red Kites, but photographs showed them to be either Black Kites or hybrids. As breeding had not been proved for many years, the population size of the Red Kite was very hard to judge, since *M. m. fasciicauda* might in fact be itself an early sign of interbreeding. C. J. Hazevoet considered that the Red Kite was gravely threatened and, at most, only a few pairs survived, Santo Antao being its last relative stronghold.

(More recent genetic work was undertaken by Johnson *et al*. (2005) on both museum specimens collected in Cape Verde between 1897 and 1932 and blood samples from live-trapped birds in Cape Verde in 2002. Both groups were compared with samples of Red Kites and Black Kites from across the geographical range (as above for Red Kites, and Cape Verde across the Mediterranean and southern Asia to north Australia for Black Kites; for both species, the Cape Verde Islands are at the extreme western end of the range). They found that the historical Cape Verde kites were Red Kites but not distinct from the rest of the Red Kites and that they were probably not a valid subspecies. The modern Cape Verde kites are Black Kites but, in common with the other Black Kites in Africa south of the Sahara, are genetically distinct from those of the Mediterranean, Asia and Australia, at the subspecific or possibly specific level. They conclude that the loss of the Cape Verde Red Kites was a range reduction but not the loss of a subspecies.)

The Red Kite's prospects before the reintroduction project
The long-term existence of any species is dependent upon maintaining as wide a distribution as possible. Once populations are fragmented or restricted, they become increasingly

Table 4.1. Summary of world breeding status of the Red Kite *Milvus milvus* in the 1980s. Under 'Extinction', XIX = nineteenth (*i.e.* 1800s). Productivity per breeding pair is the more useful measure of numbers reared, but is less widely available than the mean number of young per successful pair, which tends to underestimate the real extent of differences, as total failures are not included. Reproduced from Evans & Pienkowski (1991) with permission of *British Birds*

Area	Extinction	Estimated number of pairs 1970s	Estimated number of pairs 1980s	Trend (+, 0, -)	Productivity per: successful pair	Productivity per: breeding pair	Sample size (nests)
Sweden	*	50	>200	+	2.0	1.5	
Norway	1880s	0	0	0			
Denmark	1910s	return	10–15	+	2.1		54
Scotland	XIX	0	0	0			
England	1920	0	0	0			
Wales	–	40	50	0	1.3	0.6	676
Ireland	XIX	0	0	0			
Netherlands	1950s	0–2	0	0			
Belgium	c. 1921	1–10	15–20		2.3		19
Luxembourg	–	12–15	12–15	0			
France	–	?	2300–2900	– & 0	1.9	1.5	53
Corsica					1.9	1.3	22
Germany, W	**	2000	1700–2000	0			
Germany, E	–	?	2500	?	2.3	1.8	491
Poland	–	?	300	0 (- in W)			
USSR	–	?	<100	?-			
Czechoslovakia	–	20–50	20–25	0 (?+ in W)			
Switzerland	–	90–150	235–300	+			
Austria	1950	return	2–4	?+			
Hungary	1970s	4–5	0	–			
Romania	?1970s	c. 10	?0	–			
Bulgaria	?	0	0	0			
Yugoslavia	1960s	?0	?0	–			
Italy	–	?	150–300		0.8 †	0.7 †	
Albania	1960s	?0	?0	–			
Greece	–	0	0	0			
Midde East (see text)	–	0	0	0			
Cyprus	–	0	0	0			
Israel	–	0	0	0			
Egypt	–	0	0	0			
Tunisia	–	0	0	0			
Malta	–	0	0	0			
Algeria	XIX	0	0	0			
Morocco	–	9	?20	–			
Spain	–	?	3000	0			
Portugal	–	100–120	100	?0 ††			
Canary Is.	1960s	0	0	–			
Cape Verde Is	–	?	?<20	–			

* Formerly extended farther north
** Decline to 1960s
† Productivity figures refer only to northern Italy; productivity 2.5 young per breeding pair on Sicily; most of population is in south Italy
†† Following a large decline

vulnerable to local pressures which may result in extinction. Our geographical review gave several examples of local extinctions and re-establishments. The more that fragments are isolated, the less likely is recolonisation. The review above indicated also that the existing range of Red Kites was even more fragmented than that implied by the map in Stanley & Cramp (1980, reproduced Chapter 2). In particular, the large area marked in the USSR (now Russia, Belarus, Ukraine, Moldova, Baltic states and the states in the Caucasus) included few Red Kites, and even the Spanish population was much more fragmented than shown.

The world population of Red Kites, which was then estimated at between 11,000 and 13,000 breeding pairs (Table 4.1), had suffered major declines in range, in continuity of range, and in numbers in the nineteenth century. In the 1980s, most of the population bred in Spain, France and Germany. The numbers in these countries appeared to have been fairly stable in recent years, although there had been some local declines and perhaps some increases. There had been increases or recolonisations in at least parts of neighbouring countries, including Sweden, Denmark, Belgium, Luxembourg, Switzerland and Austria. In some of these areas, available habitat might have reached capacity.

The outlook farther east and south was bleak. There must have been major range losses, fragmentation and declines in numbers in the USSR, the Middle East and countries bordering the Mediterranean. Continued persecution, and possibly habitat loss, was probably responsible for the demise of this species in the southern and eastern regions of its range. Numbers in Poland were low. The eastern Czechoslovak (now Slovakian) population seemed to have died out, although pairs seemed to be moving into the west (now the Czech Republic) from Germany. The species had gone locally extinct in Hungary, and few if any pairs survived in the Balkans. Breeding had long ceased in Turkey, northern Iran and Syria, and few, if any, survived in the Caucasus. The fact that Red Kites were said formerly to be a common winter visitor to Greece (Lambert 1957), Israel (Shirihai in prep. [1996]) and Egypt (Morris 1904) suggested that the eastern population was once considerably larger than it had become by then. The populations in mainland Italy, Sardinia, Sicily, Mallorca and north-western Africa had been much reduced and continued to decline. The North African population appeared to be down to a small number in Morocco. The Portuguese population had possibly stabilised, but at a much-reduced level. On the Canary Islands, the Red Kite was now extinct, while on the Cape Verde Islands it was gravely threatened (with later work indicating that it was actually already extinct). Corsica remained one of the last strongholds in the region (Patrimonio 1990) outside Spain.

To put the world Red Kite population in the 1980s into perspective, it is perhaps worth comparing it with the British population of the Buzzard at the time. This was estimated as 12,000–15,000 pairs by Taylor, K. *et al.* (1988), even though the species was persecuted in some areas. Persecution of Red Kites in their wintering quarters was perhaps of great concern, especially for those breeding in northern Europe, since they might again be migrating to the Mediterranean area in large numbers as a result of changes in the methods of rubbish disposal and the decline in numbers of rubbish tips. This would have exposed them to hunting pressures in southern Europe and may have had serious consequences on the north European, and therefore world, population. Although not available at the time of our survey, in progress at around the same time and published some years later, the map by Hagemeijer & Blair (1997), reproduced as Fig. 4.1 effectively illustrates the results of our survey.

It was striking how bad the situation looked: worse than that described by Cramp & Simmons (1980) and it was clear that we should, therefore, not be complacent and assume that the fortunes of the Red Kite would continue to improve in northern Europe. Nor should it be forgotten that populations in West Germany and parts of France were now in decline. Furthermore, the political changes in central and eastern Europe (a move from Soviet Union

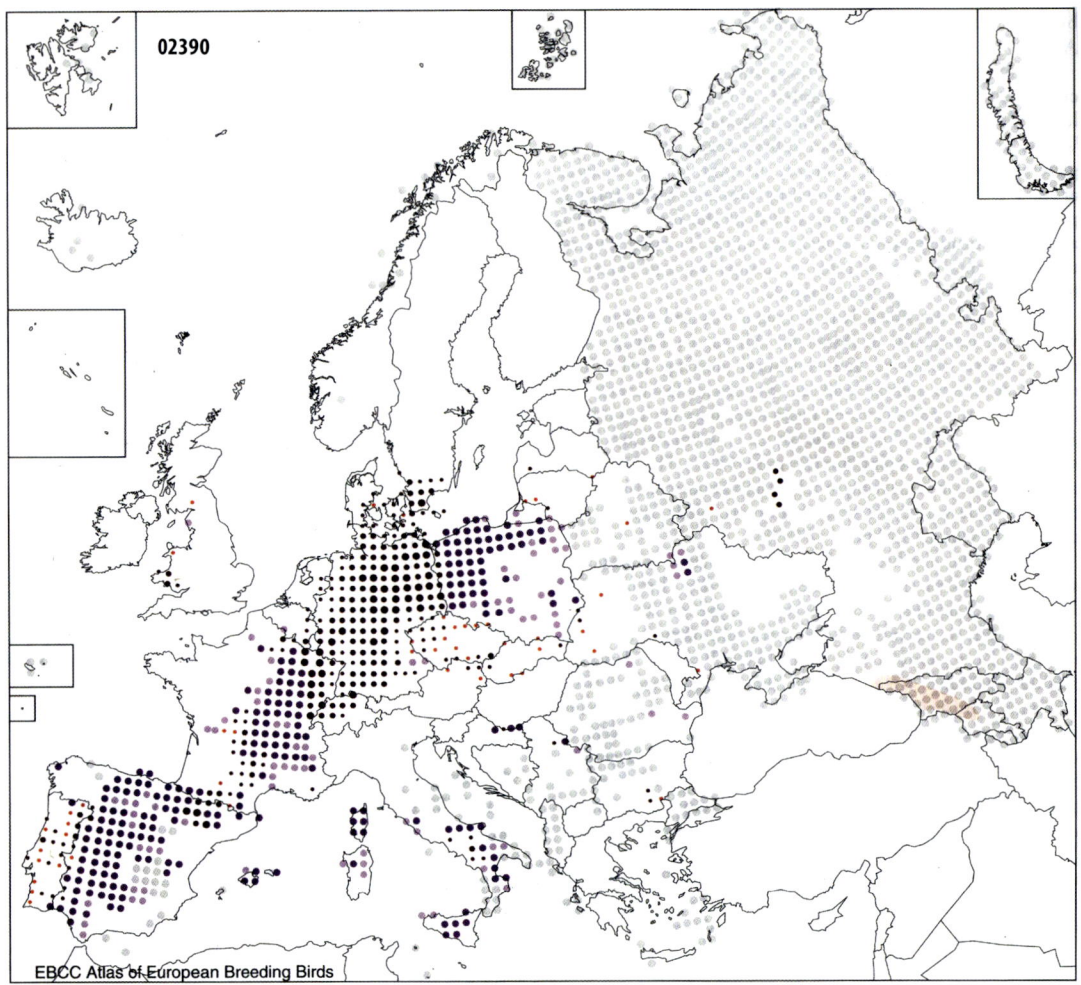

Figure 4.1. World breeding distribution Red Kites *Milvus milvus* **in the late 1980s** (Hagemeijer & Blair 1997). Brown/deep-purple = confirmed or probably breeding qualitative/semi-quantitative; light-purple/orange = possible breeding qualitative/semi-quantitative; no dot = square surveyed but Red Kites not recorded; grey = not surveyed. The size of the dot indicates estimated number of breeding pairs in the 50km x 50km square: smallest = 1–9; next = 10–99; largest = 100–999. Total population estimated as between 17,000 and 21,000 pairs. © European Bird Census Council, 1997, *The EBCC Atlas of European Breeding Birds: Their Distribution and Abundance*, T & A.D Poyser, an imprint of Bloomsbury Publishing Plc.

domination to democracies, many of which went on to join the European Union, and the collapse of Yugoslavia) were likely to lead to an intensification of agricultural methods there. Farmland with a high proportion of traditional management appears to be particularly important to Red Kites (and, indeed, other vulnerable birds), notably in eastern Germany. Census and subsequent monitoring of the Spanish, French and German populations would, therefore, be especially valuable. These, together with the small but expanding Swedish population, were now the core of the world distribution and numbers. Re-establishment in UK could make a major global contribution.

The survival of the British population in central Wales, and its slow increase in the 20th century to over 60 nesting pairs, is a tribute to the sustained efforts of many farmers and conservationists in that area. The slow rate of increase, however, could be attributed to three factors.

The use of poison baits (Davis & Newton 1981) was a threat both in Wales and in other areas, especially around the Mediterranean. Though usually directed against crows *Corvus* and Foxes *Vulpes vulpes*, carrion feeders such as kites also suffered. In 1989, at least 11 kites were killed in Wales by this activity, which accounted also for the failure of at least three nests; many other deaths were likely to have remained undetected.

Secondly, breeding productivity in Wales was one of the lowest recorded and was coupled with one of the highest rates of nest-failure (Davis & Newton 1981). This is thought to be related to the less productive environment than in the habitats used by Red Kites in France, Germany, Sweden, Denmark, Belgium and Spain, but could also be related to low genetic variation.

The third factor, egg-collecting, had possibly been reduced by nest-protection schemes, although it remained remarkably persistent.

Although there had been some expansion of the range within Wales, illegal poisoning in the area around the kites' range in Wales was probably a major limitation to further spread. The prospects of enough of the small number of surplus young moving beyond this area to start a distant re-establishment were very low. So far, it had not happened, apart from scattered unsuccessful nesting attempts in Devon, Cornwall and Cumbria, one of which was 12 years earlier and the others over 60 years before.

There would be major benefits in Britain in re-establishing Red Kites through their former range. These would include the return of a formerly widespread and important element of the wildlife; the opportunity for many people to see this most attractive raptor; the public support generated; and the encouragement of land-use practices sympathetic to wildlife. The most important contribution, however, would be to enhance the chances of world survival of this attractive species. In Britain, in collaboration with conservationists elsewhere in Europe, we now had the chance both to contribute to the survival of this rare species, and to benefit from its eventual wider presence in Britain.

Possible sources of kites

The members of the Project Team were able to combine the information on world distribution with personal knowledge and contacts with colleagues in other countries to explore the possible sources of birds. These fell into two categories:
1. the existing relict population in Wales; and
2. other countries.

In line with the guidelines, we needed to find a source population of the birds, which was healthy and had a reasonable concentration of breeding birds to make collection of young practicable. We corresponded (in those days by snail mail) with colleagues in conservation across several European countries which appeared potentially to have reasonable concentrations of Red Kites.

The Team recognised the importance of not depending on a single or very few sources of supply. This was especially important in a project which would need to be maintained with a fairly constant supply of birds over several years if it was to stand a chance of success. Secondarily, there were also potential genetic benefits in using a wide source of supply of birds (see below).

In the preliminary work before the first meeting of the Project Team, we had identified three initial possible sources of young birds. Magnus Sylvén of WWF Sweden had offered 10–12 young per year from the high productivity of the Swedish population of 150 breeding pairs. This population was itself the result of a recent conservation initiative. The East German population was large, and we understood that the scientific and conservation workers there were prepared to supply birds. However, at that time, Germany was still politically divided, and we anticipated problems with exportation. It was also possible that the workers in East Germany would come under pressure to require payment for the birds; if so, this would in turn present ethical problems for the Team. Michel Terrasse, of France, who had a major involvement in the reintroduction of vultures to the Cevennes, France (see Chapter 3), had also agreed to investigate the potential supply of Red Kites from France, and was hopeful of being able to assist.

The Project Team meeting on 20th October 1987 agreed, in the first instance, to explore further the possibilities in Sweden, which would be followed up by Roy Dennis, and East Germany, for which Ian Newton would make enquiries. They also accepted the view of the Welsh Kite Committee that it was not appropriate to explore the use of Welsh birds as the first main option.

By the time of the Project Team meeting in October 1988, the Swedish field-workers had confirmed their agreement, and I agreed to write formally to the Swedish conservation authorities for approval.

No substantive reply had been received from East Germany.

Wales

From 1986, RSPB and NCC had been taking a more proactive approach to kite conservation in Wales beyond simple nest protection, by undertaking a short-term research programme (Lovegrove *et al*. 1990). The aim of this programme was to ascertain the reasons for the high number of nest failures in the central part of the breeding range. This involved erecting miniature video cameras on selected nests to investigate the progress of individual nests during incubation and the fledging period. The cameras relayed pictures of the nest to monitors in nearby buildings, and these were also recorded on video so that they could be analysed in detail at a later date. Early indications were that food availability was the main reason why so few young fledged from nests in central Wales. The videos showed how, during times of food shortage, the stronger, older chick attacked and eventually caused the death of its fellow nestling. However, the research work demonstrated that it is possible to increase breeding success by putting out additional food for the parent birds. In some of the more fertile valleys where kites were now nesting, food shortage did not appear to be such a problem and broods of two and three chicks were a regular occurrence.

As another aspect of the research work in 1987–88, the NCC and RSPB, in conjunction with Dr Nick Fox, established that some of the many eggs which would not normally result in fledged kites could be incubated artificially. In this experimental manipulation programme, kite eggs were taken from vulnerable nests, replaced by dummy or Buzzard eggs, and hatched in an incubator. The chicks were subsequently returned to nests, when they were about a week old, ideally back to the original nests. Eggs were taken only from nests which were habitually robbed or where the parent birds had deserted. Kites from this source could potentially be used for a reintroduction programme, without any adverse effect on the size of the Welsh kite population. This action would depend, of course, on the agreement, help and co-operation of Welsh farmers and conservationists. It could also provide a potential opportunity to build on their efforts over the years.

To help both the monitoring and protection work in Wales and to check the potential supply of birds, I had been able, after the meeting of 13th March 1987 (Chapter 3), to find some funding from the NCC Chief Scientist Directorate to contract the two leading Kite workers to continue to work for the Welsh kite team after their retirement from NCC Wales.

1989

At the Project Team meeting in Inverness on 24th January 1989 we reviewed the situation. By this time, we were hoping to start the reintroductions in 1989, but we clearly needed a cut-off point. If the key elements were not in place by that time, we would need to postpone until 1990. After considering all the key stages and the time needed to put them in place, the

deadline date agreed was 15th March. It was anticipated that before this date answers would have had to have been received to outstanding questions on:
a. Source of birds
b. Transportation
c. NCC's Committee for Scotland, which had raised some issues (see Chapter 5).

All of these answers were expected by the end of February.

Roy Dennis had had some contact with East Germany. There was an estimated population of 1200–1500 pairs. It appeared that the only possibility would be through a formal approach to the Ministry of Land, Forestry and Nature Conservation. The Team agreed that no contact should be made yet but that I could write to explore if a negative response was received from Sweden. We all recognised that this potential supply could not be secured in time for the current year and would be relevant only to possibilities in future years.

Dr Leo Batten, who was in charge of bird licensing at NCC, reported that he had received an approach from a licensed bird of prey breeder in England who had expressed a desire to breed kites in captivity. However, he had no birds at present and his source would probably be West Germany. There were assorted complications in this idea, so the Team asked Leo to look into the background but otherwise to take no action at present.

Despite the enthusiasm of the Swedish field-workers, the wide consultations undertaken by the Swedish conservation authorities following my formal request (following the Project Team meeting in October 1988) revealed mixed views amongst Swedish conservationists, some very much in favour and some against. Further investigation indicated that the concerns arose mainly from the idea that the Welsh experimental activities had been more successful than anticipated and could supply all the project's needs. A Swedish ornithologist had attended a recent conference in Britain on reintroductions. The organisers had not involved those on our Project Team who had been involved in previous reintroduction work, notably the sea-eagle project (and note the kite reintroduction project was not yet public knowledge). The Swedish ornithologist had become aware of the initial success in hatching Welsh kite eggs, but not how limited the potential number of birds was. He had therefore questioned the need to import Swedish birds. Ian Newton was due to visit Sweden in late February and might be able to discuss with relevant people if contacts were arranged in advance. Roy Dennis and I would liaise over further contact if no response had been received by the expected time of mid–February.

Peter Walters Davies reported on the recent Wales Kite Committee meeting in Wales. That Committee had agreed that surplus Welsh captive-bred birds could be made available to the reintroduction project. They were also keen to continue with the egg manipulation programme. Birds were being hatched in incubators, raised by a female buzzard until about 12 days old and then distributed amongst foster kite nests. The latter exercise was difficult, expensive and the number of foster places limited. There was wide acknowledgment amongst the personnel in Wales of the fact that the eggs presently being used to produce chicks using incubators would otherwise be 'doomed', being either from 3–egg clutches (from which three young were never reared) or nests that were consistently robbed. There was a desire that some 3–5 chicks should be retained for release in Wales and therefore a surplus of 4–6 chicks could be available for the reintroduction work. However, it seemed that there was not a great deal of wider support in Wales for the relocation programme.

An underlying problem seemed to be that some of the conservation workers in Wales felt a justified "ownership" of the kites. They felt (in some cases probably unconsciously) that the kites were special not just because they were beautiful and spectacular birds that were rare because of previous human action, but because they were in Wales and in no other part of the United Kingdom. That they were, essentially, Welsh. Given that the Welsh had been less unpleasant to kites than other Britons in the past, and that they had striven so hard throughout the 20th century to save them, it was difficult to take exception to this view. It was, however, a little frustrating. The view of those concerned with the reintroduction project was rather that it provided an opportunity to build on the efforts over the years by the Welsh team. They had maintained the existence of the Red Kite in Britain. Use of artificially hatched young from Welsh eggs that would not otherwise survive provided the opportunity to enhance the prospects of the kites' survival in the long-term despite the many unforeseeable threats, by the only way possible: by widening their range. Not only would this restore the opportunity for others to enjoy kites in their neighbourhoods, but it would also provide a safeguard to the long-term survival of the Welsh population.

After a lengthy debate on the question of the use of birds reared in captivity in Wales, the Project Team decided that a meeting should be set up to air a wide range of opinion and interest in kites in Wales. At least two members of the reintroduction project team (Dr Ian Newton, myself and probably Richard Porter) would address this meeting, to be held as soon as possible, preferably in February. In advance of the meeting, Dr Newton would produce a brief description of the background to the project to be made available to those likely to attend. The purpose of the meeting would be to convince the majority of the importance of the reintroduction project in a national and international context, as well as to the Welsh population, and to arrange for this to be the priority use of Welsh-bred birds.

There were arguments for providing all the birds for the reintroduction from within Britain, *i.e.,* from Wales. However, it was clear that it would not be possible to provide enough reared birds to do this in the most effective way. In addition, there were several reasons not to make these the only, or even the main, source. These centred on our suspicions of limited genetic diversity – which proved to be correct. However, it would be useful to bring some birds from Wales to the release sites, for various reasons, including to show commitment to our generous colleagues on continental Europe.

Ian Newton and I (both of whom were then based in the Peterborough area) therefore drove over to Wales for a meeting kindly organised by our Welsh Kite Committee colleagues so that we could both brief and, more importantly, address questions from, the Welsh kite workers. The meeting seemed to go quite well, especially as we progressed through it. As Ian and I travelled the long drive back, we relaxed a little by talking about how we might eventually measure the success of the project (see Chapter 12). I recall one lighter moment when I think it was me who suggested that a good measure of success might be when persons other than the Kite Project Team claimed responsibility for it! We did not adopt that measure, although we certainly later achieved it – but I am naming no names!

At the meeting, the representatives of the Welsh Kite Committee offered to seek the views of the rest of their colleagues, the field-workers and farmers including those not at the meeting, to the relocation of some of successful rearings from their manipulation work. The Project Team, of course, strongly approved of this, as the chance of a reared kite contributing to the future well-being of the population might even be greater if it were part of the reintroduction. This was because of suspected factors including habitat quality, the intensity of illegal egg-collection and genetic diversity. Our colleagues in the Wales Kite Committee agreed and set out the position in the note (see the opposite page) to their largely voluntary team.

On 8th April 1989, I was able to update the Project Team that both Ian Newton and I had attended a special meeting of the Wales Kite Committee and that "surplus" rescued and reared kites would be available. The English and Scottish teams had agreed that these, likely to be few in number, would go to the English site, for geographical simplicity.

Ian and I had both also spoken with representatives of the Swedish authorities, Ian during a visit to Sweden, and myself taking the opportunity of discussions at meetings (mainly of European Union member states' conservation personnel in Brussels) on other topics, where key parties happened to be attending. Once the misunderstanding about the

To: ALL NEST WATCHERS

cc Kite Committee

1. As requested at the last Kite Committee, please find enclosed:
a. Your personal copy of a technical brief prepared by Dr Mike Pienkowski providing background information relating to the Red Kite Relocation Project (south-east England).
b. Five copies of an 'Information Note for Landowners', which summarises the more practical aspects of the technical brief.

2. Please retain the technical brief as a personal reference document; it provides you with all the information you are likely to require when entering into discussions with landowners. The Information Note has been drafted specifically for landowners; it explains our objectives and asks for their co-operation. Copies may be left with landowners at your discretion. A Welsh version will be available as soon as a translation can be completed.

3. The technical brief and the Information Note should be read in conjunction with my note on Procedures (Egg Manipulation 1989) sent to you with Roger Lovegrove's letter of the 6 March 1989…

29 March 1989

Information Note for Landowners from the Kite Committee

1. The very slow increase in the number of kites breeding in Wales is giving us cause for concern. Productivity (the number of chicks raised/breeding pair) is less than half that of Continental kites breeding in Sweden or Germany. The reason for this is not fully understood but we believe it is connected with persistent wet weather in spring, poor feeding conditions when the chicks are in the nest, and to some extent from the activities of egg collectors.

2. For the last two years we have been conducting an experiment to see whether we can incubate eggs artificially and raise chicks by hand before returning them to the wild at about 12 days of age. Results have been very encouraging, and in 1988 we were able to return eight chicks from nine fertile eggs taken from nests in mid Wales.

3. This year we wish to extend our experiment by returning some of the hand-reared chicks to the wild at a carefully selected location in southern England, under a controlled system of release. We wish to do this because: -
a. As an isolated breeding population, the kite in Wales is vulnerable to any adverse changes that might occur in the local environment, which could bring about its extinction. A few years ago, Peregrine Falcons were wiped out from most of North America before the effects of certain pesticides were realised. The establishment of a second breeding population in southern England would guard against this type of catastrophe.
b. When fully mature, 2–3 years after their release, kites would be breeding in a more favourable climate and better feeding conditions which should result in a higher productivity. Relatively more chicks would be raised in relation to the number of breeding pairs which, hopefully, would recolonise other areas of southern Britain, just as the Sea Eagle spread over western Scotland after juveniles had been reintroduced to the island of Rhum.

4. We would not be contemplating this experiment if there was any danger of depleting the breeding population of Welsh kites. After several years of study, we now know that kites in Wales lay more eggs than they can rear. Every year there are some nests which contain three eggs, but which for various reasons (such as food shortage) appear to be unable to raise three chicks. It is these 'wasted' eggs that we are seeking to collect. Also, in some years nests deserted by the adult kites could provide an alternative supply, as also would nests that are habitually robbed by egg collectors; if we could manage to take and hatch eggs that would otherwise have finished up in a collector's cabinet, we would be able to produce still more chicks.

5. If you have a kite nesting on your land, and our local kite watcher is of the opinion that an egg or eggs could safely be taken, we would ask for your co-operation in helping us make a success of this experiment.

numbers available from Wales had been explained, the Swedish hesitations were rapidly overcome. They had now agreed to allow up to 10 young birds to be supplied in 1989, for a pilot study. Their agreement to provide birds from their small but expanding population was because of the world importance of widening the distribution of this species through its former range. Future supply would depend on the outcome of that year's pilot. The Project Team had agreed that, for this pilot year, we would aim at similar numbers of young kites to be reared at the English and Scottish sites.

By 21st May 1989, a further update collated by myself reported that several Welsh kite eggs had been collected, although some of these were emergency rescue attempts from nests whose adults had been poisoned in that year's appalling poisoning incidents; eleven Red Kites were killed by poison. (This incident, and the at least eight nests in Wales robbed by egg-collectors in 1990, emphasised even more strongly the need to widen the range of this species.) Unfortunately, but not surprisingly, several of these eggs in 1989 were found to have died before rescue. The number of young kites available from Wales this year would be very small. In fact, in that first pilot year of 1989, the six young kites in Scotland came from Sweden, which was also the source of 4 of the 5 released in England. The other kite in England was reared from a rescued Welsh egg.

Finding sources of birds after the trial year: sources of birds for the rest of the initial programme

In November 1989, at a Project Team meeting, we reviewed the pilot year and considered continuing sources of kites. (The eventual resulting sources are summarised in Table 4.2 later in this chapter.) It was important to maintain the supply of young kites for future years. By early 1990, the review of kite distribution with which we started this chapter, having existed as a working draft for some time, had been completed, helping considerably.

We wanted to collect the birds at approximately four to six weeks of age because they could then thermo-regulate without parental brooding and could handle food themselves. This also gave them as long a period as possible to imprint on the release areas, rather than the area where they hatched.

Sweden

Swedish colleagues remained enthusiastic, although the Team noted that there could be some adverse reaction if no further birds were supplied from Wales. An approach to see if more birds could be obtained from Sweden was subject to several constraints, including the physical effort in climbing, and the logistical problem of contacting owners on whose land the kites' nests were situated. It was not possible to collect chicks over a longer period of time, because we were constrained to only one collection flight.

I agreed to draft a formal report to the Swedes indicating what we were proposing to do next year and to thank them formally on behalf of the NCC and RSPB. I would write to the Swedish authorities and Roy Dennis would contact Magnus Sylvén, asking for up to 20 birds as originally proposed, as well as fulfilling the commitment to report on progress in the first season. Roy would explore also whether assistance in the fieldwork would be helpful.

Sweden was again obliging, with up to 20 young for 1990, after previous indications from Swedish authorities to myself that this would be the case.

Germany

In respect of East Germany, Ian Newton had written a letter in 1989 and received a reply 11 months later, and no reply to a second letter. He agreed to make another formal approach to the Ministry of Land, Forestry and Conservation requesting 10 birds per year, although this would be an option probably for a future year rather than 1990 (and, indeed, was – after political changes – see Chapter 11).

France

Roy Dennis had approached Michel Terrasse in France in an earlier year. We agreed that I would make a formal approach, after Roy had telephoned to restore informal contact.

In respect of birds from continental Europe, the replies were generally quite positive and helpful. We were particularly flattered by the reply from France. As requested by the Project Team, Ian Evans and I had followed up Roy Dennis's initial contact with France. Our colleagues there had kindly canvassed their colleagues in the various areas that kites bred, and very generously shared the reply information with us. Although there were further complications to deal with there, some individual responses from kite workers had been extremely encouraging. One particularly striking one noted how the English (as the French tend to refer to the British) conservationists do not take on these things lightly and, if they had asked, there must be a good reason; and that he would like to collaborate, especially as an insurance for the future should kites meet unforeseen problems in France; and that the strongest chicks should be taken from the nests he looked after to give the best chance of success – very pleasant in view of the traditional friendly rivalry. With such positive views, we would be investigating further, but it was far too complicated to pull things together for that year.

In the end, we did not choose France, largely because we eventually realised that, although the population was healthy, it was quite scattered and the time needed and logistical complications challenging, especially when compared with the situation in Spain.

Spain

My NCC colleague in NCC Ornithology Branch, Dr Eric Bignal, had a number of contacts with Spanish bird of prey workers, having advised them on Chough *Pyrrhocorax pyrrhocorax* conservation and research, and had offered to make a number of enquiries through them, an offer which the Team keenly accepted.

Accordingly, conservation authorities in Navarra, northern Spain (and national colleagues in Madrid) also agreed to assist, with up to 20 birds, building on earlier contacts and co-operation on other species by Eric.

In the provinces of Navarra and Aragon, their Red Kite populations were comparatively large and productive (Elosegui Aldasoro 1985; Compaired Carbo *in litt.*) and could readily compensate for the loss of a small number of nestlings.

As regards sources, the most promising locations seemed to be in Sweden and in Spain. In later years, political and other changes in Navarra gave problems in the supply from there, but our Navarrese colleagues were most helpful in enlisting the help of colleagues in neighbouring Aragon, which progressively took over the supply.

Wales

In Wales, 11 eggs and 2 chicks had been collected in 1989. From these, two chicks were returned to the wild in Wales and one was released in England. All eggs were collected under the criteria agreed in 1988, although in the event not all eggs eligible for collection were obtained. Peter Walters Davies reported that the main reason for the latter was that the landowners' permissions were not granted in some cases. Peter Walters Davies concluded that the outcome of the recent meeting of Welsh kite workers, held after the Welsh Kite Committee meeting, was disappointing since no progress was made in resolving the situation regarding the non-cooperation of key kite workers. I mentioned my impression that there was no objection in principle to reintroduction, but individuals' reactions depended on subjective perceptions and influential individuals rather than on biological and conservation grounds. Richard Porter, of RSPB, made the point that no premature decision would be made regarding the Welsh situation but there was a need to know where we stood. It was agreed that, provided the other two members of the Wales Kite Committee on the Project Team agreed,

Varied Red Kite breeding habitat, Navarra, Spain [MP]

a questionnaire would be sent to every kite worker so that they could make their views clear without the constraint of a meeting. Dr Nick Fox made the point that, although criteria existed for removing eggs and young, no criteria existed for putting birds back into nests, and that manipulation should be directed at harvesting surplus birds that would otherwise perish and not as a rescue service.

Meanwhile, Reintroduction Project Officer Ian Evans pointed out that, as a Welshman who had worked with the kite team in Wales, he ought to set out the position again for his fellow-countryman kite workers. His note is set out in Annex 5.

In Wales, manipulation work continued, with the possibility that this could also result in birds contributing to the relocation exercise.

Captive breeding experiment

So far, all Red Kites released had been collected as eggs or young from the wild. The Project Team identified the importance of a diversity of sources of birds. Accordingly, the possibility of captive breeding was noted.

They also noted the possibility of importing birds as eggs if quarantine problems with the importation of young birds became excessive. However, the massive technical difficulties with the transportation of eggs, if these are to remain viable, was well recognised, and this option was not one we would have been keen to pursue.

With regard to captive breeding, Dr Nick Fox, experienced in captive rearing for conservation rescued kites in Wales, had made clear that he would be prepared to help in this regard. Dr Fox estimated that up to 12 young per year could be obtained from 3–4 pairs of captive Red Kites, given optimum conditions. The cost of acquiring each bird for breeding would be up to £300 and they would have to be imported from Europe. Dr Batten indicated that importation could potentially be granted on scientific grounds and on the basis that it would be a wise use of resources. Dr Fox made the generous offer of rearing Red Kites free of charge. The full support of the NCC and RSPB with regard to importation and to receiving all captive bred kites would be required. This did raise several important policy and precedent issues, and a lengthy debate on the question of the suitability of captive-bred birds for reintroduction schemes ensued. We concluded that captive breeding needed further evaluation by Dr Fox so that breeding could be attained as soon as possible, if it were decided to proceed. Nick Fox was asked to investigate the possible supply and report back for guidance before making any commitment. The purchase of stock from licenced breeders in other countries would have given rise to some difficulties to reconcile with policy and practices in the lead organisations and was not pursued at that time while other sources were explored.

At a later stage in 1990 during our first collection trip to Spain (see Chapter 6), another opportunity arose to explore the feasibility of using captive breeding to supplement wild-bred birds in the release programme. Dr Borja Heredia of ICONA, the Spanish federal conservation authority, drew my attention to the existence of many birds rehabilitation centres in Spain. He showed us the rescue facility for injured Red Kites run by ICONA and noted that there were other such facilities in Spain. He noted also that not all kites recovered adequately for release, usually because of wing damage. He kindly invited us to investigate the use of these for a captive breeding facility in UK. On return, we commissioned Dr Nick Fox to investigate.

With the help of Rod Hall and our arrangement with British Airways Assisting Nature Conservation (Chapter 6), Nick visited Spain and this facility in July 1990, inspected the kites and found several suitable for captive breeding. In discussion and correspondence with Dr Borja Heredia of ICONA, other rehabilitation centres and vets he arranged, in consultation with my team, to secure appropriate licences and set up a programme to test this.

Dr Heredia arranged for potentially suitable kites to be sent by rehabilitation centres to a centre near Madrid, where they were inspected again. Five kites that could not be

Above: Injured Red Kites at a rescue facility in Spain, and Dr Nick Fox interviews a candidate for his captive breeding facility (below). [MP]

rehabilitated were provided by the Grupo de Rehabilitacion de la Fauna Autoctona (GREFA) and four more by a municipal rehabilitation centre, the Buitrago Raptor Rehabilitation Centre. The birds (7 adult females and 2 adult males) were transported from Madrid to London by courtesy of the British Airways Assisting Nature Conservation programme on 16th November 1990. We contracted Dr James Kirkwood and the Zoological Society of London to provided quarantine facilities as well as checks on their health and condition, and ZSL kindly shared the costs. After quarantine was complete, the birds were transported to Nick's captive breeding facility in January. We all recognised that it would be some time before the prospects of this initiative could be assessed. A further male and female were obtained in 1991, when a released Red Kite from southern England and a wild Red Kite from Wales could not be rehabilitated, and there were a few further similar additions.

Captive breeding is an extremely difficult technique, especially with injured birds, and the use of wild stock in the release programme was more appropriate, particularly as IUCN criteria 5 and 6 were not violated. In Nick's first report after the first season noted that no nestlings had yet been reared, although two pairs had laid infertile clutches.

In April 1994, as we moved towards the end of the experimental reintroduction project, Nick summarised the situation. He currently held 8 kites, 3 pairs and 2 females imprinted (in Spain probably before arriving at the rescue centres) on humans. One male had died the previous year, but the post-mortem had not revealed a cause. Of the three pairs, all but one bird (a male) were incapacitated because of the earlier injuries which resulted in taking them to the rescue centres.

Nick continued: "One pair laid infertile eggs in 1992 but did not lay in 1993. Another pair laid two infertile eggs in 1993. … We replaced the eggs with dummies and later tried unsuccessfully to mother on a young Harris Hawk chick but they did not accept it, indeed wouldn't go near the nest. … We decided to move them this year to a totally covered pen to keep them dry. All the kites go completely useless in wet weather. They get themselves soaked and then can't fly. Worst still, their breeding drive (such as it is) ceases…

"Artificial insemination is not feasible with these pairs. They give almost no indication of when laying is imminent. They lay only a small clutch. The insemination needs to be within about 2 hours to have a chance of catching the second egg. Any small disturbance puts them right off. We have placed the two imprinted females together this year in the hope that they will stimulate each other to lay; in this case there would be a greater possibility of AI.

"We do not foresee a significant contribution coming from these birds. The only way to breed kites would be to obtain some healthy breeding stock raised properly so that they are relatively stress-free in captivity. There are no short cuts. You must decide what the priorities are. How long do you foresee a requirement for kites for release? The reintroduction programmes have been much more successful than we originally envisaged."

Nick made it clear that he was prepared to continue with better stock if that is what we wished, but we recognised that he had raised sensible questions.

We had benefitted from the services and advice from one of the most experienced captive-breeding experts well used to working with conservation projects, and investigated the challenging possibility of using the available kites, mainly those rescued but too injured to release. By this time though, we knew that the English site and probably the Scottish one were well on the road to more than self-sufficiency. The Project Team decided accordingly that it would not be necessary to add any further complications by pursuing the captive-breeding option, thanked Nick and his team for their perseverance in investigating this option and concentrated on the translocations from other populations.

Summary of sources of birds during the experimental project

Table 4.2 summarises the sources of birds during the experimental phase of the programme (incorporating some information from Evans et al. 1997). In the later operational phase of the extended programme of releases at further sites in Britain (Chapter 11), some additional sources were used, and within a few years, our initial English site was productive enough itself to be able to supply young kites for these, and soon replaced the importations from the continent.

I shall return to the challenges of permits, transportation and related matters but first I need to turn to choosing the rearing and release areas – which turned out to require at least as much diplomacy combining with the science as did the international aspects!

Table 4.2. The number and country of origin of the Red Kites released between 1989 –1994 in the initial Scottish (S) and English (E) sites. Reproduced from Evans *et al.* (1999) with permission of British Trust for Ornithology

Area	Origin	1989	1990	1991	1992	1993	1994	SubTotal	SiteTotal
S	Skane, Sweden	6 (4,2)	19 (11,8)	20 (13,7)	24 (12,12)	24 (12,11)	–	93 (52,40)*	93 (52,40)*
E	Skane, Sweden	4 (0,4)	–	–	–	–	–	4 (0,4)	
E	Wales	1 (0,1)	2 (1,1)	4 (1,3)	–	–	–	7 (2,5)	
E	Navarra, Spain	–	11 (7,4)	11 (5,6)	10 (9,11)	10 w(12,8)	–	42	
E	Aragon, Spain	–	–	–	10	10	20 (13,7)	42	93 (52,40)

Numbers of males and females are given in parentheses (males, females). We did not have this information available in the first year of the releases.
*One bird in Scotland was not identified as to sex. Separate figures not available for the two Spanish source areas.

5. Identifying the right places

Requirements for success and selecting suitable areas for rearing and release

Our preparatory work on the requirements for kite breeding to be successful enough to build up to self-sufficiency had resulted in the identification of six criteria for area assessment put before the Advisory Committee on Birds (Chapter 3). Between that meeting and the first Project Team meeting later in 1987, those who would become the Team members gathered further information to allow areas to be considered against these criteria. Such information collation included consideration of habitat continuity to facilitate spread to other areas, productivity information on other raptors, examination of records of illegal persecution, and confidential conversations with individual NCC regional staff about local conditions and the attitudes of land-owners and local residents.

At its first meeting, which I hosted at NCC's Peterborough headquarters on 20th October 1987, the Project Team considered the possible regions where a reintroduction might be attempted. Several factors could influence participants' viewpoints. These include the tendency to assume that where a threatened population still exists – or where a locally extinct one was last recorded – is its optimal habitat. We were getting increasing evidence against this assumption from both the White-tailed Eagles and the Red Kites (see above). Another is the inevitable human tendency for everyone to promote his or her favourite area. We tried to moderate such enthusiasm by utilizing the scientific information available, but without falling into the trap of waiting until everything was known with no uncertainties.

Prime criteria for a reintroduction area are reworked slightly below to make them more amenable to assessment.

(1) Any illegal persecution should be at a low level, because of the danger from poison baits. Such information collation included an examination by RSPB Species Protection staff of their records of illegal persecutions. It was recognised, however, that all Red Kites would be liable to visit areas of illegal poisoning when they dispersed from the rearing and release area.
(2) The area chosen should not be an isolated patch of good habitat in a predominantly over-intensively game-keepered or otherwise unsuitable region. This we could assess both from maps and the wide knowledge of habitats and situations across the country by the Project Team and their colleagues.
(3) The area should offer a good winter food supply as well as that in summer. Although kites disperse widely in their first year, as later confirmed by this study, they tend to return to their natal area and stay there to breed.
(4) In view of the evidence from the Welsh studies, comparisons with continental Europe, and indications from the White-tailed Eagle work, that rainfall is a major adverse factor, drier eastern areas should be preferred.
(5) The ecology of the kites is clearly similar to that of Buzzards, so that areas of high density and productivity of Buzzards should be suitable – but recognising that Buzzards were absent from many suitable areas, for the same historical reasons as for the kites.
(6) The potential attitude of the local human population should also be considered, and this is noted further below. The network of local NCC officers and many RSPB personnel would be very helpful here.

We recognised that no one area would be likely to fulfil all these features, but they should provide a useful guide.

Project Team members had been invited to propose areas of England and Scotland, after consulting confidentially (if appropriate) with colleagues. Five areas in England were suggested as possibilities but, rather surprisingly (to the English-based members at least) only one in Scotland.

It was obviously important to try to overcome any effect of personal subjective favourites of Team members. Therefore, as much information as possible was collated for each of the six areas, against the six agreed criteria. On the basis of this, the Project Team scored the short-listed areas, from 1 star (poor) to 3 stars (good) or noted that the criterion was not applicable:

Area	A	B	C	D	E	F
1. Low persecution (illegal persecution records)	***	*	*	**	***	*
2. Not isolated (habitat continuity for spread)	***	*	*	***	**	*
3. Food all year	***	***	***	**	***	***
4. Dry summers	***	***	***	***	**	**
5. Performance of buzzards	n/a	n/a	n/a	***	***	*
6. Local attitude (local staff confidential assessment)	***	**	**	**	***	**

Area A seemed best, followed by **D** and **E** next, but **E** was rather like the existing Welsh area in several respects. To detail:
Area A (Berkshire/Surrey/Buckinghamshire borders) would also catch the public's imagination as it had a historical context (just west of London and the history of city scavenging by the birds) and would publicise conservation near several large population centres.
Area B (Sussex Downs, south of London and near the south coast) had many similar features but had a history of rather more poisoning incidents. It was also rather more separated in terms of habitat continuity from other areas to which we hoped that the kites might progressively spread their breeding range if we were successful, especially as the major city area of London would lie between it and many potentially suitable areas to the north. Both these considerations applied also to **Area C** (Breckland, in East Anglia, north-east of London), because of the largely tree-less intensively farmed near prairies to its west. These former wetlands, drained centuries ago, are Britain's major areas for most cereal and vegetable production.
Area D (the Black Isle and East Inverness-shire, on the east coast of Scotland, north of Inverness) scored generally well and was considered to be a good area although, in retrospect, the level of illegal persecution seems to have been underestimated.
Area E (South Devon, in the south-west peninsula of England) scored fairly similarly to **D** but hesitations were caused by its western position and some similarities with the landscape of the existing Welsh kite breeding area.
Area F (New Forest and Dorset, near the central south coast, between areas **B** and **E**) was noted as a good raptor area, but was prone to persecution and also suffered, at the time, from overgrazing.
Area A seemed best on this assessment, with areas **D** and **E** scoring close to it. The relative lack of Buzzards in area A was not a problem, as the point was whether Buzzards were productive if they did occur. In many parts of the country, Buzzards were absent from areas of former occupation, probably linked to persecution around the edge of their reduced range impeding re-establishment (see also Chapter 12).
Area E was thought to be rather too similar to the areas in Wales where kites remained and too close to them to be the best deployment of effort. Accordingly, areas **A** and **D** were

identified as the best areas warranting further investigation. Roy Dennis agreed to do this for area **D**, while local NCC staff (coordinated by Sarah Garnett) and I looked into area **A**. Richard Porter would alert RSPB staff for area **A** that NCC was leading in that area while I would do the same for NCC staff responsible around area **D**. The need for confidentiality was stressed heavily.

The possible use of two release areas was discussed at length. Our provisional view was that simultaneous operation in two areas might have disadvantages by dividing effort. However, there would be considerable advantages in planning from the start for eventual releases in both areas, in two programmes of about 5 years each. A project in area **D** might start two years after one in area **A**, and overlap with it. And of course in time other areas would be considered ultimately aimed at linking both populations.

Timing of local information release
At the same meeting, we considered again the related issue of information release. Involvement of local people would be important, but for reasons already outlined, this would need to be progressive and carefully managed. The Team agreed to prepare a brief for local bodies, conservation trusts (wildlife trusts in modern terminology), ornithological clubs, etc., to be released as appropriate and at stages as determined by the needs of the conservation project.

We anticipated that we would not make the first public announcement until spring 1989 as the first birds were imported, assuming that we could achieve that by then. However, the basic statement would be prepared in advance, partly in case a statement had to be swiftly produced much earlier. In autumn 1988, we planned to focus press attention on the outcome of the egg manipulation programme in Wales (see Chapter 4).

We noted that the confidentiality of the reintroduction project would progressively decrease as we needed to involve more people, but we would attempt to start with a 'need-to-know' basis.

We were convinced that keeping the spread of information on the project as slow as possible during the planning stages would be important so that expectations for too rapid a result did not undermine confidence in what would anyway be a challenging and uncertain operation. We felt also that avoiding disturbance both to the birds and to the operations of the estates which made themselves available to the project would be crucial. As I explained in Chapter 3, confidentiality and secrecy would not necessarily be the best approach to adopt now, but many things were different then, including the background level of public understanding. Indeed, the very success of the Experimental Red Kite Reintroduction Project did much to improve public understanding, enabling a very different approach in future projects.

Confidentiality presents something of a problem in a big organisation, especially one whose normal culture is rather open. Once a secret is shared by more than a few people, it is really no longer a secret. Clearly, the people who are actually doing the work or dealing with landowners, etc. needed to know the full picture. Equally, the senior staff could not be left in the dark, not least because they could unwittingly make false statements. In NCC, I approached this tightrope by advising senior staff of the activity and the general area and pointing out that their regional staff were fully involved in the location but asking that they set an example in not asking for further details. With some senior staff, this worked well. For others, I had to deploy in a more constructive role the observations I had made in my period in NCC in seeing civil servants drafting answers to Parliamentary questions, and applying these. The main difficulty was a constructive one involving personal curiosity and support, although the concern of one top manager seemed to be that the project might be successful and require conservation of the kites to be built into future activities!

Site selection for rearing and release areas

In the three and a half months before the Team's next meeting in February 1988, we were busy on these aspects, as well as all the others running in parallel which are the subject of the previous and later chapters.

My regional colleagues in NCC were of great help. At that time, local officers (then called Assistant Regional Officers (AROs), but later County Officers or similar) were usually professional biologists who had learnt by experience the skills of dealing with owners and occupiers of land and other local people whose help is needed to achieve effective conservation. Most also developed excellent knowledge of the areas for which they were responsible. My earlier discussions with the Regional Officers or their deputies, as well as with the contact officers they nominated, had already provided a good start. Now, we started focussing on identifying actual landholdings within the general areas.

Peter Schofield, Regional Officer for NCC South England Region, was fully supportive. Sarah Garnett, ARO for Berkshire in that Region, identified the most promising site, Windsor Great Park. Apart from suitable habitat, this area benefited from an owner's representative, HRH The Duke of Edinburgh, with a very positive approach to conservation, and a secure situation which would aid in confidentiality and site-security. With my Regional colleagues, I outlined the idea to the estate's manager in late 1987. He soon confirmed, in January 1988, that the representative of the owner, as well as the directors of the estate management organisation, the Crown Estates Commissioners, supported the proposal.

By the next Project Team meeting, in February 1988, Sarah and I were able to confirm that we had permission to use this excellent site and that the managers and key staff were supportive, so much so that we all agreed that our next Project Team meeting in October 1988 would take place nearby, with the possibility of a site-visit. In the following months, we continued to negotiate the detailed arrangements with the estate manager, while gratefully turning our attention to more taxing problems. We had been surprised at the ease of this aspect of this part of the project. Later, we discovered why!

On the Black Isle, our RSPB Scotland colleagues reported progress in this area of relatively low human population, and few estates to work with. At the Project Team meeting, I could report that NCC's England Directorate was enthusiastic, NCC's Scotland Directorate expressed some reservations, and asked questions particularly in relationship to forestry (which we found a little puzzling but would address).

It was becoming increasingly clear that both areas seemed feasible, and there were strong reasons, especially in political and public relations terms, to proceed with both in parallel. This was agreed upon, maintaining the strong, unified project approach which had prevailed from the start.

An agenda item on progress in identified areas was included in the Project Team meeting on Thursday 6th October 1988, held near the proposed English rearing and release areas.

For that site, good local food supplies, with the possibility of additional food dumps, were clear. Roy Dennis reported that the situation with land-owners at the Scottish sites remained satisfactory. I reported on progress with the NCC Scottish Committee. Dr Peter Tilbrook, NCC Regional Officer North-West Scotland, had given his full support. The Committee supported the project although they had some reservation as to whether a start in 1989 would be feasible. They asked for a report to be certain:
a. That the goodwill of farmers in the area had been obtained;
b. That the general approval of the Scottish Landowners' Federation (SLF) had been given; and
c. That a programme for publicity and public relations had been drafted.

Views of the Black Isle rearing and release area during the Project Team's visit there on 24th January 1989 [MP & project].

It was agreed that a plan for PR should be prepared as soon as possible, preferably to be finished by Christmas so that it would be reported to the NCC Scottish Committee in the new year.

To readers more familiar with the relatively go-ahead attitude of the Scottish Parliament nowadays and Government support for nature conservation and sustainability, a word of explanation is perhaps necessary. The political situation in Scotland was very different in the 1980s to what it is in the 2020s. First, of course, there was no separate Parliament or Government for Scotland until 1999. The Government was a Department of the UK Government, known as the Scottish Office, headed by the Secretary of State for Scotland, a member of the UK Cabinet appointed by the Prime Minister. For many years up until 1959, most MPs in Scotland were from the Conservative Party, with all the rest going to the Labour Party except for one Liberal. In that year, the gradual build-up of Labour seats, particularly in the urban centres, overtook the Conservatives (still fairly strong for several years in rural seats) and kept that lead until 2015. After a general decline, the Conservative vote collapsed completely in 1997, leaving them with no MPs in Scotland. From 1964, the

Liberal Party (later the Liberal Democrats, LD) saw some 3rd-party build-ups (although overtaken for one general election, in 1974, by the Scottish National Party (SNP), which then fell back from 11 to 2 seats). In the year of the Conservative collapse of 1997, the LD became the party with second largest number of MPs (10), with SNP third (6), but Labour still had 56. This general pattern persisted until 2015, when there was an SNP landslide, with all the other three parties left with only 1 Scottish MP each. Since then, SNP has retained the majority with some variation in the numbers for the other three parties.

In 1979, a referendum on a separate Scottish Parliament failed to secure the required 40% turnout. However, this was reversed in another referendum in 1997, with a Scottish Parliament set up in 1999 (or, some would say, resumed after an adjournment in 1707), with some, but by no means all, powers devolved from the UK Parliament. A coalition of Labour and LD took power of devolved matters. In 2007, SNP took the largest number of Members of the Scottish Parliament (MSPs) and formed a minority Scottish Government, becoming a majority one from 2011 onwards.

These political changes did not all necessarily directly affect nature conservation issues but did generate changes in the approach to many aspects of policy, although often delayed some years after obvious political changes. This is related to the fact that changes in British government policies are implemented and administered through a civil service that is supposed to be politically neutral (although there seem to have been some challenges to this in recent years). The Scottish "establishment" however, includes the senior civil servants, at least some politicians and others running various boards, commercial companies or land. Scottish friends have described to me the governance of the Scottish countryside, with its many large estates, as essentially "feudal." I cannot judge how true this is or was, and there have been progressive changes in recent years, notably as management of estates has changed hands or been passed down to new generations. However, despite the earlier political changes, in the 1980s policy decisions in the countryside were certainly still dominated by land-owner interests with views that many considered to be positively Victorian and heavily based on traditional positions.

Whatever the background, a response to the clarified requests of NCC's Committee for Scotland was approved at the January 1989 meeting of the Project Team. The Committee received, for its meeting on 22nd February 1989, a report from the Team, via NCC's Regional Officer, saying:

> The Chairman of the SLF in the Highlands, Lord Strathnaver, has given his support to the project, indicating that SLF's principal concern is that the landowners whose ground would be used for the release work should be in favour of the project.
>
> A number of local landowners have been approached including all whose land is being considered as possible release sites. All have been supportive and most positively enthusiastic.
>
> The general programme for public relations, designed to embrace Scottish, English and Welsh elements, is to consult with appropriate local interests but to avoid drawing public attention to particular localities, so as to minimise disturbance both to birds and to owners/occupiers. As the contacts with local people are likely to lead to some press interest, it is planned to release a general statement in late spring without naming particular areas. This would then enable local officers to deal with their local press at appropriate times and levels of information. A general press release would again be made in July or August after the birds had fledged and again specific localities would not be mentioned.
>
> In addition to the above a leaflet giving general background information on the birds will be produced and made available to individuals involved with the release work in local areas.
>
> 2 February 1989

These points had already been sorted by the Team, but there had been some difficulties in determining precisely what the concerns of the NCC Committee for Scotland had been. Once this was clarified, answering them had presented no great problem.

There was a wide range of views to take into account, including those of estates who wanted no publicity for fear of visitors disrupting their operations and wildlife. We confirmed our view that local people should be involved and given prior notification, and that attention should be given to local media as well as national ones. A more detailed approach would be prepared jointly by RSPB and NCC before the next meeting.

For the English site, at the meeting in October 1988, a representative had described the local food source, including provision of suitable food for the growing young kites, as well as describing the other birds and mammals present within the area and showed a map highlighting the habitat distributions. With regard to security, he would identify a secluded part of the estate to be used for the kites.

During a site-visit, shortly after the Project Team meeting, Lawrence Jones-Walters (who was standing in for Sarah Garnett who was on temporary promotion elsewhere in the Region) and I discussed with the estate the best sitings for the rearing and release facilities. During the discussions, it became apparent that, despite indications to the contrary, the estate manager had simply not consulted his head gamekeeper on the proposal in the 10 months since receiving our detailed proposal, nor in the 8 months since the estate had approved it, during which time local colleagues had been in frequent contact with the estate management. The support of such key players would be essential and, not surprisingly, this individual was now rather less in favour of the project than he would have been had he been more involved since the early stages, as we had indeed been advised that he had been.

I considered that we would be better off devoting efforts to finding a new site. This was because of the difficulties in liaising effectively with the management of the original site. We could not afford the loss of the window of time, and the fact that the extremely high public profile of the estate owners could lead to some very awkward publicity, with the needs of the project becoming subordinate to other issues. NCC's Regional staff agreed and quietly started the search for alternative sites in the area.

My concern over the degree to which a complex project could be handled in collaboration with an estate with such management problems were exacerbated in the next few weeks as the head keeper's doubts obviously rippled through the system. We provided information to address the head keeper's reasonable concerns. However, the fact that his bosses had failed to consult him over the past year clearly unsettled him – as it had us! The estate manager replied generally favourably to our further information and confirmed the owner's commitment to the project, but gave signs of wanting to start discussions again, thus delaying the project for at least a year. Fortunately, by that time, about 6 weeks after we had discovered the estate manager's failure to consult his head keeper, my regional NCC colleagues had identified several other suitable sites in the area where the owners had agreed in principle and which were, frankly, even more suitable. We decided to change sites, and then had to work out how to tell the owners and managers of the original site.

This was made much simpler in that the lead representative of the original site's owner had heard one version of the confusion and wrote to NCC's then Deputy Chairman, Sir John Burnett, who had very recently added amongst his roles liaising at the highest level with certain very high profile individuals, notably the Royal Family, as these were obviously sensitive. The Deputy Chairman, of course, then consulted with NCC's Regional Officer and myself. The Regional Officer provided the Deputy Chairman with a rather more accurate account of events than had permeated from the estate manager, noting also several other recent examples of where the estate manager had not met agreements he had previously made with NCC, possibly again through failure to communicate with his staff. I must say that, in his letter, His Royal Highness clearly was trying to find a way forward to enable the project to

Views of Wormsley Park at the time of its role as a rearing and release area [MP].

go ahead at Windsor. This was greatly appreciated. However, this would have involved a year's delay and the uncertainties about management at a lower level remained.

I was summoned at very short notice to see NCC's Deputy Chairman. I had no doubt that I was being summoned for a ticking off, despite not being advised of this. So, as soon as I was admitted into his office, I said simply that everything was alright as I had sacked the estate. After he had recovered and I had convinced him that further high-profile or public communications were unlikely, we reached a satisfactory stage of mutual wariness. Fortunately, my confidence proved correct. The Deputy Chairman wrote a careful reply to the Duke, saying that we were following up the idea of alternative sites, noting that this was in line with one of the possibilities indicated by His Royal Highness.

Shortly afterwards, the Crown Estate Commissioners, embarrassed by the actions of the estate manager at Windsor, kindly offered to examine its portfolio of other estates throughout much of Britain. Although we had found a replacement site (see below), there was some advantage in a backup, so I and a regional colleague visited a senior manager at the Crown Estate, who was most helpful. I applied the area selection criteria to a range of these, combined with further experience of kite habitat I had by then gathered from various parts of Europe. Later events seemed to give some support to the selection criteria which we were using. The top of my provisional replacement site list coincided with the first site that released kites used for an overnight stop when they started dispersing from the eventual release site, so it must have looked OK to them despite its being about 100 km from the release site! This gave us some confidence that we were able to achieve something like a kite's eye view of habitats. The second in the provisional chosen list was in the general vicinity of the third release site chosen some years later (Chapter 11). I thanked the senior manager again and explained that our regional investigations had identified a new front-runner. However, he was very content for us to get back to him on a future occasion should another site be needed.

My regional colleagues' local knowledge had again produced the goods in identifying several sites. Sarah, Lawrence and I favoured one of these, Wormsley. This was the home of John Paul (later Sir Paul) Getty Jr, and I am indebted to him and his friend and one of the directors, Mr Christopher Gibbs, who made arrangements. Here, at a meeting in December, only two months after discovering the fundamental problem with the first site, we explained the situation personally, not just with the owner's representative but also with the managers of farming, forestry and game operations. We were very gratified with their constructive approaches. Not surprisingly, the head keeper had some reservations. We explained why we did not expect kites to pose difficulties in respect of pheasant operations, on the basis of their biology. These included their preference for an easy life of scavenging, rather than hunting, their preference for foraging in open ground rather than woodland where rearing of gamebirds tends to take place, and the existing knowledge of kite-pheasant interactions (see Annex 6). We pointed out, however, that we could not guarantee this. The exercise was experimental, although based on the best available information. We explained that all aspects of the operation would be under continual review. We did not expect a problem but, if one arose, we would address it. We did not know what the answer would be. However, in a military analogy, the operation was more like a campaign than a rehearsed parade. The owner's representative noted that the keeper would not be held responsible if we were wrong, and pheasant numbers fell, but he too had his professional pride. We were grateful, therefore, for his open-minded cooperation in spite of his doubts - an open-mindedness that he would deploy to assist the project's wider objectives at later stages.

There was an unexpected benefit to the unlooked-for change of site. Despite our best efforts, some information on the previously planned location had begun to leak out, some at least from non-NCC sources. One possibility might have been the local police who, in a comment to the press, had innocently given away information that they did not realise was sensitive. Fortunately, however, this local press item was not widely picked up. The policy that we had agreed was that we would neither confirm nor deny any information on rearing areas. Equally, we were not prepared to make any statements that were untrue. If questioned, we therefore, truthfully, said that an experimental reintroduction was being considered but that, if it went ahead, we would not be able to indicate areas. The fact that, even to colleagues, we continued not to deny suggestions of the original locality as the site seems to have confirmed presumptions that this was the case, and probably gave some extra protection from disturbance of the locality eventually used.

Having met in February in the general area of the proposed English site, the Project Team met on 24th–25th January 1989 at NCC's Inverness regional office and visited the Scottish area, the Black Isle. By this stage, release sites had been agreed in both English and Scottish areas. I reported, for the record that, for various reasons, a change in the location of the English release site had been made, and that this was in the same general area, although at present the precise location was not being disclosed to anyone except those immediately involved. In the Update to Project Team on 8th April 1989, it was reported that, in Scotland, consultations with local landowners and organisations had proven satisfactory. For England, we confirmed that agreement had been reached with a very suitable estate to host the project.

As will have been seen above, considerable care and research went into the selection of the release areas and the sites within them, in order to give the kites the best chance of success. We chose areas of countryside containing a mix of farmland, woodland and rough grazing. Both sites were located in the drier, more productive, eastern half of the country, and in areas with a low estimated incidence of illegal persecution, especially involving poison. In Scotland, a further selection was based on areas of high and productive Buzzard populations.

The release area (*i.e.* not just Wormsley) in England was well wooded but interspersed with extensive areas of arable land and pasture (both cattle and sheep). There were also large areas of rough grassland, parkland and a small amount of heath. This type of habitat is strikingly similar to the highly productive lowland kite habitat of parts of Sweden and Spain, but rather dissimilar to the less productive upland habitat found in Wales.

Although this chapter has pulled out the information on selection and negotiation of sites, all aspects of the experimental project were considered in parallel. The Project Team meeting in January 1989 had agreed that the key elements needed to be in place by 15th March if the project was to go ahead in 1989. The key information was expected by the end of February on important issues like the source of birds, transportation, and remaining approvals. I turn now to the second of these.

6. Collecting and importing the nestlings

The fact that our work was clearly a conservation project did not, of course, exempt it from legal requirements for licensing. Indeed, as the conservation bodies were keen to ensure the efficacy of the licencing systems, we were anxious to follow the rules fully. (During the project, I became one of NCC's two Assistant Chief Scientists, finding myself with supervision of licensing. I issued an instruction that, in cases in which NCC staff had to apply to colleagues for licences, they must be challenged at least as thoroughly as for any other applicant, and a comprehensive record must be kept, while protecting confidential material properly.)

The licensing needs (mainly where other bodies had licensing authority) did present some interesting challenges as some of these systems were designed mainly to regulate commercial trade rather than support conservation projects.

As early as the first Project Team meeting, on 20th October 1987, we reviewed the licensing requirements if a reintroduction were to proceed.

If, as seemed likely, importations of birds were to be involved, an import licence (and corresponding export licences in the country of origin) would be required under CITES (the Convention on International Trade in Endangered Species). Our colleagues at the Department of the Environment (DoE, a forerunner of Defra) would be briefed.

In addition, even for birds which might fly naturally between countries, quarantine regulations still applied if they were being carried out by human agency. The Ministry of Agriculture, Fisheries and Food (MAFF, now part of Defra) would need to be consulted on quarantine requirements and licencing. Birds require a disease-free quarantine period of isolation of 35 days prior to release. Fortunately, this period would keep the birds in captivity not too long after their fledging period. Regional Pest Officers and Government Vets would be notified at a later date.

We would need to check also whether the short period of captivity would require licensing as keepers of captive birds, and other licensing needs that we might discover in this pioneering and experimental project as we went along.

At the Project Team meeting on Thursday 6th October 1988, Dr Leo Batten, in charge of bird-related licensing and other matters at NCC, reported that he had written and sent details of the project to Dr Death, Senior Veterinary Officer at MAFF; and to the Secretary of the Animal Welfare Branch at the Department of Agriculture and Fisheries for Scotland (DAFS). Leo took the meeting through an application form he had received from MAFF. It was felt by members that this form should now be completed. MAFF would then send an inspector to discuss the project and the import of birds. No problem was envisaged. Leo would also arrange for the CITES licence required to import the kites.

At the Project Team meeting on 24th January 1989, held at the NCC offices in Inverness, Leo indicated that he was simply waiting for more information on sources, etc. before arranging for licences to be issued.

By the update to the Project Team on 8th April 1989, the NCC had issued licences to Dr Roger Bray and others for collection and rearing birds in Wales, and to myself and others to possess these birds subsequently up to release. Leo had been in touch with DoE in respect of the CITES importation licence, and RSPB had now applied for this, as the Swedish birds would arrive initially in Scotland. Roy agreed to liaise with Magnus Sylvén and ensure that he obtained a CITES export licence in Sweden. Leo would co-ordinate applications to DAFS and MAFF for permits to quarantine.

Roy had discovered that the RAF might be able to transport the birds. The Welsh kite workers had agreed to use their best efforts to persuade farmers to allow the removal of those eggs unlikely to result naturally in fledged kites, to provide for the reintroduction project. The provisional plan was to rear Swedish birds in Scotland and Welsh ones in England, although the details of this would be kept under review so that reasonable numbers would be available in both areas.

We agreed that Roy would liaise with Magnus Sylvén over collection of the Swedish birds and would confirm transport arrangements from Sweden to Britain. Wildlife Surveys (Wales) – the small company including the retired Kite Committee NCC leaders and whom NCC CSD had contracted – together with NCC and RSPB would organise the obtaining, hatching and initial rearing of the birds in Wales.

The Project Team Update on 21st May 1989 noted that Roy would copy to me the CITES importation licence and DAFS authorisations re quarantine, so that both groups had these for inspection. He would also ensure that Magnus Sylvén had obtained the necessary CITES export licence, and obtain copies for both UK teams. Roy would arrange with DAFS for quarantine inspection of Scottish cages and of the birds on arrival. Local NCC officer, Lawrence Jones-Walters, and Ian Evans would arrange local MAFF inspection of the English quarantine rearing cages.

Roy had confirmed arrangements with the RAF to transport the Swedish birds. He had arranged to join the Swedish workers for a couple of days before returning with the birds. With only one Welsh kite available (see Chapter 4), it had been agreed already that we should try to make equal numbers of birds available to both sites. Richard Porter and I would transport some of the Swedish birds to England by car on their arrival in Scotland. We confirmed other arrangements, and Roy would arrange for a supply of food to be available to accompany birds being transported to England.

Collection of kite chicks from Sweden

The Royal Air Force had kindly transported our White-tailed Eagle chicks from Norway, on their maritime patrol aircraft. The trips fitted in well with their operational and training programme in conjunction with Norway, a fellow member state of the North Atlantic Treaty Organisation (NATO). Sweden was not a member of NATO, but Denmark, very close to the area of southern Sweden from which the kites would come, was. Just a short ferry ride linked the two. (This was before the construction of the famous bridge linking the two countries, that provided such a boon to TV dramas). To avoid the special arrangements necessary for a military aircraft to land in a nation outside the military alliance, the RAF would collect the birds from near Copenhagen.

Roy Dennis of RSPB flew to Copenhagen from Aberdeen on 9th June and travelled via ferry to Lund Field Station in Sweden. Roy reported that, *"on 10 June, seven active kite nests were visited with several members of the Swedish Kite Project to ring young birds, monitor nests and select birds for translocation to Britain. Five nestlings were collected (three from nests containing three young and two from a nest of four young). They were transported in cardboard boxes to Lund Field Station. On 11–12 June, a further 12 nests in southern Scania were visited and [another] five young obtained (three singles from nests of three and two from a nest of four).*

"The selection of young was based on our previous experience with White-tailed Eagles, and from information gleaned from work on the translocation of Ospreys in North America. It was decided to take young of about four weeks, which were well feathered and able to maintain their body heat without brooding. Smaller chicks would require greater levels of artificial feeding and care, with the risk of imprinting, whilst larger chicks would be ready to fly long before they could be released from quarantine. Chicks were selected for compatibility of size so the largest chick might be taken from one nest and the smallest from the next.

RAF Nimrod overhead and lands in heavy rain. Unloading the kites in their travel boxes; and Nimrod, its pilot, Roy Dennis and one of the kites [CG, MP]

"The chicks were identified by box number and subsequently by ring number. They were kept apart in cardboard boxes and were fed by hand, twice a day, with fish and meat obtained locally. Initially, it was necessary to open the birds' bills and put food down their throats, but usually, after the first day, they swallowed the food without such assistance. The selection, feeding and care of the young were carried out by Roy Dennis, while the location of and climbing to nests were carried out by Swedish ornithologists from Scania Ornithological Society, Lund University and WWF."

The visit to Sweden provided an additional opportunity to see Swedish Red Kites in their breeding area, and to learn how they live. Regions of England and Scotland chosen for reintroductions closely resembled the area of rolling farmland and forest with rough grazings which typified Swedish kite country. The food of kites in Sweden is principally young and dead rabbits, young rooks and assorted carrion including fish. There is no conflict with farming and sporting interests, and local people are very proud of their kites. The population of kites had increased four-fold in the last two decades to over 2000 pairs. This not only reflected the sympathetic attitudes of the local population and the hard work of the Swedish conservationists but also the favourable breeding habitat.

The 10 young kites collected under special licences from nests in Sweden were transported via car ferry to the Danish Air Force base at Vaerloese, and from there to RAF Kinloss by RAF Nimrod on 13th June 1989.

Those of us at RAF Kinloss had quite a long wait. On the way back, the Nimrod was diverted on to one of its main tasks, search and rescue missions over the North Sea. We had to wait until another of the Nimrods took over and our birds could continue on their way.

Arriving at an RAF base still required all the formal legal aspects such as immigration, customs and veterinary inspections. However, these flights were booked as a one-off and so officials came out by appointment. There were certainly no long queues.

After a photo-call for local and national press, six kites were taken to the Scottish release site while Richard Porter and I loaded four into a large one-way hire-car to drive them in the rest of the day and over much of the night the 870 km to the English site, about a 10-hour drive south. Occasional stops were made to feed the kites. This was an interesting exercise in a car without breaching quarantine regulations, but we found it possible in our first attempt a little north of the English border, in a large lay-by near the small town of Locherbie, some half way to the Buckinghamshire rearing and release site.

On arrival in the very early morning, Ian Evans awaited us, and we decided to ring the birds immediately, to give them individual identities, and to minimise the number of times they needed to be handled. As a licensed bird-ringer, I had the rings and the special ring-closing pliers with me, and so did this. Unfortunately, one of the rings overlapped slightly. This happens occasionally. Being extremely tired after a very long day and night probably did not help. I did not have my special ring-opening pliers with me. Having checked that the overlapped ring was not causing any immediate problem to the bird, I decided that the safest thing would be to fetch my opening pliers, rather than improvise an alternative way of re-opening the ring – although I was not looking forward to another 4 hours of driving. One other possibility occurred to me and I forewarned Ian.

Leaving the birds in the quarantine cages (see next Chapter, 7) in the capable care of Ian, I dropped Richard at his base on my way back to my own, in Peterborough. By this time, it was a reasonable time of the morning, so I telephoned the British Trust for Ornithology to speak with Kevin Baker who operated the bird-ringing scheme for Britain and Ireland. By good fortune, the BTO was then based in Tring, a short drive from the release site. I asked him if he would like to ring a Red Kite. Most ringers like to ring as many different species as possible, and I guessed correctly that he had never ringed a kite. Having stressed the need and ensured his agreement on the need for confidentiality (which he was used to dealing with in other aspects of his job), I described the situation and he agreed readily to fix it himself that morning – thereby saving me from yet another long drive, and probably compromising local road safety. All that was left for me was to just to drop off the hire-car at my office for collection and cleaning, checking that it was not too messy given its recent cargo of feathers and fowl, and retreat home to bed.

Wales

In 1989, the English release site received a single chick from the Welsh population. The chick originated from a clutch of three eggs taken from a nest by Tony Cross (one of the many kite fieldworkers in Wales). The nest qualified for manipulation because it fitted one of the agreed criteria: persistent failure due to illegal egg-collecting. Indeed, the dummy clutch

There was lots of press interest. Then (below right), Richard Porter (far right) and I (carrying kite in box) collect the 4 kites before heading south, leaving the other 6 kites with Roy and his colleagues. [CG]

was subsequently robbed by an egg-collector and the nest was deserted. After incubation by bantam hens, two of the three eggs hatched. After 16 days, one of the chicks was returned to a foster nest in Wales, while the other chick was reared by a captive buzzard for 32 days, and then taken to the English release site on 12th June 1989, about a day before we delivered the Swedish birds.

Continuing the supply

At the Project Team meeting on 27th November 1989, this time held at RSPB HQ in Sandy, Bedfordshire, we reviewed progress in the pilot year of releases, lessons learnt and possible improvements.

Roy Dennis raised the point that a vet is required to inspect the Red Kites in the foreign country and provide written confirmation before they are legally exported so as to avoid any possible bureaucratic wrangle in this country. I reported that the health of each bird at the English release site was monitored throughout the period of captivity by Dr James Kirkwood, of the Institute of Zoology. It was agreed that Dr Kirkwood should be approached to specify veterinary requirements for the whole project.

Roy Dennis would contact Magnus Sylvén to offer help and would make a formal approach to the RAF for further help in the following year. There would be no problem with transporting the birds from Sweden, but the suggestion that they take chicks over a longer period throughout the kite breeding season was not feasible since the RAF could not make more than one flight a year.

It was agreed that the objective the following year should be to continue the releases in both areas. Dr Ian Newton said that as many birds as possible should be the aim, with a target of at least 10 birds a year for each site. The need to release as many birds as possible over a short period of time was stressed because of the length of time the birds took to mature, although the need for staggering the age structure in the population was also noted, and the inevitable mortality to birds through accident, immaturity or unwelcome malice. Constraints on the number of birds that could be released at any one site were highlighted by Dr Nick Fox, since the release cages are graded as "low grade quarantine quarters", restricting the number of birds to 10 per site, with sites located a least one mile apart. It was decided that a total of 30 birds would be sought with the view of obtaining at least 20. It was agreed that releases at both sites would continue the following year unless fewer than eight birds could be obtained. The suggestion made by Graham Elliott that it would be wise to defer the actual decision until it is known which countries can supply birds was widely accepted.

In the Project Team *Update Note* of 3rd May 1990, I was able to comment that *"Things seem to be going remarkably well - which conceals a lot of hard work by many folk, of course. Doubtless, assorted problems will arise over the next few critical weeks: good luck to all of us in dealing with them!"*

Sweden

Sweden was again obliging, generously authorising the collection of up to twenty young birds. Licences had been applied for by Magnus Sylvén and Roy Dennis, as appropriate. Veterinary inspection in Sweden was being organised. The RAF were again flying, probably on 15th June, and possibly directly from Sweden as they had been in contact with their Swedish Air Force colleagues.

Roy Dennis visited Sweden from 11th to 15th June and selected 20 young kites. He was assisted by ornithologists from the Scania Ornithological Society and again used Lund University Field Station as an excellent base. The RAF were extremely helpful and were able to collect the birds from Malmo airport – where to the Swedes' amazement we had "sent that huge aircraft for a few chicks." The Nimrod was based on the first operational jet airliner, the De Havilland Comet – certainly not huge in terms of today's airliners, but definitely so in relation to 20 boxes of kite chicks. The young kites, accompanied by Roy Dennis and David Stroud (of Ornithology Branch, NCC, who had flown out with the RAF Nimrod maritime patrol aircraft), were in Scotland two hours later, courtesy of 201 Squadron, RAF Kinloss. They were immediately transported to the release cages at the Scottish site where they were reared, the second batch of birds bringing the total number of project birds imported from Sweden so far to 30.

Wales

In Wales, manipulation work continued, largely in an attempt to overcome the problems with egg thieves. In 1990, a total of twelve eggs were taken from several nests that were at risk from egg-collectors and, indeed, two of these nests were subsequently robbed of their dummy eggs. After a period of incubation under bantam hens at the incubation facility, seven eggs hatched. Five were either returned to their original nest or placed in foster nests in Wales. Two were reared for 41 days by the same captive buzzard that reared the kite chick in 1989, before being taken to the English release site. All work regarding the artificial incubation and rearing of the young kites was undertaken by Dr Nick Fox.

Spain

Conservation authorities in Navarra, northern Spain, and in Madrid, also assisted by agreeing to supply up to 20 birds, building on earlier contacts and co-operation on other species by Dr Eric Bignal. Licence applications, as appropriate, were made in Spain by the Navarrese authorities, who were also arranging veterinary inspections. The Instituto para la Conservación de la Naturaleza (better known by its acronym ICONA), the then national Spanish natural environment body, had been advised and consulted in advance. In Britain, Richard Porter and I had arranged for corresponding permits.

The RAF, at the corresponding Nimrod base at RAF St Mawgan in Cornwall could not then assist for Spain as they were only just starting visits, following Spain's joining of NATO a few years earlier, in 1982 – but they were keen to investigate collaboration in future years.

Through the good offices of Mike Ounsted (Wildfowl & Wetland Trust), I made contact with Rod Hall who ran, largely in his own time, the remarkable programme British Airways Assisting Nature Conservation (BAANC), which he himself had set up. Rod is a remarkable man. He had, in earlier times, been a flight engineer. Early airliners needed one of these, alongside the pilot and first officer, but they had eventually been replaced as automation improved instruments and controls, allowing the pilots to incorporate the tasks in their own role.

Rod is a natural fixer. He became a casualty engineer, the person who fixes aircraft with faults, or arranges for someone else to do so, and gets parts to the correct place when the ill aircraft is away from home base. His shift pattern at British Airways gave him free time during the week. This allowed him to combine his aptitude for fixing and his knowledge of airline systems at BA with his enthusiasm for nature conservation. He set up the BAANC programme in 1983, working initially entirely on his own. Rod gained the support from the several management departments which recognised the value of the scheme.

Most aircraft (especially in those days before computerised online booking and further optimisation of airline income) depart with empty cargo space or empty seats. Rod's idea was to offer free or discounted cargo space for the shipment of equipment and wildlife species between those working overseas in the conservation field and the captive breeding centres of rare and endangered species in UK, Europe and USA. He expanded this service to providing free or discounted seats for educators and students on flights with empty seats.

BAANC gave selective support to recognised international scientific organisations and associated individuals working to advance specific wildlife conservation projects. From the original idea of giving support to species 'at risk' captive-breeding and reintroduction projects, the scheme evolved to encompass much more. This included strong emphasis on assistance for the study of species in the wild, habitat protection, wildlife officer training, conservation education and tourism, focusing on preserving the essential variety of life on earth and encouraging the responsible management and sustainable use of the earth's natural resources. British Airways World Cargo played a vital and tangible role in fulfilling the aims of the Assisting Nature Conservation scheme.

Rod arranged for British Airways to oblige, probably on 30th or 31st May 1990. There are many differences between using a military flight and a civilian, passenger-carrying airliner. The latter are subject to all sorts of regulations which do not trouble the Air Force. One that concerned us was that we were still not sure how well the young kites would fare flying unattended and out of reach in the hold in "sky-kennels." We managed to secure special exemption from the health and agricultural authorities in MAFF to carry the birds in boxes in the cabin. Rod arranged agreement with British Airways that, although they would travel as cargo, they would physically travel in boxes in the passenger cabin, occupying (once we had worked out the volume) the rear two rows of seats, with us just in front of them. The boxes, folded flat and with appropriate labels for the return, were taken out with us on the outward flights.

Although there were some arguments for mixing the birds from both sources in each release area, the present provisional consensus, for practical reasons was to put the Spanish birds in the English area and the Swedish ones in the Scottish site. The Buckinghamshire site was of course only a short drive from Heathrow.

Arrangements and permissions for collection and export from Spain had been organised with the help of Dr Borja Heredia of ICONA and the Servicio de Medio Ambiente in Navarra. By kind permission of Snr Jose Ignacio Elorrieta (Director General), Alfonso Senosiain and colleagues of Servicio de Medio Ambiente located nests of Red Kites in wide areas of Navarra in spring 1990.

As is quite usual in an operation of this scale, the team was composed of a mixture of professionals and amateurs, some of the latter being professionals working on this project in a voluntary capacity. Ian Evans stayed in the UK to ensure that the rearing cages and local arrangements were ready, and to liaise with the London Quarantine Centre at Heathrow, who are used to dealing with all sorts of creatures, both legal importations and smuggled ones intercepted and rescued. We were fortunate to have in the team Eric and Sue Bignal, who had done so much to develop the contacts as well as John Halliday, who was kindly released for about a week by the South-West Scotland Region of NCC. John had worked in Spain as well as being an outstanding fieldworker. I went along on this first visit 'to do the diplomatic bit', as Eric put it.

The British contingent was completed by my wife, Ann. She is also a graduate ecologist but, having far more patience than me, worked as a primary school teacher. By good fortune, the right time for collection of the chicks coincided with spring half-term holiday, and Ann joined us as a volunteer. NCC's Director-General was keen for a video record to be made. We could not afford to commission this professionally but Ann had some experience in this area. (Remember that this was long before 'smart' mobile phones or digital cameras, when almost everyone now has access to video recording. Then, a video camera was the size of a large briefcase, mounted on a tripod or the camera-person's shoulder.)

Rod Hall's good offices at British Airways Assisting Nature Conservation were invaluable here too. Ann's teaching commitments meant that it was already a rush to catch the last flight from London to Madrid on the Friday evening. Rail delays meant Ann's late arrival at Heathrow, where – not surprisingly at the start of the school holiday – the check-in area was solid with people. (Those people with children who suffer the congestion and higher prices of holiday dates determined by school terms can at least escape this as their children grow up; spare a thought for teachers and their spouses who suffer this until retirement!) In desperation,

TO WHOM THIS MAY CONCERN

This is to introduce Mr Mike Pienkowski, Mr J. Halliday, Mrs S. Bignal **(RRSYJL)** and Mr E. Bignal **(RSHSAL)**, who are British Airways Consultants.

The group are travelling in connection with a Nature Conservancy Council and Royal Society for the Protection of Birds project, to reintroduce the red kite (a bird of prey) to England and Scotland.

On the 31st May I will travel with them when we will return aboard the BA459 from Madrid to London with up to twenty nestling red kites. By special license these will be carried in the rear cabin of the aircraft.

I would be grateful if you would give the party every possible assistance to carry out their important mission.

With thanks,

[signature]

Rod Hall
Principal Coordinator & Development Officer
British Airways - Nature Conservation Projects

Sita:LHRZQBA

20th May 1990

Ann did just the right thing by putting her case on the ground for a moment to collect her thoughts. Even as long ago as 1990, airport and airline staff did not like cases unattached to owners, and an efficient BA employee immediately appeared to ask whether she could help. She coped well with the shock of being presented with a note on her company's own headed notepaper requesting help as necessary. Here is the one I carried; Ann had a similar one.

This was combined with Ann's request to "get me on the flight to Madrid somehow, please." After the briefest of hesitations, Ann's rescuer announced that there was a way, and Ann found herself being rushed through the special couriers' check-in procedures.

Red Kite and Griffon Vulture overhead, while Navarra team unload ladder from their Land Rover Santana. [MP]

Eric & Sue Bignal, John Halliday, Ann and I joined our Spanish colleagues in the period 25th to 31st May 1990 to inspect these nests, find others and collect nestling kites. Nests were mainly in Oak, Pine and Poplars, often along rivers where fish formed a frequent food. Nests were generally at a height of 15–20 m or more. The breeding season for kites in Spain had been poor due to adverse weather earlier. This had caused an unusually wide spread in nesting dates as well as smaller broods than usual. Both these caused extra problems – and some futile tree climbing, because it had been decided to take one young from those with more than two. However, because of the poor season and consequent challenge to the adult kites in finding food for young, our hosts decided to take one of the young of some two-chick nests.

The technique involved a volunteer (not me!) climbing (with appropriate safety equipment) to the nest, carrying a rope and soft basket. After inspecting the contents of the nest and conferring if necessary, the climber lowered any qualifying chick, safely in the basket, to those of us on the ground. After a double check there, the climber could descend. The birds were kept safely and fed at our hosts' facility. Our own habits found some difficulty in adjusting to local catering culture. Obviously, our work needed to be done in daylight and, in the heat, the best time was early in the morning. However, Spanish culture tended to work to a different schedule, it not being unusual to be still at dinner at midnight, whereas, at least in these rural areas, breakfast did not seem to exist at any workable time for us! Still, we survived even if we could not enjoy as much Spanish cuisine as we would have liked.

Despite the challenges, we collected eleven young birds. They were kept and fed at one of Servicio de Medio Ambiente's facilities, and interviews (via interpreters) and photo-calls were organised, generating much favourable coverage across the Spanish press.

We drove them to Madrid airport in the early hours of the morning of 31st May. One of the great features about using an unconventional importation route, as provided by the RAF, was that – although all legal requirements need to be fulfilled – special arrangements need to be made. These arrangements can, however, be tailored to the needs. At Kinloss, the Ministry-approved vet and the customs officials had duly appeared, had a friendly chat while we waited for the aircraft's arrival, fulfilled their functions efficiently, and left. For the birds from Spain, however, we were using a commercial airline and commercial airports. These were designed for all the normal commercial processes – but certainly not for the rare situation of importation of nestling birds for conservation purposes.

Fortunately, Rod Hall's contacts saw us through all. At Madrid, we contacted British Airways' local agent who put us in contact with their cargo agent, wisely opining that it would be virtually impossible to work through the paperwork without someone used to the normal procedures, never mind the exceptional. On advice from British Airways as to how long

Climber ascends ladder, braced by others; reaches top of ladder; climbs tree; reaches nest; and lowers nestling in basket. [AP, MP]

customs procedures might take, we had set off from Navarra to Madrid in the early hours of the morning. This was also partly to make life as comfortable as possible for the kites before the heat of the day. Those extra hours proved invaluable as we worked our way through a series of offices in the business complex at Madrid Airport, under the helpful guidance of BA's cargo agent. Clearly, he was negotiating heavily on our behalf against the natural tendency of officials when meeting the unusual to delay, however well the necessary documents had been prepared in advance. Delay was the one element that we could not endure with the young kites at risk.

After much worry, and about two hours later, we emerged with the necessary paperwork. Our colleagues had meanwhile acquired some meat and given the young birds a last feed before the flight and quarantine checks.

Our trusty cargo agent, having entered into the spirit of the occasion, negotiated special handling and guarding of the birds for the period that they left our hands for the hour or so before we rejoined them on the plane. No less than the formidable *Guardia Civil* volunteered their services. This military-based police force, modelled on the French *National*

Back on the ground but still in tree-climbing gear, with chick. Not all nests were successful: predated eggs held by Alfonso Senosian, who also holds a heathy nestling from a different nest. [MP]

Gendarmerie, is the oldest law enforcement agency in Spain and one of two national police forces. Probably the honour of Spain's image was at stake. One of the English-speaking officers asked me about the project. I explained that both Spain and Sweden were supplying birds. Clearly this had a great impact, and my Spanish policeman friend joked that the Spanish gentlemen kites were sure to impress the Swedish lady kites. I did not correct his assumptions... he may well have been proved right had they actually met!

With the kites safely in the hands of Spain's notable police force, we returned our hire cars and checked ourselves in for the flight. As we reached the departure lounge, we were met by Rod Hall and a colleague, arriving on the inbound flight for the briefest of stops to join us on the return. Rod, of course, rushed off to fix something, having already arranged special clearance for the kite team to board early.

Through BA's system and Rod's efforts, both the flight-deck and cabin crews had been given the chance well in advance to request assignment to the kite flight. They were all enthusiasts and did us proud.

The boxes were being loaded and roped in securely on the back rows of seats by the cargo handlers as we entered the front of the Boeing 757. I introduced myself to the Captain, who was already keenly investigating his unusual passengers. At his request, I gave him an outline of the project – which was to prove of great use later. Rod rejoined us, and he and his colleague distributed the leaflets we had prepared earlier to all the seats, outlining the project for the passengers on the flight. There were both our *Ornithology Note* and a specially prepared note (in English or Spanish), reproduced on page 82.

In later years, we prepared a laminated colour sheet (again in English or Spanish), including a colour photo, and notes on the main organisations involved (on pages 83 – 84).

In later years also, BA promoted both the kites and other species helped by the programme with little calendar cards illustrating the birds (page 85) and a card was placed in each seat of the flight carrying the birds, so all the passengers knew of the important role their flight was making to conservation.

Our kites in their boxes occupied the rear two rows of seats, with the kite team, together with Rod and his colleague in the next rows in front. Normal passengers filled the rest of the plane. As the checks were completed before the plane was pushed back from the terminal, a deflated tyre was detected, probably due to damage during landing on the newly resurfaced runway. Rod – an engineer – assured us that the 757 could have the wheel replaced while laden, although this would not be possible with larger aircraft. We all stayed on board while what looked like the world's largest car-jack appeared.

A new problem arose in that we lacked on-ground power for air-conditioning. This resulted from an engineer strike at the time. Whilst obviously all equipment necessary for safety was in full service, some ancillary equipment was not. We did not know how the young kites would react to the already apparent rise in temperature. Rod, ever the fixer, disappeared to join the Captain on the flight-deck to try to negotiate on the radio the loan of a ground power-generator, while the cabin crew asked me if there was anything we could do to help the kites. I recalled that, just behind the rear seats on a 757, the rear access doors opened on opposite sides of the galley. I asked if we could open the doors and move the kite boxes into the galley to benefit from a through draught of cooling air. Permission was given. We rapidly unlashed the boxes and moved them through. I now valued even more the special effort we had taken to gain exceptional licences to carry the kites in the cabin, rather than the hold, so that we could check on them during the flight.

The safety of the kites having been assured, the cabin crew then turned their attention to the comfort of the paying passengers. Cold drinks were distributed as work on wheel-changing continued outside, as I could see from my new vantage point in one of the open rear doorways. One passenger approached the rear galley to ask if he might have diet coke rather than regular. I reached to start moving kite boxes out of the way in the galley/entrance. However, the Purser politely indicated to the passenger that he wanted to avoid moving the kites more than necessary as these were clearly a priority. The passenger readily agreed to

Two collected chicks on the ground [MP] **and I place a standard wild-bird ring on a chick, so that it can be individually identified throughout its life** [EB]. **Kite nestling being prepared for feeding. Note also the initial boxes used for collection of the kites. To keep the special boxes for transporting the kites to UK clean, other boxes were used at earlier stages, boxes for whisky bottles proving particularly suitable in size and strength** [MP]. **After feeding the birds, feeding the team** [EB]

WHEN THE KITE BUILDS... WHY and HOW we restored Red Kites across Britain

Our kite-collecting team in 1990 [MP, with camera on timer]. I put one of the kite nestlings into its box for the trip to Madrid and UK that day [EB]. Alfonso and I address the press at the temporary base for the kites [EB]. Feeding kites before the journey to Madrid [MP].

make do with regular coke on this occasion. Meanwhile, I was amused to hear my earlier account to the Captain of the kite project being repeated by him – with remarkable accuracy and probably better narrative skills than me – to the passengers to relieve the boredom of the wait. Overall, it was a most impressive display of professionalism by the crew, to whom I remain indebted.

    Eventually on our way, several passengers came back to ask about the project. Unfortunately, quarantine regulations prevented our showing them the kites, but we tried to give as full account as possible and hoped that they enjoyed sharing the experience of this historic flight. As we approached Britain, Rod (the incorrigible fixer) insisted on arranging a kite's eye view for John and myself – something which would no longer be possible in these days of further security challenges. We moved to the jump seats just behind the Captain and First Officer, looking over their shoulders on the flight over the English Channel, the left turn over central London, and the final approach and landing on Heathrow's 27-Right runway. The pilots were doing remarkably little except changing radio frequencies and communicating as necessary, the plane flying automatically into Heathrow on a planned route. They commented briefly on the fact that a crew had recently flown a Boeing 747 manually all the way across the Atlantic. Other pilots were amazed that they survived the boredom without the aid of the auto-pilot. As we approached landing, the Captain asked the First Officer if he had said that he had wanted to increase his landing count. The First Officer replied "Yes. I'll fly it then" and switched to manual control. The pilot explained that, at airports rated like Heathrow, automatic landing was now so good that fully automatic landings were completely safe and the limiting factor in poor visibility related to taxiing which was as yet not automated. He added that sometimes they told the passengers that landing had been automatic, but only afterwards, as before seemed to alarm some passengers.

After landing, the Captain authorised us to return to our seats, carefully. The cabin crew reminded everyone else to stay seated as we were still taxiing, although the "kite team" had to move at this point.

I had reluctantly declined the generous offers of in-flight alcoholic refreshment, in order to retain some coherency. This was fortunate, as I found myself giving an on board interview to a journalist from a national newspaper who happened to be on the flight, making the national newspapers the next morning. We posed for a photo-call after the other passengers had left, giving a piece to camera for Sky TV and several other interviews on the ground to newspaper journalists on arrival. Again, I can only commend BAANC. Rod made it clear that we were under no pressure to give media coverage and this should never compete with the conservation purpose or the wellbeing of the birds. If it was possible to deal with the news media compatibly with that, this was fine. If not, we should decline interviews. BAANC's purpose was to help conservation; publicity was fine and welcome, but not a pre-requisite.

With the airside press satisfied, we handed the boxes of birds over to our reliable colleagues from the Animal Quarantine Service (AQS), we returned the aircraft to the incoming crew, and became normal passengers for a while. We retrieved our luggage, passed

Kite boxes, with special kite-box seat-belts on the rear row of seats on British Airways Madrid-London flight. The lids were fixed in a partly open position to allow a good air supply while keeping the birds in the dark, so that they would sit quietly. In front of the two rows of seats with kites, the NCC team: John, Eric & Sue; and, across the aisle, Rod's colleague, Ann and my seat [MP].

through immigration and customs, and were met by my NCC colleague leading on kites in my absence, David Stroud, and Richard Porter of RSPB, who had brought cars to meet us. David had arranged for our NCC pool car to be specially cleaned immediately before this use and after, to meet quarantine regulations. Eric, Sue and John headed straight off for the BA's Glasgow shuttle flight while Rod, David, Richard, Ann and I faced the next challenge.

Heathrow was said then to be the busiest airport in the world. I believe this. Most passengers see only a small part of it. We were about to be introduced to a whole new world within it: Cargo. Once again, we found ourselves in a commercial paperwork maelstrom

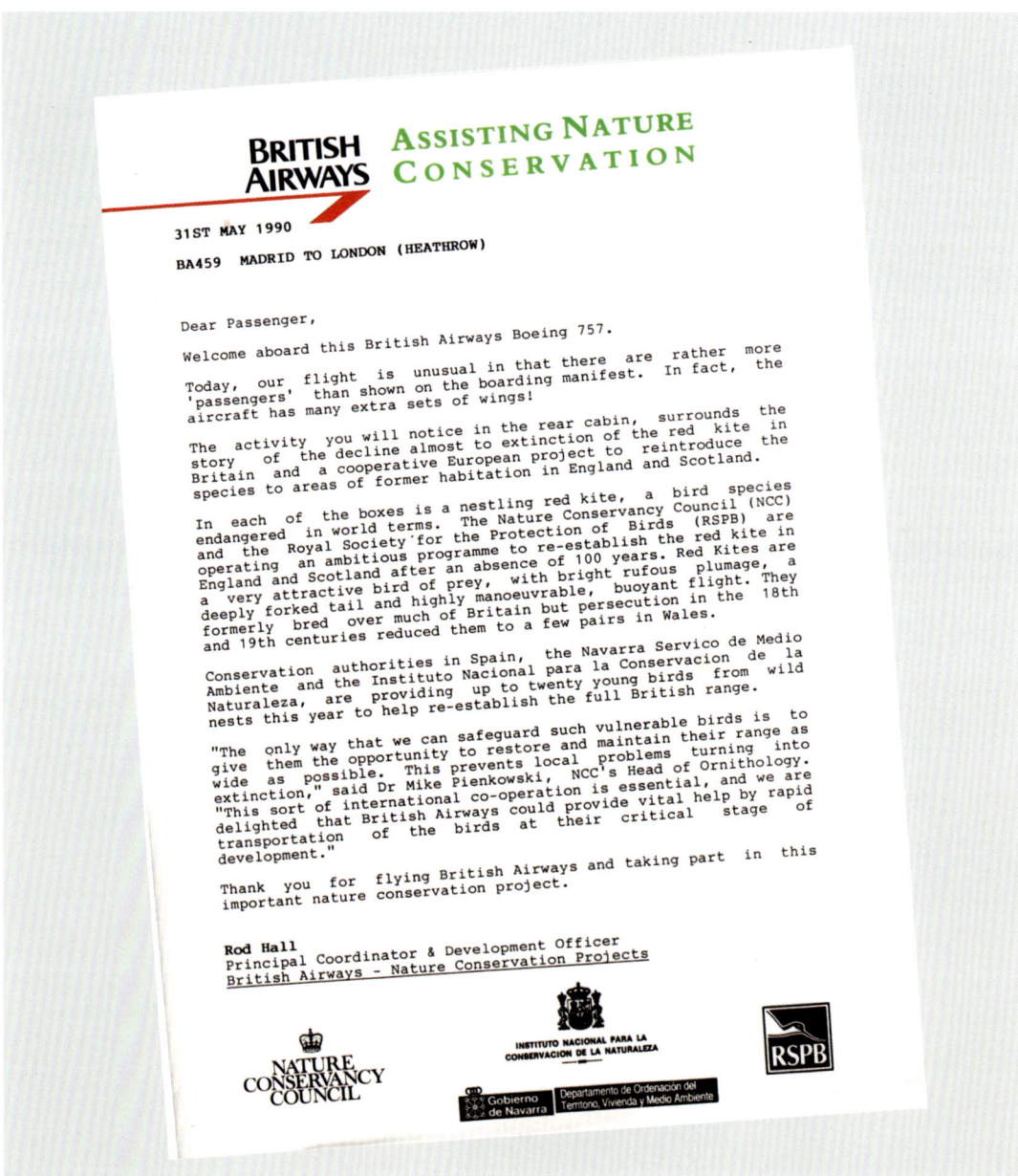

PROJECT BRIEF No.14

Red Kite

The red kite is a bird of prey, predominantly chestnut with a pale head. It is an agile flier, the forked tail twisting to give precise control as it soars and glides apparently effortlessly. Kites can take flying insects, small mammals, small birds and earthworms but feed mainly on carrion. They nest in trees and hunt over open countryside.

Red kites once ranged throughout Europe and nearby parts of Asia and Africa, but the range and numbers have declined in the East and South. The Northern and Western range has therefore become important in terms of world population: classified 'vulnerable' at only 12,000 pairs.

In the United Kingdom, red kites were formerly abundant and were even seen scavenging in the streets of London during the Middle Ages. Later, persecution by Man led to their extinction in England and Scotland by 1880. When red kites were protected in the UK at the beginning of this century, only a few pairs survived in remote parts of Wales. Today, there are 100 pairs breeding in Wales following intensive efforts to conserve them. However, natural recolonization throughout Britain is still unlikely to occur.

Milvus milvus

In 1989, after careful consideration, an experimental project to restore red kites to England and Scotland by bringing young birds from Sweden and Spain began. Initially, they are placed in aviaries to learn to feed themselves and to continue their growth. When ready to fly, coloured wing tags and small radio transmitters are fitted to enable them to be tracked after release. Once in the wild they explore the countryside and quickly learn how to find food.

Sadly, some birds have died after eating illegally poisoned carrion - a problem also for the remaining kites in Wales. However, most survive, proving that conditions are still suitable.

In 1992 and 1993, the project gained a major success when red kite pairs, formed from released birds, bred successfully in the wild in England and Scotland, the first time in more than a century. Breeding locations are, of necessity, a secret but the birds fly over hundreds of kilometres and there is increasing opportunity of unexpectedly observing these magnificent birds throughout the UK.

It will take several years of monitoring before we can be confident that these birds can establish self-sustaining populations in Britain. Their success will contribute significantly to the species' survival on a global scale.

A consequence of mutual cooperation in Nature Conservation

WHEN THE KITE BUILDS... WHY and HOW we restored Red Kites across Britain

The experimental reintroduction programme for red kite is a joint project of conservation bodies in the U.K. with the generous co-operation of organisations in Sweden and Spain.

 **JOINT NATURE CONSERVATION COMMITTEE**

The Joint Nature Conservation Committee (JNCC) was established by the Environmental Protection Act 1990 "for the purposes of nature conservation, and fostering the understanding thereof" in Great Britain as a whole and outside Great Britain. JNCC is a committee of the three country agencies (English Nature, Scottish Natural Heritage, and the Countryside Council for Wales), together with independent members and representatives from Northern Ireland and the Countryside Commission. It is supported by specialist staff. JNCC and the three country agencies carry forward duties previously undertaken by the Nature Conservancy Council (NCC), including the red kite work.

JNCC's statutory responsibilities include: the establishment of common scientific standards; the undertaking and commissioning of research; advising Ministers on the development and implementation of policies for or affecting nature conservation for Great Britain as a whole or nature conservation outside Great Britain; the provision of advice and dissemination of knowledge to any persons about nature conservation. In addition to its responsibilities in respect of the whole of Great Britain or the United Kingdom, JNCC also has the UK responsibility for European and international matters affecting nature conservation.

 THE ROYAL SOCIETY FOR THE PROTECTION OF BIRDS

The Royal Society for the protection of Birds is the charity that takes action for wild birds and the environment and is the Birdlife partner in the UK. The threats are real - pollution, destruction of heathlands, moorlands, hedgerows and estuaries, and illegal shooting, trapping and poisoning of wildlife. The RSPB is fighting these threats.

In Spain, the work is conducted with conservation authorities of the provinces of Navarra (Servicio de Medio Ambiente, Gobierno de Navarra), Aragon (Departamento de Agricultura, Ganaderia y Montes, Diputacion General de Aragon), with the cooperation of the Spanish federal conservation body, Instituto National para la Conservacion de la Naturaliza (ICONA). Transport to the UK is provided by British Airways Assisiting Nature Conservation Programme.

From Sweden, kites for the project are provided by the ornithological society in Scania, Skanes Ornitologiska Forening, and the Worldwide Fund for Nature (WWF Sweden), with the approval of the Swedish National Environment Protection Board. Transport from Sweden is provided by the British Royal Air Force.

More information on the red kite reintroduction project is available from the Joint Nature Conservation Committee, Monkstone House, City Road, Peterborough PE1 1JY. Tel: 0733 62626.

 **BRITISH AIRWAYS — ASSISTING NATURE CONSERVATION**

British Airways Assisting Nature Conservation (BAANC) was established in 1983, to give selective support to recognised international scientific organisations and associated individuals working to advance specific wildlife conservation projects. From the original ideal of giving support to species 'at risk', captive breeding and reintroduction projects, the scheme has evolved to encompass much more. Strong emphasis is now placed on assistance for the study of species in the wild, habitat protection, wildlife officer training, conservation education and tourism, focusing on preserving the essential variety of life on earth and encouraging the responsible management and sustainable use of the earth's natural resources. British Airways World Cargo plays a vital and tangible role in fulfilling the aims of Assisiting Nature Conservation scheme.

Photographs by kind permission of: C.H. Gommersall (RSPB) - Red Kite Nest & M. Wilding (RSPB) - Red Kite in Flight

 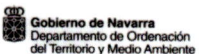  

ill-fitted to our special needs. Once again, we relied on BA's good offices and the personal presence of Rod Hall to guide us through obtaining the paperwork to allow us to retrieve our charges from the kindly hands of AQS.

We certainly found that the system at London Heathrow processed us no faster than that at Madrid's Airport. It was not designed for imports to be "walked through", as opposed to their moving at the speed of normal paperwork. Once again, the good offices of BA Cargo helped out. Despite their efforts, time dragged on. Rod duly escorted us off to one of BA's canteens for a meal break. We returned about an hour later to find at least one major problem had been identified. Heathrow's cargo system is designed for commercial trade. The kites had no commercial value. However, the computing system had simply not been programmed to allow for such a subversive concept as importing something of no financial value. The first suggested solution was to use the value that our Spanish colleagues had used to complete a similarly inappropriate commercial form. However, I realised that the

value that they had entered was the standard fine to be paid for damage to a protected bird. I was pleased that this was very high, but I could foresee a major problem if we used the same value on the importation documents, especially as I suspected that I might have to meet the tax cost personally! By this time, I had realised that the only way that we were going to be able to move the kites that evening was by declaring a value and paying VAT on it. I did not want to pay VAT on a figure of several thousands of pounds!

After some consultations, I slipped into my best public-service mode and solemnly drafted two notes. One explained the Spanish approach to valuation and indicated that an appropriate normal valuation in the circumstances was £10 per kite. The second note explained that the first note was simply for technical VAT purposes, and that the kites had no real commercial value. Having the previous week been promoted to the post of NCC's Assistant Chief Scientist, and therefore in theory responsible for some of NCC's licensing duties, I had some concern if the procedure misleadingly looked like a commercial transaction! I duly signed the notes and, in best civil service tradition, added my then rank (allegedly roughly equivalent to an army colonel) in the hope that this might help speed things along with officialdom. It seemed to work, and not more than an hour later, we were on our way to AQS with all the necessary paperwork to collect our birds.

AQS staff were, as ever, helpful and had already given the birds a superficial health check and allowed our colleagues (David and Richard) to feed them, with food supplied by Ian, so that quarantine requirements were fulfilled. So, eventually well into the evening, the birds were off on the last leg of their journey lasting less than an hour to the rearing facility in the Chilterns prepared by Ian in the previous weeks. For both them and us, it had been a long day from 3 am in Navarra to late evening in southern England. However, I have little doubt that it had been far more stressful for us than for the birds – which of course is as it should be.

Over the years Rod Hall helped with the conservation of many species of birds, mammals, reptiles and plants. Through Rod Hall's help, British Airways continued to provide invaluable assistance in this way throughout the years of importations from Spain to the first site in Buckinghamshire and beyond (see Chapter 11). He also helped in arranging a visit in 1994 by our colleagues in Spain, Alfonso Senosiain and Felix Compareo Carbo, to the English site to see the success resulting from the young kites they had provided. I was delighted to hear of his award of an MBE later that year.

We used the kite collection visits as a valuable way of giving experience and training to colleagues involved in the Red Kite project and, if there was space, others based in the region who were interested. We made sure that someone from the previous team was always included to ensure continuity. In 1991, the team included Dr Eric Bignal, Dr Ian Evans, Jonathan Spencer, and George Boobyer; in 1992, Dr Ian Evans, John Holmes and Gerald Marsh (local volunteer worker); in 1993, Dr Ian Evans, Dr Colin Galbraith, and (from English Nature) Corrina Woodall; in 1994 (the last year for the original site and also under my supervision of the project), Dr Ian Evans and English Nature's Dr Andy Clements (later CEO of the British Trust for Ornithology). In 1995 (the first year of collections for the English Midlands site – see below), Dr Ian Evans showed the new appointees for that project, Ian Carter (English Nature) and Karl Ivens (of Forest Enterprise) the ropes.

The birds were clearly supported by BA and its wonderful staff and, on the first flight no passenger had any problem. However, on one of the later flights, my colleague Jonathan Spencer told me that one passenger was overheard on disembarkation that the smell of the kites and their droppings at the back of the plane was disgusting! The smell was not something we had detected, and most passengers were interested and supportive.

By the later years of the Experimental Reintroduction Project, we had become sufficiently confident of the kite nestlings' resilience that we moved to using conventional flight-kennels, more conventionally used for small livestock, in the aircraft's hold to transport them.

British Airways Assisting Conservation continued for a time after Rod's retirement, but without his characteristic and knowledgeable management; and of course his skills as an incorrigible fixer.

In Spain, nests were located in early March, when Red Kites were in the early stages of incubation but before the nest trees had acquired foliage. In the first year, our Spanish

In 1993, having checked the resilience of the kite nestlings, we were able to switch to "sky-kennels" shipped in the hold [IE].

colleagues did this for us; in later years an early trip to do this was desirable. The main method used was to drive along a road or track, scanning the surrounding trees for likely nest structures. The best areas to find nests were in trees growing along riverbanks, as these provided the most suitable nest sites. Nest sites in large forests (especially in Navarra) were much more difficult to locate, while those close to villages were often located with help from local inhabitants. The most frequent nest trees used were Black Poplar *Populus nigra* and Oak *Quercus*. Once an occupied nest was located, a rough hand-drawn sketch map was made, to ensure that the nest could be re-found for further checks. The nestlings were collected during the last week of May or the first week of June, following the same guidelines as those used in Sweden. In Navarra, nestlings were collected from a total of 41 nests during 1991–93; single nestlings were taken from 38 broods, and two nestlings were taken from three broods (two nestlings were not released – see Chapter 7). In Aragon, nestlings were collected from a total of 23 nests during 1992–94 (some nests were 'harvested' more than once); single nestlings were collected from 30 broods, and two nestlings were collected from five broods. The average brood size of nests from which nestlings were taken was 2.4 nestlings. Depending on weather conditions and work commitments of the Spanish conservationists, it took five to seven days to collect 20 nestlings from Aragon and Navarra. After collection, the nestlings were ringed and kept together in aviaries at a raptor-rehabilitation centre in Navarra and then flown to England during the period 31st May to 8th June.

7. Rearing the kites

Previous experience and aviary design
At the first Project Team meeting on 20th October 1987, we had reviewed experience on rearing and release techniques, traditionally termed "hacking".

In the Sea-eagle Project, young birds had been put on an artificial platform in a cage made of wire-mesh stretched over a timber framework and the birds were provided with food, a widely used technique for rearing birds of prey. Bearing in mind the biology of Red Kites, tree-nesting but hunters over open country, we envisaged using "hacking cages" set in trees at the edges of clearings.

It was suggested that feeding would continue until February for each batch of introduced stock, in order to encourage them to remain in the general vicinity. The Swedes had provided long-term food-dumps of partially buried, chopped carcases. In this way, they had encouraged their birds to be less migratory, thereby avoiding poisoning and shooting in southern wintering areas, which the Swedish workers considered to be a major threat. We expected the birds in Britain to show less tendency to migrate because of the milder winters and the known flexibility in migration patterns of such birds, and felt that this technique of food-supply maintained in the long term would be undesirable in Britain (although, as birds increased later, their popularity led many local residents in the area of the English site to put out food so as to get more views of them – though not something we encouraged, for the benefit of both birds and humans). The birds would be released approximately two weeks after they were due to fledge, to fulfil the quarantine period, which for birds is 35 days after their initial inspection after importation. We planned to maintain a food supply after release; in the wild, feeding by parents may continue in that way. We were also prepared to continue providing food until the end of the winter after release, to encourage birds to remain in the general vicinity. However, this later proved unnecessary.

At the Project Team meeting on Thursday 6th October 1988, members of the Project Team considered the diagrams of the platform/cage nest prepared from Roy Dennis' notes by Sandy Collinge (not only a financial and administrative manager, but also a former draughtsperson, so keeping low the pool of people who needed to know at that stage). It was agreed that the cages should be built *in situ* and strategically placed to ensure that the cages were not in sight of each other, as there was some suggestion that unrelated birds reared together might feel as if they were siblings, which could be a possible deterrent to future pairing. Roy Dennis suggested two cage-locations separated by 1–2 km might be advantageous in some respects, and this would be necessary for quarantine purposes if more than 10 kites were being reared in any one year at one site. The cages would have to be in position by the following March–April and this would be the first job of the Project Officer(s). Roy Dennis agreed to prepare some guidelines of aspects to consider in constructing and using the cages and in subsequent practical work. Other members (particularly Peter Walter Davis) would supply suggestions to Roy. The cages were to include a small hatch in the wooden back so that food could be supplied without a human being seen, other than a gloved hand – part of our precautions to minimise the chance of the kites imprinting on humans.

After full discussions on the best conditions for the birds, it had been decided to use ground cages with raised platforms inside, rather than smaller cages in trees. *Project Team Update* note of 8th April 1989 reported that materials and cages were being built by Ian Evans, with Jonathan Spencer's assistance in many aspects. The *Project Team Update* of

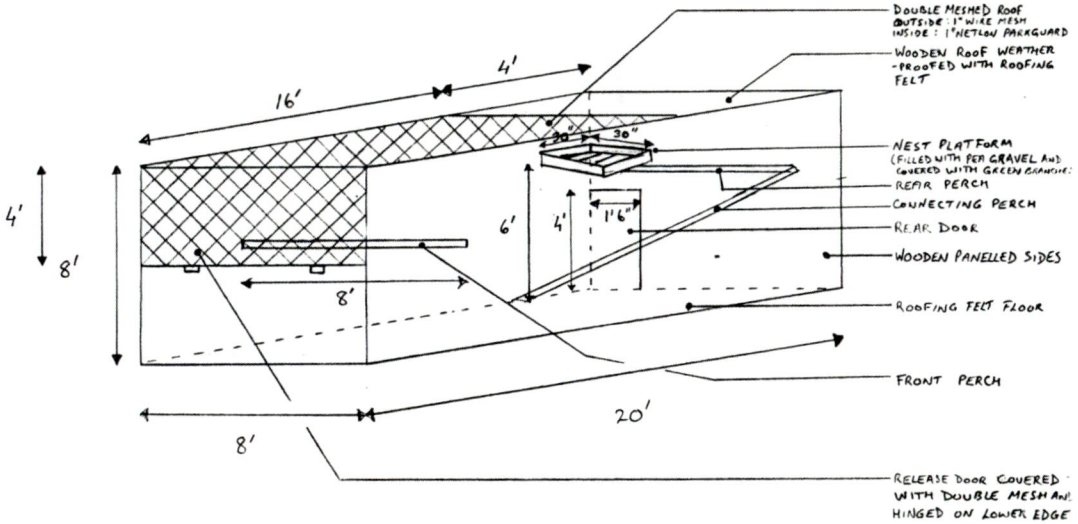

Figure 7.1. Diagrammatic plan of release cage by Sandy Collinge (Evans & Pienkowski 1989). Measurements are in feet (') and inches ("); for metric measurements, see text.

21st May 1989 noted that, in Scotland, newly appointed Dee Doody was also constructing suitable cages. We noted the need to complete the cages and arrange inspections, and for the project officers to arrange for food supplies in both areas.

Rearing and release sites

The release site in England, at Wormsley, was situated in a secluded Chilterns valley on an estate with large areas of woodland and mixed farming. The estate has a high conservation interest and had forged close links with the Nature Conservancy Council as a result of the owner's commitment to nature conservation.

Two release cages (A and B) were built, about 0.5 km apart, on a secluded part of the estate some distance away from public footpaths on opposite sites of a small valley. Cage A was situated on the edge of a wood facing a newly established field of lucerne for deer grazing. Cage B was built in an open woodland clearing on a ridge in sight of Cage A about 0.5 km away across the valley.

One of the two original 1989 cages at woodland edge in the Chilterns, with kite on one of the perches; and view, over netting roof of cage and wood-covered shelter over the platform, to surrounding countryside. [MP]

Front of the first cages at the Black Isle site; Dee Doody transfers a nestling from its travelling box to the rearing cage. [CG]

Each cage was 2.5 m high and covered an area of about 6 m by 2.5 m. Each was constructed of wood with four panelled sides. This gave protection from both hot and cold weather. The front of the cage was fitted with a 2.5 m by 1.25 m unpanelled door that was opened only on the day of release. This was covered on the outside with 2.5 cm wire mesh, and inside with 2.5 cm "Netlon Parkguard" mesh. This is a soft plastic material. The full 2.5 m width of the roof was covered with the same type of double layer for the front 5 m. In addition to safety for the birds, the double layer was required to meet quarantine regulations. A nest platform (about 0.75 m x 0.75 m) was built in a back corner of the cage. This was sheltered by a wooden section of roof 2.5 m x 2.5 m. Access to the cage was gained

Above: Ian and Ann stand beside a tree near the destroyed cage and felled in the same storm; and the new additional 1990 set of rearing cages on Portobello Farm.
Below: The surviving original 1989 cage, with two new 1990 ones added beside it, with a view of this set of cages, from a distance, showing habitat. [MP]

only at the rear, through two wooden doors (with a small compartment between so that the cage was never open to the outside). Food was placed on to the platform through a 18 cm x 8 cm hatch above the platform also at the rear of the cage, so that the human supplying this was not visible. Two horizontal perches were provided across the full 2.5 m width of the cage, near the front and rear. The rear perch was connected to the nest platform on one side and to the floor on the other by a diagonal perch, enabling a grounded bird access to the nest platform. Each cage was made fox-proof by a skirt of wire mesh around the outside edge of the cage. An inner layer of wire mesh covered the entire basal area and supported the floor of roofing felt.

Unfortunately, one of these cages was destroyed following the severe hurricane-force gales during the following winter. During early 1990, material for extra cages in both areas was acquired and cages built. In England in 1990, two more cages of the same design (but slightly larger dimensions) were built beside the surviving cage. In addition, another three cages were constructed about 1 km away. I am grateful to Viscount Richard Parker (now the Earl of Macclesfield) for permission to use the Portobello Farm, adjacent to Wormsley, for our second set of cages. All the cages survived for a further 5 years of releases at this site, until 1994.

In Scotland, two cages were constructed in 1989 and a further four in 1990. They were similar in design to those at the English site but a little smaller and squarer (3.5 m by 3 m by 2.5 m high). They were netted on the longer front section as well as half of the side. As in England, quarantine conditions required a double door. Each cage contained an artificial nest-platform in one corner, sheltered by a wooden section of the roof. Natural dead trees were installed to provide perches away from the sides of the cages. In 1990, three cages were used in the same release area as in 1989, and another three cages were located 12 km away.

All cages were inspected for quarantine purposes by veterinary officials of the Ministry of Agriculture, Fisheries and Food in England and the Department of Agriculture and Fisheries for Scotland (later Scottish Office Agriculture and Fisheries Department). Inspections took place (i) before the kites were introduced to the cages, (ii) after the kites were introduced into the cages, and (iii) at the end of the 35-day quarantine period.

Rearing kite chicks at the release site
Four Swedish kite chicks arrived at the English release site in the small hours of 14th June 1989. Two were approximately four weeks old, half feathered but still retaining a lot of down, and two were approximately six weeks old and fully feathered. The former were placed in Cage A with the four-week old Welsh chick, and the latter two were placed in Cage B. Birds in Cage A were hand-fed for the first four days, after which they fed themselves and were able to rip up skinned rabbits and squirrels and pieces of venison. The birds in Cage B were able to feed themselves and were given diced squirrel, rabbit and rook. Similar procedures were followed at the Scottish rearing and release site. Ian Evans looked after the English birds. In Scotland, in 1989 Dee Doody, and in 1990 Andy Knight, cared for the kites.

Generally, in all years and at both sites, procedures were similar to these. The kite chicks entered their quarantine quarters at 4–6 weeks old. Each bird was matched with "siblings" of similar age and size, and placed on the nest platform. Depending on numbers available, two to four nestlings were placed in each aviary. Initially the chicks were given minced rabbit, fish, squirrel, rook, carrion crow and magpie. Then, depending on age of the chicks, the food was either minced (4–7 weeks old), skinned (6–9 weeks) or given whole (after 10 weeks). The first week was the most critical as the birds adjusted, after collection, to life with no parents, and to totally new surroundings. During this period, it was necessary to make sure chicks were feeding themselves and receiving adequate food. Hand-feeding was required in some cases for a short period during the initial few days but, once birds had settled, this was discontinued, and food was supplied or removed through the small lockable hatches beside

The feeding hatch allowed Ian to supply food (not on the plate – that was just for carrying) and remove that unused, with minimal human contact. Below, the interior of a cage, showing platform, perches, ramp, netted and solid sections of the roof, and 1989 Kites A to C in residence; and kite nestling in initially rather alarming 'droopy' mode. [MP]

the nest platforms. Supply was initially twice daily, but this was reduced to a single visit per day as the birds got older. The amount of food required varied and was adjusted depending on the amount consumed. Each cage was given about one squirrel or rabbit or two rooks per day. Two chicks ate roughly two adult rooks or a three-quarter size rabbit per day. However, food consumption was variable, being greatest during the pre-fledging period, a time of rapid growth and development. By the fledging period, most of the development and growth was complete. Consequently, food consumption declined, increasing again only after fledging. Evans *et al.* (1997) give more details.

Food for the Red Kite nestlings was collected mainly from local gamekeepers and stored frozen until needed. The main food items in northern Scotland were Rabbits *Oryctolagus cuniculits* shot with a .22-calibre rifle. In addition, young crows, mainly Rooks *Corvus frugilegus*, farmed Atlantic Salmon *Salmo solar*, Trout (*Oncorhynchus mykiss* and *S. trutto*) and smaller numbers of assorted mammals (road-kills) were obtained. In southern England, fewer rifle-shot Rabbits were available and more legally trapped items (Grey Squirrels *Sciurus carolinensis*, Rabbits, mustelids and crows) were supplied by gamekeepers and were not killed specifically for the project. Trapping by gamekeepers is undertaken annually in spring as part of game management practice (mustelids and crows) and pest control (Grey Squirrels and Rabbits). Prey items killed with shotguns were avoided to prevent ingestion of lead shot.

Contact with the birds was kept to an absolute minimum, to reduce the chance of imprinting on and conditioning from their human keepers. Inspections were normally made through tiny inspection holes in the wooden-panelled sides of the aviaries, which reduced human contact considerably by providing a suitable screen. In Scotland, video cameras in each cage allowed viewing from a caravan 100 m distant; no visual contact was allowed.

A veterinary officer made at least one visit to each release site during the period of captivity to check the health of each bird. This involved taking a 2-ml blood sample from each nestling for haematological examination, sex determination and DNA 'finger-printing' studies, and a physical examination to ensure that each nestling was suitable for release.

Three imported Red Kites, representing 1.6% of the total, could not be released into the wild. One bird in Scotland, imported from Sweden in 1990, had a problem with a leg-joint; initial inflammation was treated with antibiotics by the vet, but X-rays showed that there was malformation of the joint with more bone growing on one side than the other. This resulted in a "bent" leg. Subsequently, the other leg went the same way and, despite veterinary attention, the bird died. This chick had been the smallest in a nest produced by a young pair of adults, close to a rubbish dump and very close to four other pairs of kites. Stress traces on the feathers suggested that this bird was not getting adequate food before it was collected, and it is suspected that this contributed to its problems and death. The remaining 19 birds in Scotland in 1990 were cleared from quarantine on 23rd July. The two others with problems were taken from nests in Spain and imported into England in 1991. One (the runt of a brood of three) was found to have abnormal bone growth only three days after arriving in the UK, while the other died from an acute infection (trichomoniasis, caused by the flagellate protozoan parasite *Trichomonas gallinae*) five days after importation. Two other nestlings caught this infection, but were successfully treated with antibiotics (metronidazole). It would seem that runts in litters tend to suffer early problems which cannot necessarily be cured by more than adequate food supplies later in their development – which is not really surprising.

All birds in the first year, and by far the majority throughout the project, made good progress and developed normally, although stress bars were apparent on the feathers. Stress bars are lines that run crosswise through a feather indicating an inadequate diet, high stress, or illness during the time that part of the feather was being formed. For our birds, these were attributed to the first few days of captivity, but are normal in wild birds, relating for example to bad weather on some days, perhaps leading to periods of limited food, not unusual because of the enormous nutrient requirements for feather-growth. The health of each bird at the English site in the first and all subsequent years was monitored closely by Dr James Kirkwood of the Zoological Society of London, in consultation with the vet appointed

As the kites grew, wing exercising (right) became very frequent. Below, one fully grown youngster flies up from the floor while two rest on the perch (these in 1990). Another favourite exercise was to fly up and grip the soft plastic inner netting as a sort of perch (lower right). Perhaps it was a way of exercising their talons. (1989). [MP]

A blood sample is taken; then Peter E Davis and Ian Evans attach a wing-tag. These were: orange in 1989, blue in 1990, yellow in 1991, lime green (Scotland) and black (England) in 1992, red (Scotland) and green (England) in 1993, and white (Scotland) and orange (England) in 1994. The scheme was modified in later years to the left wing indicating the region and the right the year of hatching. Below, all 5 Chiltern kites in 1989, from left: Kites A, B and the ill-fated C and, in the other cage, the two oldest youngsters, E & D. [MP]

as inspector in relation to quarantine. He found no internal parasites (gut and blood) and gave them all a clean bill of health. Blood samples were taken for health monitoring and for possible future use in DNA "finger-printing" for genetic assessment and sex determination.

As noted earlier, it was arranged that Dr James Kirkwood would specify veterinary requirements for the whole project. The care of the chicks was essentially the same in all years, the arrangements in the first year having proven very effective.

We were pleased with the feather and body condition of birds prior to release.

The first flight of each bird took place at around 8 weeks old. Prior to this, they spent most of their time lying motionless on the nest platform; with small bouts of activity at feeding and meticulous preening. Wing-flapping was also frequent, particularly near fledging. As their sense of balance developed, the birds gradually ventured on to the perches. Their first flight soon followed, after which they seldom returned to the nest platform except to feed. At this stage, the birds spent much time playing with twigs and leaves, and generally appearing inquisitive. During the period of captivity, there were no recorded instances of aggression between nestlings, even between birds of different ages. They had a habit of resting in a drooping or "floppy" position. This worried us at first, until we realised that there was nothing wrong with them; at times they simply preferred a change from the "classic" perching position. By the time of release at ten to twelve weeks old, all birds were proficient flyers and showed surprising manoeuvrability within the confines of the relatively small cage.

Marking

At the Project Team meeting on 24th January 1989 at NCC, Inverness, it was agreed that the wing-tag marking scheme for the project would effectively be an extension of the established

Robert Kenward attaches a radio to the two central tail feathers of one of the kites in 1989. The card keeps these two feathers and glue away from the others as the radio and part of the aerial is attached. The towel keeps the bird in the dark and quiet. In 1990 at our site, Robert demonstrates the technique to Dr Rhys Green of RSPB to use elsewhere. [MP]

Ready to go: Fully-grown young kites in 1990. [MP]

scheme in Wales. It was noted that the anticipated need would be for a maximum of 20 birds at each site each year for 5 years.

I agreed to obtain special approval from the British Trust for Ornithology (BTO) for use of their metal rings (of the national bird-ringing scheme) on imported and translocated birds. After collection, the birds were marked with a numbered BTO leg-ring as used for wild birds.

Prior to release (or later, near fledging of wild-bred birds), each bird was fitted with a uniquely labelled colour wing-tag. It was arranged that Peter Davis and Peter Walters Davies would supply materials and details of the tagging scheme to Roy and myself. In the early

Ready to go: Fully-grown young kite in 1991. [MB]

years, the tag shape denoted whether it was reared in Wales, England or Scotland. Tag-colour represented the year of fledging. These visual markers were especially valuable for identifying individual birds in the field without the need for capture and were designed to last for the entire life of the bird. The tags were difficult to see in flight, or when the birds were perched, and a telescope was generally required to identify the tag details.

By the *Project Team Update* note of 21st May 1989, radio-tracking equipment had been obtained for both areas. Radio-transmitters were supplied by Biotrack and Dr Robert Kenwood (of the Institute of Terrestrial Ecology), who was contracted to assist in their fitting to many of the birds. These TW2 Biotrack 19 g transmitters were attached to the central tail feathers, to aid the monitoring of movements and activity in the weeks following release. The transmitters were lost when the tail feathers were moulted but, in the first year, ceased to operate in any event after some months as the batteries ran down. This was the state of the technology available at that time. Battery life increased in the following years. All birds released between 1989 and 1993 carried transmitters, allowing monitoring for up to 12 months over a maximum range of some 40 km.

8. Release, behaviour in the wild and initial survival

All five birds at the English site were released on 1st August 1989. On the day before release, food had been placed on specially built platforms on the roofs of the cages and on another platform nearby.

We did not know how the birds would react to being released. As usual, we tried to err on the side of caution until we could build on experience. At the English site, a photographer from NCC was there to record still pictures, while an RSPB crew making a film about Red Kites in Wales wanted to film some sequences to complement their main story. We installed all these in hides with a good view, but several hours before the release to minimise the risk of disturbance.

The rest of us withdrew some hundreds of metres to another hillside with a good view of the situation, where we were joined by the estate gamekeeper and his wife, both of whom had been so helpful to us in the project. Ian Evans meanwhile stayed near the cages ready to open the doors. We stayed in communication by radios.

The behaviour of the birds was highly variable and largely unpredictable – requiring lots of patience by the photographers and occasional swift reflexes.

Prior to releases in 1990, Ian places food on platform above rearing cage. [MP]

The variability of individual behaviour on release seen in 1989 was repeated in 1990, the first year that we dared have photographers close in position: Ian unlocks first rearing cage and carefully lowers release door (left), before the first kite (Blue B) heads for the exit (centre), and out (right). [MP]

WHEN THE KITE BUILDS... WHY and HOW we restored Red Kites across Britain

The second kite (Blue A) in the same cage was more hesitant but eventually moved to the front perch, where it waited for some time before heading out. [MP]

At 06:10, I asked Ian over the radio to open Cage A. As he did so, the first kite rocketed out of the aviary and into the trees nearby. The next bird waited a few minutes before joining its fellow, as did the third bird after a rather longer wait.

We watched for some hours, to check that the birds were pretty okay and then reviewed the situation. At 14:45, I asked Ian to move about 0.5 km to the second aviary, Cage B, and to open the doors. The first occupant (wing-tagged D) was as keen to leave as its first two colleagues from the other aviary, and flew out within a few moments of opening, settling in the trees near its rearing cage. However, the final kite (E) seemed unaware that the barrier at the end of the aviary was no longer there. We waited for well over an hour before anything happened. Eventually, it flew from the aviary but it did not join the others. Instead, it flew above the trees, across the small valley and well above both the other groups (of 1 and 3 birds). The kite started circling and I recognised from my student days of learning to fly a glider that it had found a thermal – a convection cell of rising warm air heated by a hot-spot on the ground, such as a road surface heated by the sun for hours. It soared higher and higher, circling in the rising bubble of air. Clearly, acquiring flying skill was not going to be a problem. I was gratified that we had designed the aviaries to be sufficiently large for the birds to practice flying while still captive.

After five minutes, the rising kite was becoming a dot in the sky. I called to one of my colleagues, picked up one of the radio-tracking devices, and headed for one of the cars. We did

The birds in the second cage in 1990 behaved quite differently: As soon as Rod Hall (BAANC) unlocked the rearing cage and started lowering the door, the two kites left together. [MP]

After Rod opens the third cage in 1990, Kite G headed out and to the nearby trees immediately, while its fellow delayed. [MP]

In 1991 Kite 5 heads out. The radio and its forward and backward aerials can just be seen. [MP]

Kite 9 in 1991 leaves the rearing cage and into the trees. [MP]

Kite reared and released in 1991 finds a thermal to lift it higher in the air. [MP]

not want to lose track of one of our charges so quickly. However, as we headed off down the hill, the errant kite broke out of its climb and began to dive, in a long steady fall directly towards the treetops holding the group of three other kites. Perhaps it had only just seen them, or perhaps the temptation of soaring on a thermal was just too much. It was, however, encouraging to see how well 'our' kites could take to the air without lessons from parents. All the kites had emerged singly, some immediately after opening the release door, some over an hour after.

It rapidly become clear to us that our behaviour at the time of release had little effect on the kites. This meant that, in the later years, we could put our observers closer without long prior confinement in cramped hides. We could also observe the kites' behaviour more closely, as well as use the occasions as a 'thank-you' for some of our many helpers, and an opportunity for media coverage for the wider public, on whose behalf the work was, in at least some senses, done.

Two of the 1989 birds released meet together in tree above cage. Views of Kite A settled in tree and Kite B taking off from tree. [SM]

Ian Evans (right) and I track the released radio-tagged young kites. [AP]

We were able to see for example that, once the aviary end was opened, the birds did not always recognise immediately that the barrier on which they had sometimes hung by their talons was no longer there. In fact, it looked as if some were aiming to land on the mesh, only to redirect their flight in its absence, and pass through. Others appeared to view the changed appearance as rather suspicious and hesitated at the outer end of the aviary or on one of the perches, before braving the open air.

The kites usually settled happily in the trees on the edges of the clearings in which the aviaries were situated, and seemed quite unconcerned by the people, provided that these kept a reasonable distance. This was encouraging as we did not want the kites to be drawn towards human company, for their own sakes. Hence, we had gone to considerable steps to minimise human contact, and the risk of imprinting on humans.

The only slightly disconcerting feature of the close-up view of the releases concerned the first landings of some of the birds. One aspect that had not occurred to us was that the birds in their nests and aviaries had previously experienced only firm branches and had no experience in judging the rigidity of potential perches. The branches that are normally the first that a bird meets at the edge or top of a tree are rather thin and flexible. On several occasions, birds made their first landings on these, the branch in question then bending over under the birds' weight - leaving the kite hanging bat-like from the thin branch. The first time we saw this caused some worry, especially as the young kite might remain there for about 15 minutes. The bird seemed none the worse for the experience and chose a more appropriate perch for its second attempt. Indeed, the experience is probably not confined to birds reared in captivity. I have since seen a variety of young birds which had been reared in the wild make rather clumsy landings at first attempts.

Behaviour in the wild

Birds fitted with a radio-transmitter were located using a hand-held directional three-element Yagi antenna attached to a 173 MHz band receiver. Searches were undertaken by hand-held antennae and from a car with a roof-mounted omnidirectional whip antenna. In Scotland additional aerial searches were undertaken occasionally from a light aircraft. Individuals fitted solely with wing-tags were located at communal roosts from about October to February, and breeding territories from February to August. Other observations were made on a more casual basis by project fieldworkers and the general public.

Kite D (the one by itself initially) was observed feeding on the morning after release. However, Kites A, B, C and E did not feed until the third day after their release, at which time they were joined by Kite D. All five kites remained in the vicinity of the valley from where they were released until the 7th of August. During this time, the kites were seen talon-grappling in flight. They often soared to heights of a 1000ft or more but always returned to the vicinity of the release site.

The kites fed primarily on carrion. However, they were observed also feeding on insects, catching them in the air or snatching them off foliage along woodland edges, or off the ground, picking at sheep droppings (presumably for insects) and on one occasion catching a Field Vole. The kites' scavenging ability is exceedingly well-developed. It was soon found that rabbits shot by gamekeepers on neighbouring estates were very quickly discovered by the birds. The kites were even seen displacing Crows and Magpies from carrion, a trait which is very apparent in Sweden and a common strategy in carrion-feeding birds in general. You don't have to find your own carrion if you can steal it from others. In

Kite forages by flying low, scanning the ground below for carrion, worms or insects. [MP]

Kites hunt over pasture and landed on ground to feed on insects and worms. [MP]

WHEN THE KITE BUILDS... WHY and HOW we restored Red Kites across Britain

recent years young reintroduced Sea Eagles have been displacing more established but smaller Red Kites from carrion.

Dispersal in England in 1989

Between the 7th and 19th August 1989, the kites made short exploratory flights of up to 5 kilometres outside the release area, but spent most of their time within some 2 km of the release area, roosting in the vicinity of one of the cages. During this period, all birds fed regularly at the food platforms where assorted carrion (*e.g.* Carrion Crow *Corvus corone* , Rabbit, Rook *Corvus frugilegus*, Grey Squirrel and Fox) was placed daily.

On 20th August, Kites B and C left the release area entirely, finally settling at an estate on the Shropshire/Welsh border on 23rd August. Kites A, D and E remained in the release area until 4th September. During this time, they became progressively less dependent on the food put out for them on the platforms. They frequently ventured up to 16 km from the estate during the day but always returned to roost in the early evening.

Ian joked that he always kept his toothbrush in his car, as he never knew when the kites would decide to depart. Being ready and able to follow them visually and by using the radio-tracker, which had greater range than eye, but not huge at the time, greatly increased the chance of finding them. As I mentioned earlier, the first ones to depart spent their first night's roost in the vicinity of our first-reserve rearing and release site about 100 km away – really boosting our confidence in Red Kite habitat identification. The radio-tracking also put the joke on us on another occasion. In those

Kite C killed by illegal poisoning, and the radio-tracking equipment used to find it [TC]

104 *WHEN THE KITE BUILDS... WHY and HOW we restored Red Kites across Britain*

analogue radio days, only a relatively small number of different radio frequencies were available, so different studies unlikely to come into contact with others had to use the same frequencies. After losing track of some kites on one occasion, Ian picked up signals from near where he had estimated them to be in the southern Midlands. He was puzzled to find that he appeared to be tracking down to near a house: were they in trees above? Eventually, it turned out that the house was the base of another researcher working on Grey Squirrels, and one of her transmitters ready for use had accidentally switched itself on. (This was fairly common as the "off" switch was normally an external magnet which, when removed, switched the transmitter on.) Fortunately, the other researcher decided that Ian was not a stalker.

On 5th September, Kites A, D and E left the release area. Kite D returned to the release area on 6th September after travelling at least 160 km away. Kites A and E eventually settled near Ilfracombe, north Devon on 7th September and stayed in this area for six days. Unfortunately, these two birds were lost from radio contact but two kites, which were probably these released birds, were reported from Porthgwarra and Land's End, Cornwall on 29th–30th September. Kite D left the release area for the second time on 23rd September and was subsequently lost from radio contact on 27th September in south-east Devon. It was later discovered near the village of Timberscombe on Exmoor at the end of September and stayed in this area for the winter.

Meanwhile, Sir Michael Leighton and one of our kite field-workers, Tony Cross, had been monitoring the movements of Kites B and C on the Welsh border estate since 23rd August. Kite C left this estate on 11th September wandering northwards along the border and was finally lost from radio contact on 25th September at Welsh Frankton, near Oswestry. Kite C was later found on 7th November by Tony Cross near the village of Paytoe Hall, near Ludlow, following reports received from the general public. The kite was reported to have been present in the area since the end of September and was often seen following a tractor and plough like a gull. It remained in this general area until 20th November when it was found dead at Gatley Park Hall in Herefordshire, about 5 km south-east of where it was first seen in this area. This came to the Project Team's attention rather dramatically as the Wales Kite Committee was meeting that day at Rhayader. On his way to the meeting, Tony had taken the opportunity to radio-track the birds known to be in the area, and the dead bird still carried its transmitter.

The evidence and report were passed on to the authorities. The cause of death was established to be poisoning by Eldrin, an illegal pesticide. The police took this very seriously and put a senior detective in charge of the case. Cynics said that was because of the sensitivity of the case because the bird had been found on land owned by the Lord Lieutenant, the Queen's representative, in the county (although there was, and is, no suggestion that the land-owner was involved). I like to think that a senior detective was appointed because they recognised the seriousness of the case. Certainly, the quality and thoroughness of the investigation were excellent. Proving an illegal poisoning case is not easy, because of the difficulty in tracking the evidential lines. However, this dedicated team of police officers managed to secure a prosecution. One small piece in the chain was my own statement, requested to give the context and the conservation significance of the project.

After an intensive police investigation, the gamekeeper of Gatley Park pleaded guilty to two charges. He admitted storing Eldrin, a pesticide banned in 1983, at Gatley Park Estate in Hereford and Worcester. He also admitted putting it into dead Pheasants *Phasianus colchicus* and using them as bait to kill Foxes, leading to the death of the Red Kite and a dog. He was fined £600 and ordered to pay costs of £314.50. In addition, one company, one farmer and four gamekeepers were fined a total of £8000 and ordered to pay £1250 costs for storing, selling, supplying or using this pesticide. The prosecutor said that the amount of Eldrin seized was enough to kill nearly 11,000 people.

In a Scottish case a little later, the Sheriff (roughly the equivalent of an English magistrate) expressed frustration that the law did not allow him to imprison the offender and could only fine him. The Sheriff's justified outrage was largely because the offender had been training apprentice game-keepers at the time.

Kite B remained within the safe confines of Sir Michael Leighton's estate, Loton Park in Shropshire. Carrion (deer offal, Rabbits and Pheasant poults) was generously provided from when Kites B and C had arrived, and feeding was continued throughout the winter. There was no direct predation by the kites on Pheasants. Indeed, Kite B maintained its scavenging habit, competing successfully with Buzzards (which were at a very high density), Foxes and Crows. Kite B was observed frequently to fly over game coverts often before a shoot. However, the "scaring effect" that many keepers view as a major worry never materialised.

An unidentified released kite was reported only about 90 km from the release site and was present for a period 13th October to 19th November. Unfortunately, the report was received too late for investigation.

First reports in 1990 in England of an orange wing-tagged (1989) kite back near the release site some 13km to the east, was received on 16th February. The bird was last seen on 6th March but reappeared at the release site on 11th March and stayed until the end of March. At the same time, a kite had been seen regularly 19 km to the west from 26th February and another 6 km south of the release site during the same period. They clearly knew where home was in spite of their wanderings. Unfortunately, the radio transmitters were not working due to battery rundown and no close views were obtained to read tags and confirm identity. However, the timings of sightings strongly suggest that at least two different individuals were involved.

Kite D eventually left Exmoor on 1st March but was later reported on the Porlock Marshes, Somerset. An unidentified tagged bird was also later seen at Wraxall, west of Glastonbury; this may have been Kite D. Kite B finally left the estate near Shrewsbury in the last week of March.

Thus, in March, at least three, and probably all four of the remaining kites from the first English release were still alive, the fifth having been poisoned. Reports of Kite E in Breckland between 11th and 19th March may possibly refer to a Welsh bird of the same letter, but this seems unlikely. A tagged bird was also seen in the same area during the first week of May.

It was not until 13th July that another orange-tagged bird was seen, 50 km south of the release site. It stayed in the area for two weeks. This was followed by two sightings of a kite within 20 km of the release site in the first week of August.

In September, Kite B was identified in the vicinity of the release site, associating with the 1990 releases. Further reports of an unidentified individual could indicate that it had spent much of the summer in the vicinity. The bird had clearly moulted successfully, as it was now in distinctly red plumage, markedly brighter than the young birds.

Most, if not all, of the four surviving kites from 1989 had returned to the general vicinity of the release area in the spring or summer at one-year-old in 1990.

Release and dispersal in Scotland in 1989

In Scotland, the birds were cleared from quarantine restrictions on 19th July 1989. Early the following morning the cage holding the three oldest kites was opened, and the three birds emerged singly, settling to perch within 150 metres of the cage. The second cage was opened early on 23rd July and the three younger birds flew out to join the others. All six spent most of the day perched in a large Scots Pine directly in front of the cages. In the evening, all fed on food provided on the roof of the cage, where the older three had already fed just before release of the young ones.

All six kites remained within 500 m of the cages, feeding from the roof of the cage in the early morning and late evening. They spent most of the day sitting in trees, on fences or flying within a few hundred metres of the cages. They were seen also to forage for invertebrates in the forestry clear-fell area to the rear of the cages. They all became very possessive of a deer's head, put out for them in one of the fields, and defended it vigorously against Crows and Buzzards. They all fed well and regularly from the roof of the cages on Rabbit and fish. In the next six days, their exploratory flights took them up to 9 kilometres from the cages and up to 1000 ft. (300m) altitude. From 7th August, they started staying away and were well able to feed independently.

Their subsequent movements were as follows:

Kite 1 set up territory nearby on the Black Isle, mainly in company with Kite 5. On 2nd and 3rd October, both birds flew down the Great Glen to an area about 70 km south-west. They returned on 5th October and stayed in an area of farmland, forest and rough grazing about 5 km by 3 km. Kite 1 was illegally killed after eating a Pheasant laced with alphachloralose, whose use is banned for this purpose. It was found dead at Avoch on 1st December but, despite intensive police enquiries, no prosecution could be pursued due to lack of evidence.

Kite 2 travelled widely in Easter Ross in August and September, moving to Banffshire on 26th August. It moved back to the Elgin area, Morayshire on 27th August and remained there throughout the winter. It was last seen on 15th March when it apparently moved west.

Kite 3 flew inland in Ross-shire and then turned south to be seen in Fife on 12th August. On 25th August, it was located near Crieff, Perthshire and remained there until at least 16th April. It returned on 15th September and wintered again in the same locality.

Kite 4 arrived in Orkney on 15th August and, after departing from the islands on 27th August, it spent one day at the release cages. On 16th October, it was located near Biggar, Lanarkshire and set up a winter range, where it remained until at least 26th February. It returned to this same locality on 17th September for its second winter.

Kite 5 travelled with Kite 1 from August to October. It was apparently present with that bird on 27th October and may have been there on 19th November.

Kite 6 went to Nairnshire in late August and early September; and this was probably the bird seen in the Great Glen on 14th October and at the Mull of Kintyre on 19th October. It was located on the island of Islay, Argyllshire on 20th October, where it spent the winter. It was last seen there on 10th March. On 16th March, it arrived in Morayshire, where the wing-tag was read on 19th March.

Sightings in late March, April and May indicated the presence of three kites, probably four and possibly even five in Moray, Nairn, East Inverness and Easter Ross. Usually observers failed to see wing-tags, although orange wing-tags were seen on several occasions; the radios were well past their working life. (Longer-life batteries were used on birds released in 1990.) Two birds were present in Easter Ross in June and July, on one occasion raiding a rookery. Scattered reports came from other areas. The return of these kites to the general area and even to the release cages was very encouraging for the future.

Summary of the first year

All the young developed well in their quarantine cages and were duly released. They flew strongly, catching flying insects within a few hours of release. The birds fared even better than expected in dealing with natural conditions; they rapidly became independent of supplied food and started to range widely. However, one bird in Scotland and one in England (after moving a considerable distance) subsequently died due to illegal poisoning. Police investigations followed. Although the release sites were chosen to minimise such risks, kites' range over hundreds of kilometres while young and may encounter problem areas at these times before settling in safer areas. The fact that at least 11 kites of the native Welsh population of about 50 pairs were poisoned in their main breeding area in 1989 stressed the need to expand the range of this species. In addition, other initiatives were in hand to reduce the incidence of illegal poisoning – which threatens much wildlife.

All the 9 non-poisoned birds are thought to have survived their first winter, the most testing time for any young bird. This was better than we could reasonably have expected. We needed to consolidate on this pilot year, and boost the numbers brought in each year.

When the Project Team reviewed progress in November 1989, the pilot year, we agreed the use of radio-transmitters for the following year. However, due to the trade-off between range and duration, Dr Ken Smith, of RSPB's research department, would evaluate the benefits of increased duration versus shorter range with the view of making recommendations for the project the following year. Peter Walters Davies passed on the offer from Peter E. Davies to make wing-tags

Views of kite hunting for small prey over a field at Wormsley where a Rook is also foraging. [MP]

and to coordinate the colour-coding scheme. The need to monitor the release sites after mid-February was stressed, although it was realised that individuals may not return for up to 3 years.

In the Project Team *Update* of 3rd May 1990, we were able to make an assessment of the status of the birds released the previous year. Apart from the one bird from each release site which had met their ends at the hand of humans (with prosecutions still pending in the English/Welsh borders case), the others seemed to be doing remarkably well. Almost all were thought to be alive and well, and several at least seemed to have a good idea of where home was. This boded well.

Orders were being placed for radios, and Robert Kenward retained to do the fitting in England, and at the same time give further training to both NCC and RSPB personnel, thereby covering Scottish needs. Wildlife Surveys Wales (the two Peters) were organising tags.

Releases in 1990

The 1990 kites in England were released in two batches of six and seven birds at 10:00 on 10th July 1990 and 11:00 on 19th July respectively. Each of three cages at each of the two locations was opened in turn and most birds left almost immediately, settling within 3 km of the cages. The birds remained close to the release areas for several days, spending most of their time perching in the trees. As time progressed, their flights became progressively longer, higher and more wide-ranging. A detailed account of the release would only reiterate what has already been described, since most of the events and behaviour recorded during this release period closely paralleled those of the previous year. The birds from the cage opened later integrated very quickly with the first group and were observed flying together on 19th July and feeding on 25th July. However, one bird (M) did prove to be an exception since, on the fifth day after release, it left the area. Radio contact was achieved again on 1st August on the north Norfolk coast after reports received from the general public. It was monitored by Norman Sills (RSPB Warden) until 19th August when the bird dropped the tail feather carrying the radio. No foul play was suspected as sporadic reports of a Red Kite in that general area continued.

As time progressed, the twelve birds remaining at the release site gradually relied less and less on the assorted carrion (Rabbits, Crows, Magpies *Pica pica*, Foxes *etc.*) put out for them, finally becoming fully independent after 10th August. During this period, they ranged more widely (up to 32 km per day) and roosted in several widely separated places a few kilometres from the release area. On 5th September 1990, Kites B and X left the general release area. Reports were received on 8th October that Kite X was found in Shropshire only a few days after its departure, caught on a fence from which it was released. However, most birds remained in the area of the release site for longer than in 1989. It is not known whether this was related to the larger number present, the more sedentary Spanish populations from which they were drawn, or the presence of at least one of the 1-year-old birds from the releases the previous year, which was associating with them. In October, Kite J was found dead locally and it is likely that this was poisoned. However, most birds fared well, even in severe winter weather. One of the 1990 releases which ranged more widely did probably suffer from bad weather: it was found dead 270 km south in Seine-Maritime, France. The person reported the find, P. Boilet, after "*une grosse tempête*" (a very severe storm). In early 1991, at least 8 of the birds were in the same general vicinity, and some showed some preliminary signs of associating in pairs.

Releases in Scotland (where the Swedish birds were slightly younger than the Spanish ones in England) started on 25th July and continued until 2nd August. The young kites stayed near the release areas for a longer period than in 1989; again, this may be due to the larger number present. They all took to the wild extremely well, finding their own food as well as returning to eat dead Rabbits from the release sites. Buzzards also acquired this habit, and the kites were often seen flying and fighting with Buzzards and Crows.

The kites started to range more widely in early August and, from mid-August, went further afield. Departures usually took the form of birds spiralling higher and higher over the release areas on fine days, usually between 10:00 and noon, then setting off at high altitude. Reports from the general public were again very good, and the project was becoming very well-received, with good press coverage as well as news features on BBC and commercial television.

Most of the Scottish birds remained in Easter Ross and the East Inverness area throughout August and September, with some evidence of a south-westerly movement. One bird was found

At least 5 kites were hunting, alongside a flock of Black-headed Gulls in late winter in north Northamptonshire. Earthworms and other small prey were seen to be taken from this ploughed field. Included are kites hunting from the air and on the ground, and catching a small item. [MP]

dead of natural causes with a broken wing at the end of September. The rest dispersed in Scotland and beyond. Four moved north, one travelling as far as Caithness. Two remained to winter in south-eastern Sutherland. One bird moved east and returned in late December to the release area. Four to five birds set up winter ranges along the River Spey, three of them together at the RSPB Insh Marshes reserve. Two birds moved to the Hebridean islands of Islay and Jura, where one remained to winter on Islay. One moved to a new winter range in Perthshire, not far from the 1989 bird. Four other birds were recorded from Tayside and, in December, several kites were reported in SW Scotland and the north of England. Kite 9, last seen in Sutherland on 15th September, was located in Wharfedale, Yorkshire in late December. The dispersal of the 1990 kites followed the pattern as the previous year. The birds had clearly shown their ability to survive and to choose suitable winter territories. Essentially similar patterns of movement were seen in later years.

Survival

Before 1st July 1995, a total of 14 Red Kites originating from the study area in England, and 17 originating from the study area in Scotland, were recovered dead. The majority of recoveries were birds in their first year. In both countries, birds found dead from natural or unknown causes were closer (median distance 3.8 km, range 1–272 km) to the release or nest sites than those which were poisoned (median distance 73.7 km, range 5.3–806 km). There was no additional significant effect of country or an interaction between country and cause of death (Evans *et al*. 1999).

I return to the subject of survival rates in Chapter 9.

Rehabilitation

Five Red Kites from the study area in southern England were captured and taken into captivity for veterinary treatment in 1989–94. Two (both in their first year) were not rehabilitated as one died before treatment for aspergillosis and the injuries of the other prevented rehabilitation. One Red Kite, of Welsh origin and released in 1991, was found in May 1993, unable to fly due to severely bruised carpal joints. After treatment, it was rehabilitated in June 1993 and bred unsuccessfully in 1994 and again, successfully, in 1995. One wild-raised Red Kite (offspring of the 1992 cohort) was thought to have the symptoms of trichomoniasis (caused by the flagellate protozoan parasite *Trichomonas gallinae*) while it was still a chick. After treatment, it was returned to its nest in southern England where it fledged successfully. It bred successfully in 1994 and 1995, illustrating that such interventions can make a material contribution to species recovery. Another wild-raised Red Kite (this time offspring of the the 1994 cohort) was found caught in a fence in July 1994 soon after fledging. It was treated with antibiotics and rehabilitated in August 1994. Only one Red Kite was treated in Scotland in 1989–94. This bird, in its third year, was found at a garden bird table in southern Scotland at Inverleithen, Galashiels, suffering from alpha-chloralose poisoning, another recorded incidence of kite poisoning since the start of the project. It recovered and was rehabilitated in the study area in northern Scotland.

Effects of the kites on Game

At no time did any kite from the English site venture into any of the nearby Pheasant release pens, and no confirmed kills attributable to kites were recorded. Disturbance to poults was observed by Ian Evans on two occasions, but in both cases the poults ran or flew from the field edge into cover less than 3 m away. On no occasion was the poult pursued. Disturbance to poults was witnessed on a single occasion only, by the estate shepherd. These disturbances were similar to that seen when a kite flew over Crows and Magpies and when Pheasants are disturbed by humans or vehicles.

One incident worth noting was witnessed by the farm tractor driver, a farming student and Ian Evans. In this case, a kite flew low over a release pen and then flew low over an adjacent stubble field towards a feeding Pheasant poult. When the kite reached the poult, it landed beside it. However, when the poult raised its head, the kite flew off. Ian had seen kites on several occasions feeding on dead poults in this field, and this had not evidently scared the poults feeding in this field or those in the release pen. This same pen was less than half a mile (well under 1 km) from the wood where all three kites present at the time regularly roosted, and each bird spent quite a lot of time in this area.

At the English site, where the release area included Pheasant rearing sites, the effects of this bird of prey with large wingspan on game was found to be negligible. There was sometimes an apparent scaring effect on young Pheasant poults unaccustomed to seeing bird-of-prey silhouettes in the sky; they sometimes reacted by running for the nearest cover. However, this effect was short-lived, and poults soon ignored the kites. Wild birds seemed to take even less notice of the kites. During the project, kites landing beside cock and hen Pheasants were seen to cause no obvious signs of alarm. The same applied to kites flying over, and feeding in, fields containing over 50 Pheasants. There were several records of kites feeding on Pheasant poults, but in nearly every case the poults had been killed by something else and the kites were merely scavenging. There were only two cases where the poults' death could not be ascertained.

As noted earlier, the kites fed primarily on carrion, but were observed feeding also on insects and worms.

If kites were detrimental to game, one would have expected a greater incidence of kills both inside and outside release pens. Large number of kites were released in a comparatively small area where several thousand Pheasants were also being released but no kills were recorded. However, it is very easy for an observer to assume that a kite in close proximity to a release pen is hunting live Pheasants as opposed to scavenging dead ones.

After the second year of releases (1990), the helpful and open-minded head gamekeeper at the first English rearing and release site (whom we can now credit as Gavin Jones at Wormsley) published a very supportive letter in the *Shooting Times and Countryside Magazine* of 11th–17th October 1990:

> **Red kites: a keeper's welcome**
> Sir, - Following attempts by the Nature Conservancy Council and the Royal Society for the Protection of Birds to re-introduce the red kite to former breeding haunts in England and Scotland, more and more keepers will be coming into contact with these birds in the very near future. As a consequence, I think that this is an appropriate time, as headkeeper on one of the estates where a number of kites have been released during the past two years, to report the effects of these large predators on gamebirds.
> Initially, I must admit that I was very sceptical that such a large bird of prey was a scavenger, and fully expected the release pens to resemble a battlefield. However, after two years I can safely say that the effect of kites on the shoot has been negligible. There have been a few heart-stopping moments when I have found a pack of kites feeding on a dead pheasant poult near a pen. In nearly all cases the cause of death was determined and could not be blamed on the kites – they were simply scavenging.
> Indeed their presence around a pen tends to indicate that something else is killing poults, since as soon as the problem is rectified the kites drift away from the pen.
> I also thought the scaring effect of a large silhouette in the sky would be a severe problem. However, wild birds tend to ignore kites even at close quarters, and partridge numbers are still increasing on the estate. The only scaring is apparent when the poults are first put to wood, in which case they react by running for cover. It takes about a week for them to adapt.
> On no occasion have I, or my underkeepers, seen a kite killing anything, although 1 have seen them attacking crows and magpies which seem to enjoy every opportunity they can get to mob the kite.
> The kite's ability to find carrion is very highly developed as I first discovered after shooting a carrion crow one evening and not picking it up. Next morning there were five kites feeding on the remains, which perhaps makes a good point for not using poison, as these birds are extremely susceptible to this illegal practice.
> Blaming the red kite for scaring and killing poults is all too easy, especially by the inexperienced who have had little contact with the bird. Such views will only encourage bad practices which will reflect very badly on the gamekeeping profession and give the anti-shooting lobby yet more ground on which to undermine our sport.
>
> The name and address of this correspondent have been withheld to preserve the site's secrecy.

Dispersal overall

In southern England, as previously reported by Evans *et al.* (1999), some 37.1% of the 1989–92 kite cohorts left the intensive study area in their first year (*i.e.* moved more than 50 km). Most dispersed soon after their release in late summer (69.6%), while the remainder (40.4%) dispersed after spending their first winter within the English study area. Reports were received from as far afield as Cornwall, Wales, East Anglia and northern France (Fig. 8.1). The Red Kites of Swedish origin left the English study area on dry sunny days in August and September. Three birds dispersed in a south-westerly direction and one in a north-westerly direction. All four are thought to have returned in the following spring and summer. Two juvenile Red Kites of Welsh origin also left the English study area in August and September but dispersed in a north-westerly direction, while two left in April and May in a southerly direction and a north-easterly direction, respectively. None was recorded subsequently in southern England (and one was known to be dead). Juvenile Red Kites of Spanish origin dispersed in all directions from the study area in August and September, and also between March and June. Some were not observed in the English study area for almost two years, although some were resighted there only a few weeks after their initial departure. These movements and their timing were confirmed by radio-telemetry. Of the birds from the 1989–92 cohorts that left the English study area, 27.3% returned and subsequently entered the breeding population.

From the study area in northern Scotland just over 60% of the birds (60.9%) from the 1989–92 cohorts dispersed in their first year, mainly in a southerly or south-westerly direction. The majority of birds (90.5%) left during late summer/early winter, while the remainder (9.5%) dispersed in the following spring. They were reported from south and southwest Scotland, Wales, Northern Ireland, the Republic of Ireland and Cornwall (Fig. 8.1). In the following spring, Red Kites that had dispersed the previous autumn returned to the Scottish study area, and in 1994 16.7% of the birds from the 1989–92 cohorts that dispersed, bred in the Scottish study area.

As the project progressed, a smaller proportion of Red Kites dispersed from the Scottish study area (Table 8.1). The proportion dispersing from the English study area was most marked in 1989 when mainly Swedish birds were released. The proportion then declined to a relatively constant level in 1990–93 when mainly Spanish birds were released. Overall, a greater proportion of Red Kites (in the 1989–92 cohorts) dispersed from the study area in Scotland compared with the English study area. In the English study area, there was a sex bias in dispersal, since over two-thirds of the Red Kites that left there were female.

The data on dispersal were expressed also in terms of the maximum distance moved between the site of release/fledging and records during the first year of life (Table 8.2). There were annual differences in the extent of movements from the two study areas, with birds tending to be found further away during the early years of the project. There was also a tendency for females to travel

Table 8.1. Percentage of released Red Kites which moved >50 km from their release areas in their first-year. Reproduced from Evans et al. (1999) with permission of British Trust for Ornithology

	England		Scotland	
Cohort/sex	Sample size	Percent moving >50 km	Sample size	Percent moving >50 km
1989	5	100.0	6	100.0
1990	13	38.5	19	78.9
1991	15	40.0	20	60.0
1992	20	35.0	24	37.7
1993	20	35.0	24	25.0
Male	35	28.6	52	42.3
Female	38	52.6	40	57.5

Difference between countries in dispersal statistically significant: $\chi2 = 6.53$, df = 1, $P < 0.05$
Difference in dispersal between sexes in England statistically significant: $\chi2 = 6.25$, df = 1, $P < 0.05$
Decline in dispersal between years in Scotland highly statistically significant: $\chi2 = 21.4$, df = 4, $P < 0.001$

Figure 8.1. Furthest locations of Red Kites marked as nestlings in aviaries or at nest sites within their respective release areas in England and Scotland 1989–1994, and reported subsequently outside these areas. Only one location per bird is plotted, although each location can refer to more than one bird. One other Red Kite released in England was recovered 15 km north of Rouen, France (from Evans *et al*. 1999).

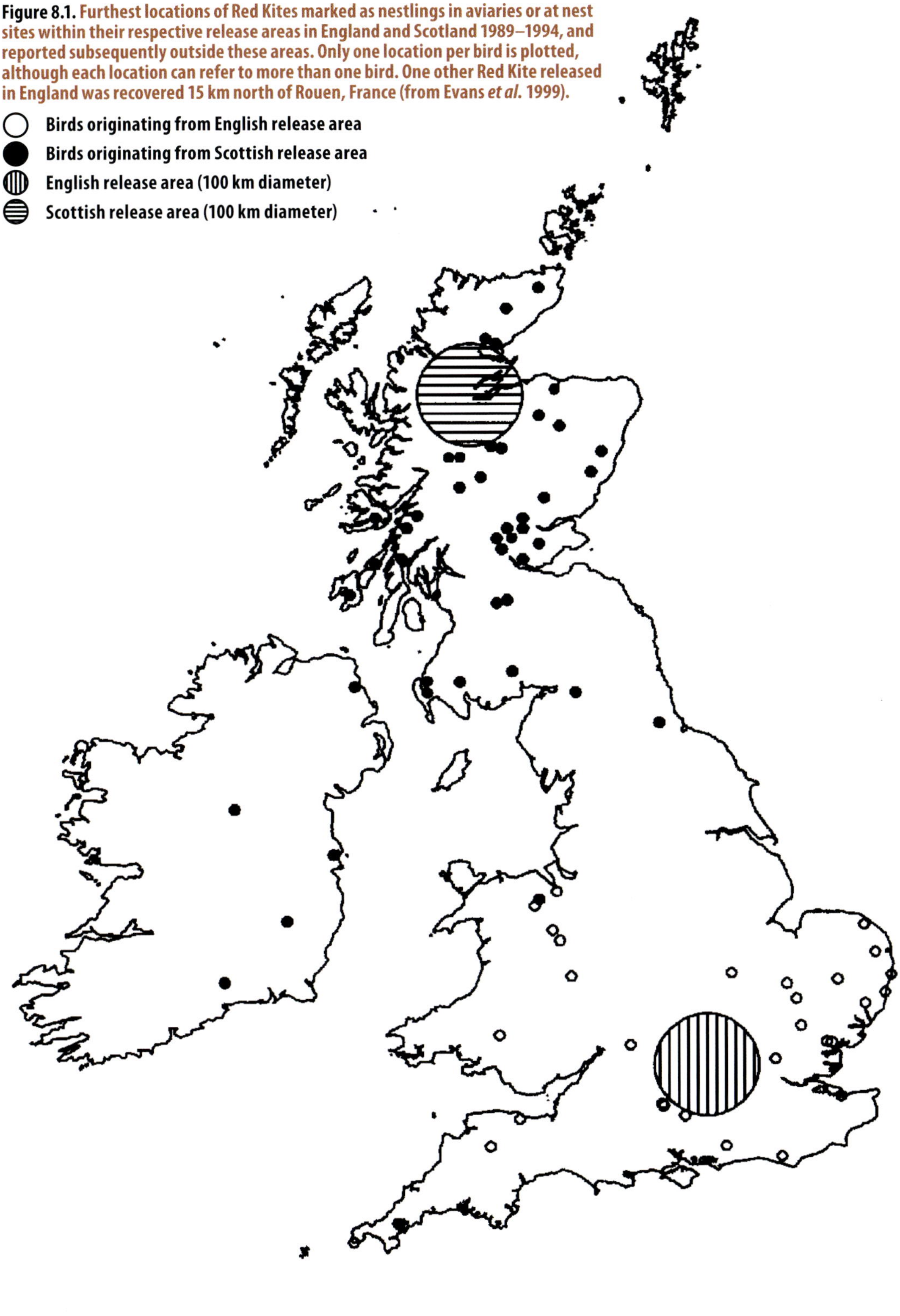

○ Birds originating from English release area
● Birds originating from Scottish release area
▮ English release area (100 km diameter)
⊜ Scottish release area (100 km diameter)

Table 8.2. Median maximum distances (km) moved during the first year of life by individual Red Kites released in England (E) and Scotland (S). Reproduced from Evans *et al.* (1999) with permission of British Trust for Ornithology

Cohort/Sex	Median maximum distance (km)		Range (km)		Sample size	
	E	S	E	S	E	S
1989	197	108	185–379	55–225	5	6
1990	15	100	9–272	7–640	13	19
1991	55	80	10–226	10–830	15	20
1992	9	26	3–126	5–470	20	24
1993	10	19	5–189	5–532	20	23
Female	21	80	3–379	5–830	38	40
Male	12	45	6–189	7–480	35	52

further than males, and for Scottish birds to travel further than those originating from England. A comparison between the distance moved by released and wild-raised Red Kites in the 1992 and 1993 cohorts in England revealed no significant difference (Evans *et al.* 1999).

As numbers built up near the release sites, the highly social nature of Red Kites became more evident. Particularly in winter, large numbers of kites gather at communal roosts that become traditional, with over 200 having been seen circling together over a wood in the Chilterns. These tend to be young birds as some adults roost near to their nest sites throughout the year. These large roosts may, however, be near a nest site.

The kites benefit from foraging in loose groups as that improves the chance of finding food and carcases found may be enough to feed several kites. The kites spread out from such roosts as part of this process. Radio-tracking has shown that individual kites tend to range over an area of about 6–7 km across during the course of a winter, with the roost within that area.

The roosts tend to break up in spring as pairs move to find potential breeding sites. They are not territorial, except for defending a small area around the nest site.

All birds need to replace their feathers, in the case of flight feathers normally once per year. Some birds, such as some ducks with safe – usually remote – rich feeding areas, can moult and re-grow all their flight feathers simultaneously, with a period of flightlessness. This would not work for Red Kites, because they need to fly in order to find food. In common with other birds of prey, kites moult slowly so as to leave only small gaps in the wings and tail, thereby minimising the advrse effects on flying performance. This bird, in early August, is in the middle of the moulting period, generally within late spring to autumn. Its 7th primary feather (the one behind the longest feather in each wing) is not quite fully grown. The outermost tail feathers (when fully grown, the longest) are clearly still growing, and the central tail feathers appear to have been recently dropped. [MP]

Red Kite at Wormsley in March carries in its talons moss for nest lining. [MP]

9. Kites breeding in the wild

As early as the first meeting of the Project Team on 20th October 1987 at NCC HQ in Peterborough, we started thinking about the situation in the hoped-for post-experimental-project phase. We recognised the potential need for nest-protection but opted not to discuss this item at length at that meeting, noting it would need attention later. It was, however,

The area of re-established kites first nesting in the wild in the Chilterns, with one of the first nests, in 1991, in tree – and the tree. [MP]

generally agreed that it was appropriate for protection efforts for the Welsh population to be maintained during the reintroduction programme. Announcements about monitoring and tagging were considered important, particularly in the counties in the vicinity of the English release areas just west of London, where sightings by birdwatchers and public at large could be expected.

On the basis of experience, especially with the White-tailed Eagles in Scotland, it was hoped that up to 20 birds per year, for possibly five years, in each area, would be an appropriate number for release. Targets would need to be set and sequential criteria for success were identified: (a) birds becoming self-sufficient and surviving the winter; (b) birds attempting to breed; (c) successful breeding; and (d) establishing and spreading of the recovering population.

Our techniques for finding breeding pairs evolved and settled rapidly. The radio-tagging facilitated the location of individuals on a daily basis until the first moult, usually during the following June–July when the transmitter was lost. Occasionally, this feather alone was lost. In the first year, batteries tended to fail before then. In later years we adopted systems that gave lower-range detection but longer battery life. Thus, as pair formation and home range establishment often took place between January and May in their first year (*i.e.* usually before the radio transmitter was lost), pairs could be detected by radio-tracking. Consequently, when radio

Ian Evans climbs to inspect one of the first two nests, in 1991, but these were unsuccessful, with crows predating eggs at this one. [MP]

WHEN THE KITE BUILDS... WHY and HOW we restored Red Kites across Britain 117 fixes (taken every 1–3 days) for a particular bird centred on a single location for at least 2 weeks during the breeding period, a search for a possible nest was undertaken. Breeding behaviour (carrying nest materials, copulation, displaying) was also noted in the area where a pair was known to have settled, and the identity of the pair was confirmed by wing-tag observation where possible.

When breeding was confirmed, monitoring by radio-telemetry was complemented by nest-site visits undertaken on a weekly basis. All located progeny produced by pairs released in 1991–1994 were ringed and wing-tagged and a 2-ml blood sample was taken before fledging. Molecular analyses of samples taken from both released and naturally fledged young were undertaken in 1995 to determine sex, confirm parentage and estimate the level of genetic variation in the new population (see Cordero el al. 1997 for technical details, and Evans et al. 1998 for more of the results).

We did not know, until analyses became possible much later, that no males were released in England and only two females in Scotland in the first year of importations. We now know, in retrospect, that no heterosexual pairs were possible in England in 1990. The first pairs of Red Kites established in southern England were detected in early March 1991, when two pairs, composed entirely of 1-year-old birds, started roosting regularly in the vicinity of their prospective nest sites. Nest building was observed on 26th April 1991. One pair (HT38604 and HT38606) had started incubation by 10th May but failed on 22nd May. The other pair (HT38601 and HT58602) started incubation around 14th May but failed on 10th June. Inspection of the eggshell remains in the deserted nests suggested that the first pair had laid at least one egg and the second female had laid at least two. The latter clutch had been eaten by a Carrion Crow *Convus corone* (published earlier by Evans et al. 1998).

In 1992, 4 pairs were on territories near the English site, and all bred successfully, rearing a total of 8 chicks, the first wild-raised birds in England for well over a century. The same year saw also a pair on territory in Scotland for the first time. This, the only nesting pair at the time, successfully reared one chick, the first wild-bred in Scotland, and as for England, the first for about a century.

Our press-release was picked up widely by the national and regional press:

9 July 1992
RED KITES BREED AGAIN IN ENGLAND AND SCOTLAND
Red kites have bred successfully in England and Scotland for the first time in more than a century, the Joint Nature Conservation Committee and the Royal Society for the Protection of Birds have announced.

The major breakthrough for these rare birds of prey has come with at least nine young flying from nests in the past few days, including eight in England and one in Scotland.

Red kites were once common in England and Scotland but had disappeared by 1890 as a result of persecution by man. In a joint reintroduction scheme, young red kites from Spain, Sweden and Wales have been released in England and Scotland by the JNCC and the RSPB to re-establish breeding populations.

Young birds have been released over the last three years. Many have now become adults and several have formed pairs and nested some distance from the release sites. Breeding locations are being kept secret to avoid endangering the success of this important project.

Dr Mike Pienkowski, a director of JNCC, said: "We have achieved a major target in the recovery of red kites in Britain more rapidly than we dared hope. Our goal is to ensure that self-sustaining populations are established which enable this magnificent bird to spread over large areas of the British countryside."

Barbara Young, RSPB Chief Executive, said: "We are delighted that our actions to conserve red kites are showing such early success, despite the loss of several birds to illegal poisoning. Close teamwork with the JNCC has been a major factor in co-ordinating international action to help this globally threatened bird."

The only native red kites in Britain are confined to central Wales where 70–80 pairs are breeding. Persecution is still a major threat to red kites and is one of the factors preventing Welsh kites increasing their range. The reintroduction project has already been jeopardised by the death of five birds from illegal poisoning.

Successful breeding in the wild occurred from 1992 and every year afterwards: adult incubating eggs in nest. [PS]

Nests are large and untidy, and usually close to the edge of a wood or near a large clearing. They are built of sticks lodged in the fork of a tree and often decorated.

Age of first breeding

Our observational monitoring, together with the genetic work we had commissioned from Nottingham University, allowed us to amplify the story later in relation to the performance of 1-year-old birds attempting to breed. Our results on breeding performance in the years 1991–94 were detailed by Evans *et al.* (1998), on which this section is based.

The number of pairs of Red Kites attempting to breed in southern England has increased each year since 1991, when breeding was first detected (Table 9.1). However, the number of pairs

Two small chicks in nest; and larger chick in nest near the original nesting site, which had been unsuccessful in 1991. [PS]

Table 9.1. Number of pairs of Red Kites found in southern England. Figures in parentheses refer to pairs containing at least one 1-year-old bird. Reproduced from Evans *et al.* (1998) by permission of the British Ornithologists' Union and Wiley © BOU

Year	No. of pairs on territory	No. of territorial pairs laying eggs	No. of breeding pairs rearing young	No. of young fledged
1991	2 (2)	2 (2)	0 (1)	0 (0)
1992	7 (5)	4 (2)	4 (2)	9 (3)
1993	12 (3)	9 (1)	8 (1)	14 (2)
1994	22 (2)	20 (1)	17 (0)	37 (0)

Table 9.2. Composition and breeding success of pairs containing 1-year-old Red Kites. Male of each pair listed first. Reproduced from Evans *et al.* (1998) by permission of the British Ornithologists' Union and Wiley © BOU

Year	Individual (ring number)	Sex	Age (years)	Fate/progeny
1991	HT38604	M	1	Failed during incubation
	HT38606	F	1	
	HT38601	M	1	Failed during incubation
	HT38602	F	1	
1992	HT38622	M	1	Young ringed as HT43959
	HT38614	F	1	
	HT38603	M	2	Young ringed as HT43957 & HT43958
	HT38621	F	1	
	HT38609	M	2	Home range established
	HT38613	F	1	
	HT38611	M	1	Home range established
	HT38626	F	1	
	HT38620	M	1	Nest built
	HT38610	F	1	
1993	HT38631	M	1	Young ringed as HT41985 & HT43986
	HT38639	F	1	
	HT38643	M	1	Nest built
	HT38633	F	1	
	HT38637	M	1	Home range established
	HT38645	F	1	
1994	HT43963	M	1	Nest built
	HT43962	M behaving as F	1	
	HT43969	M	1	Home range established
	HT43976	F	1	

Two fairly well grown chicks, one unhatched egg and an item of human underwear; and two nearly fully grown chicks on nest [PS]

composed of 1-year-old birds did not follow this pattern but declined from 1992 (Table 9.2). This coincided with an increase in the number of adult birds (due to ageing) in the population, although a period of cold, wet weather during the spring of 1993 reduced breeding success and may have also influenced the number of 1-year-old Red Kites attempting to breed.

The 12 pairs composed of at least one yearling bird were significantly less successful at breeding than the 31 pairs composed entirely of adults (*i.e.* 2 years old or older): 58% of breeding attempts by l-year-old birds failed before egg laying, compared with 3% of those pairs composed entirely of adult birds. From 1991 to 1994, 60% of the five breeding pairs composed of 1-year-old birds produced young compared with 87% of the 30 adult breeding pairs, but this difference was not statistically significant. The five breeding pairs containing 1-year-old birds also produced fewer young (1.7 young/successful pair) than the 30 pairs composed entirely of adults (2.1 young/successful pair), but this difference too was not significant. During 1989–1994, only one Red Kite of Welsh origin, out of seven, attempted to breed in its first year in southern England, while 22 of the 62 birds of Spanish origin attempted to breed when 1-year old. The composition of each pair detected in 1991–1994, where one or both members were 1-year old, is summarized in Table 9.2.

As one expects, the breeding performance of birds of prey – and of many other animals – tends to increase with experience. However, with the population at very low levels after local extinction and the start of reintroduction, competition was also very low. With this factor acting in favour in the early years, some exceptional performances were evident.

One-year-old Red Kites establishing a nesting territory but not producing eggs

In April 1992, one male (HT39609) hatched and released in 1990 established a home range with a female (HT38613) hatched and released in 1991. However, the attempt failed and the pair had broken up by 5th May. Two other pairs of 1-year-old birds also established nesting territories. Two of these birds (HT38620 and HT38610) built a nest 46 km from the release area in early May but did not lay eggs. The second pair of 1-year-old Red Kites (HT38611 and HT38626) established a home range 55 km from the point of release but did not build any nest. They were first detected in a home range on 5th May, but the female (of Welsh origin) was found dead on 26th June and the male had deserted.

In 1993, a pair of 1-year-old Red Kites (HT38637 and HT38645) were first seen carrying nest material at a nest site on 3rd April but broke up soon after they were seen copulating on 29th April.

Another 1-year-old pair (HT38643 and HT38633) established on 6th April. On 3rd May, they were located at a nest, but a week later, the nest was occupied by a pair of Buzzards, and it was clear that the Red Kite pair had broken up.

In 1994, two pairs of 1-year-old Red Kites were known to have established home ranges. One pair (HT43963 and HT43962) were seen nest building and defending the nest territory during April but broke up on 7th May when HT43963 dispersed. Genetic fingerprinting studies proved that both members of this pair were male, which was surprising since their behaviour suggested that HT43963 was male and HT43962 was female. The other 1-year-old pair (HT43969 and HT43976) began frequenting their home range in mid-February but returned to the communal roost in the evening. On 23rd April, the pair was seen displaying and carrying nest material into a wood, but breeding did not take place.

One-year-old Red Kites laying eggs but not producing young

The first pairs of Red Kites established in southern England were detected by radio telemetry in early March 1991, when two pairs, composed entirely of 1-year-old birds, started roosting regularly in the vicinity of their prospective nest sites. These events are described at the start of this chapter, above.

One-year-old Red Kites rearing young

In 1992, male HT38603 (hatched and released in 1990) established a home range in an area that he had frequented in the previous summer, bred successfully with female HT38621 (hatched and released in 1991) and reared two young. The female was first located in the nest area with the male at the beginning of January 1992, and incubation was confirmed on 22nd April. In 1993, the pair bred but did not rear any young, while in 1994 they reared two young.

A pair of 1-year-old Red Kites (HT38622 and HT38614) also bred in 1992. However, their association was not detected until the beginning of April, when they started roosting together at

Virtually fully grown chick "branching" away from the nest [PS]

the nest site. Nest building was observed on 6th May, and the female was first seen incubating on 12th May A single chick (HT43959) fledged from this nest between 4th and 10th August.

In 1993, HT38631 and HT38639 (both hatched and released in 1992) roosted at the main communal roost during January, February and early March. After 21st March, both were regularly recorded in the vicinity of the nest site, and on 21st April the female was found incubating. Two eggs were laid, and the pair was successful in rearing two young.

What the analysis of first-year breeding performance tells us more generally

In all three pairs in which one or both partners were only one-year old, genetic analysis showed that the young were, indeed, the biological progeny of the respective partners. This is important to establish as, for Red Kites (in common with almost every animal species studied), some young have been recorded as the result of extra-pair copulations. As Evans *et al.* (1998) noted, this provides confirmation that 1-year-old Red Kites of both sexes do have the ability to breed even when fitted with a tail-mounted radio transmitter.

It is clear from the results presented that both male and female Red Kites can reach sexual maturity at 1 year of age, produce fertile eggs and rear young. However, in comparison with adult breeding pairs in southern England, pairs that contained 1-year-old birds were less successful at nesting and rearing young. This is consistent with findings for other raptor species (Newton 1979) and some other kinds of birds (reviewed in Newton 1989).

Body condition plays an important role in determining whether breeding takes place in some raptors (Newton 1979). In diurnal raptors, such as the Sparrowhawk *Accipiter nisus* (Newton 1986) and Kestrel *Falco tinnunculus* (Village 1990), the male provides most of the food for the female during the period prior to egg laying. If insufficient food is provided, the female will not be able to attain sufficient condition to breed. In Red Kites, the female is also fed by the male during the pre-laying period, and radio-telemetry has shown that, during this period, she becomes increasingly dependent on the male and tends to remain near the nest site. The ability of the male to provide sufficient food for himself and the female depends partly on his own foraging skill, which is enhanced by experience, and partly on the quality of his home range. The observation that first-year birds breed more successfully within the same home range in subsequent breeding attempts suggests that foraging skills, together with experience of or acquaintance with a home range, are important attributes.

Interesting nest contents with the chicks: (above) with food (deer leg) and decoration (part of a teddy bear); (below) with decoration, not food – a dog's toy rather than an edible Cornish pasty [PS]

Differences in foraging tactics have been observed between individual Red Kites. Heredia *et al.* (1991) found that some breeding pairs in Spain remained close to their nest sites within their home range during winter and foraged within this relatively small area. This ensured that the pair did not lose their nesting territory to other Red Kites and increased their knowledge and experience of this area. In contrast, migrant Red Kites present in the same locality during winter did not occupy or defend a home range. They tended to roost communally and forage gregariously over comparatively larger areas for less predictable food resources (which could be shared with other Red Kites) and for which an intimate knowledge of particular areas is less useful. In southern England, juvenile Red Kites, in particular, foraged gregariously and roosted communally during winter. Any 1-year-old Red Kite that establishes a home range in spring must therefore change from being gregarious to being territorial. However, 1-year-old Red Kites will initially be relatively inexperienced at maintaining, and finding food within, a home range. This inexperience is probably why few 1-year-old pairs succeed at breeding (*i.e.* producing eggs). However, establishing a home range at 1-year old, even without breeding, could be advantageous since it would allow the male, in particular, to become better acquainted with an area, and this experience could be beneficial in food provisioning and facilitate occupancy and successful breeding in subsequent years.

Red Kites may not have been previously reported as breeding in their first year in some parts of their range because all nesting territories were occupied and defended by more experienced adult birds. In other raptors when there has been a shortage of adult recruits (or an excess of vacant nesting territories), as in persecuted populations, juveniles have been able to breed because of reduced intraspecific competition (Newton 1979). Competitive exclusion by adults may thus act chiefly in delaying breeding of 1-year-old Red Kites in populations where there is an excess of adult recruits relative to vacant nesting territories, as in Spain, France and Germany (Evans & Pienkowski 1991).

When Red Kites, mainly of Spanish origin, were first released in southern England, and of Swedish origin in northern Scotland, 1-year-old Red Kites had little or no competition with adults, and all potential home ranges (and the nesting territories which they contained) were empty. Hence 1-year-old birds were free to choose the best nesting territories. However, since 1991, the number of adult Red Kites occupying nesting territories in southern England has increased, and the number of 1-year-old Red Kites occupying nesting territories declined. A core breeding range developed as a result of the high degree of philopatry exhibited by the released population. This development is not unique, since the distance between place of birth/rearing and place of first breeding is within the range recorded for Red Kites breeding in Wales (Newton *et al.* 1989, 1994).

Range expansion tends to be on a rolling front, with colonization occurring in areas adjacent to peripheral nesting territories (Newton *et al.* 1994). Hence, in the first few years, it was unlikely that competitive exclusion prevented or delayed breeding by 1-year-old Red Kites in southern England because only a relatively small area was occupied by breeding adults. Because Red Kites breed up to 55 km from where they were reared (N. Snell, M. McQuaid & P. Stevens, unpubl.), there was a large peripheral area of suitable breeding habitat, and this probably remains the case at the edge of the spreading breeding concentrations. Competition for vacant nesting territories with older Red Kites may influence where 1-year-old Red Kites can settle.

In Wales, competitive exclusion and competition for vacant nesting territories do not explain entirely why no 1-year-old Red Kite has been recorded breeding. The population was relatively small, and large areas of vacant habitat that have been occupied historically existed close to the relict breeding range. However, the quality of the habitat in Wales is poor in terms of food supply, and this, together with an unfavourable climate, has a major influence on both breeding productivity (Newton *et al.* 1994) and the age when breeding first takes place (Newton 1979, Newton *et al.* 1989). There may also be a genetic component, since in southern England the breeding performance of Red Kites taken from heterozygous populations is better than that of Red Kites taken from less heterozygous populations, such as in Wales (Cordero *et al.* 1997).

It is likely that habitat quality is the ultimate factor in determining whether and how well Red Kites can breed in a particular environment. However, individual experience, climate and the level of competition provide the fine tuning in determining at what age an individual breeds, and this, in turn, may be influenced by the genetic fitness of the individual.

Build-up of breeding numbers

The number of breeding pairs increased annually (Figure 9.1, Table 9.3). In 1994, six wild-raised Red Kites (the first offspring from nests established by released birds) bred for the first time in southern England. These birds were in four pairs (two pairs composed of wild-raised birds – one

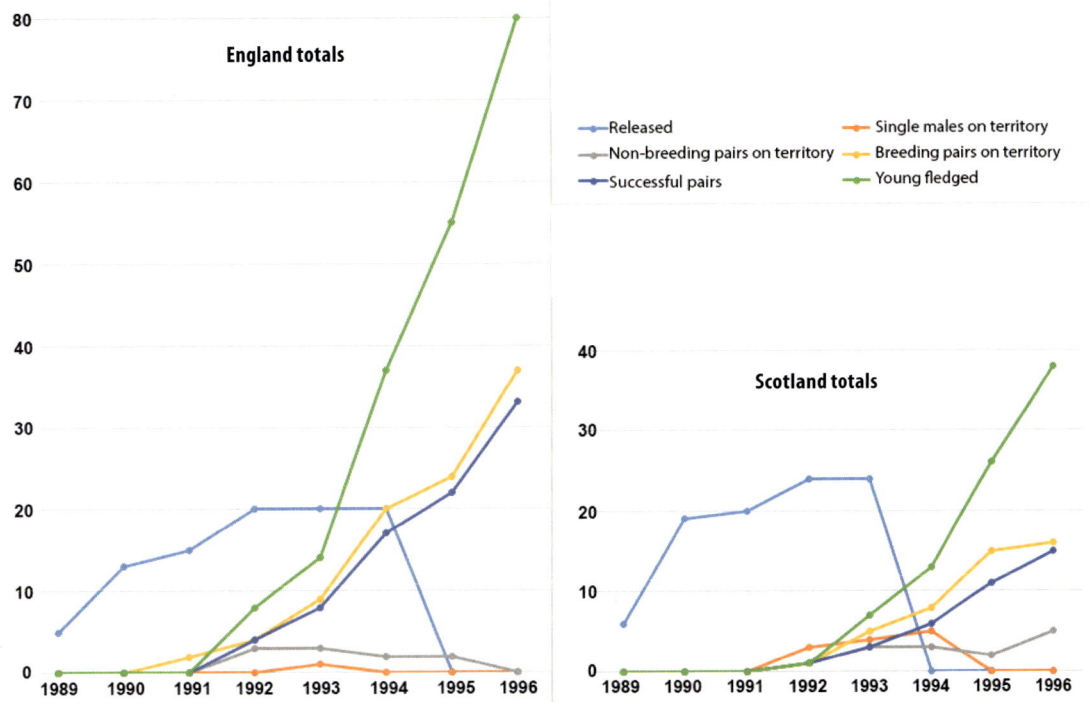

Figure 9.1. Initial outcomes of first phase, to 1996. (The two graphs are drawn at the same scale.)

Table 9.3. Summary of numbers of Red Kites released and their subsequent breeding performance 1989–1996, at the first English (E) and Scottish (S) sites. Combined from Evans *et al.* (1999) with permission of British Trust for Ornithology

Year	Released		Single males on territory		Non-breeding pairs on territory		Breeding pairs on territory		Successful pairs		Young fledged	
	E	S	E	S	E	S	E	S	E	S	E	S
1989	5	6	0	0	0	0	0	0	0	0	0	0
1990	13	19	0	0	0	0	0	0	0	0	0	0
1991	15	20	0	0	0	0	2	0	0	0	0	0
1992	20	24	0	3	3	1	4	1	4	1	8	1
1993	20	24	1	4	3	3	9	5	8	3	14	7
1994	20	0	0	5	2	3	20	8	17	6	37	13
1995	0	0	0	0	2	2	24	15	22	11	55	26
1996	0	0	0	0	0	5	37	16	33	15	80	38
Total	93	93	1	12	10	14	96	45	84	36	194	85

comprising a brother and sister – and two pairs composed of one wild-raised and one released bird) and reared a total of six young. In northern Scotland, an unsuccessful pair in 1994 included a wild-raised bird, reared in 1993. (The following sections are based on analyses which were commissioned towards the end of the Experimental Project; there are more details in Evans *et al.* 1999.)

In 1993, there was excitement in Suffolk where a pair of untagged kites raised two young. It was not clear whether these were released birds which had lost their tags or birds from the Continent. However, there was evidence that the rapid build-up of the English site was enhancing prospects of re-linking to the Continental population. In addition to the released birds, an immigrant adult female believed to have come from the continent bred with a released bird in the English study area during 1993–95 (P.J. Cordero, pers. comm.), while an immigrant juvenile Red Kite was observed with released and wild-raised birds in the winter of 1993/94.

By 1995, 26 pairs were located in southern England and 17 pairs in northern Scotland (Table 9.3). Not all pairs in England were located and it was estimated that about 30 pairs (excluding first-year breeders) bred. This estimate is based upon the number of males (in their second year or older) present in the winter roosts in February 1995, prior to pair establishment and an excess of females (in their second year or older). It is likely that over 60 young were reared based on the then current breeding performance.

Differences in performance at the Scottish and English sites

During 1991–95, there were fewer breeding attempts in Scotland than in England (Tables 9.3 & 9.4). This resulted in 47 chicks fledging in Scotland in 1991–95, compared to at least 115 in England.

This was the start of a steady build-up in both areas, with the English population increasing rather more rapidly than the Scottish one on all measures (Figure 9.1, Table 9.3). Why should this be?

The actual breeding performance of Red Kites in England and Scotland did not differ significantly (Table 9.4).

Evans *et al.* (1999) indicated that there were no significant differences between England and Scotland for either clutch and brood survival (Table 9.4). Clutch size varied from two to four eggs whereas the number of young fledged per nest varied between one and three in England, and one and four in Scotland. Male Red Kites bred for the first time in England when they were one to three years old, while females bred at one to two years old. In Scotland, males bred for the first time at two to four years old, and females at one to two years old (Table 9.5). There was no difference in the mean age of first breeding between male and female Red Kites (in the 1989–92 cohorts) in England, although in Scotland females initiated breeding at a significantly younger age than males.

Table 9.4. Breeding statistics of Red Kites in England in 1991–95 and Scotland in 1992–95. Reproduced from Evans *et al.* (1999) with permission of British Trust for Ornithology

	England	Scotland
Known number of clutches laid (includes replacements)	59	29
Known number of replacement clutches laid	0	1
Clutch survival (%)	89.6 (80.3–100.0)	77.7 (63.2–95.4)
Brood survival (%)	91.3 (80.3–100.0)	87.2 (74.5–100.0)
Nest survival (%)	80.3 (67.1–96.1)	67.2 (51.5–87.5)
Clutches not fledging young (%)	13.6	27.6
Clutches fledging at least one chick (%)	86.4	72.4
Mean clutch size	2.9 ± 0.4 (n = 8)	3.0 ± 0.8 (n = 24)
Mean number of young fledged/breeding pair	1.9 (n = 59)	1.6 (n = 29)
Mean number of young fledged/successful pair	2.3 ± 0.7 (n = 49)	2.2 ± 0.9 (n = 21)

95% confidence limits are given for clutch, brood and nest survival. Standard deviations (±sd) are given for clutch and brood size; n = sample size.

As kite numbers increased, multi-bird interactions increased, especially as nests were being established. Here, two pictures of three kites interacting. [MP]

Table 9.5. Breeding parameters of male and female Red Kites in England in 1991–95 and Scotland in 1992–95 (sample sizes in parentheses). Reproduced from Evans *et al.* (1999) with permission of British Trust for Ornithology

	England		Scotland	
	Male	Female	Male	Female
Mean number of young by one-year old birds	0.8 (4)	1.0 (5)	- (0)	0.5 (4)
Mean number of young by two-year old birds	1.8 (23)	1.7 (27)	0.9 (8)	1.6 (14)
Mean number of young by three-year old birds	2.2 (19)	2.5 (17)	1.9 (13)	1.7 (7)
Mean number of young by older birds	2.3 (13)	3.0 (7)	1.9 (8)	2.8 (4)
Proportion of sex in 1992–94 cohorts at fledging	0.383	0.617		
Mean age (years) of first breeding (1989–92 cohorts)	1.9	1.8	2.6	1.7
Range in age (years) of first breeding (1989–92 cohorts)	1–3	1–2	2–4	1–2

Tagged chicks – showing the later tagging system, where the yellow left wing-tag indicates the Chilterns and the red right one 2012. The year code repeats after about 9 years, as tags tend not to survive that long. The lower part of a tag is marked with the colour on the other wing in case only one tag is seen. [PS]

The size of broods at fledging was correlated with the age of the mother and to a lesser extent with the age of the father (Table 9.5).

The difference in rate of population growth in England and Scotland can be accounted for by differences in survival rate. Evans *et al.* (1999) analysed the survival of released and the wild-bred kites in the two areas, by age-group (Table 9.6), and over two time periods, the first including just released birds and the latter including both released and wild-bred (Table 9.7).

Minimum annual survival values (expressed as a percentage of birds known to have survived from one year to the next) were determined from radio-telemetry data and wing-tag observations for released and wild-raised birds. When a settled bird disappeared in a particular year, it was never detected later in a subsequent year.

In England, 80.4% of Red Kites that were released or wild-raised during 1989–94 survived their first year, while in Scotland, 51.6% of the birds released in 1989–93 survived (Table 9.6). This difference was statistically significant. There was also a significant difference between the 1989–94 cohorts, with survival being higher during the latter part of the release scheme than during the earlier part (Table 9.7). There was no difference between the survival of male and female Red Kites, when tested either independently or in combination with other factors. Despite the lack of significant differences, the small differences in survival did result in changes in the sex ratio. In England, the loss of females in the 1989–92 cohorts changed the sex ratio from an excess of females at release to an equal number of males and females in the adult population in 1994. In Scotland, more males were released and this led to an imbalance in the sex ratio of adult birds in 1994. There was no difference in survival rates of released birds compared with naturally raised birds for those years (1992–94) when both groups of birds were present. This applied even when the effects of country and cohort had been accounted for in the analysis.

Second-year survival was also found to differ between countries, with English Red Kites surviving highly significantly better than Scottish birds (Table 9.6). However, there were no differences in survival between year-cohorts (Table 9.7). Second-year birds also had a highly significantly better survival rate than first-year birds after the effects of country and year had

Table 9.6. Annual minimum survival of each age-group of released and wild-raised fledged Red Kites for England and Scotland
(Sample sizes in parentheses; the range of hatching years of survival included in each category is indicated in the Cohorts rows.) Reproduced from Evans *et al.* (1999) with permission of British Trust for Ornithology

Category	Sex	First year	Second year	Third year	Fourth year	Fifth year
England						
Released and wild-raised	Male	83.1% (71)	96.8% (31)	100% (20)		
		100% (10)	100% (4)			
	Female	78.0% (82)	92.5% (40)	85.7% (21)	100% (7)	100% (1)
	Both sexes	80.4% (153)	94.4% (71)	92.7% (41)	100.0% (17)	100.0% (5)
	Cohorts	1989–94	1989–93	1989–92	1989–91	1989–90
Released	Male	83.3% (48)	96.3% (27)	100% (18)	100% (10)	100% (4)
	Female	68.9% (45)	87.5% (24)	80.0% (15)		
		100% (7)				
		100% (1)				
	Cohorts	1989–94	1989–93	1989–92	1989–91	1989–90
Wild-raised	Male	82.6% (23)	100% (4)	100% (2)		
	Female	89.2% (37)	100% (16)	100% (6)		
	Cohorts	1992–94	1992–93	1992		
Scotland						
Released	Male	50.0% (52)	65.4% (26)	93.3% (15)	100.0% (7)	66.7% (3)
	Female	52.5% (40)	71.4% (21)	80.0% (10)	75.0% (4)	100.0% (1)
	Both sexes	51.6% (93)*	66.7% (48)*			
		88.0% (25)				
		90.9% (11)				
		75.0% (4)				
	Cohorts	1989–93	1989–93	1989–92	1989–91	1989–90
Wild-raised	Both sexes	42.9% (21)	100% (5)	100% (1)		
	Cohorts	1992–94	1992–93	1992		

The numbers alive at the beginning of each year are given in parentheses. The wild-raised birds in Scotland were not identified as to sex. *Includes one kite not sexed.

Table 9.7. Annual minimal survival of first- and second-year Red Kites in England (E) and Scotland (S). Reproduced from Evans *et al.* (1999) with permission of British Trust for Ornithology

		1989–91			1992–93		
Annual survival		Number released	1st-year survival	2nd-year survival	Number released or wild-raised	1st-year survival	2nd-year survival
Both sexes	E	33	63.6% (21)	90.5% (19)	63	79.4% (50)	96.0% (48)
	S	45	46.7% (21)	66.7% (14)	56*	57.1% (32)*	71.9% (23)
Male	E	14	71.4% (10)	100% (10)	26	80.8% (21)	95.2% (20)
	S	28	42.9% (12)	66.7% (8)	26	61.5% (16)	68.8% (11)
Female	E	19	57.9% (11)	81.8% (9)	37	78.4% (29)	96.6% (28)
	S	17	52.9% (9)	66.7% (6)	26	57.7% (15)	80.0% (12)

*The wild-raised birds in Scotland and one released kite were not identified as to sex.

been taken into account (Table 9.6). The survival of the older age groups was commonly 100% in England and Scotland. Clearly, a larger sample size would be required to achieve more realistic estimates for adult survival.

The project demonstrated that naturalized breeding populations of Red Kites could be established in England and Scotland by translocation. However, releasing equal numbers of birds and use of the same methods at each release site had not achieved similar results, possibly because the birds originated from different source populations and probably because the release environments differed.

Feisty chick threatens researcher fetching it for ringing and tagging. [PS]

Red Kites in Sweden (Kjellén 1994), in common with other raptors in northern latitudes (Newton 1979), migrate from their breeding areas in autumn and return in spring, presumably to avoid the harsh winter. The Red Kites of Swedish origin, released mainly in Scotland, appear to have retained the migratory instincts in terms of the timing and direction of movement. However, it is also possible that the longer movements were a consequence of where they were released rather than the origin of the birds. Juvenile Red Kites of Spanish and Welsh origins, which dispersed from the study area in southern England, differed in that their movements were not directional, seasonal or as far. This behaviour is similar to that recorded in Wales, where Red Kites were also known to disperse in all directions during their prebreeding years (Newton *et al.* 1994).

In Sweden, winter feeding was believed to have helped increase the over-wintering Red Kite population (Sylvén 1984) and similar results may have been achieved in Scotland by food-provisioning near release and roost sites during the winters of 1991/92 and 1992/93. In contrast, no supplementary feeding during the winter was undertaken in southern England, but released and wild-raised Red Kites dispersed similar distances and initiated dispersal mainly in late summer and spring during their first year. It is likely, therefore, that Red Kites may display different dispersal behaviour depending on the source population from which the translocated birds were taken, and the environment in which they are released. For instance, the proportion of juveniles of Swedish origin dispersing declined as a breeding population developed in northern Scotland. A similar pattern occurred in Sweden, as migratory behaviour was more prevalent when the population was very small but over-wintering became more frequent as the population increased (Kjellén 1995). Hence, there may be an alternative explanation for the increased tendency for migratory Red Kites to over-winter within their breeding areas, since increased population size may be linked to improved foraging efficiency, irrespective of food provisioning. This is because carrion, important in winter (Walters-Davies & Davis 1973; Davis & Davis 1981; Blanco *et al.* 1987), is irregularly distributed both spatially and temporally. By forming loose groups as opposed to foraging individually, Red Kites can search larger areas more efficiently for food (Heredia *et al.* 1991; Hiraldo *et al.* 1993). Individual Red Kites of Spanish and Welsh origins exhibited similar dispersal behaviour to that described in sedentary Buzzard populations, where a proportion of the annual production of juveniles displayed a mixed dispersal strategy (Walls & Kenward 1995; Davis & Davis 1992). It is therefore possible that autumn dispersal displayed by some of the Red Kites, taken from non-migratory populations, is related to residual migratory behaviour as some individuals returned in the following spring. Another possible factor as population size increases could be a need to be present at and defend a good territory, at risk of loss if one migrates. However, if some dispersing individuals settled and bred in other subpopulations (as may well have been the case when Red Kite populations were more widespread in Britain – and has been seen between the release areas as these increased), such behaviour would enhance genetic heterogeneity in Red Kite populations.

"I'm not dropping this!" Early season chase, lasting several minutes – but the kite holding the branch in both talons retained it through all the aerobatics, in the Chilterns. [MP]

In this study, Red Kites released in northern Scotland suffered greater losses and this led to a smaller breeding population establishing there compared to southern England. However, in comparison with the native population of Red Kites in Wales (Newton 1979), birds released in Scotland were surviving at least as well if not better. Nevertheless, once Red Kites reached adulthood, when dispersal was less likely, survival was very high in both England and Scotland, and similar to other raptors (Newton *et al.* 1989).

It is likely that some birds died undetected. Most of the Red Kites known to have been poisoned by pesticide-laced baits, or deliberately killed, were killed after dispersing. Several other Red Kites were also suspected of being killed deliberately or poisoned but there was insufficient proof for them to be included in this analysis. This suggests that, outside the areas where Red Kites were studied intensively, the actual number of deaths caused by persecution was larger than that recorded. Two incidents of illegal poisoning were also recorded within the intensive study areas in 1989–90 but none was recorded from 1991 to 1994, probably because the majority of countryside users gradually accepted that Red Kites did not harm their interests. However, this acceptance has not been universal. In 1995 and 1996, when Red Kites could no longer be located by radio-telemetry, persecution was again recorded within the intensive study area of southern England (Smith 1997). A vital element in future Red Kite conservation work must therefore be to encourage more people who use the countryside to accept Red Kites. For example, a government-led campaign against illegal poisoning of wildlife in the UK, like that initiated in the later stages of our Experimental project (Holmes *et al.* 1994), seemed to help to reduce this form of persecution, and may do so in the future. In addition, by educating the public to report suspected poisoning incidents, deaths caused by the abuse, misuse and approved use of certain pesticides can be highlighted and may lead to action to reduce their damage to the environment. There are signs of this, as discussed in Chapter 12, but vigilance needs to continue.

Rehabilitation of sick or injured birds played a minor role in the establishment and maintenance of the populations due to the small number of Red Kites taken into captivity when ill or injured. In England, at least two Red Kites that received treatment entered the breeding population, suggesting that rehabilitation can be of value when breeding populations are small. Other studies (Radler 1992; Chapter 4) suggest, however, that establishing populations only from sick or injured wild birds is not effective, since these birds are likely to be less fit and their offspring are likely to have poorer chances of survival. In this study, from the rehabilitation work and post-mortems undertaken, it was clear that Red Kites are vulnerable to a range of accidents and diseases, but the risks that these posed to the viability of Red Kite translocatiom programmes in the UK were insufficient to warrant concern.

One important factor affecting the population dynamics of small populations is the sex ratio (Ballou 1995). In this project, the chicks taken for translocation could not be sexed at the time of collection. However, sex determination after collection revealed that roughly equal numbers of males and females were released (except in the first year). Even so, a small bias in sex ratio during the early stages of the project did lead some males to remain unpaired in Scotland.

For several years, the naturalized breeding populations were still largely confined to relatively small areas of southern England and northern Scotland, despite wide-ranging dispersal by released and wild-raised Red Kites during the first few years of life. This high degree of natal philopatry, the propensity of birds to return to the area where they were born, is exhibited by Red Kite populations elsewhere (Newton *et al.* 1989) and by other raptors (Newton 1979; Davis & Davis 1992; Walls & Kenwood 1995). It is considered to hinder recolonization (Dennis 1995; Walls & Kenwood 1995). However, in suitable habitats Red Kites will breed at relatively high densities without affecting breeding productivity (Kjellén 1996; Newton *et al.* 1996) or population growth (Kjellén 1996). The ranges of the naturalized Red Kite populations in England and Scotland might therefore have been expanding relatively slowly at that time because the breeding populations were still achieving the carrying capacity of the then occupied habitats.

The productivity of the populations in England and Scotland were similar. In comparison with the native population in Wales (Newton *et al.* 1989, 1994), naturalized pairs laid larger clutches (14% more eggs), fledged on average one-and-a-half times more young per breeding pair, and had started breeding at one year old (Evans *et al.* 1998). These data show that the naturalized Red Kite populations, re-established in lowland districts of England and Scotland by translocation of continental birds, were by then expected to make a major contribution to range recovery in the UK, complementing the conservation action that was continuing in Wales.

Both naturalized populations in England and Scotland were by then self-sustaining, as their survival and reproduction levels were similar to or better than those of the – at last – expanding population in Wales. Predictions of population growth suggested that the English population would grow faster than the Scottish, due mainly to higher rates of survival; reproductive success was similarly high in both countries. There was therefore a need to focus on minimizing persecution (Cadbury 1992), particularly in areas where Red Kites were now recolonizing (Elliott & Avery 1991).

In every category in Table 9.7, survival rates at the English site were higher (or the same if both were 100%) than at the Scottish one. As discussed above, this could be due to various causes but, as later pointed out by Orr-Ewing (undated but written after 2012): "*The greatest threat to the Scottish Red Kite reintroduction remains illegal persecution (notably illegal poisoning), despite the fact that Red Kites pose little or no threats to any land use interests. Red Kites are primarily scavengers in Scotland, although they will also take some live prey including voles, other small mammals and birds. The Black Isle population of Red Kites has suffered in particular from illegal persecution. In 2012 there were only 52 pairs laying eggs in the Black Isle area, whereas by comparison the Chilterns population in the south of England (which involved release of the same initial number of birds [over roughly the same time period], and the established populations have similar productivity), now stands at between 900 and 1000 breeding pairs. During the period 1999–2006, an estimated 166 red kites from the Black Isle population were illegally poisoned and differential rates of illegal poisoning are confirmed to explain the difference between growth rates of the two red kite populations (Smart et al. 2010)."*

Chapters 10 and 12 look further at this problem and addressing it.

Breeding dispersal

All breeding attempts (nests with clutches) in the Experimental Reintroduction project were recorded within about 50 km of the release areas. At least 40 occupied territories were located in England and 34 in Scotland during 1991–95. In a small establishing population, the dispersal distances to nesting locations from place of rearing of the males and females are not independent. For the years 1991–94 in England and 1992–95 in Scotland, there was a slight difference between countries, with Scottish birds dispersing slightly further than the English birds (Table 9.8). There was no effect of year, showing that there was no significant expansion of range in these early years as the populations grew. Nest sites were not fixed and pairs would shift to new nests within a territory and to new territories between years. The distance moved by pairs between nesting attempts in succeeding years ranged from 0 to 55 km, although the majority of breeding pairs moved less than 6 km. In England, where pair composition between successive years did not change between 1992 and 1995, 56.2% of successful pairs returned the following year to breed again in the same nest. In Scotland, during the same period, only one successful breeding pair (out of 15) returned to the nest it had used previously. Pairs vacated territories in England following breeding failure (five cases) and as a result of the loss of the female partner through death (two cases) or through infidelity (two cases). In three cases, vacated territories were taken over by new pairs which bred successfully in the nest built by

Table 9.8. Natal dispersal distances (km) by male and female Red Kites in England and Scotland (the distances between the place of release or nest of birth to where the bird first bred). Reproduced from Evans *et al.* (1999) with permission of British Trust for Ornithology

Country	Sex	Median distance (km)	Range (km)	Sample size
England	Male	4.2	0.6–8.1	18
	Female	4.1	0.8–8.3	15
Scotland	Male	5.6	0.6–27.9	15
	Female	9.4	1.1–18.5	16

the previous pair. Some successful pairs in both areas moved only relatively short distances (*i.e.* up to 400 m) to a new nest site, often within the same wood. One English pair moved 400 m between years and built a nest within 100 m of the nest of another pair. This was the closest inter-neighbour distance recorded by then for Red Kites in the UK. Both pairs bred successfully.

Changes in pair composition between years occurred in eight pairs, out of 21 pairs that held territory in two or more years in southern England during 1991–94, and in two pairs (out of 16 that held territory in two or more years) in northern Scotland during 1992–95. In three cases in England and one in Scotland, the change was due to the death of the female. In the six other cases, the males lost their mates to other males (five in England and one in Scotland). These changes in pair composition occurred after establishment of a nesting territory, and in two cases after successful breeding. It appears that the females left the males, as the estranged male then attempted to attract another female to the established territory and, in four of the six cases, they succeeded.

In summer, farming activities give feeding opportunities for kites, gulls, corvids and other birds by exposing and disturbing insects, earthworms, small mammals etc. This is both by harvesting cereals and grass (left field in top left) and ploughing (right rear field). Kites hunt over these (middle left). In the series of pictures in the centre, a kite carefully removes straw and other unwanted material from its catch. Bottom right: a young kite gains experience in such manipulation. [MP]

Population growth

Using the information gathered during the experimental project up to 1995, computer simulations (Evans *et al.* 1999) indicated that both populations in southern England and northern Scotland would increase exponentially (until other factors limited). Assuming an equal sex ratio and a stable age distribution, the English population was predicted to increase by 3.94% per annum, and the Scottish population by 2.02% per annum. At these rates, the population were estimated to exceed 100 breeding pairs in England by the year 1998 and in Scotland by 2007.

If releases had been suspended in southern England in 1992 when the initial population size was 42 individuals, the model predicted that the population would exceed 100 breeding pairs in the year 2000 (with the same assumptions). Similarly, annual supplements of ten male and ten female Red Kite nestlings for two, three and five years in southern England after 1994 would have achieved 100 pairs in 1998; making virtually no difference in the longer term.

Determining when to stop releases is an important aspect of any translocation scheme. In this project, population models of the Red Kite population in southern England suggested that releases could have been suspended in 1992 (when the size of the population was similar to the 1994 Scottish population) or perhaps even sooner. However, in practice, a time-lag exists between release and breeding, and this delays assessment of population performance. In addition, small naturalized populations with little or no natural immigration are less able to compensate for detrimental stochastic effects and this increases their probability of extinction (Green, Pienkowski & Love 1996). Stochastic effects refer to fluctuations around the average. At high population sizes, average values generally work well but, with small population sizes, fluctuations around the average can reduce the population to zero, from which it cannot, of course, recover. Consequently, releases should be suspended only at the point when performance (in terms of survival and reproduction) of the naturalized population can be reliably established and when further releases contribute little to the population's rate of growth. In order to reach this conclusion, it is essential that long-term monitoring of basic survival and breeding parameters is an integral part of any release scheme. This project has demonstrated that such data can be used to assess what current action is required, and also to predict future population sizes, and of course to set objectives on which further conservation action can be based.

It was considered unlikely that the growth rates then estimated would apply in the long term (particularly in England), since environmental and competition factors would vary, both temporally and spatially, and influence population growth in a complex manner. However, the models available back then were useful in setting short-term targets or expectations which could then be compared with observed future population levels.

What was happening in Wales?

Sixty–three pairs of kites were proved to breed in Wales in 1990, by far the most successful season since records began. Forty–five of the nests were successful in rearing a total of 70 young, 22 more than the previous record of 1989. It was the first season since 1954, when 11 pairs reared 13 young, that the number of young reared exceeded the number of breeding pairs. Apart from the 63 breeding pairs, 18 other pairs were found, most of which built nests but did not lay. Two or three may have laid and failed swiftly, though most pairs certainly did not. In addition, at least

Table 9.9. Population data for Red Kites in Wales for four years

Year	Breeding Pairs	Other Pairs	Total Pairs	Unmated Birds	Successful Pairs	Young Flew	Total birds in:	
							April	August
1987	43	15	59	40	27	39	158	196
1988	47	19	67	41	27	38	175	211
1989	53	17	70	58	33	48	198	235
1990	63	18	81	58	45	70	220	286

Young kite rapidly acquiring high-performance flying ability as it hunts for food. [MP]

58 non-breeding birds were identified in spring, giving a minimum population in April 1990 of 220 birds – the first time the figure had exceeded 200 since records began. By August, after deducting known casualties, the population estimate was 286 birds.

In contrast to 1989, 1990 was a quiet season for poisoning incidents, probably due in part to a publicity campaign run by RSPB, NCC and ADAS in the early spring, following the appalling year before. The deaths of two birds near Tregaron in May and July were suspicious, but both were too decayed for analysis when they were found. The death of a fledged juvenile in July was still being investigated. An old female taken into care in the summer could not be returned to the wild due to an infection of the lungs. Despite the encouraging success that year, it was still a question of 'what might have been,' for 1990 turned out to be one of the worst years on record for loss of clutches to egg-collectors. Eight (possibly ten) nests were robbed by egg collectors although two of these had been manipulated and the kite eggs replaced by those of Buzzards. Although there had been no prosecutions, one collector seen near three robbed kite sites in April was later caught at an Osprey site in Scotland.

In 1992, the new Countryside Council for Wales, which had taken over from the NCC, abolished the Wales Kite Committee, their role being taken over, alongside other matters, by routine RSPB/CCW liaison meetings. CCW and RSPB would participate in JNCC's Red Kite reintroduction liaison meetings. Existing field-season contractors would be invited to provide monitoring services for 4 months per year. It was concluded that the kite manipulation work on eggs and young had been adequately researched and could be drawn on in the future if necessary and would cease after 1992. It was agreed also that Welsh kites would no longer be used for releases in England and Scotland.

10. Education and public awareness

Opportunities and expectations

It did not come naturally to NCC or RSPB to keep the plans confidential but, with the level of public awareness at the time, some 35 years ago, and our wish to get these birds re-established near centres of human population, gradual release of information seemed both necessary and desirable.... and the only practicable approach. We wanted to move as soon as we could to increase public awareness, support and engagement.

We did not want to lose any of our birds to illegal poisoning. However, with its prevalence amongst a minority of gamekeepers, we expected this to be inevitable. We wanted to mitigate any such losses by increasing public awareness of this unnecessary, indiscriminate and illegal practice – and to help reduce this activity to extinction.

At the Project Team meeting on Thursday 6th October 1988, the minutes note:

1. *The timing of the press release on the kites was thought to be crucial. Several views were discussed, including those of the estate, who want no publicity at all. Mr Porter to draft a project programme of PR and project management generally, with options, and to send to Dr Pienkowski to add an NCC view, with an attempt to produce joint proposals.*
2. *It was agreed that the local people should become involved, as appropriate by prior notification of the project. Attention should be paid to the needs of local newspapers as well as the national ones.* [Recall that there were few TV and radio channels, and no world-wide web or social media at the time.]
3. *It was suggested that NCC/RSPB should video the activities of the kites from the start. Arrangements could be made within the organisations for the use of equipment.* [Not a simple operation back then.]
4. *It was agreed that care should be used in relation to sponsorship and that initiatives should be agreed between NCC and RSPB before any approaches are made.*

A few months later at the Project Team meeting on 24th January 1989, held at NCC, Inverness:

There was a lengthy discussion on the question of publicity and particularly the timing of press releases. To some extent this has been overtaken by the publicity statement submitted to the Committee for Scotland and members [were] invited to comment on this. Assuming it is acceptable, then following action points arise.
a. *Preparation of background leaflet.*
b. *Drafting of initial and second press releases.*
c. *Decision on timing of initial press release.*

With such a spectacular bird, the opportunities for news media attention is great, giving the potential for getting across some important information. Red Kite in north Northamptonshire. [MP]

Red Kite in north Northamptonshire. [MP]

In the *Update to Project Team 8 April 1989*, under "Public relations", I noted:
On more private relations, I have updated the briefing note prepared earlier by RFP [Richard Porter]. This has been supplied to Welsh workers for their own use, together with a 1-page extract (prepared by PWD [Peter Walters Davies]) which can be passed at kite workers' discretion to farmers with kites on their land…
On wider PR, RFP and I are discussing currently with RSPB and NCC press staff. You will recall the need to allow for local requirements whilst ensuring that any public comment in one of the reintroduction areas does not cause problems in the other area, nor in the source areas (Wales & Sweden). I shall be in touch further on this aspect soon. The present preferred scheme (as noted in the minutes of the last meeting), may be developed as follows.
1. *A general press release probably in late May. This, and any subsequent discussions, will not give information on sites. Indeed, there is no real reason to indicate that there is more than one area.*

2. Following this, more local statements may be made in the two areas, as appropriate. As I understand at present, it seems more likely that colleagues in Scotland will wish for early publicity than will those in England. In any event, it is essential in this joint programme that action is co-ordinated. If this scheme does in fact take place, it would probably be desirable for any local Scottish statement not to indicate that there is also an English area.
3. If successful, the flying birds will become obvious (in July/August). We would obviously envisage a press release, etc at this time, and indeed request sightings of the birds. However, even then we would not favour indicating the actual release site to minimise disturbance in future years. For example, for the English site at that stage, we would envisage referring to "western Home Counties" or some such.

In the *Project Team Update 21 May 1989*, the section on "Public relations" noted:

The discussions between NCC and RSPB, including respective press officers have now taken place. A schedule of press information has now been agreed within the framework agreed by the Project Team, and taking account of other constraints including the timing of the RAF flight.

The agreed initial press release is attached [follows]. This is for release on 5 JUNE AND MUST NOT BE PASSED ON TO ANYONE BEFORE THEN. The release will be made by NCC's Press Officer on joint NCC/RSPB paper printed by RSPB. Sites are to be referred to only as somewhere in England (not even specifying south) and in Scotland. (I understand that the Scottish site may already be more widely known: could RHD/AJW [Roy Dennis/ Jeff Watson] please advise me of the present situation and what they wish to do in this respect in the future. Whatever is decided for Scotland, it is important that no indications are given as to the area of the English site, in view of the numbers of people in the vicinity.)

Those press expressing interest in response to the initial press release will be invited to witness and photograph the arrival of the birds at Kinloss; this will also be mentioned in the initial press release. No information as to the areas of the rearing sites will be given.

A further national press release will be made after the birds fledge. Subsequently, some provision for photography at a food dump, probably at the Scottish site, may be made – but no offer of this should be made at the time of the birds' arrival, in case of unforeseen difficulties.

Action required
1. MWP/RFP to continue to liaise with Press Officers.

The press release read:

Confidential till 5 June 89

Red Kites return

An ambitious project aimed at securing the future of one of Britain's rarest birds of prey begins this summer.

The joint programme, run by the Nature Conservancy Council and the Royal Society for the Protection of Birds, will attempt to re-establish the red kite in England and Scotland after an absence of 100 years.

The red kite was formerly widespread through England, Scotland and Wales. In the 19th century persecution led to it disappearing from England and Scotland by 1890. A few pairs were remaining in Wales at the beginning of the 20th century and only special protection enabled them to increase to about 45 pairs today.

In this experimental project, NCC and RSPB plan to release young kites in suitable areas of England and Scotland. It is hoped that these birds will establish themselves to form new centres of population.

Dr Mike Pienkowski, NCC's head of ornithology said, "Despite the efforts of farmers and conservationists in central Wales the British population of kites has been increasing very slowly and it is showing few signs of expanding its distribution. With such a restricted population occupying only a small part of its potential range it is extremely vulnerable to extinction. By expanding its range through reintroduction it will have a greater chance of surviving."

The young birds will come from Sweden and Wales but the exact locations where they are to be released are being kept secret to minimise disturbance. The Swedish kites are being flown to Britain by the RAF and will arrive at Kinloss on Tuesday 13 June.

Richard Porter, RSPB's head of species protection said, "The reintroduction of bird species has been well studied, and in Britain it has been successfully tried with the white-tailed eagle. Swedish conservationists have agreed to supply young kites from their small but expanding population and the Welsh young will be birds that have hatched from artificially incubated eggs that would otherwise not have survived."

ends

For further information contact: …

Additional notes
1. The reintroduction of any species to Britain will only be supported by NCC and RSPB when strict criteria are satisfied. The red kite is rare and threatened in world terms and is one of the few bird species which meet these criteria. Both organisations consider it a conservation priority to help expand the population by introducing it back to its former breeding range.
2. Ten Swedish kites are being flown here and will spend five weeks in quarantine before their release.
3. In 1988, work by RSPB and NCC in Wales established that some of the many eggs which would not normally result in fledged kites could be incubated artificially. Young kites reared in this way can be used in this project without adversely affecting the size of the Welsh kite population.
4. The project to reintroduce the white-tailed eagle to Scotland was run jointly by NCC, RSPB and other wildlife bodies. It involved using young eagles from Norway which were flown over and released, just as the kites will be. In 1985, ten years after the start of the eagle project the first young were reared successfully in the wild and this success has been repeated each year since.

The Progress Report no 1, November 1989 reported, under "6. Public Relations":
6.1 Poisoning: It was agreed that steps should be taken to raise the public profile of this. Mr Walters-Davies informed the committee that MAFF was to start a publicity campaign against the illegal misuse of poisons, since it has a bearing on the conservation of kites. Dr Pienkowski and Dr Batten noted that poisoning of birds of prey generally was under active consideration by NCC's Advisory Committee on Birds. Any announcements on poisonings of kites should be fully coordinated between NCC and RSPB.
6.2 Sightings: A press release for requests of sightings was advised in England as well as informing bird clubs, regional RSPB and NCC offices. Any sightings in England to be directed to Chris Monk (Dr Pienkowski's assistant) at NCC Headquarters, Peterborough. Sightings in Scotland to be directed to Mr Dennis. Mr Elliott agreed to draft a press release and send to Dr Pienkowski. Dr Evans to contact local bird clubs, etc.
6.3 RSPB Film: The film unit based at Sandy is currently preparing to make a film about the red kite. The joint nature of both work in Wales and the reintroductions project was stressed and should be noted by the film-makers. Mr Porter confirmed that a script would be made available for comment by NCC.
6.4 Kite Fact Sheet: The need for an information leaflet, consisting of a sketch (possibly supplied by Dee Doody) with text, to be given to the general public to aid identification and possibly increase sightings was agreed.

In 1990, our importation of kites from Spain on a regular passenger-carrying scheduled British Airways flight from Madrid to London Heathrow generated more public attention, especially as a journalist happened to be on the flight. A Sky News film crew interviewed me on arrival on the tarmac at Heathrow.

As we progressively established that a moderate number of people near the release did not give the kites any problem, we arranged for the press to be present, by prior arrangement, at releases on condition of confidentiality of the location of the release site. I am pleased to say that, to my knowledge, the press never breached this agreement. As we still tried to manage the numbers present as we gained experience, we sometimes asked the newspapers to provide us with their photographers' images for project use, to avoid having our own photographer present, which was again readily agreed.

In 1993, BBC television asked to film at one of the releases, and broadcast this on their Sunday *Countryfile* programme.

The first Chilterns release in 1989: NCC photographer Steve Moore organises his hide (left) **near the rearing cage** (right). **Beyond Steve is the hide of the RSPB film-makers, shown below after release from captivity.** [MP]

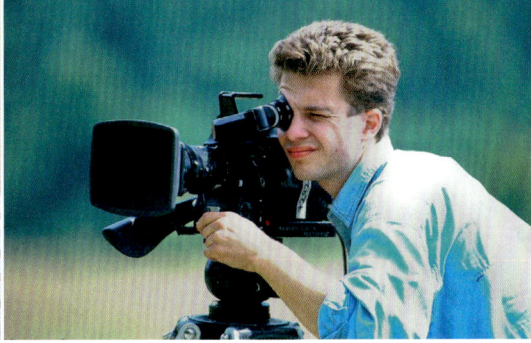

Our most ambitious release event was in 1994, the final year of releases in the Chilterns. We arranged to involve a Government Minister, Lord Arran, Parliamentary Under-Secretary of State for Environment, with wider press coverage – albeit still with the site-confidentiality in place. I was, however, aware that the circulation of papers within ministries is a huge issue, and the sensitivity of the information might not be understood by all the people seeing the message. Accordingly, I found myself waiting at a layby near a junction off the M40 motorway for a ministerial car. I had the impression that the Minister understood why I had not given directions to the site, rather than my comment "it will be easier to guide you" – even if some of his rather grumpy officials did not.

We arrived at the nearest point on the track that a car could reach to be met by the Land-Rover which was to have carried us the last half-mile to near the cages. It had its bonnet raised with my colleagues frantically trying to replace a broken fan-belt. The Minister, fortunately a countryman himself, asked how far it was and said, "Let's walk." So we did, and this provided a good opportunity to go over possible lines that he might like to use in his answers after he gave a prepared speech when he joined in releasing the birds. Some ideas he felt would not work well but others he was fortunately very happy with.

In sight of the cages, I gave a prepared explanation to the waiting press:

Minister, Ladies and Gentlemen,
On behalf of the Joint Nature Conservation Committee, I would like to welcome you to the joint JNCC/RSPB red kite experimental reintroduction project, and particularly welcome the Right Honourable Lord Arran, Parliamentary Under-Secretary of State for Environment, and the Earl of Cranbrook, the Chairman of English Nature. My name is Mike Pienkowski and I am Director Life Sciences for the JNCC (the Government's statutory advisor on nature conservation at national and international levels).

In a few minutes, I shall invite Lord Arran to join my colleagues in releasing some of the Red Kites. He will speak to us, and there will be a chance then for you to ask questions of both of us. First, I have been asked to give some background to what is becoming a major conservation success story.

Reintroduction projects are difficult. To succeed, they must be well planned and closely monitored. We need monitoring to know what happens; to adjust what we do; and to set standards for the future.
All reintroduction proposals should take into account a set of internationally agreed criteria. These include:
- *there should be a clear understanding of why the species was lost to the area;*
- *the factors causing extinction should have been rectified;*
- *there should be sufficient suitable habitats available; and*
- *the transfer of animals for reintroduction should not prejudice the survival of the source population.*

We should remember that it is even more important to prevent the loss of our native wildlife, rather than having to take heroic steps to reinstate parts of it. The Minister will tell us later about an initiative to help sustain the kites and other species.

We should only try to reintroduce species which are threatened and where natural recolonisation is unlikely.

You will recognise that, having been trained as a scientist, I put all the provisos in first; now to the more interesting bit.

Seven years ago, I chaired a group of colleagues from the statutory conservation bodies and RSPB to consider the feasibility of re-establishing Red Kites. We decided that we should try. This was not just because kites are highly attractive birds whose re-establishment would enhance the countryside for all to enjoy. Their world range is small, and they are still declining in some parts. Therefore, re-establishment in Britain, if it could be achieved, would be a valuable contribution to conserving world biodiversity.

After two years of study and planning, we released the first imported Red Kites to England and Scotland 5 years ago. The birds have done even better than we dared to hope. In 1992, the project gained a major success when Red Kites bred successfully in the wild in England and Scotland for the first time in more than a century. And this year, for the first time, young kites hatched and reared in the wild, as a result of our reintroduction efforts, have themselves nested and raised young kites.

This is a good point to stress the partnerships on which this project depends. We are extremely grateful for the responsible international outlook of our conservation colleagues in Spain and Sweden in supplying birds. The RAF and British Airways have helped with transport, and the estates, farmers and keepers in this area – all of whom have to stay anonymous of course – have been immensely supportive. So have many others, including our friends in the statutory and voluntary conservation bodies, and in the Department.

Finally, I should say that the work needs to continue. We are investigating how best to help the kites re-establish themselves throughout more of the country, so that as many people as possible can see these magnificent birds as a spectacular, but normal, part of our countryside – as they should be.

Thank you for your attention. I invite the Minister to join Dr Ian Evans, our project officer, to go over to the aviaries and help release some of the birds imported from Spain this year. The kites are now fully grown and past their quarantine period. You will see that the aviaries are large enough for the birds to try out flying. But once the aviaries are open – and once they realise this – they will be making their first long flights. Our experience is that they are generally pretty good at this. However, like most young birds on their first solos, it takes them a bit of practice to get the hang of landing. Let's see.

Lord Arran then spoke:

Ladies and Gentlemen,
Welcome to this secret location "somewhere in southern England". You may ask why the secret? This is one of the release sites that is the focus of an important and exciting experiment undertaken by the Joint Nature Conservation Committee and the Royal Society for the Protectlon of Birds. They are finding out how to re-establish the Red Kite, one of Britain's rarest and most attractive birds. The sites are kept secret in the welfare interests of the birds.

Red Kites were once very common in Britain. The kites were so common in the Middle Ages that they scavenged city streets for refuse. Today they occupy only a minute fragment of their former range: a legacy of past human persecution. Red Kites are rare and vulnerable throughout their world range. By demonstrating how we can make Red Kites common again in Britain we are making an important contribution to the global conservation of this species; helping to safeguard a part of the world biodiversity.

The battle to save the Red Kite in Britain began at the beginning of this century when the entire British population consisted only a few pairs which survived in the remote hills of central Wales. The action undertaken in Wales has improved the conservation status of the species and has saved it from almost certain extinction in Britain. However, re-colonisation of former nesting areas in England and Scotland which still remain suitable for Red Kites is unlikely to occur naturally.

It is against this background, that the option of establishing additional population centres of Red Kites in England and Scotland was considered as the best means of enhancing the future of this threatened species. The Red Kite is one of only a few birds in Britain that are suitable for reintroduction, as determined against internationally agreed criteria. The decision to release Red Kites into the wild was taken after much careful thought. The methodology for establishing Red Kite populations was completely unknown. For this reason, JNCC and RSPB embarked upon this experimental reintroduction project in 1989.

As a result of this programme, Red Kites have been imported annually into Britain from Spain and Sweden, and after completing quarantine, have been released into the wild from this secret release site in southern England and from another in northern Scotland. The project achieved its first major success in 1992 when reintroduced birds bred successfully in the wild in England and Scotland for the first time in over a century. Today, the project is in its sixth year and I am delighted to announce that this year the kites have bred more successfully than we could have expected. Twenty-eight pairs have successfully reared 50 young in England and Scotland. This is a remarkable success story which is a credit to the efforts of JNCC and RSPB.

So much has been achieved in such a short time. The project has made an important contribution to the conservation and restoration of our natural heritage and has forged partnerships between voluntary bodies, statutory agencies, government and commercial companies as well as promoting international co-operation between conservationists in the UK, Spain and Sweden. Our thanks must go to the many landowners, farmers and gamekeepers who are contributing to the success of this project by their responsible and positive attitude.

We are releasing 10 young Red Kites here today, and a further 10 in the next few days, which will ensure that the breeding populations that are now firmly established will be able to expand and recolonise new areas, giving many people the opportunity to see these magnificent birds. Careful monitoring will continue as the experimental work is integrated operationally into a much wider recovery programme.

Despite all our hard work to conserve the Red Kite in this country, our efforts may be jeopardised by a small minority of people who persist in poisoning these birds illegally.

In the last two years alone, eleven Red Kites were poisoned. We know that a number of these were birds from the release programme. The illegal poisoning of Red Kites and other rare birds of prey continues and it is one of the reasons why these birds are not recolonising many parts of their traditional ranges.

It is not just birds of prey that are poisoned illegally. Hedgehogs [*Erinaceus europaeus*], deer, pet dogs and cats have been killed. In 1993 alone, some 275 wild animals and pets were killed by illegal poisoning.

Because of the number of animals being killed, the Government started the "stop illegal poisoning campaign" in 1991. The Campaign aims:
- to persuade the perpetrators to use legal control methods rather than abuse pesticides; and
- to encourage the public both to report suspected poisoning incidents and to respect legal control methods.

It is supported by a wide range of interest groups, including agricultural, agrochemical, conservation and gamekeeping organisations and the Police. Past campaign material has been directed at farmers, gamekeepers and the general public.

Today, I would like to announce the publication of a new leaflet which doubles as a poster. It has been designed with young people in mind but I hope it will appeal to the public at large. The leaflet describes the problem of illegal poisoning, and explains how everyone can help stamp out this practice by following our action plan:
- recognise a poisoning incident;
- protect the evidence and ensure safety;
- report the incident;
- respect legal methods of pest control.

All incidents reported WILL be followed-up and, where necessary, appropriate action WILL be taken. Anyone convicted of illegal poisoning can be fined up to £5000 and in some cases can go to prison. There is a free phone number which can be used at any time to report a suspicious incident. This is 0800 321600 [still operational]. A word of caution, though. DON'T TOUCH a dead animal or suspected poisoned bait. It could be very dangerous. Leave it to the experts. Also,

A few examples of the great amount of coverage by UK and country newspapers during the project.

there are legal methods of pest control (such as cage traps for some pest birds). It is important not to interfere with them because it may only encourage illegal methods which are far more dangerous and cruel.

Together with the leaflet, we are launching four new, free postcards showing examples of wildlife and pets at risk from illegal poisoning. Stocks of these can be obtained from my Department [of Environment] and MAFF [Ministry of Agriculture, Fisheries and Food].

Encouragingly, there are signs of a decline in the number of illegal poisoning incidents since the start of the campaign in 1991, but we cannot afford to be complacent – illegal poisoning is still a major threat to wildlife and pets.

The summer holidays are upon us with millions of people visiting the countryside on day trips and holidays. We must be vigilant and help stamp out illegal poisoning by following the action plan and reporting incidents on the freephone number. If we can stop this illegal poisoning, we may one day all have a chance to see the beauty of the kites as they wheel and soar in our skies.

The information pack provided further information on all, and much national news media coverage followed.

Many TV and radio programmes featured the experimental project once we made it public. In 1997, BBC's *Blue Peter*, the famous children's television programme, featured the Red Kite Reintroduction Project in southern England. As one of the UK's most successful and high profile conservation stories, the project continued to attract considerable media coverage, including regular pieces on radio and TV even after releases ended at the original sites.

And perhaps the ultimate in entering public awareness, a Red Kite featured in "Roger the Dodger" in the famous and long-lived children's comic *Beano*, Issue 2754 on 29th April 1995! Jonathan Spencer told me that in 2020 he saw some graffiti in London of a Red Kite, while on his way to an international meeting on captive breeding and reintroductions! They are firmly part of popular culture now.

Poisoning

The background to the then situation with wildlife poisoning was set out in one of the earliest *JNCC Vertebrate Notes* (the successor to NCC's *Ornithology Notes*). A few of the key points include:

Illegal poisoning incidents involve birds, wild mammals such as Foxes and Badgers Meles meles, *and animals such as cats and dogs. Protected wildlife may be the intended target of poisoned baits or it may be the victim of illegal baits aimed at killing Crows* Corvus corone, *Magpies or Foxes which are often perceived as pests by farmers and gamekeepers and which can be legally killed using other methods. The laying of poisoned baits such as rabbit carcasses and injected eggs also threatens the lives of humans; one gamekeeper has died as a result of this practice. It is illegal to poison any wild bird species. It is also illegal to lay poisoned baits for other wildlife, except to poison invertebrate pests and rats and mice. Poisons laid for rodent pests however must be inaccessible to other wildlife.*

Birds of prey are among the most vulnerable species. Two globally threatened bird species, the Red Kite and White-tailed Eagle have also been affected. 25 Red Kites were poisoned between 1979 and 1990 and the species continued to fall victim to this type of persecution (Cadbury 1992, Fletcher et al. 1991, 1992). A Government campaign to raise awareness and encourage reporting of illegal poisoning incidents had the support of a wide range of shooting, farming and other countryside and nature conservation organisations.

Reported incidents probably represented the tip of the iceberg, while only a fraction of those reported result in successful prosecutions because of the difficulty in obtaining sufficient evidence. However, the campaign had some successes. The National Pesticides Retrieval Scheme, organised by the British Agrochemicals Association during 1991, allowed farmers and gamekeepers to safely dispose of unwanted and illegal pesticides which could potentially have been used to poison

Kite C of the first year of releases was poisoned illegally when it dispersed into the Welsh borders, which had so long been a barrier to the spread of kites and buzzards from Wales into England. It was the first of too many of the released birds to be poisoned. However, the publicity of these events probably helped change attitudes and reduce such illegal activity. [TC]

wildlife. Around 6,000 individuals surrendered unwanted pesticides with some 300,000 litres of product being collected. Between March 1991 and the end of 1992 there were 13 prosecutions in Britain, compared with just 14 in the preceding five years.

As I noted earlier, most gamekeepers and farmers were law-abiding, and I quoted earlier (Chapter 8) the generous published letter from the head keeper at the estate of our first English rearing and release site. Similarly, in the second release year, 1990, BASC (the British Association for Shooting and Conservation) issued a statement:

Keepers support for red kites

Earlier this year at the Gamekeepers' Day over 100 gamekeepers lent their support to the NCC and RSPB's initiative to reintroduce Red Kites in Britain. Twenty of these birds have recently been flown in from Sweden and together with eleven from Spain and two from Wales, they will be released shortly at locations in England and Scotland.

"Red Kites are very restricted in their range in Britain and this initiative to release birds into other areas is an important piece of positive conservation work" said Peter Fox, BASC's Head of Conservation.

Last year eleven Red Kites from Sweden were released but within six months two of these birds where found poisoned. "The issue of persecution of birds of prey continues to divide the shooting and conservation world and all of us working for wildlife conservation should strive to eradicate this practice.

"One of the main aims of the BASC is to foster a better understanding between conservationists and sportsmen and is well placed to attempt to find long term solutions to benefit both," he added.

In the aftermath of the misfortune of losing to poisoning in their first few months at least 2 (18%) of the 11 individuals reintroduced in the first year (1989), we were very fortunate in our secondary aim of changing public attitudes to illegal poisoning.

These cases (and those which followed) generated huge public and press outrage. For some (slightly illogical but understandable) reason, the public felt that poisoning birds which were part of a reintroduction exercise was even worse than poisoning birds here naturally. I suppose that this is because they recognised the reintroduction as an attempt to put right what previous humans had put wrong, and that interfering with this was doubly wrong. In addition, these birds have a presence and support. They have a link to people's aspirations, either directly or via the press coverage. Reducing persecution at large must be one of the most tangible benefits of reintroductions. The birds or mammals become persons in the public mind – so the impact is even greater should they be poisoned or shot.

In a few cases, it seems that some kite deaths resulted from incredibly ill-informed attempts to help the kites. A researcher investigating a high incidence of poisoning cases near one release area interviewed farm-workers where rats were being poisoned legally. One worker clearly did not understand the underlying reasons for the requirement to bury poisoned rats. He proudly announced that, instead, he threw the dead rats on to the flat roof of a shed – because he wanted to help the kites by supplying extra food!

Without a doubt, whilst illegal poisoning continues, looking back over more than 30 years, it is at a much lower level now and an even larger majority of game-keepers, farmers and land-owners are opposed to it, and the general public find it a loathsome practice. This has had beneficial outcomes (see Chapter 12). Whilst we cannot prove that the Experimental Red Kite Reintroduction Project made a major contribution to this, it does seem highly likely.

11. From experimental success to operational delivery

In the pre-planning stages of the Kite programme, we had noted that releases of White-tailed Eagles had been spread over a decade but that the progress to establishment had been very slow. As the plans for Red Kites developed we hoped to achieve more progress in a shorter time, because:
- Red Kites tend to mature at far younger age than the eagles;
- we planned to release them in more productive areas; and
- we considered that rearing and releasing a similar number of young birds but over a much shorter period would be more likely to help the birds progress, partly for social interaction reasons.

Because of the many uncertainties and unknowns, we deliberately ran this as more of a military campaign than a military parade. We did not lay down firmly the duration of the experimental project. However, as matters evolved, we had in our minds something like 5 or 6 years of releases (depending partly on the availability of young birds to release between 80 and 100 at each site), followed by a year or two of continued monitoring, putting the end of the experimental project in the mid-1990s, the releases having started in 1989.

The challenge of the Government's destruction of the Nature Conservancy Council

There were major organisational changes in the UK statutory nature conservation bodies during our project, from which we did our best to shelter the project.

The trigger that set the UK Government off on that attack on nature conservation was the issue of the peatlands of Caithness and Sutherland, the Flow Country in the far north of the Scottish mainland. These were described accurately as the last remaining essentially natural terrestrial ecosystem in UK, the UK's equivalent of the Amazonian rain-forest. This has become even more evident more recently, as healthy peatbogs have been shown to bind even more carbon than do forests. To today's reader, it may be inconceivable that the UK Government was subsidising the destruction of this invaluable ecosystem for no public benefit but the further enrichment of rich people via tax breaks and creative accounting – but that was certainly the case.

In the 1970s, the Government's Forestry Commission had assured the Nature Conservancy Council that afforestation of the Flow Country would be technically impossible for the foreseeable future. However, in the late 1970s and early 1980s, new techniques allowed deep ploughing of peat for tree planting, and the Forestry Act and tax laws allowed huge profits to be made, whether or not the trees grew. Very soon, these peatlands (and others across UK) were being rapidly destroyed, mainly by deep ploughing and draining so that exotic conifers could be planted. Although most of these would not grow to produce a timber crop, a few private forestry companies could legally operate the Government's Foresty Commission subsidies and tax-breaks so that this became a hugely profitable investment for rich people, many of whom probably believed that they were doing something good for the environment. The four of us scientific conservationists in NCC who led on the issue were at last able to be more open about this case in a memorial volume to our Chief Scientist, Dr Derek Ratcliffe, who had championed our work (Stroud *et al*. 2015). Our chapter was entitled: *The Flow Country: battles fought, war won, organisation lost.*

The Nature Conservancy Council had the statutory right to disagree publicly with Government, although it was obviously reluctant to do so, because its governing Council members were appointed by Government and its funding provided by the Treasury via a Government Ministry. So, as the issue developed in the 1980s, NCC officers, as well as undertaking scientific surveys and study, initially used internal government channels to warn about the issue and recommended

Subsidised destruction of UK's last natural terrestrial ecosystem: aerial views of parts of the Flow Country [MP]:

1. Highly productive patterned natural bogs, locking up carbon even faster than tropical forests

2. Poorly growing plantations of monoculture exotic conifers beyond, with new deep ploughing in the foreground surrounding the bog-system

3. Poorly growing plantations of monoculture exotic conifers surround the last remnants of a natural bog and disrupt its hydrology.

4. Bog destroyed by deep ploughing. Not only does this destroy the native wildlife but it stops carbon-capture and adds to the problem by releasing the previously locked carbon back to the atmosphere.

strongly a change of course. These even included a meeting in September 1986 between NCC's Chairman, Sir William Wilkinson, and the then Secretary of State for the Environment, Rt Hon Nicholas Ridley MP. However, this process got nowhere, and Government published in mid-1986 a report on future afforestation in the Flow Country.

An extra challenge was that the top staff (but not the ones on the ground) of the Scottish directorate of the Nature Conservancy Council were, at the time, one of the remaining strongholds of the feudal landowner supporting elements of the old Scottish establishment. Remember that this was years before devolution, and the Scottish directorate was answerable to Council but frequently took an anti-conservation line. At the time, the overall Scottish administration was a department of the UK Government, the Scottish Office.

Eventually, at the request of the NCC Chief Scientist, Dr Derek Ratcliffe with the support of the Chairman, the four us who led the scientific cases (and authored the then draft *Birds, Bogs and Forestry*) presented the case to a joint session of NCC's Governing Council and that of the Countryside Commission for Scotland, at Battleby, Perthshire, on the 14th October 1986. After the presentation to the Councils of both organisations, the members of CCS withdrew, to allow NCC to discuss its course of action. As they left, CCS Council commented that they had missed this issue and the chance to take their own action, but that they hoped NCC would not miss it. A rather tense debate followed with the Scottish hierarchy of NCC fighting a strong rearguard action resisting a crucial conservation initiative. Council, under the inspired leadership of former banker (when there were still many respectable ones), Sir William Wilkinson, over-ruled this and decided to go public by publishing our document once it had been finalised (Stroud *et al.* 1987).

We circulated a draft widely for peer-review in November 1986, and met regional colleagues in Inverness that month for another strategy meeting.

In December, our long-term questioning of the supposed economics of forestry was supported by the National Audit Office which, in its normal, understated – but absolutely damning – review, questioned the economic justification of investing further public funds in afforestation in northern Scotland (NAO 1986) and the Forestry Commission's accounting systems.

On 23rd June 1987, we published *Birds, Bogs and Forestry*. The authors wanted to launch it near the area concerned, in Wick or perhaps Inverness or Edinburgh. However, the Scottish hierarchy, still resisting its governing Council decision and stung by the decision to publish the report, refused to host the launch in Scotland, so London it was – giving rise to the main criticism of the book by its opponents in the press: that it was not launched in Scotland!

On 23rd February 1988, amid a continuing barrage of press, radio and television protest about the destruction of the Flow Country, the Secretary of State for Scotland, Rt Hon. Malcolm Rifkind MP, announced protection of half the remaining peatlands of Caithness and Sutherland. On 15th March, Chancellor of the Exchequer, the Rt Hon Nigel Lawson MP, announced changes in the tax regime relating to afforestation. In May, our second full scientific report, *The Flow Country* (Lindsay *et al.* 1988), was published, concentrating on the vegetation and ecology itself, rather than its imminent destruction

We followed up with many meetings with the Scottish Office, the Highlands Regional Council and others, usually having to listen to the senior NCC Scotland officials starting off with the words *"I am directed by my Council to…"*, thereby making it clear that they disagreed with what they were saying, and we then had to try to recover the ground throughout the rest of the meeting. On one occasion, the Chief Scientist of the Department of the Environment, who was present, had to remind the Scottish Office that the NCC was the statutory advisor to both, as the Scottish Office had fielded another scientist clearly retained by them to try to undermine our scientific evidence and that of our allies in the conservation NGOs, such as the RSPB.

However, the corner had been turned. In November 1988, local councils and the Scottish Office set up working parties on a new land-use strategy. And NCC set up a Caithness and Sutherland Peatlands Project Team, based in the region.

The Scottish Office officials (to whom the Scottish NCC top officials had attached themselves) hated the NCC as a whole, and the Chief Scientist Directorate in particular, for saving the Flow Country. They persuaded the then Secretary of State for Scotland to press to split the NCC into separate, independent country bodies (years before devolution, so that the complicated situation would arise that three different bodies would then be advising the one government in Westminster). One of the arguments they used was that the legislation would be simple and quick to pass. In fact, it was one of the longest periods of debates ever, with strong opposition from the House of Lords and almost every conservation NGO and many scientific bodies in the country. The Scottish Secretary persuaded the Environment Secretary to go along with this – which was probably not difficult as the late Nicholas Ridley was one of the strangest of appointments in Mrs Thatcher's administration. He fundamentally opposed regulation – which was by far the biggest role of the then Department of the Environment.

The decisions were made without any consultation with NCC itself, and NCC's Chairman was advised by message carried by a government despatch rider (which I had not known still existed). By coincidence, this news came in just as we were completing a meeting of NCC's Advisory Committee on Birds. On 11th July 1989, the Government announced the breakup of the Nature Conservancy Council. In its place three separate organisations were to arise, covering England, Scotland and Wales.

I reflected later that the UK government normally disrupted its own nature conservation agency every 8 years. Like the National Health Service and the National Parks, such an agency was one of the ideas developed by government committees and advisors in the darkest days of the 2nd World War, to make Britain a better place after the war, and to be put into action in the years immediately following its conclusion. So, the Nature Conservancy came into being in 1949 under the aegis of the Privy Council. (The UK Nature Conservancy pre-dated the unrelated US NGO of the same name by two years.) As far as I know (I was only 6), no major change was imposed after the first 8 years in 1957. However, 8 years later in 1965, it was placed in the Natural Environment Research Council, but as a semi-separate body which NERC needed to maintain under statute. This was a fairly crazy arrangement, as it put the national conservation function under a body devoted to research. As the Nature Conservancy was widely regarded as a successful body, both the government departments for science and for the environment wanted to claim it. This resulted (after the rapidly developing tradition of disruption every 8 years) in the 1973 Nature Conservancy Council Act, which split the Nature Conservancy in two, into a research arm staying in NERC as the Institute for Terrestrial Ecology (which many years later NERC merged with its Institute of Hydrology to make the Centre for Ecology and Hydrology, which it is now in the process of privatising). The conservation arm of the NC became the Nature Conservancy Council, an independent agency of the Department of the Environment. (By chance, I was affected a little by this. As a recent graduate in 1972, I had a short-term research contract which was issued by NC but my report had to go to ITE.) Eight years later, in 1981, the entire work of NCC was disrupted yet again by the poorly conceived 1981 Wildlife and Countryside Act. And again, 8 years later to the decision to break up NCC, with the emergence of English Nature (now Natural England), NCC for Scotland, a year later becoming Scottish Natural Heritage (now NatureScot) and the Countryside Council for Wales (now Natural Resources Wales). It sometimes surprises me that my colleagues were able to get so much achieved during this continual governmental disruption. The 8-year cycle broke down somewhat after 1989 as the cycle of disruption became more frequent but less regular.

Reorganising a government agency is a major disruption, wasting an immense amount of time and effort that could otherwise be devoted to its real purpose, in this case nature conservation. But that is what petty governmental spite can do – instead of wise governance. All sorts of work need to be diverted into this, rather than environmental and conservation action. As one almost trivial example, I recall having to apologise for not being able to add an interested member of the public to a circulation list for a category of publication, simply because updating the lists was one of the activities that top management had decided to cut, because of staff-redeployment!

In his Chairman's Review to the NCC's 15th Report (on 1st April 1988 to 31st March 1989), Sir William Wilkinson (1989) was able to report:

"A solution to the problems in the Flow Country appears to have been reached and it is pleasing that the Secretary of State has recognised the international importance of this area of Caithness and Sutherland. The report of the Highland Regional Council's working party provided a sensible working framework. Although we remain concerned that many fine areas of blanket bog remain under threat, at least the strategy will divert forestry away from the more sensitive zones. We are grateful to the Department for finding the additional resources necessary to help us implement the strategy and the necessary scientific work to support it."

However, he underlined at the start of his report:

"Last year in my review I struck an optimistic note. This year I am concerned that nature conservation generally faces great difficulties. The Government's proposal in particular to split NCC into separate organisations for England, Scotland and Wales, linking the last two with the Countryside Commissions in those countries, represents a serious threat to the nation's independent voice on nature conservation. As the changes are framed at present, I fear that the NCC's scientific competence, its standing as an independent adviser, both nationally and internationally, and its overall efficiency will be seriously reduced. I shall not dwell on the details of the proposed changes here since much water will have flowed under the bridge before this Report is published, but I do look, however, to the new Secretary of State and his team to recognise the dangers, to see that there is an inescapable need for a body with responsibilities for GB as a whole and also to ensure that Britain's

international standing in wildlife conservation is not lost and its responsibilities met in full. This is not just a self-interested plea for the status quo; *it is significant that virtually all of the voluntary organisations engaged in one aspect or other of nature conservation, distinguished scientists and conservationists, and representatives of many other interests have expressed their deep concern about the implications of the proposals as announced. I very much hope that at a time of unprecedented opportunity for nature conservation, with environment at the top of the political and public agendas, both here and in Europe as a whole, the Government will consider very carefully and ensure that the final results will bring substantial improvements for the delivery of nature conservation in all three countries of Great Britain, and possibly in Northern Ireland as well.*

"After a number of years of expansion in line with the growing public interest in conservation issues and increasing responsibilities, the NCC faces a significant reduction in resources and more cuts are scheduled to follow. Work programmes will have to be curtailed, including those for marine and urban nature conservation and staff numbers reduced to levels which will impair overall efficiency and ability to respond to problems at a time of ever increasing demands for our services. This is a matter for regret, though the dedication and professionalism of NCC's staff will, as always, disguise the full extent of the shortfall."

As usual, Sir William's analysis was very perceptive. His arguments, and much wider support, did at least generate a GB body to maintain standards, but it was subordinate to those whose standards it was supposed to maintain (see below). And, as William feared, the next 20 years saw a progressive decrease in the independence of the governmental conservation bodies. They immediately lost the right (and duty) to disagree publicly with Government and, in the following years, all but one of them lost the ability to comment independently on policy matters – a consequence, it seems, of progressive loss of competence and expertise by central government departments, and an increasing fear of openness and accountability.

Most of the very professional and committed NCC staff wanted desperately to keep the key work going while having to consider applying for jobs in the new structures. There would be separate bodies for England, Scotland and Wales. Northern Ireland had not been part of NCC but the body there had worked closely with it. At a late stage, as the legislation crawled its way through Parliament, it dawned on the politicians and senior officials that the single UK Government could not take advice on one topic from three separate bodies. Two paragraph numbers were left with no text initially, to allow space for some provision for some structure. This was eventually filled by a requirement being placed on the three country agencies to form the Joint Nature Conservation Committee (JNCC), with a governing council formed of 2 representatives from each, plus two from the Northern Ireland body, together with four independent senior scientists appointed by Government, one of these being the Chairman. Staff were to be on secondment from the country agencies, an arrangement that anyone with appropriate experience knew to be crazy, and something which had to be changed by further legislation several years later, though not before it had done serious damage.

An early consequence of the Government announcement was on my own work. Our deeply respected and experienced Chief Scientist had been nearing retirement. A recruitment exercise had been undertaken and a replacement appointed. However, in view of Derek Ratcliffe's huge experience, a quite exceptional overlap period of several months with his successor was arranged. This ended on 7th July 1989 when Derek retired – 4 days before UK Government announced the unanticipated break-up of NCC. The new Chief Scientist, Dr Peter Bridgewater, obviously saw little future in NCC's successor bodies, and quietly found himself another senior post in Australia (where he had previously worked) and left soon after. The NCC's Director-General then transferred the previous Assistant Chief Scientist (then Director of another division) into the Chief Scientist role and replaced him with one of the two Assistant Chief Scientists, creating a vacancy at that level.

I had no wish to leave as Head of Ornithology Branch and did not intend to apply to be Assistant Chief Scientist. However, several other Heads of Chief Scientist Directorate Branches urged me to do so, as one fairly new recruit heading one of the other branches clearly would do so, and several of us had serious doubts about that person's ability to fulfil the role. So, my application went in with some reluctance. So shortly before the first kite collection visit to Spain, I became one of NCC's two Assistant Chief Scientists. My colleague, Dr Keith Duff, was trained as a geologist, so the terrestrial biology branches came into my orbit – including mine, as it remained until we could appoint a replacement Head.

I had no wish to undermine my successor, appointed a few weeks later, and so made a point of referring to him any ornithological enquiries that still came to me. However, we had only just over a year to go before implementation of the new organisations, when there would be yet more changes of management. Consequently, for those projects that I had been managing directly, rather than delegated to one of my senior staff, I carefully considered the stage that they were at. One to keep was NCC's largest contract, with the British Trust for Ornithology, which was due for renewal and we were part way through complex but positive negotiations. Another was the Red Kite project, well advanced and of great personal interest. I decided to keep managing the kite project, continuing to enlist the help of several members of Ornithology Branch staff, particularly David Stroud who had already been heavily involved. We got the project through this major change without any negative impact.

NCC also received approval for a new post, Director of Reorganisation. This post and its staff were filled mainly by existing administrative staff, but with few, if any, of the scientific staff. They followed the classic route of commissioning consultants. I did not understand the obsession of bringing in people who know nothing of the work of an organisation, the qualities of the personnel involved, nor with any commitment to being present when the consequences of their recommendations become evident. Possibly it was an expression of the even greater incompetence of the people bringing in the consultants. I well recall the definition of consultant provided to me some years later by a very able and very eloquent Polish scientific civil servant when, in another role (not as a consultant!), I was working with her on the environmental possibilities in Poland joining the European Union: *"A consultant is someone brought in, at great expense using resources I could deploy much more usefully, to get in my way and tell me what I already knew."*

I am told (by my daughter – who is a management consultant specialising in change) that things have moved on since the 1980s and 1990s; I hope so! She tells me that, in the present competitive world, *"a good consultant is someone brought in to help guide or manage a situation that the organisation does not have the capability to address. The role of the consultant is to seek to understand (before being understood) the nature of the challenge and to devise and implement a strategy to resolve it, whilst making sure the recipients are receptive to the change. The good consultant leaves the organisation with the challenge completed and a clear plan for the customer to improve or build on the activity in the future. You know, a bit like how you did with the Red Kite project."*

I was in one of NCC's Scottish offices, I think advising the Flow Country team, when I took a phone call from the Reorganisation Director, asking me to act as Implementation Officer for JNCC. This was a role, supported by a couple of staff, to set up the structure and systems for the new body before governing councils or staff had been appointed. Several senior staff were involved in similar roles for all the new bodies. I did not really want a second job, especially as I was still carrying elements of the original Ornithology role as well as Assistant Chief Scientist. However, for various reasons (see below), it was important to maintain good relations with the Reorganisation Directorate. So, I accepted. Only one of the senior staff filling two jobs received two salaries – and it was certainly not me!

The Reorganisation Directorate was responsible for the allocation of existing and continuing work between the four successor bodies. At this time, with the kite importations just started, most non-scientific staff still associated kites with Wales, and we duly noted the proposed allocation of the Experimental Reintroduction Project to the new Countryside Council for Wales. This would, of course, have been disastrous as the Welsh staff were obviously concentrating on kite conservation in Wales. All the staff running the English project and supporting the Scottish project would have been detached from the project itself... and were certainly not planning to move to Wales. It took quite a lot of explanation and persuasion to get the allocation changed to JNCC, where it seemed that most of the staff experienced with this would be based. We would of course be working with regional colleagues in what would become English Nature.

A great deal of my time was needed to brief the newly appointed Chairman and then the new Chief Officer of JNCC, as well as recruiting and interviewing other potential JNCC staff, and liaising with the Department of the Environment (usually to little effect) to improve the legislation. I also had to sort out my own role: the fact that I was Implementation Officer did not guarantee a long-term role. There was one Director role under the JNCC Chief Officer, and I applied for that, but also for a couple of posts in the new English Nature. After interviews, I was offered a choice of the JNCC Director role and a role at equivalent rank in English Nature. I opted for the JNCC role as, otherwise, there would be no director-level post-occupant in JNCC from the NCC Chief Scientist Directorate, the nearest thing to its functional predecessor. My boss and now the designate Chief Executive of English Nature, Dr Derek Langslow, gave me the impression that this was some form of treason, or at least lunacy, on my part.

Priorities for the Chief Scientist Directorate in the last couple of years of NCC were to ensure completed projects were written up and published, continuing work and contracts were handed over in good order to successor bodies and morale was maintained. It is to the credit of the professionalism of NCC personnel at all levels, these were largely achieved.

The new bodies took over from NCC on 1st April 1991. At JNCC, as Director Life Sciences and Resources, I supervised the branches concerned with terrestrial conservation, as well as the administrative, financial and public awareness sections. We had not been allowed to appoint the other director post that had been planned, so the Chief Officer looked after the Earth Science, Marine and International branches. Fortunately, mobile phones had just come into common business use (although it was some years before they became toys for everyone); otherwise I would never have been able to leave the office, with only the Chief Officer and one director to manage all.

As I, and others, had warned Department of Environment officials, the three new country bodies did not like being forced by law to form a Joint Committee. However, the top officials in some of those new agencies now decided to take out their frustrations on the JNCC staff – who were, by law, their own staff. This was the worst and most destructive – and most pointless – sustained behaviour I have ever seen in a lifetime of public service. Nature conservation certainly did not benefit. In a reflective mode of dark humour, we noted the Inverse Size Rule. The smallest entity, our colleagues in Northern Ireland, were a dream to deal with. They were a tiny and under-resourced unit who valued our input. At the time, things were very difficult generally in Northern Ireland, and they were past masters at balancing matters in all sorts of dimensions. They were so welcoming that we held our first Annual Report launch there, attended by the Secretary of State for Northern Ireland and colleagues from the Republic, as the omens for hosting an amicable meeting from the GB countries were distinctly negative. Colleagues in the Countryside Council for Wales were generally pragmatic, and we did quite a lot of joint work contracted by them. The Nature Conservancy Council for Scotland (renamed after a year as Scottish Natural Heritage) were strained in their relations at top level. Partly this was due to a hang-over from the strong linkage of the heads of that organisation to Scottish Office officials. However, we could sometimes get NCCS/SNH to co-operate if they thought this would score points against English Nature. Even though English Nature was JNCC's majority shareholder and we made it clear that they were welcome to any credit for what we achieved (and our staff were working well with their scientific and regional staff), we could almost never get the top officials of English Nature to work in a collegiate way. This was noticed by senior Department of Environment officials, who tried to help, but the system that they had set up tended to thwart this. Relations with conservation NGOs in those early years were excellent, however, as they were with most working-level scientific staff in the country agencies; it was good to have some friends.

As a very welcome surprise present at my departure event in April 1995, my friends and colleagues at JNCC commissioned from Philip Snow (www.snowartandbooks.co.uk) these superb Red Kite Studies Britain & Europe 1980–1995. The tag on one kite reads "MP ONE".

Things did not need to be so antagonistic and aggressive. In the same period, I led for Great Britain in twice yearly meetings with the Republic of Ireland and Northern Ireland to coordinate conservation work across the island group as wildlife did not recognise the various boundaries. Despite the politically and sometimes violently troubled times, the group remained friendly, cooperative and effective throughout.

The negative attitude from the country agencies leaderships was manifest in JNCC's governing Committee itself, where they had the majority. Even when agreement was reached in the Committee, country representatives often tried later to renege on decisions. It reached the stage that half of each Committee meeting was taken up with arguments about the minutes of the previous one, feeding back the ill-feeling and distrust. After consulting JNCC's Chairman, the Earl of Selborne, I placed a very large and obvious recording machine (still tape then) at the centre of the Committee table. This stopped the ridiculous time-waste on the minutes. My staff did not change their minuting procedure; they continued to work from notes, rather than from the recordings (which is a horribly slow way of producing minutes), but the fact that the participants knew that we had their words on tape to back the minutes stopped the nonsense.

Whilst we did not mind being criticised for some of our conservation work being less successful than we hoped (a relatively rare event), we gained the distinct impression that we were criticised even more for getting things right – simply because our "owners" did not want JNCC and its staff to work successfully. This was essentially corporate abuse, and caused severe stress, which could have led to work failures. Several of our branch heads in the first years were the leading conservation ecologists in their fields, with worldwide reputations, people like Dr George Peterken of Woodlands, Dr Don Jefferies of Vertebrates and Terrestrial Pollution, Dr Pat Doody at Coastal Conservation, Dr Roger Mitchell and Dr Keith Hiscock at Marine, Dr Chris Newbold at Aquatic Pollution and Wetlands, Dr John Hopkins at Biotopes Conservation, Margaret Palmer at Species Conservation, Dr Tim Reed at Environmental Audit & Information Systems and the Seabirds Team with Mark Tasker. These distinguished persons, and newer branch-heads, including Dr Colin Galbraith at Ornithology & Landscape Ecology, would be abused by people on the Committee who knew far less about the topics than them. I took to briefing these colleagues to allow the comments to wash over them and I would sort out the situation later, so that they could get on with their important work. Thus I, and the Head of Administration who reported to me, spent a lot of our time being the buffers between some of those running some of the country agencies and our key professional specialists, so that the latter could get on with their conservation work. The lack of professionalism amongst some of the senior personnel in the country agencies was profoundly frustrating to those of us working hard to achieve our conservation goals – and, in some case caused more than frustration. During my four years as JNCC Director, three successive Heads of Administration were made seriously ill under the unreasonable pressures from the country agencies. I am grateful to them and feel somewhat guilty, although they had my unwavering support throughout and I was not the source of the stress. It was a dark time, but we managed to avoid it affecting the kite project (and much other work).

Management of the Experimental Red Kite Project

In this poisonous atmosphere, I recognised early that I could not spend as much time as earlier on the Red Kite project as I had hoped and, anyway, I had intended to start passing day-to-day management over as soon as JNCC staffing stabilised. I retained the chair of the Project Team, and visited the project when I could, as it was still within my overall responsibility and high profile. However, I handed much of the project over to the newly appointed Head of JNCC's Ornithology and Landscape Ecology Branch, Dr Colin Galbraith, who I had some years earlier recruited into NCC in my Ornithology Branch. He was supported by David Stroud, a long-term member of the former NCC Ornithology Branch, who had been involved in the Kite project from fairly early days. Dr Ian Evans remained as Project Officer, and the involvement of local former NCC, and now English Nature, regional staff remained strong.

Again, we managed to prevent the trauma of NCC's enforced and destructive reorganisation to impact negatively on the Red Kite project.

Progress by 1994–5

In spite of all the disruption, 1994–5 was a key year for both the kites and for me. This was about the scheduled end of the experimental project. It was also when (rather belatedly to my mind) the top managers of the country agencies realised that they could get me out of JNCC. After all, English Nature was theoretically my employer. They were required to offer me a post at equivalent grade in English Nature itself and tell me what the options were 6 months in advance. They totally failed in the latter requirement and, anyway, I was not very keen on going to work with people who had been trying to undermine my colleagues for the last few years. I quietly applied for a few senior posts in other conservation or science organisations and was in the running for three of these. I accepted one, and negotiated a secondment out of English Nature (which provided a better financial deal for the bodies concerned) and became Head of International Legislation and Funding at RSPB, and later the Director of the European Forum on Nature Conservation and Pastoralism, finally becoming Chairman of the UK Overseas Territories Conservation Forum.

Kites seem to generate a strong mobbing reaction in other birds, like a flock of Jackdaws *Corvus monedula* including this close one. However, these cause little trouble to the buoyant and manoeuvrable kites. [MP]

By 1995, The Experimental Reintroduction of the Red Kite to England and Scotland project had clearly been successful, with the following objectives achieved:

1. Obtaining an adequate supply of young birds from suitable source populations and transporting them safely to the release sites;
2. Successful rearing and release of Red Kites into the wild;
3. Survival through the post-fledging period (a time when they are still normally dependent on their parents) to independence;
4. Successful integration back into the wild and winter survival;
5. Demonstration that birds which have dispersed very widely can and will return to the release area even after an absence of several months;
6. Breeding successfully, and producing offspring that also breed successfully;
7. Establishing self-sustaining populations of Red Kites in England and Scotland.

It was clear that it was time to move from an experimental to an operational phase. With the success of the project, English Nature HQ were keen to take it over. We had full confidence in the English Nature regional colleagues with whom we had been working for some time, so we arranged in 1994–5 to transfer the programme in 1995 from JNCC to English Nature, with RSPB continuing their partnership role. My colleagues Colin Galbraith and David Stroud remained available to advise and Ian Evans remained involved. In addition, English Nature later appointed a new Project Officer, Ian Carter, who subsequently provided a first-hand account of this later operational phase (Carter 2001).

In Scotland, RSPB and SNH reached agreement in 1994 on the formation of a partnership for the monitoring of the released kites in Scotland, jointly funded by both bodies.

Kites do most of their foraging at low level, scanning the ground for carrion and small animals. This one in the Chilterns in November hunts over a field below the height of the field-boundary hedgerow behind. [MP]

Operational phase

Before I left, there was a key job in using the results of the Experimental Reintroduction to recommend future actions. My initial view, given that the re-established populations were clearly self-supporting and increasing, had been that we should leave them to spread, provided that we monitored and, if necessary later, stepped up protection or other measures. This was partly on the grounds of an 'elegance' of approach: stepping in enough to overcome human-made problems and then handing back to natural processes. It was also on the grounds of deployment of resources. Generally speaking, conservation resources spent on one project are not available to others – and there are always other high-priority needs waiting to be addressed.

In this context, I had always been aware, especially while Head of Ornithology Branch at NCC, that some other specialists regarded bird work with envy because of birds' public popularity. They were perceived as gaining disproportional resources, especially in the voluntary sector. I recognised the truth of that but argued that, rather than suppress this public interest, we should use bird conservation as a pioneer, leveraging public interest into other wildlife conservation activity. This should lead to more levelling up, rather than levelling down. I think that some of my colleagues in other specialisms began to see the benefits of that approach, and actions subsequently bore this out. Some are evident in the following chapter. Other examples include the spread of the sort of bird atlas and census work we commissioned from the British Trust for Ornithology to other taxa, the introduction of Important Plant Areas, modelled on Important Bird Areas, for example, and the progressive introduction, as data became available, of non-bird criteria into selection of Wetlands of International Importance under the Ramsar Convention. Indeed, the Parties to the Convention eventually dropped usage of the original last four words ("especially as Waterfowl Habitat"), leaving the working title as the "Ramsar Convention on Wetlands of International Importance." (Incidentally, Ramsar is the city in

Over to the next field… and behind the trees. The kites' low-level hunting technique means that, when they are not thermalling, they are often hidden or viewed just through trees. [MP]

Iran where the Convention was signed, not an abbreviation; so, only the initial R should be capitalised.)

With this background, I did not want the continuing Red Kite work to generate negative feelings amongst those working on the conservation of other wildlife. In fact, we had been so successful in securing voluntary support from NGOs, business and individuals that most continuing Red Kite conservation work did not depend on the public purse. During the Experimental Reintroduction project, the main cost to the public purse had been the cost of employing one project officer. The RSPB had met equivalent costs in Scotland and, as explained in earlier chapters, most other costs were donated. In fact, the real cost of even the one post to the public purse was more than offset by the voluntary unpaid overtime worked by most staff. We know this because one of the early innovations of Sir William when he became Chairman was to introduce time-recording (and relating this to the work being done), much to the disgust of staff. Sir William had recognised that NCC was hugely under-resourced and needed evidence. Admittedly, had the trained scientists been consulted by the administrators who implemented this, we could have designed a far more efficient sampling-based approach, rather than everyone counting all their time. Nevertheless, William soon proved the value by securing increased resources for nature conservation by using this evidence.

In the event, a few months before the announcement of NCC's end, the Government imposed a staff inspection on NCC. These exercises were not to investigate the performance of staff but the need for the posts that the staff fill. At least in the eyes of those being inspected, such staff inspections are viewed as one of Government's ways of cutting posts. In fact, most of NCC survived this inspection unscathed, and I managed to persuade the inspectors that all that Ornithology Branch did was needed by statute or Government policy, and my staff were working, on average, nearly twice the hours paid for. As a result, we were in the rare position of having the Treasury staff inspectors recommending two extra permanent posts for my Branch. We never got them, as reorganisation of the NCC intervened. Rather like Monty Python's view of the Spanish Inquisition, there was no escape from the negative aspects of staff inspection, it seems.

However, despite the disruption of the destruction of NCC, we managed to retain the enthusiasm of staff, at least in the first years. On many an occasion when I finished work in the evening at JNCC, I would walk around our offices to discover large numbers of our scientists and conservationists still at work long after hours. I had to encourage them to go home to their families.

My earlier thoughts about further releases were only provisional views and we needed evidence against which to assess options. Although numbers and breeding production were increasing rapidly, the rate of spread was rather slow. This was not totally surprising because, if you are a creature of a fairly stable habitat, the place most likely for successfully breeding is probably near where you yourself were successfully reared. So, Colin Galbraith and I asked Ian Evans to review the evidence relevant to future options. The need for such a review was agreed by the Project Team at its meeting on 12th April 1994.

Ian Evans (1994) reported that:

Published research indicates that the population of Red Kites in Wales is very philopatric, since mean dispersal distances between places of birth and first breeding are 7 km for males (range 1.0– 22.0 km) and 8 km for females (range 0.5–32.5 km). In England, mean dispersal distance between the point of release and first successful breeding for the released birds is 2.12 km for both males and females (range 0.58–5.83 km), although this should increase as more and more territories become occupied. One pair did attempt to breed in their first-year at 45.8 km from the point of release, but subsequently moved to only 5.83 km from the point of release and bred successfully in their second year. Another first year pair occupied a territory 53.2 km from the point of release but breeding was not attempted as the female was probably poisoned. In the following year the male found a new mate and bred successfully at only 2.08 km from the point of release. For this reason, I anticipate that, by 1996, the nucleus breeding population now establishing in England will still remain within 50 km of the current point of release. However, if this population increases two-fold between 1996 and 1999, then areas greater than 50 km from the point of release should begin to be recolonised.

Ian set out various options, and concluded:

Based on current estimates, it seems most appropriate to establish a new release site between 80–140km from the current point. This would mean that a new site would be located either in Wiltshire, Midlands (Northamptonshire/Leicestershire) or East Anglia (Norfolk/Suffolk border). The release scheme should ideally release 60–80 birds or 20 annually for a 3–4 year period, i.e. from 1994–1996/7. Full breeding potential would be reached by 2000. By analysing the performance of the two established population centres we should be able to judge optimum distances where release points should be placed. We could then advise other organisations/individuals to set-up their own red kite release schemes based on our recommendations and guidance.

Juvenile Red Kites, until their moult at about 1-year-old, have duller upper plumage than adults, white patches among the red-brown on the belly, more dark markings on the head and, very distinctively, white tips to the greater upper wing covert feathers, giving a white band at the forward edge of the dark flight feathers. [MP]

Colin and I concurred with Ian's conclusions, and I favoured the Midlands site, because it allowed far greater potential for spread throughout Great Britain. However, as we were about to pass the operational lead to the country agencies, it would not be our decision; we could only advise.

We recognised, however, that the top personnel in the country agencies were keen to undertake further work on Red Kites, so as to associate their new organisations with what was by now perceived as a highly successful and popular project. We wanted to ensure that the best use of this was made for effective conservation.

As the various related studies that we had undertaken or commissioned to assess the project and provide a scientific basis for future actions came to at least preliminary conclusions, we were confirmed in our view that the first two sites were self-supporting. Our colleagues in Scotland had decided not to release more kites in 1994 and we decided that the releases at the first English site would end in 1994, taking the total number of releases at each site to about (or, as it turned out, exactly) the same, 93 kites in each.

With this further input, Ian, Colin and I revised Ian's draft to prepare a paper for the Project Team and consulted members on various aspects. We took out the specific area recommendations, as we thought it better to allow discussion towards the logical conclusion. We supplied members of the Team the revised paper to start considering well before the meeting itself:

REINTRODUCTION OF RED KITES TO ENGLAND AND SCOTLAND: FUTURE OPTIONS

This discussion paper considers the objectives of red kite conservation action in the UK and, in the light of these, assesses options for future red kite work. Operational aspects of potential future reintroduction work are outlined for discussion.

OBJECTIVES FOR CONSERVATION ACTION OF RED KITES IN THE UK

The objectives of the UK action plan for the red kite, as agreed by the action plan process with RSPB and the statutory conservation organisations in September 1991, are:
1. In the short term, to maintain the annual red kite population increase at more than 5% per annum which should result in 100 breeding pairs by 1997.
2. In the long term to see the red kite re-established throughout its former range in the United Kingdom.

To assist in achieving these objectives, a joint (J)NCC/RSPB experimental reintroduction project was initiated in 1989 to determine if and how red kite population centres could be established in former areas of the red kite's range in the UK. Objective 1 was achieved ahead of schedule, since the red kite population in Wales achieved a mean annual rate increase of 10% between 1991–1993 and as a result there were 102 breeding pairs in 1993. In addition, a further 14 pairs were established by the joint (J)NCC/RSPB experimental reintroduction project in England (9 pairs) and Scotland (5 pairs). These populations increased again in 1994 to 106 breeding pairs (producing 98 young) in Wales, 20 pairs (producing 37 young) in England and 8 pairs (producing 13 young) in Scotland. The present UK breeding population is 134 pairs.

Kite departs from a winter roost, leaving one of its fellows. [MP]

Objective 2 remains to be achieved. The BTO atlas data demonstrated that in 1991, breeding occurred in 45 10-km squares in Wales, an increase of 26 10-km squares since the previous atlas in 1976. In England and Scotland, less than 10 10-km squares are currently occupied by breeding pairs, hence the current breeding range (1994) in the UK is unlikely to be greater than 60 10-km squares. Making an arbitrary assumption that 50% of the 2800 10-km squares in Britain are suitable for breeding (which is less than the number of squares occupied currently by the buzzard), then only 4% of, what might be, the potential breeding range in Britain is currently occupied.

It is important to note that, as population density varies from one area to the next, increases in UK population size may not result in the same proportional increase in UK population range. In addition, optimum breeding densities in each 10-km square are achieved by colonisation and infilling over a period of several years. It will be difficult therefore to predict future population range size and distribution from current breeding parameters.

REVISED OBJECTIVES
The Red Kite Action Plan is due to be reviewed in 1995 and a set of revised objectives need to be agreed. It is recommended that the new objectives are as follows:
1. In the short term, ensure that the UK red kite population exceeds 325 breeding pairs by the year 2000.
2. To ensure that, by 2020, the range of the red kite becomes linked with Wales and England, and England and Scotland.
3. In the long term, ensure that the red kite population colonise all suitable habitats in the UK.

FUTURE OPTIONS FOR THE EXPERIMENTAL RED KITE REINTRODUCTION PROJECT IN THE UK
This section assesses three options for consideration taking into account the biological objectives outlined above. This assessment assumes that:
- A mean growth rate of population size in Wales is maintained at 10% per annum.
- The existing breeding populations in England and Scotland are self-sustaining and are able to increase without the need for further releases at release sites used during 1989–1994.
- A mean first breeding age of 2 years and mean productivity of 1.5 young/breeding pair for released populations in England and Scotland.
- No colonisation of areas greater than 50km from existing release sites before the year 2000.
- Releasing ~100 juvenile red kites over a 5-year period will produce between 15–40 pairs over a 7–8 year period (an extra 2–3 years is required for released birds to enter breeding population).
- A population of 100 pairs will occupy about 40 10km squares or an area of 35km radius assuming a circular and even expansion.

OPTION 1: do no more releases
Based on current population growth rates, if further releases are suspended, a maximum of 190 breeding pairs in Wales (assuming that 10% annual increase is sustained), 90 breeding pairs in England and 25 breeding pairs in Scotland could be attained by 2000.

Problems:
1. One or both of the existing translocated populations may not be fully self-sustaining and may progressively decline leading to the experimental reintroduction project to be judged as largely wasted effort.
2. Population targets in either England or Scotland, or both, will not be achieved.
3. If the established translocated populations decline, then the causal factors need to be identified and rectified in order to prevent further declines. Consequently, the need for further releases cannot be ruled out in the future.
4. Population in Wales may stabilise or decline.
5. Total population will remain vulnerable to unforeseen events
6. Lose links to source populations in Spain and Sweden.

Benefit:
1. Saves money and effort.

OPTION 2: continue releases at the existing release sites
By 2000: up to 190 breeding pairs in Wales (assuming that 10% annual increase is sustained). If translocations continue in 1995–2000 at existing sites, then a maximum of 110 breeding pairs in England and 45 breeding pairs in Scotland (based on current population growth rates) could be attained.

Pair of kites in the Chilterns explore potential nesting areas in February. [MP]

Problems:
1. Will incur financial commitment.
2. Will waste valuable resources if established populations are self-sustaining and able to expand by themselves.
3. Will not achieve objective 2 within the specified time scale.

Benefit:
1. Maximises the success of the existing release sites.

OPTION 3: commence releases at one or more new sites
By 2000: a maximum of 190 breeding pairs in Wales (assuming that 10% annual increase is sustained). If further reintroductions are initiated at two new sites between 1995–1996 in England and Scotland, at least 100km from existing release sites (to encourage natural linkage of populations since maximum distance from place of birth to first breeding is 50km), then up to 110 pairs in England and 45 pairs in Scotland could be attained in a total of four population centres.

Six of a larger group of kites in the Chilterns thermal above a roost and feeding area in November. [MP]

Problems:
1. Will incur similar financial commitment as Option 2 once new release sites are established.
2. New sites may not be successful or may require more time (and birds) to establish self-sustaining and expanding populations than existing sites.

Benefits:
1. Will maintain programme continuity with conservationists in Spain and Sweden, and others providing logistical support to the project.
2. Will enable achievement of objective 2.

RECOMMENDATION FOR FUTURE ACTION ON RED KITE REINTRODUCTIONS IN THE UK
The following section recommends the action on red kite reintroduction judged most likely to achieve red kite population objectives within the time scale proposed in the revised objectives above.

Reintroductions
- Option 3 above is considered to be the only option likely to enable the achievement of the revised objectives proposed above, within the time scale specified by objectives 1 and 2.

- Implementation of option 3 relies on the establishment of at least two [further]release sites, one in England and one in Scotland by 1996. No change in the existing methodology for establishing population centres is proposed. It is assumed that the population centres now established in England and Scotland are self-sustaining and able to expand without the need for further releases. However, if the populations begin to decline, appropriate remedial action will be undertaken.
- Operational aspects of future releases need to be agreed by the Project Team and should include:
  (a) Criteria for release site selection.
  (b) Source of release stock to be used (e.g. continue with translocations from the continent, undertake nest manipulation or captive breeding options).
  (c) Criteria for establishing when translocated populations are self-sustaining.
- This action should be undertaken by a consortium of JNCC/RSPB/EN/SNH. The Project Team should consider options for taking this forward.

Monitoring

An effective UK monitoring strategy must be agreed between JNCC, RSPB, EN, SNH and CCW in advance of any further releases. This needs to:
- Develop compatible methods of data collection, storage, analysis and dissemination.
- Agree on a clear division of labour between JNCC, RSPB, EN, SNH and CCW.
- Agree on the level of involvement by volunteers and other organisations.
- Agree threshold population levels when funding for full annual coverage of breeding pairs is replaced by sample monitoring.
- Develop appropriate monitoring techniques to further the conservation of red kites in the UK.

Public affairs strategy

A UK public affairs strategy must be agreed between JNCC, RSPB, EN, SNH and CCW in advance of any further releases. This needs to:
- Agree the extent to which release sites and breeding areas/localities should be kept confidential.

Red Kite in Chilterns in November [MP]

- Agree a procedure on press releases and other media opportunities.
- Determine what audiences need to be targeted and define what supporting material is required, e.g. leaflets, videos, TV and radio programmes, newsletters.
- Agree criteria under which it might be appropriate to set up public viewing schemes.
- Agree strategy for managing birdwatcher pressure to protect the birds and the goodwill of local people.
- Define a clear division of labour between JNCC, RSPB, EN, SNH and CCW.
- Promote the red kite as a flagship, especially in relation to illegal poisoning and public image of raptors.

Nest Protection
A nest protection strategy must be agreed between JNCC, RSPB, EN, SNH and CCW. This needs to:
- Define criteria which must be met to justify actions to protect red kite nests from human threat.
- Consider division of labour including the role of volunteers in any nest protection work.

Funding
This has yet to be agreed by JNCC, RSPB, EN, SNH and CCW.

The paper by Ian, Colin and myself was considered at the Red Kite Project Team meeting at JNCC's Peterborough HQ on 10th November 1994. This was, in fact, the last formal meeting of the Team, as the Experimental Project would be ending in 1995, and we needed to make clear recommendations for the operational phase. The Project Team itself would continue into 1995, to follow up action points from the meeting, wrap up the Experimental project, and hand over smoothly to continuing operational elements.

The minutes of the meeting record (in part):

6 & 8. Discuss future action for 1995–1999 and discuss mechanisms for reviewing UK Red Kite Action Plan
A future options paper was circulated to the Project Team before the meeting and a further copy is attached with these minutes.
The Project Team decided that the following revised objectives should be incorporated into the UK action plan. These objectives are:
- *In the long term, ensure that the red kite breeding population occupies all suitable habitats in the UK.*
- *By the year 2000, ensure that there are at least 5 expanding population centres of red kites, at a minimum distance of 100km apart, totalling at least 350 breeding pairs, in the UK.*

The Project Team recognised that population genetics need to be considered. The Welsh population is known to be inbred, whereas Spanish and German populations are highly heterozygous. The Swedish population had been through a genetic bottle neck as a result of heavy persecution in the last century and was not as genetically diverse as the Spanish and German populations. In addition, the objectives of the reintroduction need to take account of both numbers and range, since action which achieved the widest and contiguous range provided the best means of safeguarding red kites in both UK and global terms. It was recommended that range should be expressed in terms of population centres rather than numbers of 10-km squares occupied as this would avoid setting numerical targets. In terms of cost it was pointed out that a vast amount of financial and human resources had been expended in safeguarding one natural population centre in the UK which still remains extremely vulnerable. The current experimental work was undertaken partly to ease this pressure by developing a technique to establish other population centres and thereby reduce the overall resource commitment for red kites in the long term.

The Project Team judged that Option 3, from the discussion paper, was the most appropriate action to achieve objectives 1 and 2 and recommended that 2 new population centres should be established in the UK between 1995 and 2000 to promote linkage between existing breeding populations in England, Scotland and Wales. Further releases at existing release sites are to be suspended but it is essential to continue monitoring the established breeding populations in order to assess progress, and fulfil the remit of this experimental project in standard setting. The Project Team recognised that it was crucial to maintain continuity in both human resources and source of birds. For this reason, a new release site should be established in England in 1995 with the intention of releasing 20 birds per year for 5 years. Mark Avery saw JNCC involvement as very important as it could utilise its contacts in Spain to secure a further supply of birds.

Action: JNCC to maintain contacts and organise supply of red kites from Spain.

Ian Evans suggested that a new site should be at least 100km from the existing population centre in England either to the north or south-west. The distance was based on the fact that the maximum distance red kites have nested from the current release site is 50km. Hence two populations 100km apart are more likely to become linked within a reasonable time scale. Releasing red kites near the south coast may prove problematical as birds may be more likely to disperse to the continent and hence would be difficult to monitor. The Project Team agreed with Ian Newton that a new release site would be best placed in the E. Midlands, possibly Northamptonshire or Leicestershire.

Action: EN to discuss location with JNCC and RSPB.

It is unlikely that further supplies from Sweden can be secured and for this reason a new supply from another donor population should be investigated. Work on the definition and resourcing of a new release site in Scotland should be undertaken during 1995 with the intention of releasing red kites in 1996. Meanwhile, the potential of increasing number of birds supplied by Spanish conservationists should be investigated, before other sources are explored.

Action: SNH, RSPB and JNCC to explore the potential for a second Scottish release site, to start operation in 1996. The Tay region looks to be the most likely.

The range of tasks that now need to be undertaken were considered and include:
- Analysis of work to date
- Co-ordinating supply of release stock
- Monitoring of existing established populations
- Establishing a new release site
- Release activities
- Monitoring new releases

After discussion, the Project Team agreed that the financial and human resources required for this level of work are beyond the scope of any single individual and probably the available resources of a single organisation. For this reason, EN, JNCC and RSPB need to reach agreement on funding and the division of labour required by each organisation to fulfil all the existing and proposed commitments. It is important to continue the successful co-operation to date, however. RSPB would be against taking any new work forward if it prejudiced the outputs of the current work. For this reason, it is a high priority to complete the analysis of the current work and publish its findings.

Action: Colin Galbraith, Mark Avery and Phil Grice to discuss and report back to the Project Team within one month.

A public relations strategy is now urgently required incorporating the existing and future population centres.

Action: Colin Galbraith to set up a working group to co-ordinate P.R. at local, national and international levels.

A revised UK Red Kite Action Plan will now be prepared.

Action: Nicola Crockford to circulate first draft to Project Team after Christmas.

The Chairman thanked everyone for their attendance and contributions.

As a result, new release centres were established in 1995 in Rockingham Forest, Northamptonshire, a joint project between Forestry Enterprise, RSPB and EN, and in 1996 in Perthshire, Scotland. Later release centres were established in Yorkshire, Dumfries & Galloway, near Gateshead, Aberdeen, the Republic of Ireland, Northern Ireland and the Lake District.

As will be seen from the rest of this chapter, our paper (based on the experience of our experimental project) set the structure for the next two decades. So, with the undoubted success of our experimental project, the experience of its personnel, the keen-ness of the top staff in the new agencies to join something already successful, enthusiastic staff and keen-ness to participate by the public, enterprises and NGOs, the releases in additional areas proved very worthwhile, and certainly increased the rate of spread. I often look out of my home-office window in central Peterborough, in East Anglia, to see a Red Kite overhead, I think a member of at least one pair that breed in the city (2021).

Red Kite passes my neighbour's chimney, and scans the ground for food in the old cemetery with mature vegetation across road from my home. Views of kites flying low while hunting are often through the branches of trees. [MP]

Update on Wales and the first English and Scottish sites

In 1993 for the first time for well over a century, over 100 pairs of kites had nested in Wales.

The *Red kite monitoring report 1995* (Anon. 1995) – based on the UK Red Kite co-ordination meeting held on 23rd October 1995 – reported that:

> *In [1995 in] Wales, nest protection involving the army, voluntary watchers and members of the monitoring team, resulted in no proven egg robberies. Likewise, in England and Scotland there were no nest failures due to human interference and the nest site locations were kept confidential. However, one of the English nests failed due to disturbance by a woodman working too close to the nest, due to the landowner not informing him in time of the nest location.*
>
> *In addition to the 1994 released kite being shot (but not killed) in southern England, one of the kites released in 1995 in the Midlands [see below] has been poisoned with alphachloralose and investigations are in progress. Another kite was poisoned by the legal use of phorate pesticide. This brings the total poisoned to five. In advance of the Midlands release, all relevant landowners and game interests were contacted with an information note. Liaison is ongoing: only two keepers local to the release area expressed initial concern. In Wales, two kites were poisoned although at least one of these cases was accidental death due to misuse of sheep dip. …*

Red Kites are thriving near the original Chilterns release site. [MP; also images on following pages]

Southern England: monitoring was by a contractor, two volunteers and JNCC. 42 of the 55 young were ringed and wing-tagged. It is thought that at least 4 other pairs, [with] 5–10 young, may have been missed. A monitoring strategy was developed for 1996, involving a part-time contractor (1 day per week in winter and 2.5 days per week in the breeding season).

[Midlands] RSPB Central England Regional Office has received a positive response to a questionnaire sent to c800 local members to recruit suitable volunteers to help monitor.

Wales: monitoring was patchy with about 70% of young colour-ringed.

A Scottish red kite newsletter was produced. Plans for a UK one are likely to be shelved, at least for 1995.

Summary: *Further excellent progress (UK population increase 16% in 1995 compared with 13% in 1994), with the Welsh population's range expansion and milestone of over 100 chicks produced, good breeding success of the reintroduced populations including recruitment of British-bred birds into the breeding population and the establishment of a new release site and successful release of 10 Spanish kites. Plans for a new Scottish release site are progressing well. Little progress on landuse policy actions in the absence of detailed knowledge about the requirements of red kites. Nest protection, with the help of the army in Wales and confidentiality in England and Scotland, successful; no nests were robbed. At least one kite illegally poisoned (English Midlands released bird).*

Future Action
Aim to translocate 20 birds annually to the Midlands site for the next four years. Establish a new Scottish release site in 1996, with annual releases for up to five years to give a total of 100 birds released. Consider establishing a third release site in England. Develop a UK monitoring strategy. Increase efforts to monitor lead levels in red kites and develop guidelines for supplementary feeding to reduce lead intake.

Wales
CCW/RSPB reported in 1995:

In Wales, the "Kite Country Project", [set up in 1994 and] launched in May [1995], is on target to attract 105,000 visitors to its 6 centres, an average 100% increase in visitor numbers on 1994, with an estimated third (ca 1,000) of these being new visitors attracted in response to the extensive media coverage. It is estimated that eight new jobs have been created directly and 10 jobs indirectly while 22 jobs have been safeguarded. A "Green Guide to Kite Country" was published with extensive information on public and other green transport. No detrimental effects on kite populations.

The *Red Kite Project, Wales* reported in December 1997:

The Red Kite project shows how wildlife tourism and farming can stimulate a rural economy. Mid-Wales is an area of low wages, declining employment in agriculture and economic stagnation. It also supports remnants of the native population of Red Kite, a rare bird of prey.

The Kite Country Project was launched as a partnership of various local councils, tourism and countryside bodies and the RSPB. It is supported by [European Union] Objective 5b money, the Welsh Office and private sector sources. The aim is to increase tourism to the region, promote wildlife and environmentally-friendly farming, and encourage visitors to stay longer and so spend more in the local economy.

The project has set up six visitor centres, installed remote video technology and special feeding stations so that the birds can be observed without disturbance; set up interpretation panels; developed community partnerships for green tourism; and promoted a stay-on-a-farm scheme with 130 farms as participants.

The impacts have been substantial. In 1995–96, there were 148,000 visitors to the Kite Country centres. They spent £5.4 million in the mid-Wales economy during these visits, about half of which has been attributed to the presence of the kites. A third of the visits are during winter, formerly a very low season for tourism. People who come tend to stay longer and come back more often. The project has created and/or safeguarded 114 jobs in the local community, and created a further 14 directly through employment of staff and contractors.

1995 was also the best breeding year seen [so far] for the Red Kite, with 120 pairs fledging 112 young.

In 1996, the Welsh population numbered 127 pairs, 88 of which raised 115 young.

During winter months feeding stations provide visitors with superb close-up views of kites. In

several visitor centres modern technology has been used to provide information on red kites and enable visitors to observe them at close quarters. The technology includes computer-based maps, interactive CD-ROMs and closed-circuit television pictures of nesting kites.

Scotland

The *Red Kite Project in Scotland in 1997* by Lorcan O'Toole, Brian Etheridge, Colin Crooke and Paul Walton (1998) reported:

27 of the 93 wild-bred, Swedish born, juvenile Red Kites released at two localities in close proximity on the Black Isle, Highland Region in the 5 years 1989–93 were still alive and bred in the release area in 1997. 16 kites had by then been recovered dead. The fate of the remaining 50 kites is unknown but the majority were likely to be dead by then. Up to 1997, 126 Red Kites had been reared in the wild in North Scotland. During 1997 at least 89 of these wild-bred chicks were known to be still alive. Nine of these birds had been recovered dead (five poisoned), and a minimum of 24 had now bred as first generation Scottish Red Kites.

A further increase in the number of pairs breeding was recorded in 1997. However, clutch sizes were smaller than the previous year. Prolonged periods of continuous heavy rain during critical hatching and nestling stages led to a number of total failures, and a reduction in the average brood size at successful nests. All 28 surviving adults which bred in 1996 remained faithful to their mates and nesting territories in 1997. There were 15 successful nests in 1996 and 10 of these nests were re-used in 1997. At the five sites where the previous year's nest was not re-used, it was believed that 3 pairs moved because of human disturbance in the vicinity during March. All pairs that moved bred successfully.

Breeding Results 1997:
Average clutch size (from a sample of 10 nests):	2.9
Average number of fledged young per successful pair	2.1
Average number fledged young per pair which laid eggs	1.7
Proportion of breeding pairs which fledged young	83%
Number of young wing tagged (of 39 total fledged)	33

Mortality and Survival
In the last Newsletter, we reported on the 100% survival of the 15 pairs that bred in the previous year (1995). This high survival was not maintained through to 1997; 4 of the 32 identified adults which bred in 1996 were missing from their established sites this spring (1 male from 1991 and 3 females from 1992 and 1993). With the exception of one of the females they had been replaced by new first time breeders. Assuming the 4 missing birds are dead, the annual survival of breeding adults between 1996 and 1997 is 87.5%. In 1997, 6 dead (3, possibly 4 birds poisoned) and 1 injured kite have been reported by the public: 6 of these 7 birds were in their first year.

Winter roosts
Three communal roosts were visited during the year and were occupied in both winter periods (1996/97 & 1997/98) by red kites. Two were in the core area of the Black Isle and held up to 10 birds each, consisting mainly of known breeders and only a few immatures. The third and largest roost was at the edge of sheep walk and hill ground in Easter Ross and held up to 21 birds in the 96/97 winter and 40 birds during the 97/98 winter. In both periods it was largely composed of first and second year non-breeders. Of the 19 first-time breeders recorded in 1997, 15 were seen at this major roost during January and February 1997. The total count of birds using these roosts in December 1997, compared with the estimated population, suggest that other undiscovered roosts probably exist in the area.

Public viewing
A new red kite viewing facility was established in the Tourist Information Centre at North Kessock (1 mile north of Inverness) on the Black Isle in 1997. Closed circuit TV cameras were placed at two kite nests which contained small young. One camera, with the aid of a micro-wave link, transmitted live

Adult on nest in Beech, the tree species most used in the Chilterns [PS]

Kites are very able in controlling flight while doing something else. This Chilterns bird circled in a thermal for well over a minute with its head down while adjusting something on its leg. Similar position is used to feed in flight while holding food in the bird's talons. [MP]

pictures to the centre, while the other recorded video footage on a daily update basis. Unprecedented images of nesting Scottish red kites resulted. This innovative facility is designed to provide a visitor attraction which not only raises awareness of the species, but also minimises any disturbance. This development is part of the RSPB/Scottish Tourist Board 'Birds of Prey' initiative which seeks to link a network of sites across Scotland, where raptors can be viewed using closed circuit technology.
This new Red Kite Viewing facility was made possible by the support of the Highlands of Scotland Tourist Board, a grant of £10,000 from [European Union] Leader II and similar assistance from Ross & Cromarty Enterprise and the Highland Council.

The December 1999 issue of British Wildlife reported, in its News section: *"Today is quite a significant day in the life of Blue left/Orange right, which is a Red Kite* Milvus milvus *reared on the Black Isle, just north of Inverness, in July 1997. Its sibling stayed around and bred this year near the natal nest. However, our hero decided that Scotland was not the place to be and it was found in Iceland in December 1997 - this was further north than any other Red Kite had ever flown and a journey of over 1,000km. The local farmer fed it meat scraps, and the Icelandic birdwatchers were thrilled, but eventually the bird got covered in Fulmar* Fulmarus gladalis *oil and was taken into care. It was then decided that the best course of action was to repatriate the bird to Scotland, where it would be able to find a mate! The flight back, courtesy of IcelandAir, will be much less taxing than the trans-oceanic flight, under its own power, that it undertook in 1997. The reintroduction of the species into England and Scotland has been successful beyond belief; since it first bred in 1992, no fewer than 223 chicks have fledged from nests on the Black Isle!"*

In 2001, the Scottish Ornithologists' Club reported from the *RSPB/SNH Red Kite North Scotland Newsletter 2000*:

At least five Red Kites have been killed as a result of eating poisoned bait in the Highlands in the last 12 months. All the poisoning incidents were on or next to sporting estates, but enquiries by the Police and officials from the Scottish Executive Rural Affairs Department (SERAD) have so far been inconclusive.

The poison used, carbofuran, is more toxic than strychnine; both the poisoned bait and the victim pose a risk to members of the public who come across them. It is particularly disheartening that the very reason the species became extinct in Scotland 120 years ago is still the main cause of death today. There are many estates and farmers who go out of their way to look after the kites, and they are being let down by a selfish minority.

Nevertheless, 2000 was the most successful year for kites since the reintroduction project started, 11 years ago. In North Scotland, 36 territorial pairs were located, 32 of which bred, all but two successfully. A record 74 young fledged. Across the UK, 431 pairs were found.

Red Kites habitually decorate their nests, and a number of unusual items were found during nest visits. These included: a white handkerchief, a black woollen hat, a patterned curtain, a woollen sock with a hole in the toe, a detachable hood from an anorak, a hand towel, a Carlsberg lager bar-cloth and a black plastic Labrador dog! An active nest of House Sparrow [Passer domesticus] was found in the foundations of one kite nest.

Remains of food items found in the nests were primarily Rabbits (often the staple diet), but also a Brown Hare [Lepus europaeus], lambs' tails (complete with docking rings), a couple of Hedgehogs, Feral Pigeons [Columba livia], Hooded Crows [Corvus cornix], Red Deer [Cervus elaphus] carrion, a young Common Starling [Sturnus vulgaris] and thrush [Turdus sp.], the wing of a female Common Pheasant, many Brown Rats [Rattus norvegicus], a male Eurasian Sparrowhawk, an adult Common Shelduck [Tadorna tadorna] and the front leg of a Sheep [Ovis aries]. Three Red Kite chicks died in 2000 as a result of ingesting rats poisoned with second generation anticoagulant rodenticides.

Away from the core area, one bird (Blue/ pink '5'), tagged on the Black Isle on 22 June 2000, and seen at a communal roost there in November, subsequently took a trip to Devon, where it was seen on 28 January 2001. Apparently unimpressed with England, it travelled the 735 km back to the Black Isle in two days! Allowing for eight daylight hours of flying each day, a direct path over the Bristol Channel, West Wales, 170 km crossing of the Irish Sea to Dumfries and Galloway and onward to the Black Isle, represents an average speed of 46 km/hour.

Most SOC members will have heard of the male Red Kite that was tagged as a chick in 1997, subsequently wandering to the south coast of Iceland, where it survived primarily on scraps put out by farmers until it was picked up, disabled by fulmar oil, in September 1999. It was taken into care and released back onto the Black Isle on 1 March 2000. Sadly, he was found dead 7 weeks later, 40 km away. It has not been possible to determine the cause of death.

Kites possibly too popular in south England

In 2004, a report local to the first English release area indicated: *"The red kite is a highly social bird in winter and large numbers gather in the late afternoon to roost. Over 200 birds have been counted in the air together in the Chilterns, forming one of the most impressive wildlife spectacles in England. Windy days offer the best prospects as the kites spend much more time in the air, using their long wings and forked tail to fly effortlessly over the countryside. Communal roosting is probably an adaptation to allow more efficient foraging. Kites leave the roosts in loose groups to begin searching for food and when one bird locates a food source, the others are able to converge to share in the feast. Communal roosts may also provide other benefits such as a place where birds can interact and perhaps meet up with potential future mates. Thanks to the continued success of the red kite reintroduction programme, this spectacular bird is becoming a familiar sight in parts of England, and even a regular visitor to gardens but it was not always so. After centuries of persecution by landowners, the bird was almost wiped out by the end of the 19th century. In order to restore its numbers, the Nature Conservancy Council (now English Nature in England) and the*

Two Chiltern kites fell through the tree with locked talons, bounced off a bush, landed and continued fighting on the garden lawn. [GW]

RSPB began a reintroduction programme in 1989. Fifteen years later, populations in the Chilterns are well established, with 177 pairs found in 2003, and more than 1,000 birds in total. Two more projects have since been carried out, with birds from the Chilterns and Spain released between 1995 and 1998."

The success of the first English release site and the popularity of the birds had given rise to a new problem. The team put out a new message:

When millions of us put out food for birds in our garden, the last thing we expect is a visit from a bird of prey. Increasingly, however, people on the edges of villages and towns in the Chilterns are putting out food specifically for this purpose. The contrast between past and present could not be more striking. Actively persecuted in the 19th Century, the birds are now viewed as a spectacle, diving down to snatch up food from within feet of the kitchen.

Avoid providing too much supplementary food for kites as it may prevent the birds from recolonising new areas and can cause nutritional problems if food is of poor quality. Experts at the Zoological Society of London's Institute of Zoology found that several nestlings in the Chilterns this year were suffering from a growth problem known as metabolic bone disease. Thus nutrition, and inappropriate food put out to feed kites, may be a factor. To avoid such problems, a few simple guidelines are shown below:

Feeding Red Kites

Provide only small amounts of food for kites so they continue to forage for natural food. Feeding in the afternoons only will enable birds to forage naturally in the first part of the day.
- *Avoid processed meats which may have potentially harmful additives such as salt.*
- *Limit the use of butcher's offcuts which may be excessively fatty with little skin or bone from which kites derive important nutrients.*
- *Whole or chopped animal carcasses are suitable for feeding kites. Dead mice may be ordered from a specialist supplier or road kills can be used, provided that sensible hygiene precautions are taken.*
- *Be aware that food provided for kites may attract crows or rats which is likely to be unpopular with neighbours.*

In fact, the best thing by far is to avoid providing food to the kites.

Overall progress

A series of Red Kite guided walks and other opportunities were soon regularly taking place at each of the release sites.

Red Kite numbers continued to recover. In 2002, in England and Scotland these were higher than any year since the start of the re-establishment scheme, with 227 pairs rearing at least 392 young. The Welsh population had continued to recover and was estimated at more than 300 pairs, an increase of over 250% since 1990. Moving it from the red to the amber list of birds of conservation concern recognised the recent recovery of its population. However, despite excellent breeding success, the Scottish population was increasing at a very slow rate. Few young birds were surviving long enough to breed, and there were concerns over deliberate poisoning of birds and the effects of second-generation rodenticides in the food chain. Since birds of prey are high in the food chain, they will always be susceptible to these effects.

Later progress at the Chilterns site

Pete Stevens (2012), who was one of the early volunteer helpers as we started the work in the Chilterns, lives locally and reported the situation up to 2011:

Pairs continued to be very productive in subsequent years, producing around 45% more young per successful nest than pairs in Wales as well as breeding at a younger age. Between 1992 and 2006 the average brood size was 2.07 chicks compared to 1.43 in Wales at around the same time, 1991 to 1999 (Cross & Davies 2005). The Chiltern broods included eight broods of four chicks, something that had not been recorded in Wales before 2011, when a single brood of four was found (Welsh Kite Trust). This high productivity resulted in a rapidly expanding population with the number of pairs increasing by approximately 26% each year up until at least 2004. So successful was the release programme that, by 1997, there were enough breeding pairs (over 50) to allow some chicks to be taken from nests for other release projects. Between 1997 and 2009 a total of 291 young kites were taken from nests in the Chilterns for release in Northamptonshire, Yorkshire, Dumfries & Galloway, Northumberland and Aberdeenshire. Despite this, numbers continued to increase and the breeding range expanded into all of the counties surrounding the Chilterns, including Berkshire, Hampshire, Wiltshire and Hertfordshire. In 2004 there were an estimated 201 breeding pairs in the Chilterns and surrounding areas (Carter & Whitlow 2005). Nest monitoring by the Southern England Kite Group (SEKG) has largely been confined to a relatively small core area centred near the Oxfordshire county boundary in the south west corner of Buckinghamshire. There were at least 92 pairs in this area of the county in 2011. It has not been possible to provide an accurate population estimate for the whole of the county

Chilterns kite scans the ground for food. [MP]

Chilterns kite [MP]

for 2011 because nest densities vary so much and very little fieldwork was carried out by the SEKG in the outlying areas, away from the core area. However, it appears that the population is still increasing and spreading to new areas.

Given the rate of population growth, it is perhaps surprising that kites are still scarce in the north of the county. There were very few winter records north of Milton Keynes and breeding was confirmed only in 3 tetrads north of Whitchurch. However, this is almost certainly due to Red Kites tendency to breed close to their natal area. Like the kites in Wales, Chiltern kites normally return to breed close to their natal area. For the most part, they have expanded their breeding range on a "rolling front", rather than striking out into distant unoccupied areas (Newton et al. 1994). This has resulted in the development of a core area with an increasing density of breeding pairs close to where the birds were released. The confirmed breeding records ... clearly shows this core area in the south-west corner of Buckinghamshire where artificial feeding is probably helping to maintain a high density of breeding pairs. Kites are now a common sight in towns and villages in this area of the county where they have become regular visitors to gardens, as many people now provide them with food. Although most pairs nest in the mature beech woods that are widespread in the south of the county, some pairs were recorded nesting in gardens and in isolated clumps of trees close to main roads, probably because food was being provided nearby. Red Kites build a large stick nest often adapting the disused nest of Carrion Crows, Buzzards and Squirrel dreys. Around 85 % of the nests monitored by the SEKG were in beech trees. The highest nest density recorded during the [2007–2011] atlas period was close to the original release site where 14 pairs nested in a single tetrad [2km x 2km National Grid square used in the atlas work]. Three of these were in beech trees within 90 metres of each other. Brood sizes in the densely populated areas have generally been smaller, probably because of competition for food. In 2011 a sample of 53 nests within 7 km of the release site had an average brood of 1.42 chicks per nest while a sample of 24 nests more than 7 km from the release site, where densities are lower, had an average brood size of 2.17.

Red Kites are gregarious birds. They are often seen feeding in groups where food is plentiful and gather at dusk to form communal roosts. Communal roosts have been recorded in all seasons in the Chilterns but the largest gatherings are found in the autumn and winter when over 200 birds have been recorded roosting together. These can be a spectacular sight with large numbers of birds wheeling above a favoured wood at dusk making a shrill mewing call. To add to the spectacle, they are sometimes joined by other raptors and ravens [Corvus corax]. Counts at roosts in the Chilterns appear to have peaked between 2004 and 2005 when there were two main roosts within 6 km of the release site and a higher proportion of first year birds in the core area. The number of roosts has increased since then but the number in each has generally decreased, with most of the larger roosts being found away from the core area. Between November 2008 and February 2009, a sample of 18 roosts counted by the SEKG had an average of 31 birds. The largest of these was recorded near Marlow where 79 birds were counted on 21st January 2009. Availability of food probably influences the size of these communal roosts as some of the largest were recorded close to where birds were being provided with food.

Gatherings at feeding sites can also be large and have included: over 60 following a plough near Turville, over 40 at an unofficial feeding station near Stokenchurch and several counts of over 20 at landfill sites near Beaconsfield and Calvert. The landfill site counts included 54 at Springfield Quarry on 2nd February 2011 and 44 at Hedgerley on 2nd January 2011, but it seems likely that EU regulations limiting the dumping of waste to landfill will reduce numbers at these sites in the future. Numbers are already down at Springfield Quarry where the dumping of waste was suspended in the summer of 2011.

Once they have established a breeding territory, Red Kites in Buckinghamshire are largely sedentary, spending the winter on or near their summer ranges, though a few shift to places with more reliable food supplies. Most movement occurs during the first year, generally during late summer/autumn or the following spring/early summer after the birds have wintered in their natal area. Although most of these movements are within 40 km from their natal areas, first year birds have been recorded visiting Wales, Yorkshire, East Midlands, West Sussex and Wiltshire. A nestling tagged near Fawley, in the Chilterns, on 5th June 2009 was recorded visiting the Argaty feeding station in Perth & Kinross, central Scotland, on 15th August 2010. Kites visiting Buckinghamshire from outside the area have included birds from Dumfries & Galloway, Yorkshire, Northumberland, Wales, East Midlands, West Sussex, Wiltshire and Hampshire. One of the young kites taken for release in Yorkshire in 2002 returned to Buckinghamshire twice during its first year and, on both occasions, it made the journey south in a single day.

Pete (Stevens 2017) updated the situation:

Red Kites in the Chilterns continued to produce small broods in 2017. It was the 11th consecutive year with low productivity and the worst on record. In the sample of 78 nests which were climbed to, the average brood was 1.21 chicks per nest (94/78). This was marginally down on the previous low of 1.27, recorded in 2012, and last year's average of 1.28 chicks per nest (106/83). Comparing results to earlier years (1992–2006), brood sizes were down by approx 41%, with only two broods of 3 recorded in 2017 (2.6 %) compared to 31% between 1992 and 2006. We recorded also quite a difference in [chick] size in many of the nests with more than one chick, so it is likely that broods would have been even smaller had we been able to delay climbing until the chicks were close to fledging. Of the 171 breeding pairs located, at least 101 produced young and 57 failed. The outcome of the remaining 13 is unknown.

As in previous years, we are recording smaller broods in the core area compared to those further out but the difference is becoming less pronounced than it used to be. This is probably because nest densities have continued to increase outside the core area and this has increased competition for food to levels approaching those in the core area. Using the same circular boundary as in previous years, the average brood in a sample of 44 nests in the core area, (i.e. less than 7 km from the main release site) was 1.11 chicks (49/44). There was one brood of 3 and two broods of 2 in the sample. All

Red Kites and Buzzards are uneasy when too close together. The highly manoeuvrable kites tend to dive at buzzards and seem to dominate most encounters. [MP]

of the others had a single chick each. The average brood in a sample of 34 nests, more than 7 km from the release site, was 1.32 chicks (45/34). These included one brood of 3 chicks, ten broods of 2 and 23 singles.

As our monitoring was restricted to a relatively small area, it has not been possible to estimate accurately the number of pairs in the Chilterns and surrounding area using the data we have collected. However, in their 2016 report, the joint BTO/JNCC/RSPB Breeding Bird Survey (BBS, https://www.bto.org/volunteer-surveys/bbs) published estimates for the increase in numbers over the 20 years between 1995 and 2015. In the results for the south east of England, it is estimated that Red Kite numbers increased by 10,584% (up from 8,613% in the previous year). This is less than the estimate published in the 2014 report (12,975%) but still indicates a rapid population growth. An increase of 10,584% over 20 years is equivalent to an annual growth rate of 26.3%. Assuming breeding pairs have increased at this rate then the population in the south east of England would have been 2564 pairs in 2015, increasing to 4090 pairs by 2017. These estimates apply to the whole of the area where kites have spread to from the Chilterns, not just the Chilterns. They were obtained by scaling up from the number of pairs recorded in the Chilterns in 1995.

The farmer leasing agricultural land at Wormsley mentioned to me in 2022 that he and his wife had noticed more dead kites in recent years, possibly reflecting recently fledged birds being able to secure less food.

The decrease in productivity per nest (and possibly initial young survival) in the exceptionally high breeding densities in an increasing circle around the release site is to be expected, and should help encourage the spread of the breeding range. Despite the reduction in productivity per pair, the exceptionally high density of pairs mean that the total productivity of these areas remains high.

As Pete Stevens noted, the success of the project meant that, as numbers increased, assessing the population size becomes more difficult. There are also marked seasonal variations in visibility of the kites. Generally, they are most obvious in the winter, when more effort is needed to find food, nesting sites are being claimed or reclaimed, and deciduous trees lack leaves. As nesting and chick-rearing occur in the spring and early summer, the kites tend to make themselves less obvious, aided by trees becoming covered in dense vegetation. In fact, it is possible at that season to drive the country lanes in an area of high kite density but see none, whereas many would be seen on the same route in winter. Even in late summer, the picture is confused by the kites taking advantage of feeding opportunities provided by farming operations revealing small prey. These activities vary in timing across an area.

I update the general situation in the next and final chapter, but first I need to address the later release sites.

The English Midlands reintroduction 1995–1998

Carter & Ivens (1998) noted, referring to the situation from 1995:

The experimental project has been a great success and two breeding populations of red kites are now established, in addition to the native Welsh birds. Although the numbers of breeding pairs have increased in each of these populations over the last few years, they remain relatively small and isolated, and therefore vulnerable. Chance events such as an outbreak of disease or a series of poor breeding seasons could seriously affect the long-term survival of the red kite in Britain. It was therefore agreed, that in order to secure the future of the red kite in Britain, at least two further populations should be established.

The RSPB and English Nature (as part of its Species Recovery Programme) have already begun to reintroduce kites at a new site in the English Midlands. … It is hoped that birds from the new populations will link up with populations already established and eventually occupy all suitable areas in Britain.

The release sites and breeding areas will be kept confidential in order to prevent disturbance and stop local landowners being inconvenienced by large numbers of visitors coming into the area to see

Six Red Kites, part of a larger winter flock, thermal above a village church spire in north Northamptonshire. [MP]

As in other areas, the success of the Northamptonshire kites has not been without setbacks. One hazard here is the narrow main road with heavy traffic passing through their main area. Animals hit by vehicles are a major food source for the kites, especially in winter. However, the kites are not adapted to land animals moving as fast as speeding motor vehicles! Although the kites' huge lift-to-weight ratio and manoeuvrability lead to most escapes (as I have seen), sometimes they do not make it, as here. [MP]

kites. However, people can play an important role in the project by keeping an eye out for kites and reporting casual sightings…

The *Red kite monitoring report 1995* (Anon. 1995) reported that the new release site had been established in the English Midlands in a project funded by EN and RSPB, with EN taking the operational lead. The Midlands project started in 1995 and the same methods were used to establish a breeding population of kites in this area. Forestry Enterprise joined in the project. Ten young kites imported from Spain (Segovia and Salamanca), plus a kite released in the southern area in 1994 which had been shot and rehabilitated by the Institute of Zoology, were successfully released.

In 1996, 15 birds came from Spain and one from Wales. In 1997, 10 birds came from each of central Spain and 10 from birds breeding near the southern England release site, where the population was more than self-supporting and increasing rapidly. All 20 young birds released in 1998 were from the well established Southern English population. As the Central England team commented, it was an indication of how successful the project had been in southern England that these chicks could be taken without threatening the southern population. No releases took place in 1999 as it was thought that the Midlands population should be able to increase and spread naturally, without further birds being added to the population. The situation would, however, be reviewed each year with the option of releasing further kites if this was felt necessary. As in the first sites, the kites released in the Midlands were taken from nests as chicks at about five weeks old. The cages and procedures followed those used in the earlier sites.

The 1995 report continued:

Much positive publicity [was] generated by the Midlands release, around which a ministerial media event was organised: two TV features are in production, including a feature on Heart of the Country *to be screened in January 1996. There was also news coverage of the arrival of the birds at Heathrow and the transfer of the shot bird from London Zoo. Two press releases were produced (re: the release and 1995 breeding season results). Articles produced for Birdwatchers Yearbook, British Wildlife and English Nature magazine. A colour leaflet was produced for public distribution.*

In advance of the release, a news item requesting sightings was published in most Midlands Wildlife Trust and bird club newsletters, plus at least 11 national magazines, but no unaccounted for bird has yet been re-located as a result. An aerial survey, in collaboration with the ITE and RSPB buzzard projects helped locate one bird in the Brecon Beacons. The location of four of the eleven birds is unknown. A 1995 Scottish-bred bird has joined the roost.

A safer food source. A Northamptonshire kite moves its talons forward ready to grasp a flying insect (out of focus nearer the camera). [MP]

The *Red Kite newsletter (England) Summer 1997* (Anon. 1997) recalled earlier results to place new information in context:

Winter wanderings…

Monitoring has shown that most kites overwinter in the areas where they were reared or released. There are, however, a few kites which seem to have an irresistible wanderlust in their first year of life.

Chicks born in southern England during 1996 have been reported as far afield as Yorkshire and mid-Wales. Some of the young kites released in the Midlands last year have also turned up in Welsh valleys and a few joined up with the population in southern England.

All the red kites released in the Midlands carry radio transmitters. During aerial surveys, signals can be picked up by researchers from up to 30 miles away enabling them to search a wide area in a relatively short space of time. The information they provide is extremely valuable in tracing the birds' movements.

During September, after the breeding season has finished, kites begin to gather in large communal roosts, mostly made up of younger birds. These are often in small woods which are used year after year. It's possible that large roosts are a social highlight in the lives of these youngsters, a place to meet potential future mates.

Roosting together is thought to be an adaptation for finding food as birds can keep an eye on each other and when they see their companions fly down to food they fly in to join them.

A review of progress in 1999 noted that several of the eleven 1995 releases dispersed soon after being released never to be seen again but most remained in the area and three were still going strong four years after their first flight. Another bird, having initially dispersed to north Wales, then headed south to join up with birds from the re-introduced southern England population. Two of this year-group of kites were found dead, one in southern England, and another found illegally poisoned with alphachloralose in Lincolnshire in 1995. In 1996, a pair of kites built a nest and laid eggs in the Midlands for the first time in well over 100 years. The eggs did not hatch and no chicks were reared.

A higher proportion of the 18 birds released in 1996 dispersed away from the Midlands following release and many of these failed to return. One bird that did stay was illegally poisoned, not far from the release site, with the highly toxic chemical mevinphos in the spring of 1997. One of the birds that wandered away from the area fared no better, being found dead under power-lines in central Wales. The carcass was too decomposed to establish a cause of death but it seems likely that it was electrocuted as it tried to perch on the power-lines. By the spring of 1999 only three of the 18 birds released were still present in the Midlands.

Twelve of the 20 birds released in 1997 remained within the Midlands during their first winter, joining up with other kites released in previous years. The other eight birds dispersed and were reported from as far apart as central Wales, the east coast of England, north Yorkshire and Beachy Head on the Sussex coast. One of the eight dispersing birds was found dead under power-lines in north Wales only two weeks after being released, the scorch marks on the feet showed that it had been electrocuted. Power-lines can be a considerable hazard for birds of prey as their wing-span can be large enough to cross two wires as they land or take off. In poor visibility there is also the risk that they may not see the wires and injure themselves by flying into them. As most Red Kites breed for the first time when they are two years old, the ten birds from this group still present in the Midlands were expected to pair up and establish territories in the spring of 1999.

Hard left turn as a Northamptonshire kite spots potential food. Note on this and other images that, like many other birds, kites head-stabilise, *i.e.* hold their head in the same position to keep their eyes on an object however their body twists to change direction. [MP]

The final 21 kites released in the Midlands in 1998 brought the overall release total to 70 birds. By March 1999, 17 out of the 21 birds were still present in the Midlands, together with about 30 other kites from previous years. Of the four that dispersed, one spent much of the winter near Horsey in east Norfolk but was later found dead in Berkshire the following spring. During the 1999 summer, the young kites became much more mobile and six moved south to join up with kites in southern England.

Twelve of the 16 Midlands chicks in 1999 were fitted with long-term radio-transmitters while they were still in the nest. The improved (and lighter) technology then available allowed their progress to be followed for about three years before the batteries ran down. Early the following year, 11 out of the 12 birds were still alive and well in the area and formed part of a Midlands population then estimated at some 60 birds. The 1999 wild-reared chicks were also given coloured wing tags, white on the left wing and black on the right wing, with letters from A to P identifying each individual. This work revealed that some pairs breeding in the Midlands might have gone undetected as up to ten young kites without wing-tags were seen following the breeding season. It is also possible that these birds were immigrants from other areas as young kites can move large distances away from their nest-sites and are clearly attracted to concentrations of other Red Kites.

With the intensive project now having continued far longer than originally planned, the wing-tag colours then used each year had to become part of a modified scheme involving kites in several new other areas. Using this scheme, the colour of the tag on the left wing indicated the area where the bird was fledged or released. The colour for the Midlands was white and this did not change from year to year. The colour of the right wing-tag indicated the year in which the kite was born. This was the same across all the different areas in each year; tags for 1999 were black.

The 1999 breeding season was much better than the rather poor second year of wild-breeding, when only three chicks were reared. Ten pairs held territories at the beginning of the season, seven of these laid eggs and six were successful, rearing a total of 16 young. A few details of each of the breeding kite pairs found in 1999 are given below, as an example of the variation at this and other areas.

Pair 1 (untagged kite and Black 28): This pair built a nest about 10m high in a small Scot's Pine tree near the edge of a wood about 800m away from a site that was used in 1997 and 1998. Black 28 was a wild-fledged bird from southern England that joined the Midlands population in 1998. The origin of the untagged bird was not known for certain but the team suspected that it was a female from the 1995 releases that had bred in this area over the preceding two years and had now lost both wing-tags. All three eggs hatched and a regular supply of food brought in by the adults ensured that all three chicks fledged successfully. The adults from this pair spent much time around a nearby pheasant laying pen and were quick to exploit any dead birds found inside the pen.

Pair 2: This pair were the only surviving pair of birds that were definitely released in 1995 in the first year of releases in this area. They bred successfully in the same wood for the third year running, again building a new nest close to those used in previous years. The nest was in an Oak tree along the same wide woodland ride as the previous year. For the third year in succession, two eggs hatched and, for the first time, both chicks fledged successfully when about eight weeks old.

Pair 3 (both untagged): This pair involved the same untagged adult kites that had bred in the area over the previous two years and that, for the third time in as many years, moved to a new wood this year. This was unusual behaviour as kites normally remained faithful to the same site, using it for breeding year after year. A nest was built high up in a Larch tree but, after the female had been sitting for about two weeks, the nest slipped from its supporting branches and was abandoned by the pair. Some weeks later a new nest was found in the same wood, and a new clutch of eggs was laid. Three chicks were reared and all fledged from the nest successfully.

Pair 4: Both of these 1997-released birds were breeding for the first time, occupying a site in a Forest Enterprise wood used by a different pair in 1998. A rather flimsy nest was built about 12m high in a larch tree and two eggs laid by mid-April. Only one egg hatched and the single chick grew quickly and had left the nest by early July. A study by a student at Anglia Polytechnic University showed that the adults spent almost all their time close to the nest site and only rarely left the area to search for food. Having only a single chick to feed meant they were left with plenty of time on their hands.

Pair 5 (untagged kite and 1997 release): This pair nested in the same section of a Wildlife Trust wood that had been used by other pairs of kites over the previous two years. The nest was well-secured in a substantial fork near to the top of a large Oak. Previous attempts at this site had ended in failure but this year a brood of four chicks was reared and all fledged successfully. A brood of this size is particularly impressive as at least one of the pair was only two years old and making its first breeding attempt.

Pair 6 (1997 releases): Also first time breeders, this pair chose a site in a small deciduous wood on the edge of parkland. The nest was situated in a fork close to the trunk about 15m up in

Family life: nest in north Northamptonshire, with two views of female incubating, and male brings in branch for structural addition and later small food items for chicks – manoeuvring tightly as he dives into nest area. [MP]

a Sycamore tree. Three chicks fledged from the nest but one was found dead shortly afterwards near to the nest tree. A post-mortem showed that the bird had several fractures in its wings and legs that had partly healed and so had occurred while the bird was still alive. It is not clear whether this individual had some form of genetic disorder or if the bones had been weakened by an imbalance in the diet, possibly in conflict with siblings. The other two chicks from the brood were healthy and became independent of the adults about four weeks after their first flight.

Pair 7 (black 17 and red C): The site selected by this pair was well outside the area where kites are normally found in the Midlands. This is the first Midlands pair where it is known for sure that both birds were wild-fledged individuals rather than releases. Both were 1997 birds, red C being one of a brood of four fledged in the Midlands and black 17 the male of the pair, one of 100 chicks fledged from wild nests in southern England in 1997. Unfortunately, the nest, situated in a mature Oak, became dislodged after heavy rain and strong winds in late May and a dead chick and a smashed egg were found on the ground below.

The tabulation below shows the numbers of birds released in the Midlands and growth in the breeding population since the project began.

	1995	1996	1997	1998	1999
No. released	11	18	20	21	–
Territorial pairs	–	1	5	8	10
Breeding pairs	–	–	4	4	7
Young fledged	–	–	8	3	16

By 2004, an expanding population of 24 pairs existed in Rockingham Forest, north Northamptonshire, near the release site.

The Central Scotland reintroduction 1996–2001

In 1995 RSPB and SNH agreed, in line with our recommendations at the end of the experimental project, to establish a second release site in Scotland. This began in 1996, with the intention of establishing a breeding population in Central Scotland (and the 4th new one in GB) by introducing around 100 Red Kites, over a 4– to 5–year period. RSPB/SNH budgeted for 50:50 funding of this, hoping to use German birds (a potential source considered early in the original experimental project but not then practicable).

37 young Red Kites from Sachsen-Anhalt, Germany were released in Central Scotland in 1996 and 1997 (O'Toole *et al.* (1998). The team are very grateful to the people of Sachsen-Anhalt, and particularly Prof. Dr Stubbe of Martin Luther University, Halle and Herr Schonbrodt, Sachsen-Anhalt Regional Director for Nature Conservation. They helped in many ways and continued to monitor the nests from which the donor stock were removed. The plan was to release up to 100 Red Kite chicks from the Sachsen-Anhalt Region between 1996–2000.

The patterns of rearing and release and subsequent monitoring, as well as the patterns of illegal poisoning, were very similar to those of the earlier sites.

Of the small number of kites that dispersed more than 50 km, the majority appeared to have dispersed down the west coast through Ayrshire and Galloway. Some remained in the Southwest of Scotland, while others crossed over to Northern Ireland and beyond or continued as far south as Devon in England. This ultimate long-distance flyer was Yellow 2, released in central Scotland on 1st August 1996. Four months later it was recorded in south Devon. In the second year of releases, kites were tracked to the Mull of Galloway and County Donegal, Republic of Ireland. These dispersing birds generally moved quickly southwards to over-winter in England and Ireland.

In both Scottish release areas, some first-year Red Kites left their nesting or release areas and dispersed for their first winter. Most headed south or south-west (Fig. 11.1). The Black Isle kites often spent their first winter in Perthshire, or went further south like the Central Scotland birds, towards Ayrshire and Dumfries. Some of these birds continued to reach England, Wales,

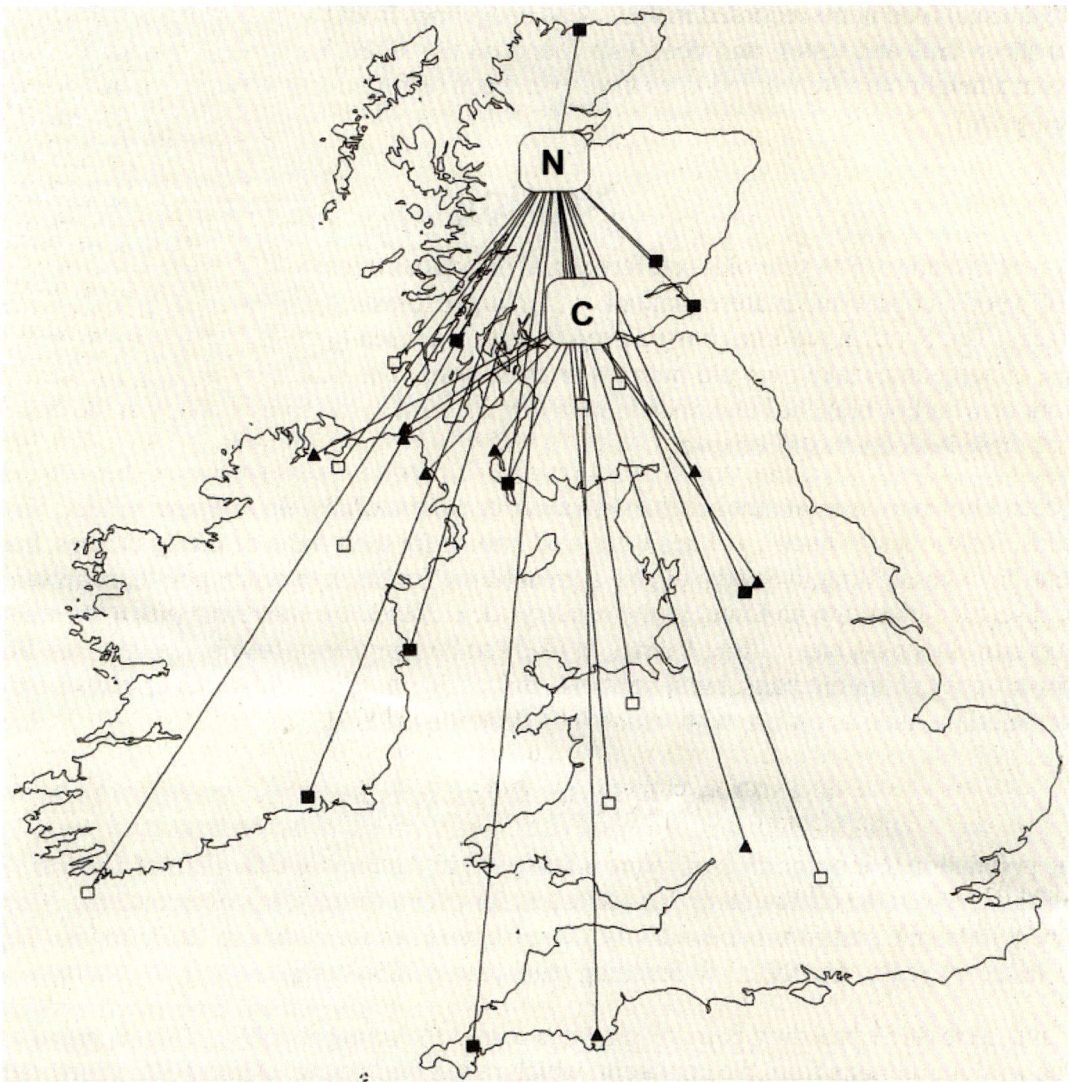

Figure 11.1. Map of typical movements of released ■ and wild-bred □ kites from northern Scotland (N), and of released ▲ kites from central Scotland (C) 1989–1997. From O'Toole et al. (1998)

Northern Ireland and the Republic of Ireland. At least 10% of first year Scottish kites crossed over to Ireland each winter.

The birds began to return north between February and May. Most returned to their original nest or release site and eventually tried to nest in the same area. However, some birds spent up to two years away from their place of origin and a few probably settled in various other parts of Scotland.

A total of 103 birds were eventually imported from eastern Germany, reared and released between 1996 and 2001 (Orr-Ewing undated). In the final year, in June 2001, the birds included 13 Red Kite chicks seized by police from traders who had illegally taken them from the wild in Saxony. The German authorities offered them to the re-introduction programme in central Scotland. Duncan Orr-Ewing, who had been with the project since 1991, accompanied them via Glasgow Airport. The seizures of 80 birds, of which the kites were a small part, included Golden

Eagles *Aquila chrysaetos*, Goshawks and Peregrine Falcons, part of an international black market involving organised criminals.

The Yorkshire reintroduction 1999–2003

The Yorkshire Red Kite Project was the fifth release site and began on Harewood Estate, near Leeds in West Yorkshire in 1999. By this time, the now well-established Southern English (now identified as the Chilterns) population had been so successful that it had been supplying chicks for the last two years of the Midlands releases. The Chilterns site was able to supply, from 1999 to 2003, a total of 68 young birds for release in Yorkshire. This figure was supplemented by an older rehabilitated bird, also from the Chilterns, and an untagged bird of unknown origin, both of which arrived in late 1999.

The Yorkshire project rapidly resulted in the establishment of a small breeding population. In 2003, the last year of releases, 16 breeding pairs were found (Yorkshire Red Kites 2020).

The Dumfries & Galloway (SW Scotland) reintroduction 2001–2005

Between 2001 and 2005, 104 Red Kites were released near Laurieston (Dumfries and Galloway), using donor stock from the first two re-introduction sites, the Chilterns and northern Scotland (Orr-Ewing undated).

The 'Galloway Kite Trail', around Loch Ken, recognised these birds as a source of nature-based tourism to benefit local communities in the area. In so doing, the trail helped to strengthen the 'ownership' of the kites by local communities and tourist operators. Developed by RSPB Scotland, with assistance from Making Tracks, Scottish Natural Heritage, Forestry Commission Scotland, Dumfries & Galloway Raptor Study Group and local businesses, the trail included various facilities around the loch such as footpaths, viewpoints, information points, CCTV (on nest sites), release cages and RSPB Scotland's Ken-Dee Marshes Reserve, all of which are good places to see kites and other wildlife. A feeding station with a hide was established at Bellymack Hill Farm near Laurieston, and over 30 kites have often been seen together during the winter months. In the early years, these included many of the birds released in 2003 as well as adult birds and individuals that arrived from other reintroduced populations. The trail helped to secure the local population of kites by making them a financial asset to the area that benefitted local businesses.

The Northumbria (NE England) reintroduction 2004–2006

Over 2004–2006, English Nature, the RSPB, Gateshead Council, Northumbrian Water, the National Trust and Forest Enterprise introduced 94 kites from the Chilterns population to release pens in the Derwent Valley, near Gateshead. Central to the project was a community initiative intended to make kites accessible to large numbers of people. The birds are establishing, but perhaps rather more slowly than in some other earlier sites. There are indications that this is due to persecution (Friends of Red Kites 2021).

Looking back to the original press statements about this plan in 2003 and 2004, I was fascinated to see that the project would go ahead *"subject to funding"* and *"Thanks to Gateshead Council and the Heritage Lottery Fund, this now has £750,000 worth of funding to last over several years."* After allowing for inflation, this would have been the equivalent of about £400,000 in 1987. When RSPB colleagues and NCC estimated the costs we thought we might need about £15,000 per year for each initial site. The 2004 figure would have been equivalent to over 25 years of operation! I know that our teams then tried to minimise costs to get more conservation for our 'buck' – but I had not realised that we were that good!

Aberdeen reintroductions 2007–2009

With the objective *"To create a self-sustaining population of Red Kites on the outskirts of Aberdeen which the people of Aberdeen can enjoy and be proud of"*, 101 Red Kites were released in the area from 2007–2009. These came from donor stock in the Chilterns and central Scotland.

The birds first bred successfully in 2009. Following this successful reintroduction programme, they rapidly became a common sight once more in both City and Shire. The population grew year on year, with a minimum of 35 breeding pairs established in the north east of Scotland by 2016. They ranged from the edge of the Cairngorms National Park to Aberdeen City and spread south into Angus. By 2021, Aberdeen Red Kites had raised more than 300 chicks in the wild.

A farm on the edge of Aberdeen, VSA Easter Anguston Farm, provided the release site for the reintroduction which was supported through funding and partnership support from The National Lottery through the Heritage Lottery Fund, Aberdeen Greenspace Trust Ltd through the Landfill Communities Fund, and Scottish Natural Heritage, with further donations from local business supporters.

Republic of Ireland 2006–2011

The project to restore Red Kites to Ireland was initiated in 2007. Once common and widespread, they became extinct in Ireland in the 18th or early 19th century, due to persecution, poisoning and woodland clearance. This international, co-operative project was managed by the Golden Eagle Trust in partnership with the National Parks and Wildlife Service and the Welsh Kite Trust. In May 2007, the Irish Minister for the Environment, Heritage and Local Government announced an agreement to bring at least 100 birds from Wales to restock the population as part of a 5-year programme in the Wicklow Mountains. 107 Red Kites were imported from Wales and released in Co. Wicklow from 2007, when 30 arrived. A further 53 chicks were reintroduced in Co. Dublin in 2011, making 160 in total.

First breeding was recorded in 2009 when two pairs were known to have built nests and laid eggs. Unfortunately, neither of these pairs produced any young, but young were reared the following year. In Wicklow, the first Irish-hatched Red Kite reared a brood of young in 2012, signifying the first time a wholly native Red Kite had been recorded breeding in Ireland since the early 19th century. In some years, there were problems reducing success, including poor weather conditions. However, survival rates have been very high. While most of the released birds have taken up permanent residence in the vicinity, a number of the more adventurous birds had been spotted further afield. Kites from Wicklow had been sighted in Kerry, Leitrim, Dublin, Sligo and Antrim. Then there were an estimated 50+ birds still resident in Co. Wicklow, including a number of birds that were released in Northern Ireland which subsequently found their way to Wicklow.

Golden Eagle Trust Red Kite project manager Damian Clarke said *"The discovery of the first Red Kite chicks in over two hundred years was a significant milestone for Irish biodiversity. To see chicks in a typical Wicklow landscape reaffirms my belief that these birds will thrive here once*

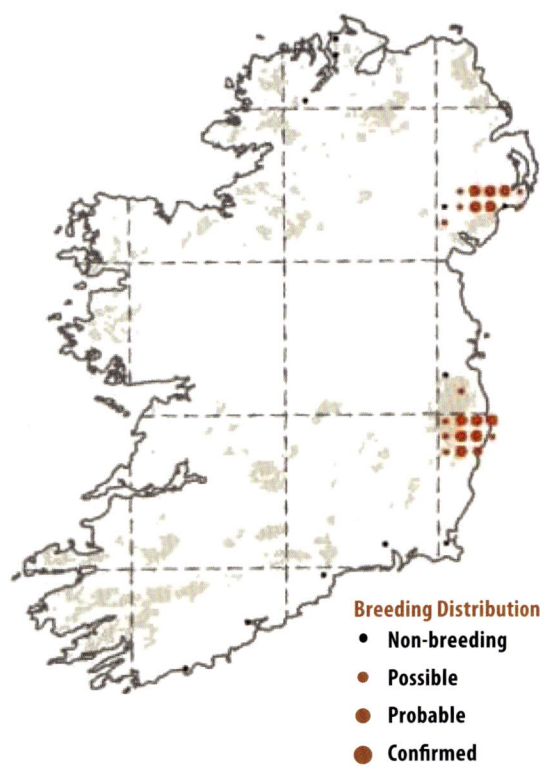

Figure 11.2. In 2011, kites breeding on the island of Ireland were still confined to the east coast, close to the original reintroduction sites in Counties Wicklow, Dublin (and Down in the North). Monitored by Countryside Bird Survey. Reproduced with the approval of BirdWatch Ireland and BTO from Bird Atlas 2007–11 (Balmer *et al.* 2013), which was a joint project between BTO, BirdWatch Ireland and the Scottish Ornithologists' Club.

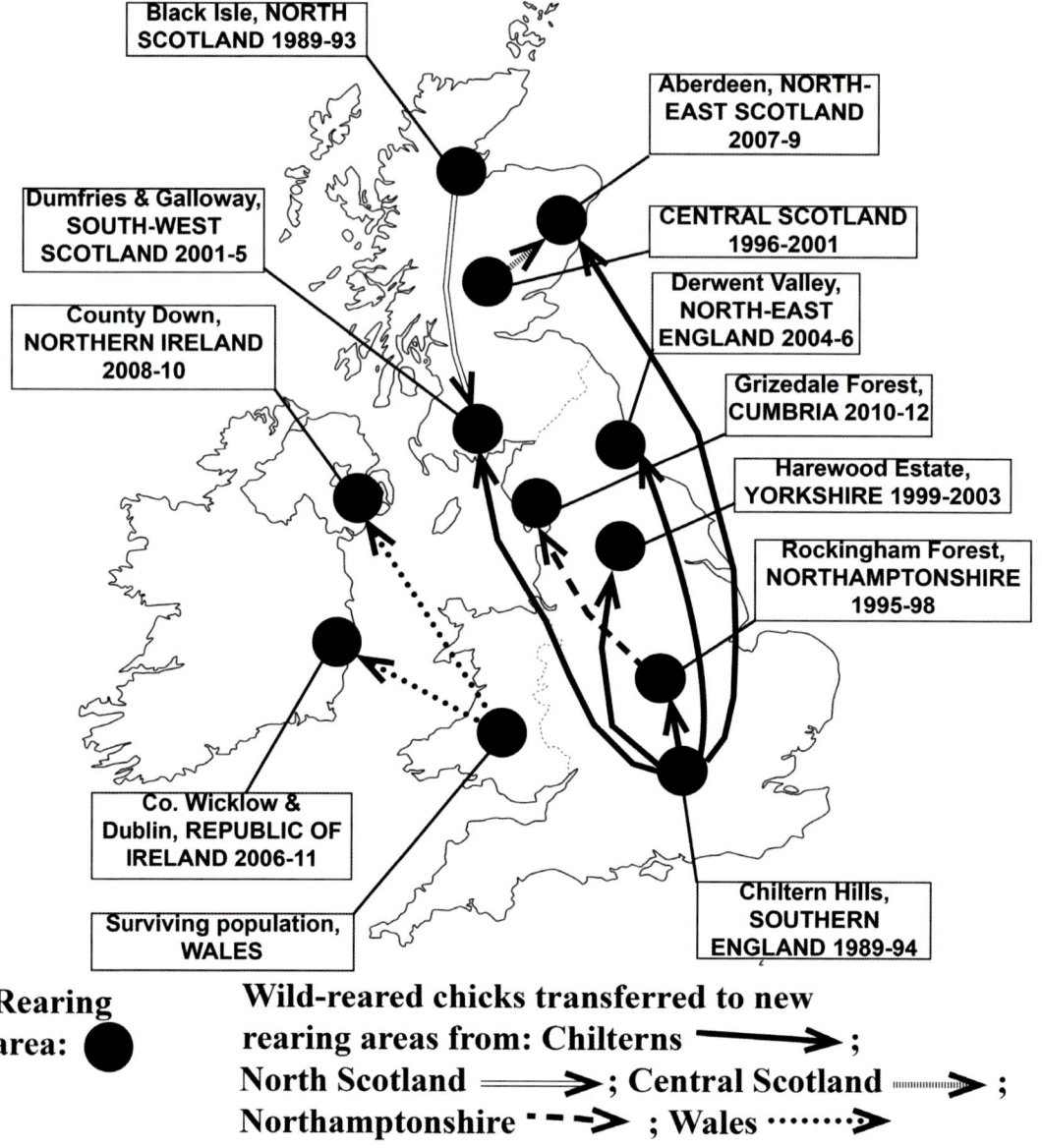

Figure 11.3. Rearing areas (named) and the years of releases at each. Broad arrows show main sources and destinations of wild-reared translocations within Britain and Ireland after first two areas established mainly with young from overseas.

given the chance. It is my hope that the Red Kite will with time once again be a common sight throughout Ireland. These Irish-bred chicks are the first sign of that becoming a reality" (Golden Eagle Trust 2010; BirdWatch Ireland).

Northern Ireland 2008–2010

It is highly likely the Red Kites bred in Northern Ireland until the mid-18th century. Due to the momentum and experience gained from recent successful reintroductions in England and Scotland, the stage was set for this large-scale species recovery project to be rolled out in Northern Ireland and the Republic of Ireland, first in County Wicklow in 2007 and then in

County Down in 2008 as it was unlikely Red Kites would naturally re-colonise here in the near future.

During the reintroduction projects in England and Wales, the Welsh population had recovered considerably and was estimated at around 900 pairs in 2009. In June 2008, a visit by Northern Ireland conservationists to Wales collected the donor stock for the Northern Ireland Red Kites reintroduction project with partners Welsh Kite Trust and Golden Eagle Trust. A total of 27 kite chicks were collected, and all were successfully released into County Down in the first of three years of the release programme, with 26 and 27 further birds imported in the following two years, respectively.

In July 2010, five Red Kites successfully fledged from four nests in County Down. All parent birds were those released in 2008. In 2013, for the first time, a Red Kite which was born and reared in Northern Ireland was confirmed to be breeding, at a site on the southern edges of the Mournes.

Below and next page: young Red Kites on early foraging flights July and August in North Northamptonshire [MP]

Another 13 nests were also located, and, of these, 17 chicks fledged successfully from seven nests. In 2017, 20 pairs were found with 13 of these fledging 28 chicks. By 2020, there were around 24 breeding pairs in Northern Ireland. The Red Kite project officer and volunteers continued to monitor closely the progress of the Red Kite population and work to raise awareness of these birds to address the ongoing threat of wildlife crime.

The 'RKites Project' was organised by RSPB, Welsh Kite Trust and Golden Eagle Trust, with the support and assistance of the Northern Ireland Raptor Study Group and the Mourne Heritage Trust, and funded by: the Heritage Lottery Fund (HLF); Ulster Wildlife Trust's Landfill Communities Fund grant scheme provided by Down, Newry and Mourne District Council, Armagh, Banbridge Craigavon Borough Council; Quinn Environmental Ltd; Ernest Kleinwort Foundation; Garfield Weston Foundation; Heritage Council; and Northern Ireland Environment Agency.

Lake District 2010–2012

Between 2010 and 2012, 90 Red Kites were translocated from the Central England (Rockingham Forest, Northamptonshire) to re-establish a population in Grizedale Forest, in the Lake District of Cumbria, by the Forest Enterprise England. The Grizedale programme was the tenth reintroduction of Red Kites into different regions of the UK, and the final reintroduction phase in England.

Forestry Commission Wildlife ranger Iain Yoxall, project manager for the Grizedale Red Kite Release Project, said: *"It is a real conservation coup for the area and it will help to establish the Red Kites in the largest region in England from which the species is absent, a process which could take decades naturally"* (*The Westmorland Gazette* 17th June 2010). The first wild-bred chicks were produced in 2014.

Review

It will be apparent that the last few reintroductions within Great Britain had far stronger declared public amenity and awareness objectives, in comparison to national and international ones. There is nothing inherently wrong with that, especially if the resourcing is from local sources. However, we have probably reached the stage that further translocations are probably unnecessary and might start to become counter-productive, distracting resources from other raptor conservation initiatives or wildlife conservation projects. However, there are lots of other possibilities that conservation bodies and the public can turn to, and are so doing. I mention some of these in the final Chapter.

We have gone from a relict and inbred population hanging on in Wales, international decline and long absence in most of UK to a restored, recovering and thriving population, constituting a major part of the world population. No more needs to be done now bar the ever-required vigilance re persecution, poisoning and other modern pressures experienced by all birds of prey. A job well done!

12. What are the outcomes?

Natural England chair Tony Juniper said: "Red Kites are one of our most majestic birds of prey with a beautiful plumage, and are easily recognisable thanks to their soaring flight and mewing call. Persecuted to near extinction, they have made a triumphant comeback in England over the past three decades. Thanks to this pioneering reintroduction programme in the Chilterns, increased legal protection and collaboration amongst partners, the Red Kite stands out as a true conservation success story. The flagship Red Kite reintroduction project paved the way for further species reintroductions, helping to reverse the historic deterioration of our natural environment and our precious species that inhabit it." (Natural England 2020)

Jeff Knott, RSPB operations director for Central and Eastern England said: "The Red Kite [re-]introduction project has been a fantastic example of conservation in action and is the result of really effective partnership working, which we're proud to be part of. It's been amazing to see a species once persecuted to near extinction in this country, brought back and welcomed by local communities, with local economies reaping the dividends of the return of this iconic species. In the 1980s, anyone wanting to see a Red Kite had to make a special pilgrimage to a handful of sites. Today it is a daily sight for millions of people. In a few short decades we have taken a species from the brink of extinction, to the UK being home to almost 10% of the entire world population. It might be the biggest species success story in UK conservation history!"

Danny Heptinstall, Senior International Biodiversity Adviser at the JNCC, said: "Thirty years ago the reintroduction of a lost species was a radical act. Thanks to pioneering projects

One of the first reared Red Kite chicks in 1989 shortly before release [MP]

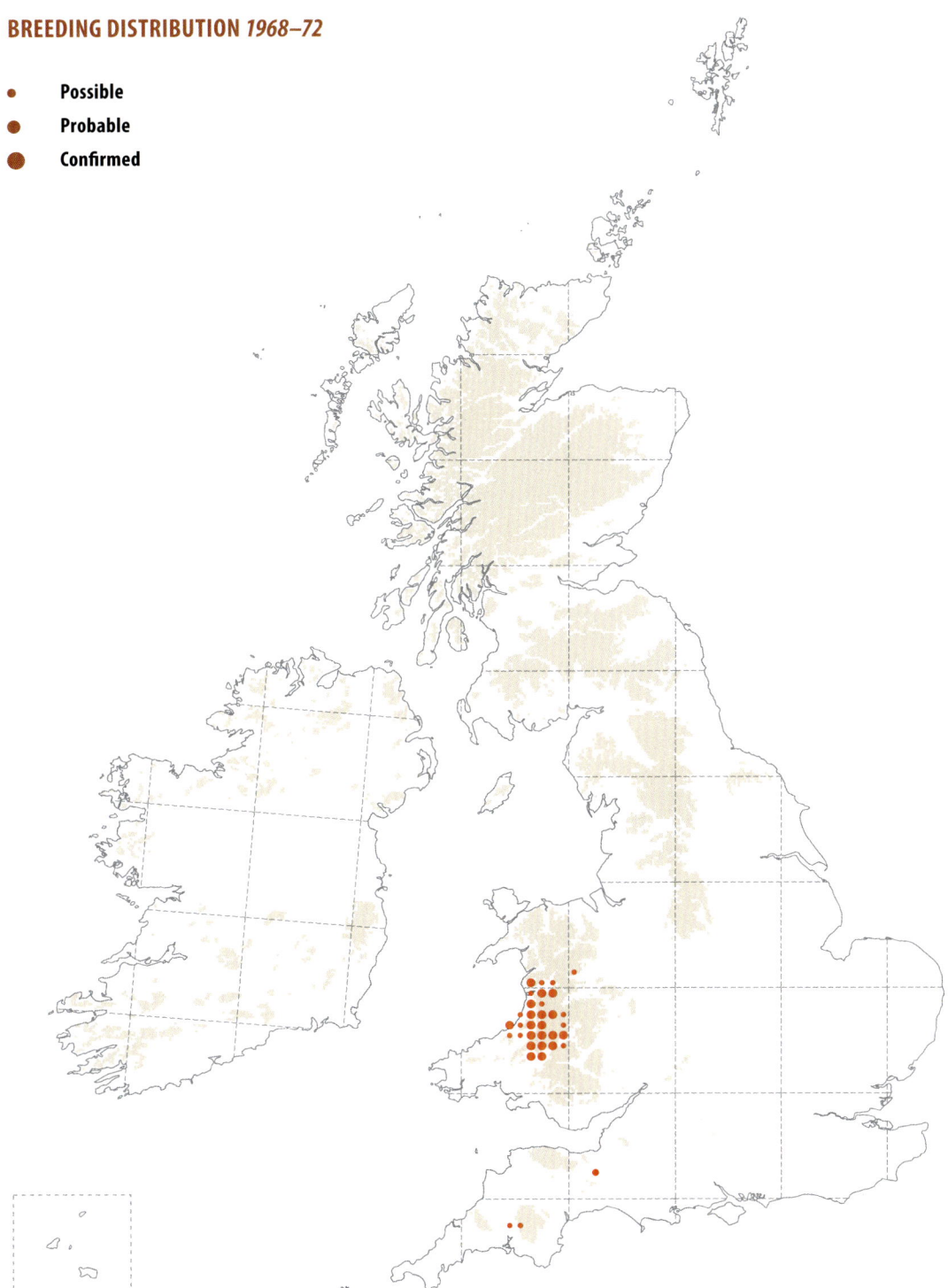

Figure 12.1. Red Kite breeding distribution 1968–72. (Note that the 10-km square data was not published precisely in the original Atlas – see Chapter 2 – in order to protect the kites, especially their nests.) Reproduced from *The Atlas of Breeding Birds in Britain and Ireland* (Sharrock 1976), which was a joint project between BTO and the Irish Wildbird Conservancy.

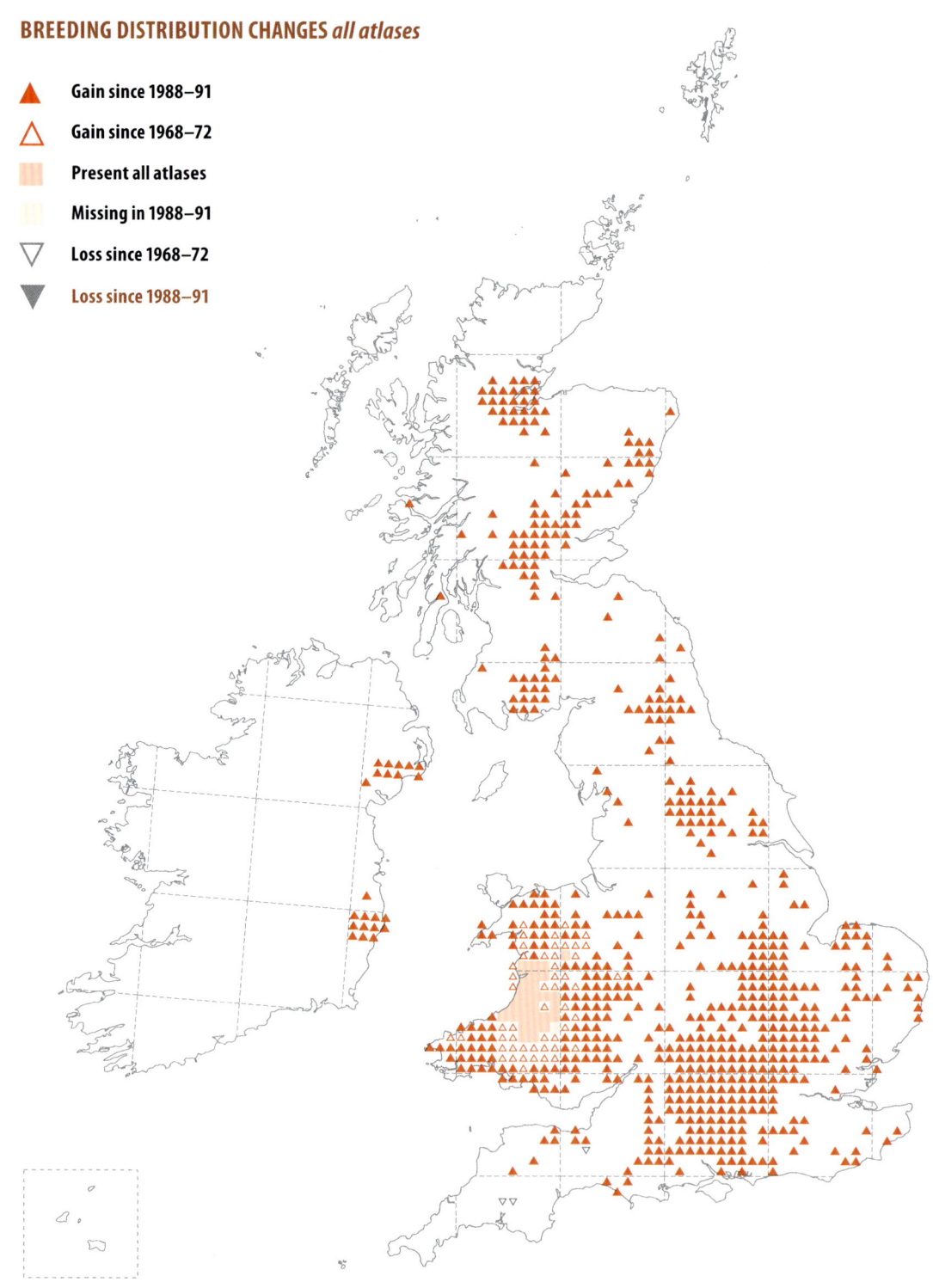

Figure 12.2. Changes in Red Kite breeding distributions from 1968–72 & 1988–91 to 2007–11. Reproduced from Bird Atlas 2007–11 (Balmer *et al.* 2013), which was a joint project between BTO, BirdWatch Ireland and the Scottish Ornithologists' Club

WINTER DISTRIBUTION 1981–84

● **Present**

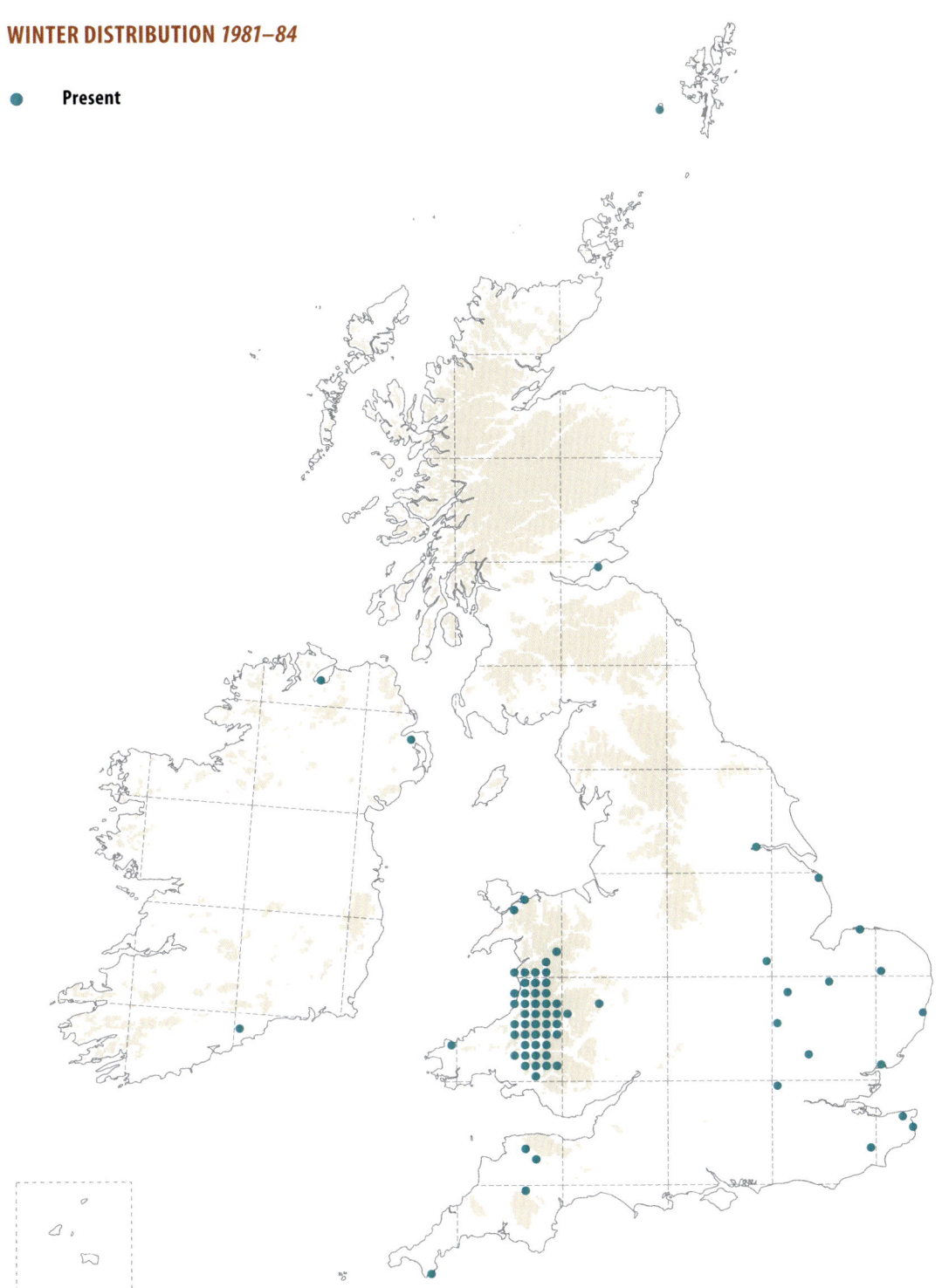

Figure 12.3. Red Kite winter distribution 1981–84. Reproduced from *The Atlas of Wintering Birds in Britain and Ireland* (Lack 1986), which was a joint project between BTO and the Irish Wildbird Conservancy.

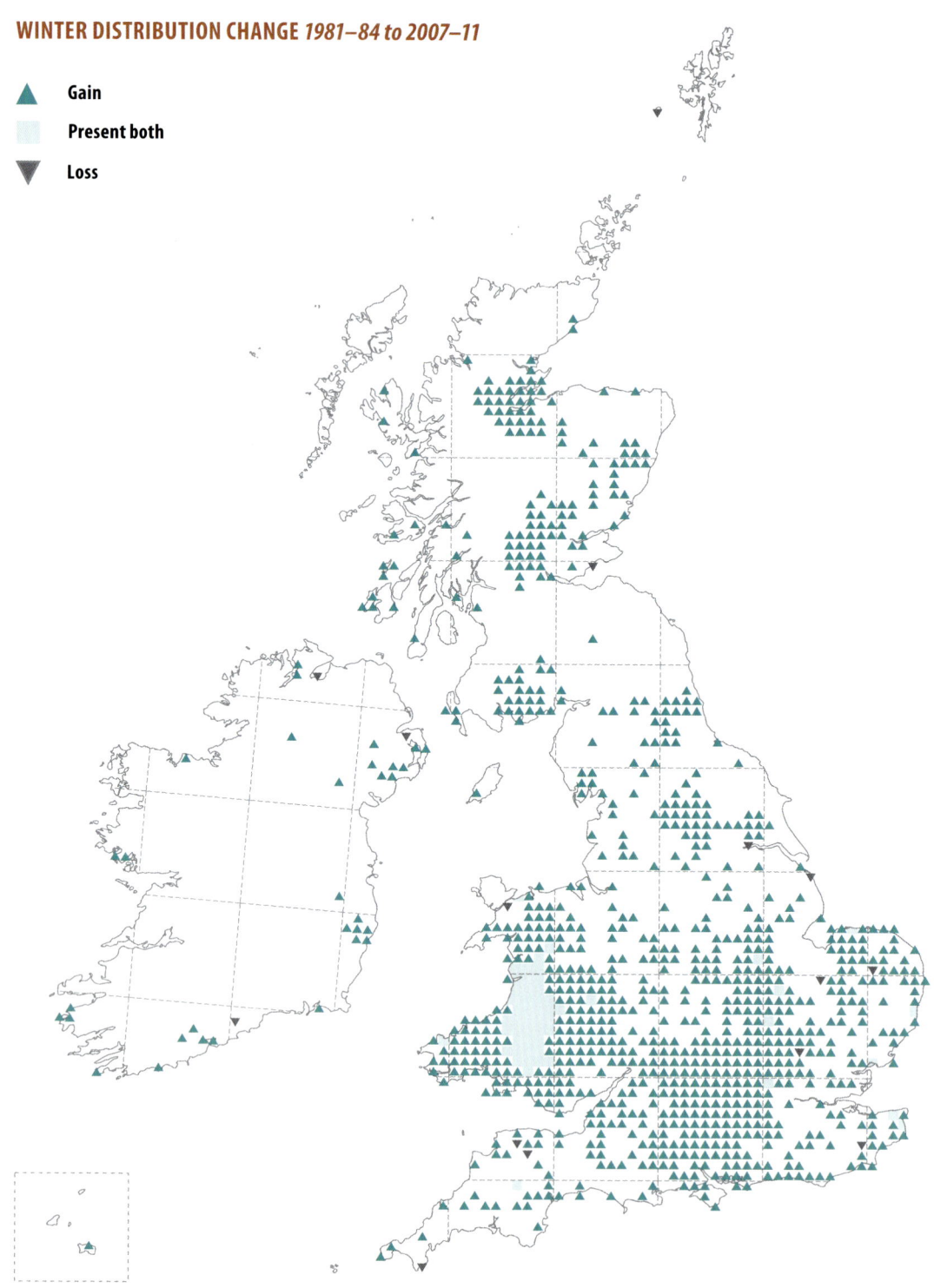

Figure 12.4. Changes in Red Kite winter distribution from 1981–84 to 2007–11, from the BTO Atlas data. Reproduced from Bird Atlas 2007–11 (Balmer *et al.* 2013), which was a joint project between BTO, BirdWatch Ireland and the Scottish Ornithologists' Club

like the Chiltern Red Kites, it is now a standard tool in the nature conservation toolkit. In 1990, the UK had only a few dozen Red Kites, 30 years later there are over 10,000. JNCC is delighted to have played its part in this ground-breaking conservation success story, and look forward to the continuing success of the project and others like it."

The press release went on "The re-introduction of Red Kites was a trail-blazing project, and paved the way for successful reintroductions of bird species licensed by Natural England, including White-tailed Eagles to help establish a breeding population in southern England (https://naturalengland.blog.gov.uk/2019/04/02/natural-england-issues-licence-to-release-white-tailed-eagles/). Natural England is also involved in a number of initiatives to help ensure Hen Harriers recover through the Hen Harrier Recovery Plan (https://www.gov.uk/government/publications/increasing-hen-harrier-populations-in-england-action-plan) including a southern re-introduction."

Of course, the references are to England, because of the destructive and damaging split of the old NCC into country agencies (Chapter 11); RSPB and NCC had originally strived to stress the combined English/Scottish/ Welsh project. And success has been achieved across the British Isles, in the Republic of Ireland, Northern Ireland, Wales, England and Scotland.

It is very satisfying that the pioneering work is appreciated, even with slight misapprehensions. Are these assessments correct?

Strictly speaking, and keeping an eye on the grammar, they probably are. However, had Jeff Knott omitted "species" out of "the biggest species success story in UK conservation history", I would have had to argue. Looking only at projects with which I have had personal involvement, I would argue that the saving of the Flow Country, UK's only remaining extensive basically natural ecosystem (see *e.g.* Stroud *et al.* 2015 & Chapter 11) ranked much higher. In a similar way, the decades-long – and not yet complete – fight to stop intertidal areas being squeezed between rising sea-levels due to human-induced climate-change and fixed (or even expanding) hard human-made sea-walls defending land claimed from the intertidal has made major progress. Interestingly, both peatlands and coastal wetlands are now recognised as amongst humanity's strongest allies to fight further climate-change. Both are perhaps stronger contestants for most successful conservation projects than the Red Kite programme.

Red Kite of the increasing north Northamptonshire population [MP]

We should remember too that it is even more important to prevent the loss of our native wildlife, rather than having to take heroic steps to reinstate it.

It is often quoted that the then Chinese Premier Zhou Enlai, when asked in October 1971 by Henry Kissinger about the impact of the French revolution, answered "it is too early to say." However, it seems that he may have been referring to the Paris student riots of 1968 (only 3 years earlier), rather than the storming of the Bastille and the French Revolution of 1789, almost 200 years earlier. Whichever is correct, I think that, 35 years on, we can reliably assess the outcomes of the Experimental Red Kite Reintroduction project and the activities that it has led to. I turn now to the several aspects of this:

- Re-establishment of the Red Kite;
- Reduced persecution of birds of prey;
- The attitudes to ecosystem restoration;
- Facilitating appropriate reintroductions and recovery programmes more generally for other species of wildlife;
- Public Attitudes & Perceptions.

I start with the core objective of re-establishing Red Kites in England and Scotland.

Outcome: re-establishment of the Red Kite

The success of the project can be demonstrated by the results of the periodic breeding atlases, organised roughly every 20 years by the British Trust for Ornithology, BirdWatch Ireland (and its predecessors) and the Scottish Ornithologists' Club. From the Red Kites' restricted breeding in central Wales around 1970 (Fig. 12.1) and 1990, to the very widespread of about 2010 (Fig. 12.2, and further spread since). This is reflected too in the winter atlases of the 1980s and about 2010 (Figs 12.3 & 12.4).

The BTO also makes available maps of records gathered for all its many surveys (Fig. 12.5). I think that we can conclude, from that for records between 2016 and 2019, that the project has resulted in a distribution throughout almost all of Great Britain and adjacent islands and spreading also in the island of Ireland (which not all the BTO surveys cover in full).

The suitability of area selection and other conservation measures is supported by the rapid rates of increase, as already evident in the early years (Figure 12.6 – RSPB undated2). These were at the upper end of the possible range that we estimated at the start of the project.

As noted above, by 2020, the total UK population had reached about 1800 pairs. As the population size and distribution increased, precise counts of pairs and nests became impracticable, but the British Trust for Ornithology's surveys, part commissioned by UK government

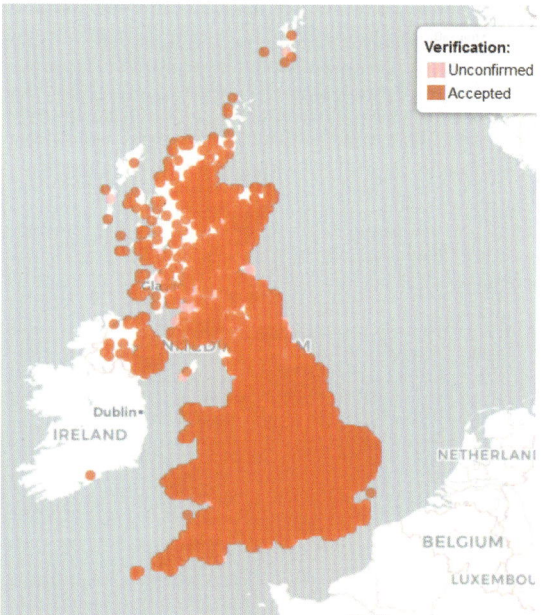

Figure 12.5. Red Kite distribution (essentially in Great Britain and Northern Ireland, according to all BTO surveys 2016–2019, which do not generally include information from the Republic of Ireland). Collated by the National Biodiversity Network Trust (https://nbnatlas.org/) and reproduced by permission of the British Trust for Ornithology

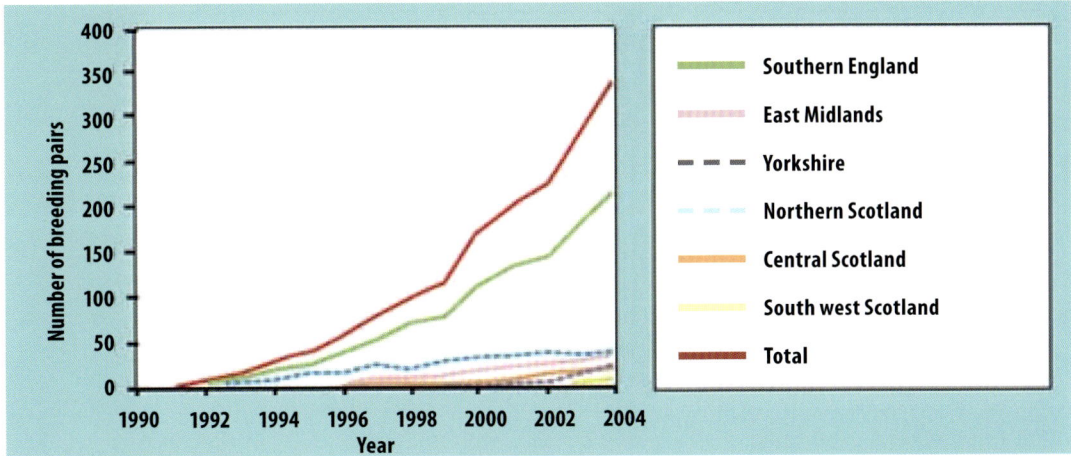

Figure 12.6. Red Kite breeding populations in release areas 1991–2004.

conservation agencies, kept track of the situation. One of these is the Breeding Bird Survey (BBS), which was started while I managed this contract from NCC with BTO. The results of this for Red Kites show the continuing trend in population increase (Fig. 12.7).

By 2020, there were nearly 2000 breeding pairs in England, and over 10,000 individuals in UK, representing about 10% of the world population.

In terms of stages, the project has established that:

Figure 12.7. Index of Red Kite population size 1994–2019, from BTO Breeding Birds Survey. Reproduced by permission of the British Trust for Ornithology

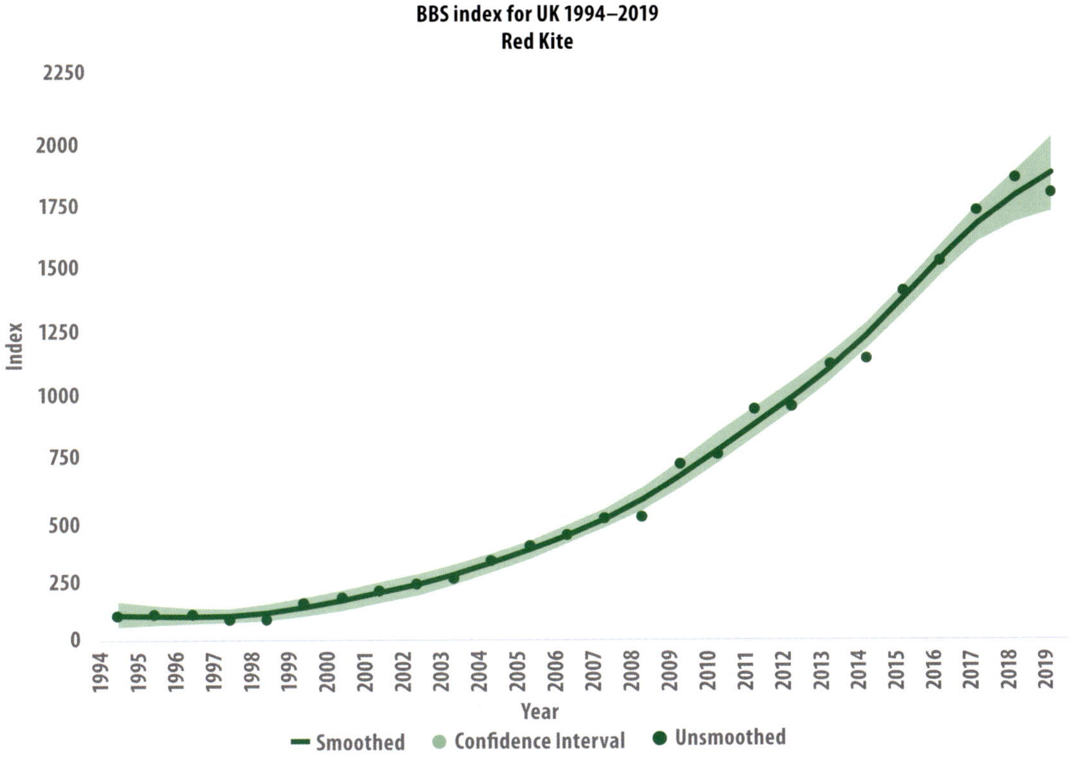

1. The Red Kite can be translocated and released into the wild successfully and without jeopardising donor populations, demonstrating that such a scheme is practical using the techniques developed.
2. The released Red Kites have become fully integrated and self-supporting in the wild, with a high survival rate.
3. The breeding performance of successful pairs established by the reintroduction project is at least as good as the populations from which the released birds were taken, demonstrating the suitability of the environments into which they have been released.
4. "Home-grown" chicks reared in the wild by pairs established by the release programme have recruited into the successful breeding population, as have their offspring.
5. Self-sustaining population centres have been established, with the earliest of these rapidly becoming productive enough to provide young for new release centres.
6. Illegal persecution (including poisoning) does not at present threaten the released populations with extinction, but measures must continue to stamp it out as it is still a major cause of mortality.
7. The spread and increase of the population has been so effective that the UK population now constitutes about 10% of the global population.
8. This success has depended on strong international co-operation with several other European nations, as well as huge collaboration by volunteers, commercial bodies, NGOs and governmental bodies (with their personnel often acting in their own time) – and its shared success has added support for wildlife and its conservation.
9. The importance of spreading the range as a form of international insurance for the survival of the species has been established, illustrated by declines in populations in Continental Europe since our survey in the 1980s. As the Yorkshire Red Kites (2020) team commented, "It is a salutary thought that Red Kite numbers have plummeted in some parts of Europe, especially Spain. It is fortunate that the timing of the initial English releases preceded the onset of this problem; otherwise the Spanish authorities might not have allowed the relocation of some of their young birds to kick-start the now burgeoning population here." As this book was being finalised came news of even more direct evidence of this (see below).
10. We managed to maintain the programme despite the disruptive and destructive reorganisation by the UK Government of its conservation agency which ran over almost the same period as the experimental project.

Why has the project been successful? Colleagues and I think that several key elements have been:

1. There were clear objectives, not driven by methods, nor imposed (rather than flexible) time-schedule, but instead a flexible, learning approach was adopted (see below).
2. We learnt from experience, both with the White-tailed Eagle and with that of others working with raptors elsewhere.
3. The work was informed by the best information available from international science and experience: looking at studies where the birds occur and do well, rather than assuming that the marginal areas where they happened to have survived human persecution were the best areas; care was taken to avoid imprinting on humans; research was undertaken on sources and distribution; and we attempted to overcome personal subjective views by using selection criteria for rearing birds and selecting release areas.
4. We adopted a flexible approach, with monitoring. Like the Sea-eagle project, the experimental kite project was monitored carefully throughout, so that progress could be checked and any necessary modifications could be made according to emerging experience and evidence.

5. Cooperation: we were determined to sustain the cooperative approach: between NCC and RSPB, between the project teams in Scotland, England and Wales, and with our friends and colleagues in other nations, as well as many other individuals and organisations who donated their time and help. We considered this essential for success – as well as for a pleasant life. We achieved this, despite the disruption of NCC's reorganisation. The good collegiate approach that we had all built up in the first years of the experimental project meant that individuals from successor bodies maintained strong commitment and support to the project even if some top managers in new organisations were more interested in objectives other than nature conservation.
6. Careful use of public involvement – as open as possible but without letting media messages have undue influence on the project. This is for proper openness of public information balanced with security of the birds, but also to enthuse the public with a real positive contribution to UK and world conservation, as well as involvement in the project and its successors in various ways – and helping to change attitudes to illegal persecution of this and other species.

This project illustrates the need to avoid a parochial or nationalistic approach to conservation. Birds range widely. For birds of prey and others with wide ranges, population sizes will always be relatively small and vulnerable. Effective conservation planning needs to be at least at a national and often a European or even wider scale – while taking local views fully into account. It is because of the world importance of widening the kites' distribution throughout its former range that Swedish and Spanish, and later German, conservationists agreed to help (as earlier the French had done, although for reasons of practicability that offer was not taken up). We are helping each other to ensure the survival of these birds for the long-term future.

This is underlined by the news, as the text of this book was being finalised in 2022, that young kites from the English population are being exported to Spain. As noted earlier, the population has been declining in Spain because of the poisoning of animal carcasses, sometimes to protect lambs from foxes. However, Alfonso Godino, the project manager of

Red Kites in a thermal over Wormsley. [MP]

Acción por el Mundo Salvaje (Amus), one of the reintroduction partners in Spain, reported that the Spanish kites can thrive again because tough measures – including prison sentences for illegal poisoning – have now reduced Red Kite mortality. He said: "Illegal poisoning will never disappear but the level has decreased a lot over the last decade." He added: "It's really amazing that this one action – the reintroduction in England – can get a lovely reaction even three decades later."

Addressing the illegal persecution was the principal secondary objective of the earlier exercise in Britain.

Outcome: reduced persecution of birds of prey
As noted in Chapters 3 and 8–11, a major aim of the project was to help reduce persecution of birds of prey. It is not possible to prove a link from the project to this aspect, but some circumstantial evidence is strong.

Kite poisoning
As I reported earlier, there is a particular risk in the initial period, when wide wandering by immatures is to be expected. Even in the first year of releases, one kite each in Scotland and England (out of six and five, respectively, released in 1989) was killed by illegally laid poisons. The one from England had unfortunately strayed into the Welsh borders, an area with a high incidence of poisoning. As noted above, a contributory factor in limiting the spread eastwards to England of Red Kites and Buzzards seemed to be the intensity of illegal poisoning along the English/Welsh borders (Newton 1979). Because of the low productivity then of Welsh kites, this was probably a proportionately more important factor constraining Buzzards, for which more young birds would be available to spread.

The poisoning of kites, including the ones we reared and released, continued through the project and beyond – but the publicity given to these seemed to be changing attitudes, both in the public and amongst those conducting this activity. We stressed throughout that we knew that this activity was confined to a minority of the farming and game-keeping communities – but a small number can have a huge effect. We are grateful to the many who operate responsibly for their pressure on those who do not.

The Red Kites' successful re-establishment has been due in part to their ability to adapt to our modern countryside. As scavengers, this exposes them to poisoned rodents and inappropriate food put out in gardens. It had been known for many years that some modern anticoagulant rodenticides are so toxic that they pose a risk to other animals that feed on poisoned rodents. Red Kites in England are known to have been killed in this way, and some dead birds have been found with obvious internal bleeding. Many of the poisoning cases involved the use of alphachloralose, a rodenticide left illegally on bait in the open. In 1998, a man was fined £1000 after burying a kite, not realising it had a still-working radio-transmitter on its tail.

Between 1998 and 2001, around 30 incidents were reported involving birds of prey, especially Red Kites and Buzzards, where it is likely that rodenticides were the cause of death. Kites are especially vulnerable to this threat because they often feed around human settlements where rats are regularly controlled using poison. And, being scavengers, they take dead rats that are likely to have been poisoned. In 2000, at least 9 kites were poisoned, and at least 100 over the ten years to then.

There has been a shift of attitudes during the period of the projects but, with small populations, the activities of a small number of people can have large impacts. 2001 saw such a set-back. RSPB reported the worst spate of illegal poisoning since the start of the project in 1989, with 36% of the birds in the Black Isle lost in a 12-month period. In 2002, two found dead in North Yorkshire were the latest of more than 20 that had been killed in the previous two years by eating carrion laced with poison.

Kite C from the first year of releases illegally poisoned in Herefordshire [TC]

2010 saw the needless death of a brood of 2 young Red Kites. Local RSPB staff found the 5-week-old chicks in a nest in the outskirts of Muir of Ord (Ross-shire). They were in a weak condition, coughing up blood and their bodies were covered in blood, which was leaking from their feathers. These signs are consistent with poisoning from an anti-coagulant rodenticide. Attempts to save the young birds by local veterinary staff were in vain and they died in convulsions. It is likely that the chicks died accidentally after they were fed poisoned rats by their parents.

Following this incident, RSPB Scotland (and with English Nature south of the border) again urged anyone who lives in areas where Kites nest not to use rodenticides at this time of year. If this is not possible, in order to reduce the risk to birds of prey people were encouraged to:

- consider alternative forms of control such as trapping or the use of less toxic poisons based on warfarin or coumatetralyl, where resistance is not a problem (The use of warfarin poses much less of a threat to Red Kites than the use of other anticoagulant rodenticides that are 100–600 times more toxic.);
- follow the product label instructions carefully whenever poisons are used, ensuring that none of the rodenticide can reach an external source; and
- carry out regular searches for dead rodents and dispose of the bodies safely by burning or burying.

The conservation bodies noted a positive response by Rentokil, a leading pest control company, saying that it would reduce its use of rodenticides by 75% when carrying out rat control programmes. They considered this a very welcome move and should help Red Kites, as well as Barn Owls, Kestrels, Buzzards and Polecats *Mustela putorius*.

We considered too that the general situation was improving – while stressing the need for continued effort. This is illustrated by Orr-Ewing's (undated) comparison of performance between the first English and first Scottish release areas (Chapter 9).

I looked for other evidence for changes in the situation, preferably by ultimate consequences, rather than indirect indicators. Here is one.

The case of Buzzards

In a review, Evans (1995) noted that Buzzards had once been distributed throughout Britain but, by 1915, persecution had reduced their breeding range to areas of Cornwall, Devon, Hampshire, the upland of Wales, Cumbria, Kirkcudbrightshire, Ayrshire, the western Highlands and inner isles of Scotland (Tubbs 1974). A reduction in persecution since 1915 had allowed the population to expand eastwards through natural recolonisation, although continued persecution was considered to be preventing full recovery (Swann & Etheridge 1995). A review of reports of buzzard persecution between 1975 and 1989 showed that this species was significantly more likely to be reported poisoned from the eastern edge of its UK breeding range (Elliot & Avery 1991). Illegal poisoning is thought to have limited the eastward spread of this species.

Buzzard just west of Peterborough in 2022. For decades, this species was rarely seen in this region but now is becoming increasingly common. [MP]

Several efforts to reintroduce Buzzards in eastern Britain had been undertaken in the past. For example, in 1939 six young Buzzards (obtained from western counties) were released in Surrey (Harvey 1939). Appeals were made to everyone 'to spare these birds from gun and trap' but the re-establishment attempt failed. More recently, detailed research had been undertaken on Buzzards in Dorset in order to provide quantitative data on dispersal, social, habitat usage and population dynamics behaviour (Walls & Kenward 1994b). This work was an essential pre-requisite for an experimental study investigating how to re-establish Buzzard populations and if there were factors other than persecution preventing the restoration of former range (Walls & Kenward 1994a). Newton (1979) showed strong evidence that gamekeeping activities were restricting the Buzzard's range.

The results of the breeding bird atlases maps for Buzzards are striking. In the first Atlas (1968–1972, Fig. 12.8), most of England was devoid of Buzzards, except the south-west peninsula, Cumbria and the far north of Northumberland. The distribution border close to the Welsh border was extremely sharply defined for a natural distribution. Twenty years later, in the 1988–1991 survey (Fig. 12.9) as we started the Red Kite project, there was little change, except for some spread in parts of Scotland, particularly the south and in Northern Ireland.

By 20 years later (2008–2011), the change was dramatic (Fig. 12.10). Buzzards had spread as breeding birds throughout Great Britain, much of the island of Ireland, and some of

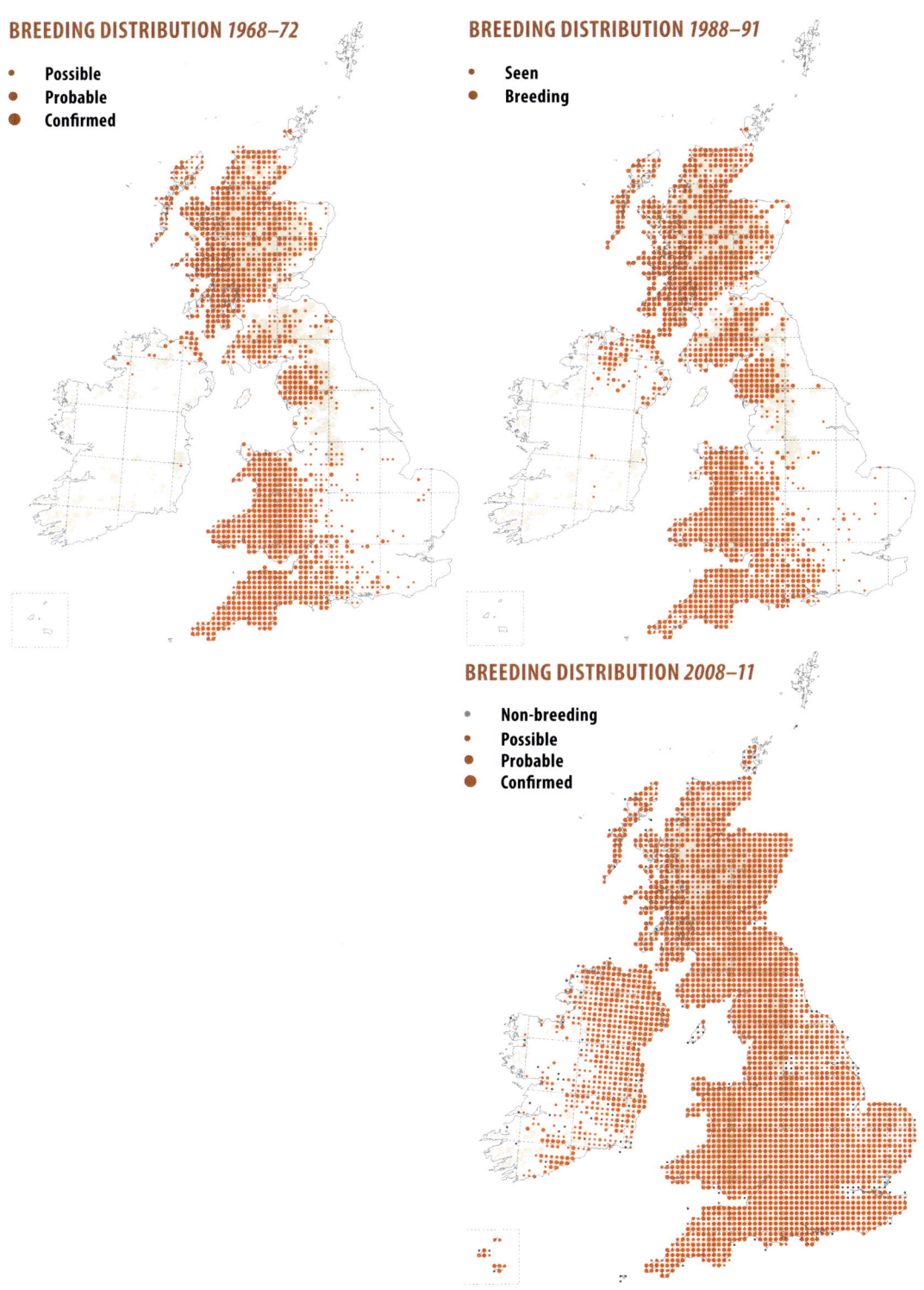

Figures 12.8–12.10. Buzzard breeding distributions 1968–72, 1988–91 and 2007–11. Reproduced from Bird Atlas 2007–11 (Balmer *et al.* 2013), which was a joint project between BTO, BirdWatch Ireland and the Scottish Ornithologists' Club

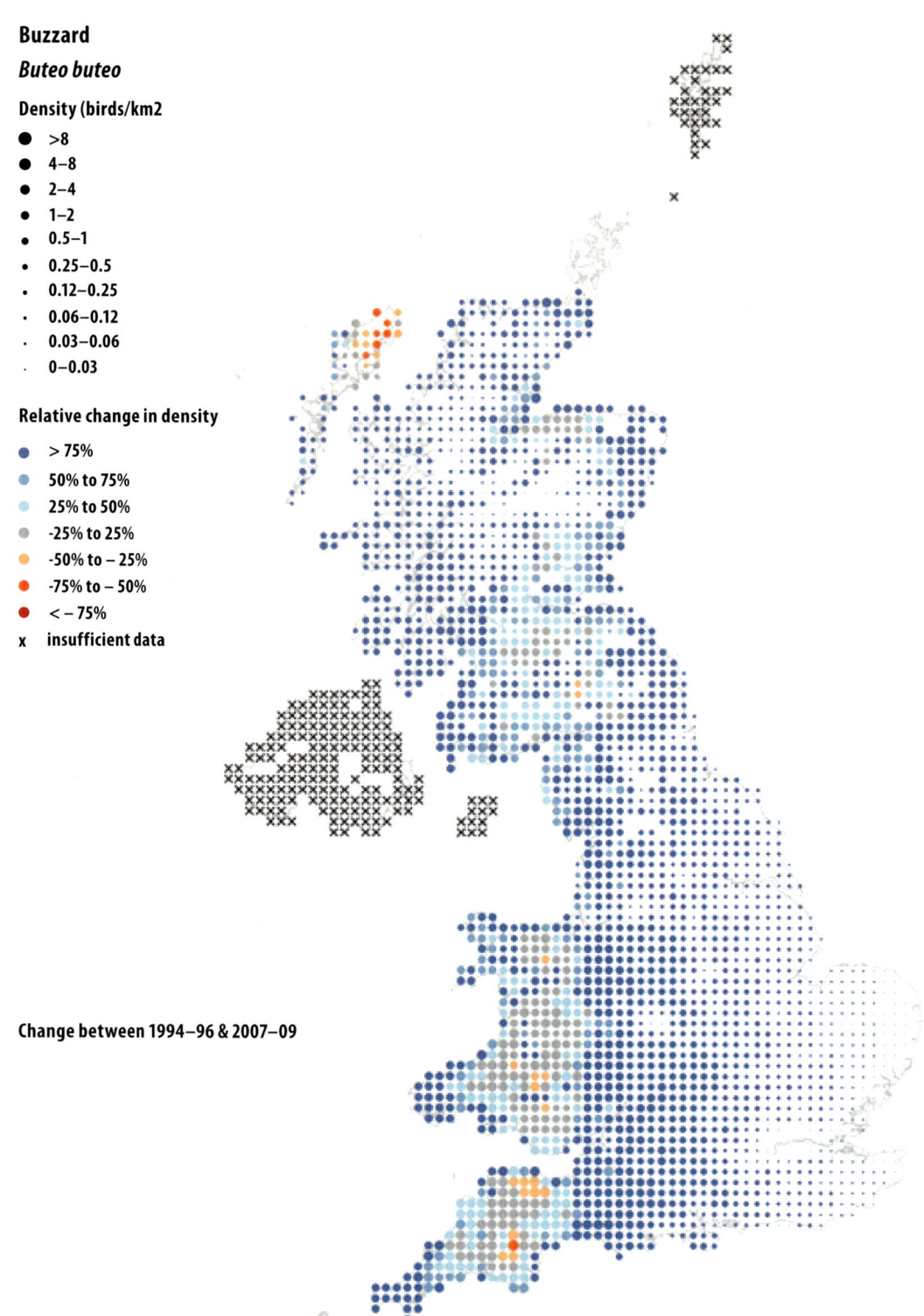

Figure 12.11. **Buzzard changes in breeding densities 1994–96 to 2007–8** (Source: BTO/JNCC/RSPB Breeding Bird Survey). Downloaded, with permission, from: www.bto.org/our-science/projects/breeding-bird-survey/latest-results/maps-population-density-and-trends

the smaller islands, even including the Channel Islands. The changes in winter distributions approximately match this.

The situation is striking too when one looks at the density and change map covering roughly the same period (Fig. 12.11). The drastic increase east of the Welsh border is particularly clear, and there are indications of a progressive spread eastwards. It is notable that the gaps centred on the major cities, London, Birmingham and Manchester, are also evident. A few other major gaps in the new main distribution may reflect pockets of continued illegal poisoning. The low numbers in the east of England probably relate to the Buzzards only just reaching there. This Breeding Bird Survey data reflects also increasing numbers over this period.

The state of the UK's birds 2000 (Anon. 2000) noted that the numbers of several rare birds of prey had recovered since the 1980s (Fig. 12.12). These included particularly Red Kite, Goshawk, Marsh Harrier and Osprey, as well as, less rapidly, Honey Buzzard *Pernis apivorus* and White-tailed Eagle. They noted that the spectacular rise in Red Kite numbers was thanks to protection in Wales and the highly successful reintroduction programme in England and Scotland; and White-tailed Eagles due to the reintroduction programme. The Montagu's Harrier *Circus pygargus* population remained dangerously low, as it had been for many years. Although not illustrated, Hen Harrier *Circus cyaneus* populations remained flat, numbers continuing to be limited by human persecution associated with grouse-management for shooting. The numbers of young Hen Harriers raised on grouse moors were very low, acting as a barrier to recovery. Extinction as a breeding species in England was noted as a real possibility. Among the more common birds of prey, the Hobby *Falco subbuteo* and Buzzard had increased most dramatically in recent years. They considered that the welcome rise in

Figure 12.12. Numbers of breeding pairs of rarer raptors in Britain 1970–2000 (Source: Anon. 2000). Reproduced by permission of the British Trust for Ornithology

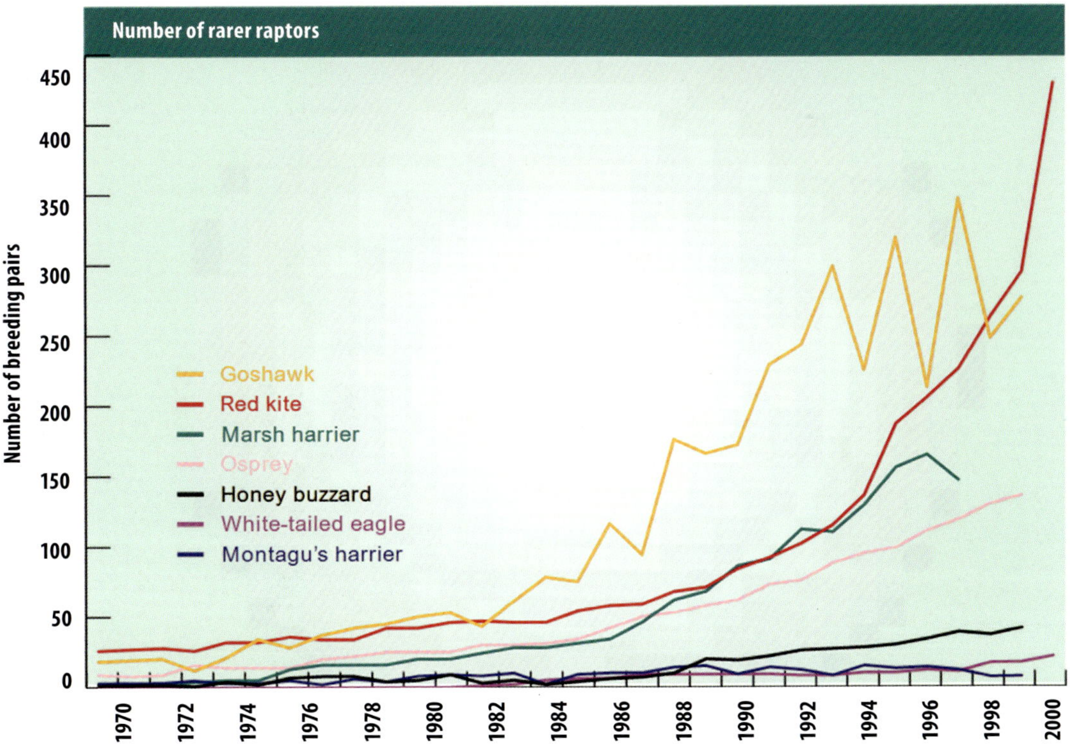

Male (above left) and female (below) Marsh Harriers hunting over their preferred terrain; their numbers in Britain have shown modest recovery, although habitat is now much reduced. The numbers and distributions of Montagu's Harrier (above right: a male being 'mobbed' by a Lapwing to chase it from its breeding area) and Hen Harrier remain extremely concerning. [MP]

numbers of Hobbies might partly be the result of the increased availability of habitat for their favoured prey, dragonflies. Buzzards and Sparrowhawks had both started to spread eastwards in Britain (see above) as part of a recovery from the effects of the organochlorine pesticides in the 1950s and 1960s, helped now by lower levels of illegal persecution in lowland areas. The BTO's monitoring programme showed Sparrowhawk numbers to have stabilised. Other sources of information, however, pointed to local population declines in the 1990s. The Kestrel was the only common raptor in long-term decline. The numbers had fallen by a third since the mid-1970s, the authors noting this as another clear signal that farmland was becoming a poorer place for birds.

The state of the UK's birds 2020 (Burns et al. 2020) noted continuing trends, with increases in both the long and short term obvious for most birds of prey. They concluded that a release from historic levels of persecution and the impacts of organochloride pesticides has allowed raptors such as Ospreys, Peregrines and Marsh Harriers to recover. However, Hen Harriers remained a notable exception, with a lack of recovery, and indeed a short-term decline, caused by illegal persecution continuing. The recent downturn in Montagu's Harriers was a worrying development for this, the rarest of UK's breeding raptors. So, there was still clearly work to do, especially in harrier habitat, where illegal poisoning remained intense.

Outcome: the attitudes to ecosystem restoration

As my project colleagues and I have said repeatedly, we should remember that it is far more important to prevent the loss of our native wildlife than to have to take heroic steps to reinstate parts of it. We have also stressed that it is essential that suitable habitat exists or can be regenerated before reintroductions are attempted. There is some evidence that the success of the Red Kite project stimulated both conservationists and the wider public to try to restore degraded habitats.

This was reflected in 2003, in the news section (pp. 434–5) of *British Wildlife* August 2003 issue, which noted:

Reintroduction has proved overwhelmingly successfully for Red Kites in Britain. Restoring the numbers of other species, however, will require changes in habitat management. A classic example of this is actions to restore the fortunes of farmland birds through management of farmland, largely by means of agri-environment schemes. The first assessment of the impact of the pilot UK Arable Stewardship Scheme gives some cause for optimism. The pilot, in two areas of England (East Anglia and West Midlands), tested such options as winter stubble, wildlife seed mixtures, undersown spring cereal, and field margins. Bird surveys on farms in and out of the scheme showed constant positive effects on granivorous passerines (species such as Linnet Carduelis cannabina, *Yellowhammer* Emberiza citrinella *and Tree Sparrow* Passer montanus*): these occurred in higher numbers in winter on scheme farms than on 'control' farms, probably benefitting from more food in winter in stubbles and wildlife seed mixtures. This was the case, however, only in one pilot area, and other target species, such as Lapwing* Vanellus vanellus *and Skylark* Alauda arvensis, *did not appear to benefit. It may be that simple measures of bird numbers are not adequate, or that there was not enough time for options to develop, but few believe that there will be a quick 'fix' to this problem (Bird Study 50: 131–141).*

Habitat management is also the key to maintaining populations of breeding waders in lowland wet meadows. A recent survey of English sites by BTO, funded by RSPB, English Nature and DEFRA, suggests that the need for such action is urgent. A 2002 re-survey of sites covered in 1982 showed declines of around 40% in Lapwing and Curlew Numenius arquata *numbers, a 20% decline in breeding Redshanks* Tringa totanus *and a staggering 60% decline in Snipe* Gallinago gallinago *numbers. Breeding populations are now concentrated at a handful of sites such as the Nene and Ouse Washes, the Somerset Levels and the Lower Derwent Valley. In fact, 90% of the Snipe recorded in 2002 were on just 3% of the sites covered – a huge concentration that leaves this species extremely vulnerable to massive declines if one or two of these sites are lost (BTO News 247).*

Choughs foraging on sandy coastal heath on the island of Islay, Scottish Inner Hebrides. [MP]

The case of the Chough

In Chapter 3, I outlined our efforts in NCC's Ornithology Branch to deter well-meaning but inappropriate attempts to reintroduce species for which the conditions were not yet suitable. We were certainly not against Chough conservation. In fact, one member of Ornithology Branch, Dr Eric Bignal, was based on – and still lives on – Islay, a stronghold of the Chough. He was already an internationally respected expert on Choughs, and their continued survival on Islay is very much down to him. He and I also responded to a request to NCC from the Chief Executive of the very successful Manx Airways (and later also of Loganair), Terry Liddiard, to design a Manx bird conservation project for them to sponsor, which led us to found the Manx Chough Project.

In Cornwall, the Chough is culturally important, featuring on the county's coat of arms. Cornish legend tells that King Arthur, on his death in battle, was transformed into a chough, 'talons and beaks all red with blood'. In the 1600s, 'Cornish choughs' was a common nickname for the Cornish people, and was used by Shakespeare and other playwrights several times (Deacon 2020). However, the last Cornish Chough had died in 1973, leaving the county devoid of its 'national' symbol. Over the next few years, occasional Choughs would be reported, blown in by storms from Brittany or Wales, and sometimes staying a few months.

The situation for Choughs in 1989 was outlined in our *Ornithology Note 14: Bird Reintroduction schemes in Britain* (Pienkowski 1989):

Chough
There are current proposals to reintroduce choughs to Cornwall, where it is a county emblem. The chough was more widely distributed in Britain in the 19th century and occurred along the south coast of England and around the southwest peninsula. Cornwall was a stronghold but a decline, which began in the latter part of the 18th century, culminated in local extinction (as a breeding bird) in 1947. The general consensus of opinion is that a combination of persecution, particularly between 1870 and 1900, and land-use changes brought about the declines. Nationally this manifested itself as a westward contraction. Protection (initially partial) since 1900, together with maintenance of suitable agricultural land-use has resulted in recoveries notably in the Isle of Man and some parts of Wales, e.g. Bardsey Island and Ramsay, and on the island of Islay, the Scottish stronghold. Pairs still reach the Cornish coast, but do not establish there.

The chough is a good "flagship" for some of the pastoral, low-intensity agricultural landscapes which we would wish to conserve in several parts of Europe. For this reason, NCC's Ornithology Branch sponsored a successful workshop on choughs and land-use in the EEC in autumn 1988, and the proceedings will appear in summer 1989 (Bignal & Curtis 1989). The proposals can be assessed on the basis of this, and other detailed studies. NCC has given modest support to studies of habitat suitability in Cornwall. The present indications are that it is not suitable, but could be reinstated. The need for reintroduction of choughs is also questionable, in that Cornwall is well within the range of normal movements and, indeed, birds do occur there from time to time. One worrying feature is that pressure to obtain birds to release in Cornwall could adversely affect other populations, such as that on Islay which is currently the source of the natural spread in the Hebrides. One magazine article recently submitted by the Cornish project appeared (unintentionally) to incite illegal collecting.

At present, this proposal fails to fulfil criterion 2 as there seem to be prospects of birds reaching the area naturally, 3 and 4. There are also concerns about 6. Again, it is appropriate here to put effort into habitat re-establishment. Only when the habitat is suitable and sufficient to support the social groups which are an important feature of chough's biology would it be appropriate to consider if reintroduction is necessary.

This later proved correct. For example, at first, we had to point out the dangers of suggestions of release of choughs in west Cornwall. However, some of the proponents of this took our concerns to heart and researched the needs of these birds. This led to initial work on coastal habitat restoration, to make the environment more suitable for choughs and other species either lost or endangered in the area (summary in Hales 2021).

For Choughs to thrive, they require management at a landscape scale. Most of the Choughs breed on or close to the coast but there are also pairs inland, particularly in Wales and the Isle of Man. In autumn and winter, flocks roam over considerable distances to find food and are more likely to use inland and upland areas. As primarily invertebrate feeders, Choughs need access to the soil and a mosaic of vegetation with lots of short and open areas in which to feed. Grazing is crucial in keeping coastal and upland habitats in good condition for Choughs. Young Choughs seek out the invertebrates in animal dung as an easy food source and, in some areas, they feed along the strandline on sand-hoppers. During autumn and winter months, arable land is important for choughs where they eat grain and forage for invertebrates in the open soil. They also need safe places to nest. Choughs use sea-caves, old mine-workings, abandoned buildings and even modern agricultural barns. In some areas, they use specially made nest-boxes and ledges.

Work with farmers increased the amount and quality of chough-friendly habitat around the coastal fringe, partly as a side-effect of the National Trust's attempts to encourage wildflowers and rare plants that also flourish in this habitat. This was achieved through advisory work with farmers and landowners and by using agri-environment schemes to fund management, as well as promoting awareness of why managed habitats are good for wildlife and how they are great for people too.

In 2001, a small group of three to five Choughs arrived in Cornwall. Three of the birds took up residence on The Lizard, the UK's most southerly point, and looked set to stay. It was at this time that foot-and-mouth disease took hold of the country, and all access to the countryside was immediately restricted. This made it almost impossible to observe the incomers, but also allowed the Choughs to explore without undue harassment. Two of the birds formed a pair. In 2002, this pair nested and produced three young, the first choughs to be hatched in the wild in Cornwall in over 50 years,

In response to this event, three organisations, the RSPB, English Nature and the National Trust, formed the Cornwall Chough Project. 24-hour surveillance of the nest-site was organised to protect the choughs from any unwanted attention during the breeding season.

The Cornwall Chough Project also kept chough-watchers up to date with regular postings on its blog at http://www.cornishchoughs.org/. Many of the watches are undertaken by local volunteers giving their time to support the choughs, including staff from Paradise Park where Operation Chough is based.

The Cornwall Chough Project reported a steady increase in breeding performance of Red-billed Choughs in Cornwall, reaching 17 chicks fledged from 5 nests in 2014 and 13 chicks fledged from 8 nests in 2015, with 12 pairs in 2020.

Although there is an expansion of nesting pairs, many of these are related as the population is the result of breeding from just three founders. Operation Chough is making captive bred birds available for release in Cornwall to secure the future of the current population, if necessary for demographic or genetic reasons.

On Jersey in recent years, Choughs have formed a flagship part in their ecosystem restoration project, "Birds on the Edge" (undated) to save coastal birds and habitats from extinction, by the States of Jersey, Durrell Wildlife Conservation Trust and the Jersey National Trust, on which the following is based. This programme of habitat restoration on the island's coastline aims:
- To return the Red-billed Chough to its former home
- To highlight the coastland restoration work
- To become a flagship and focus for the state of the natural environment in Jersey.

Jersey's north coast farmland is epitomised by small sloping fields running down to the cliffs' edges. This area is often wild and can never have been easy to farm productively. However, in its heyday with un-intensive farming techniques and numerous hedges, shrubby areas between the fields and sheep-grazed grasslands, it must have been a haven for many species of farmland birds. Sadly, the area entered a steep decline in fortunes as these forms of farming became less profitable. The abandoned fields were quickly overrun by bracken and the dense stands of this fern offer little feeding opportunity for birds. Accordingly, many species once common in these fields have declined and several have died out altogether. The Yellowhammer *Emberiza citronella* was common between Grève de Lecq and Bouley Bay as recently as the 1980s. Now it is extinct here, its distinctive song, rendered as *"a little bit of bread and no cheese"* no longer heard. The last pair was recorded in 2005. Similarly, Turtle Dove *Streptopelia turtur*, Skylark *Alauda arvensis* and Stonechat *Saxicola rubecula* have declined and may be lost, while Meadow Pipit *Anthus pratensis* and Linnet *Carduelis cannabina*, once widespread, now thrive only at a handful of protected sites. Historical numbers of Choughs in Jersey are unknown, but, once found on several areas of the Island's coastline, the species became locally extinct by 1900. A similar pattern of extinction was recorded in all the other Channel Islands and the last attempted breeding may have been in Guernsey in 1929. Now the nearest colonies of Chough to Jersey were in Brittany where there are around 50 pairs and in Cornwall, where the species was doing well since naturally recolonising, and on the Gower Peninsula and Pembrokeshire in west Wales.

The *Birds on the Edge* project is using Choughs as flagships of innovative schemes for an improving environment and an increased understanding of the benefit of this to all islanders. Areas of the north coast are being actively managed to remove the bracken as well as reinstating former farming practices such as sheep-grazing to benefit wildlife. With sufficient areas of former farmland restored, Choughs are being re-established using birds reared at Jersey Zoo (Durrell's headquarters) and at Paradise Park in Cornwall.

In 2013, the first release began with seven birds. By 2015, a further 13 birds had joined the wild flock at Sorel. After only a year in the wild, and in only their first breeding attempt, 2015 saw three nesting pairs, and one pair succeeded in raising a chick – the first in Jersey for over 100 years. By 2020, the numbers had reached at least 12 chicks from at least 7 nests, and wild-bred young had themselves produced young.

Corncrakes

Along with Red Kite and White-tailed Eagles, Corncrakes *Crex crex* were the third globally vulnerable bird species in UK in the 1980s. RSPB and others have been putting major effort and resources into restoring Corncrakes. This has been via a variety of approaches, including habitat management, exploration with farmers on farming techniques, captive breeding and regional reintroductions.

Corncrakes are related to Moorhens *Gallinula chloropus*, Coots *Fulica atra* and rails but differ from most members of the family in that they live on dry land. Corncrakes are surprisingly small; they are only a little bigger than Blackbirds *Turdus merula*. They are very secretive, spending most of their time hidden in tall vegetation, with presence betrayed only by the rasping call. In flight, their bright chestnut wings and trailing legs are unmistakable. They are summer visitors and migrate to Africa for the winter.

The species started declining in western Europe in the mid 19th century, coinciding with the start of the mechanisation of agricultural systems and earlier cutting of the hay harvest. Since the 1950s the rate of decline accelerated, coinciding with a period when the majority of hay fields were changed to silage production, which allowed even earlier cutting dates, and often production of two crops per season. In many areas cutting is now so early that suitable nesting habitat no longer exists in the breeding season. Major investment in drainage schemes in the 1980s allowed silage production to spread to many poorly drained areas in Scotland and Ireland, which until then had remained untouched.

This was first noticeable in Britain, Ireland, Fennoscandia and west-central Europe and, since 1970, the decline spread through most of the European range of the species, including some of its east European strongholds. During 1970–1990 all countries except Sweden and Finland recorded declines in excess of 20% (in ten countries more than 50%).

A male Corncrake makes a rare emergence from deep in the meadow grasses and scrub to make his crex-crex call, one of very few bird species to sing just its scientific name. [MP]

In Britain, the decline started in south-east England in the mid-19th century and gradually spread north and west. By the late 1930s, Corncrakes were absent from much of England and southern Wales, and large parts of Scotland. Only in the northern and western islands were they still abundant. In Ireland the decline started later and spread more slowly, though more recent decline since 1988 has been dramatic.

The speed at which agricultural changes can affect the corncrake is illustrated by the 80% decline in numbers in Northern Ireland in three years (1988–1991), which coincided with earlier cutting dates as farmers were encouraged to produce silage instead of hay and increased sheep stocking which resulted in further loss of hay meadows.

In Britain and Ireland there have been unprecedented declines in numbers throughout the range of the species, accompanied with 76% contraction in range since 1970. By the 1990s, the annual decline was so great that, had it continued, the species would have gone extinct in the British Isles within 10–20 years. As a result of conservation measures in the core areas, the decline was finally halted with the lowest point in Britain in 1993 with 480 calling males, and in Republic of Ireland in 1994 with 129 calling males. Since then numbers in Britain have increased with just under 900 males recorded in 2019.

In Northern Ireland Corncrakes were still widespread at the time of the 1968–71 *Atlas*, but by mid-1980s their range had contracted to the western counties, particularly Co. Fermanagh. In recent years the range has contracted further with only a small number recorded annually.

Reintroductions are rather challenging in this species. With current numbers and distributions, captive-breeding is probably the only practicable course. The species is a long-distance migrant and, at least in evolutionary terms, its habitat is fairly mobile geographically in time. Therefore, young birds are less likely to return to where they were reared than were, for example, Red Kites. The RSPB, in conjunction with others, has made major efforts here during the last two decades, but I think that the jury is still out on whether the limited successes have the potential for wider use. However, they wisely did not put all their eggs in one basket. Their other techniques have shown some recovery in core areas, but not yet a re-spread of range (RSPB, undated1; Wotton *et al.* 2015). Habitat management is key.

The situation more generally

The Corncrake illustrates a wider problem. Whilst it is pleasing that the situation for Red Kites and other predators and scavengers is improving, largely because of the decline in illegal poisoning, the situation in the countryside more generally gives rise to concern. For example, Burns *et al.* (2020) reported: *"New figures from the Avian Population Estimates Panel (APEP) suggest that there are 83 million pairs of native breeding birds in the UK. This is 19 million pairs fewer than when widespread monitoring began in the late 1960s. This figure is similar to that presented in* The state of the UK's birds 2012, *based on the previous APEP report, suggesting that, in terms of total breeding bird numbers, the period of relative stability that began in the 1990s is continuing.*

"The farmland indicator continues to decline, despite widespread uptake of agri-environment schemes and other bespoke conservation initiatives. In 2019, the indicator stood at 45% of its 1970 value, with a decline of 5% in the short term (2013 to 2018). Specialist farmland species within the farmland indicator include some of our fastest declining birds, such as turtle doves [Streptopelia turtur] *and grey partridges* [Perdix perdix].

"Species in the wetland indicator show a mix of trends within a long-term average decline of 12% . When further split into wetland type, birds of wet grassland show strong declines (lapwings [Vanellus vanellus]*, redshanks* [Tringa totanus]*, snipe* [Gallinago gallinago]*), whereas birds of slow or standing water show an increase, driven by increased numbers of mallards* [Anas platyrhynchos] *and tufted ducks* [Aythya fuligula]*."*

Formerly widespread and familiar species being lost from our countryside: (left) Curlew in song-flight and pair guarding their hidden chicks; (right) Lapwings in song-flight and catching a worm. [MP]

The intensification of agriculture (see, *e.g.*, Pain & Pienkowski 1997), involving heavy use of fertilizers and pesticides, deep drainage, over-winter cropping with early harvest, increasingly large and fast machinery *etc.*, has led to a heavy toll on wildlife. The Corncrake decline was an early consequence, but the losses even during the recent decades of my lifetime are striking. Looking at my old specialism of waders, a well recognised sequence of loss of breeding species has been evident across the country. The loss of Snipe has been followed by Redshank, then Curlew and now Lapwing. Some countries have retained high breeding densities of some of these species on productive farmland. Several of these are around the Baltic, where over-winter crops may be less dominant. There must be lessons to learn here.

Outcome: facilitating appropriate reintroductions and recovery programmes more generally for other species of wildlife – the lessons from the Kite programme
In Chapters 3 and 11, I explained that the legislation badly written by central government departments had so distorted the budget of NCC that it had no allocation for species recovery, and we had to find a reason to provide the modest funds needed for the kite project from the research budget. Recovery programmes were already being discussed by scientific conservationists in both the statutory and voluntary bodies. However, a boost was needed to get that into the budgets of the statutory bodies. By the time of the setting up of the successor bodies to NCC, the success of the Red Kite Experimental Reintroduction project was already evident. The leaders of the successor bodies, as well as the relevant NGOs, made sure that they had restoration budgets and programmes. Indeed, when part of the kite project transferred

from JNCC to English Nature several years later, it was retrospectively added to their species recovery programme.

Of course, the trick of a really successful species recovery project is to generate benefits for wider conservation gains. This might be in terms of habitat improvement or public attitude for other species in the ecosystem, or breaking new ground for them. In the Red Kite project, we did both. As Danny Heptinstall, of JNCC, said in 2020: "Thirty years ago the reintroduction of a lost species was a radical act. Thanks to pioneering projects like the Red Kites, it is now a standard tool in the nature conservation toolkit."

We can look briefly at some of the consequences, at least partly due to this project, for other species.

White-tailed Eagle

Our Red Kite exercise benefitted, of course, from our experience in running the White-tailed Eagle introduction. We were able to repay the complement in at least three ways: the benefit to anti-poisoning attitudes which arose at least in part from the Red Kite project; the numbers to be released; and considerations of release areas.

In fact, as Chairman of the Sea Eagle Project Team from 1987, I was responsible for supervising a review of this project in parallel with setting up the Red Kite project. In the case of the eagle, we wanted to work out how the project was progressing and whether further importations were needed following the end of the first phase of releases in 1985. Figure 3.1 in Chapter 3 was generated from that review.

In addition to continuing to contract John Love to coordinate survey and monitoring work, collate sightings, assess numbers, estimate ranges, locate eyries, monitor performance, liaise with land-owners and others with an interest, organise protection, disseminate information, *etc.* the Project Team set in train various reviews to answer key questions which would determine future actions. These included a review by John Love and myself of data on performance over the years, including in relation to age and time since release (some early birds were kept in captivity for some months or even years before release) to correct any errors in earlier collating. This was to feed into mathematical modelling by Dr Rhys Green of RSPB. Rhys's modelling indicated that the chance of long-term survival of the establishing population would be greatly increased by introducing 8 male and 8 female young eagles in each of the 3 years 1995–1997 (Green, Pienkowski & Love 1996). On the bases of these various analyses, we supported the more recent style of release after shorter, rather than longer, periods of captivity, and saw advantages in aiming to release the same number of birds over fewer years. We had rapidly reached similar conclusion with the Red Kite releases in progress by this time, and knew from experience with that project that we could handle more young birds per year than had the earlier eagle importations. We also knew from the kite work that it is possible to reduce the human contact of the kites during quarantine more than previously used with the eagles.

Two White-tailed Eagle chicks in a Norwegian nest [JL]

Other studies by Dr Bob Furness (Glasgow University), Mick Marquis and others did not support (partly because of limited data) any suggestions that various pollutants were affecting breeding success. NCC and RSPB also collaborated from 1990 in attempts to install hidden video cameras and recorders at nest sites to secure further information on the causes of nest-failure. Video equipment in those days was far

Red-tagged released juvenile White-tailed Eagle on the shore at Kinloch, Isle of Rum [JL]

"Flying barn door": member of Pair 6 formed from the reared and released White-tailed Eagles, Scottish Hebrides [JL]

less portable than nowadays, and I recall spending a few days with colleagues in the Scottish Small Isles laboriously carrying heavy car batteries strapped to my rucksack frame over the hills to set this up. We investigated electronic tags to help follow the birds but discovered that, at that stage, development did not allow for long enough useful tag-life. The video systems were plagued by technical failures, flooding by heavy rain, inadequate sunlight for our early solar power system, and failure of the eagles to use some of their previously used nest-sites – but you can't win them all!

During this period, we were delighted by the major step forward in 1991 when four pairs of eagles raised a record seven young. In the press release, we were keen both to celebrate the success but also to stress that we were still in for a long haul. Accordingly: "*Dr Mike Pienkowski, JNCC Director Life Sciences, said: 'This success is particularly exciting as it follows a poor year in 1990. These young are a just reward for all the effort and goodwill put into the project from individuals and organisations both locally and internationally.'* Graham Wynne, RSPB Director Conservation, said: *'Although too soon to judge the overall success of the project, this year's results are very promising. Careful monitoring and protection wlll be needed for many years to come before this magnificent bird can truly be said to have returned.'*"

At the Project Team meeting in November 1991, we reviewed the results of the various studies and agreed to explore securing further young eagles from Norway in the light of the studies outlined above. A key aspect was the analysis (later published as Green, Pienkowski & Love 1996, and mentioned in Chapter 9) addressing the issue that small naturalized populations with little or no natural immigration are less able to compensate for detrimental effects and this increases their probability of extinction, and further releases would be advisable. This required investigations of the potential supply, transport, cost, timing, strategy and release locations. For the last mentioned, we would need to stay, for the present, in western Scotland because the purpose was to strengthen the resilience of the population starting to establish. We were looking for the future at more easterly sites, based partly on the kite research.

We developed better field recording forms (still paper in those days). We agreed to collect feathers and blood samples when possible systematically to explore for individual identification, DNA analysis, presence of heavy metals etc, some of this building on the kite experience. We agreed on a form of release of information for the BTO Atlas in a way that would be useful for that but not pose a risk to the birds. We also set up investigations of the potential in new legislation to allow payments to farmers as an incentive to take a positive approach to eagles settling on their land.

Released White-tailed Eagle "Sula" on nest in Scottish Hebrides [JL]

Raven "mobbing" White-tailed Eagle shows the enormous size of the latter. [MP]

Following NCC's reorganisation, I agreed with my SNH colleagues that JNCC would continue the project lead, with strong SNH and RSPB involvement (effectively reflecting the continuing roles of existing Sea Eagle Team personnel), but that we would plan to transfer the lead to SNH in 1993. This timing was built into the various studies we had commissioned, so that we could hand the project over with a clear direction agreed for the project to continue.

I had to fend off some over-enthusiastic requests by certain Nature Conservancy Council for Scotland (renamed the following year as Scottish Natural Heritage) senior staff in 1991 to bring this date forward and to transfer some aspects to staff not previously involved before these planned matters were resolved, but this was achieved. I am pleased to say that, shortly before the handover, the senior SNH officer (who had not previously been involved with the eagles) taking over responsibility wrote to me: "The project seems to have run extremely smoothly thanks to the dedication of John Love and the supervision from yourself."

Meanwhile, during 1992, we arranged for members of the Team, particularly Roy Dennis, John Love and Rhys Green, to draft operational plans to implement the provisional decisions of the Team. These were then considered in discussions during the year and at the Project Team meeting in Inverness in August that year, when I was able to welcome increased SNH representation to ease the transition to come in the next few months. After considering Rhys Green's further analysis, the Team confirmed the wish to import more eagles and to start this in 1993, if possible. We applied a technique similar to that developed earlier for the kites to be as objective as possible in identifying the best release areas in the region. We agreed on a plan for farmers assisting eagles on the land they worked.

Following the meeting, I advised colleagues in the Department of the Environment that further importations would be needed and therefore an application for CITES licences would be coming, probably from SNH. I arranged for JNCC to fund a visit by Roy Dennis (no longer on RSPB's staff but with their approval) to Norway in early 1992 to explore importing more birds, and John Love would advise on the basis of his earlier and continuing contacts.

Early in 1993, as planned, I handed over the project lead to SNH, who had appointed Professor George Dunnet to chair it. I arranged for JNCC to continue to be involved to support, and appointed Dr Colin Galbraith to this role.

Between 1993 and 1998, a further 58 young eagles that hatched in nests in Norway were released in Wester Ross by Scottish Natural Heritage (SNH), in collaboration with RSPB.

White-tailed Eagle [MP]

In 2000, the 100th sea-eagle chick was reared. There were then 19 breeding pairs, of which 12 had produced chicks. However, four nest-sites were responsible for 75% of the chicks since the first success in 1985 (10 years after start of reintroduction). So matters were not yet secure.

With the early results of the later releases, the slow but steady upward trend in numbers of White-tailed Eagles continued in 2002, with 26 territorial pairs found in the Highlands and Islands of Scotland. Unfortunately, illegal persecution remained a problem, and a real threat to the future of the population. Two birds were found poisoned in 2002 – the loss of a breeding male was particularly significant. The prospects for a continued recovery looked quite good, however, as long as persecution could be checked. The low productivity and slow maturity of these large birds meant that future increase was likely to be a slow process; they remained vulnerable.

Taking on further of our recommendations, both on a more easterly location and more young released per year, a third phase of the reintroduction project took place on the east coast of Scotland between 2007 and 2012. A total of 85 young birds were released. In 2013, the first pair of birds from the east coast project bred successfully fledging a single chick. This was the first pair to breed in that part of Scotland for more than 200 years. A similar project took place in Ireland from 2007 to 2011 when 100 young birds were released in Killarney National Park, Co Kerry with the first successful breeding also taking place in 2013. The Irish project extended to Munster in 2021 (Anon. 2021a).

There are now more than 100 territorial pairs in Scotland. The recovery in Britain is reflected across many other parts of Europe, particularly around the Baltic. While the population remains small, the potential impacts of persecution, disturbance and egg collecting remain high.

At least seven White-tailed Eagles have been killed illegally since the start of the project and at least four clutches of eggs have been stolen. Nevertheless, the population continues to grow and is calculated to be self-sustaining.

Increasingly close partnership working between the conservation bodies, police and local communities – combined with the introduction of custodial sentences for convictions of wildlife crime – appears to have neutralised the impact of egg-collectors during a critical stage of population growth. There have been no known nest robberies since 2000.

The concerns of sheep-farmers have been addressed by maintaining close liaison with farmers and crofters and by implementing research and management schemes. Projects on Skye and Mull have raised the profile of White-tailed Eagles by encouraging the public to see the birds safely. The high level of interest shown by visitors has encouraged the community to value White-tailed Eagles more highly and the public sites may well have taken the pressure off nests otherwise vulnerable to disturbance.

An invitation from my colleague in the earlier Experimental Red Kite project, Jonathan Spencer, to Roy Dennis to address his then colleagues in Forest Enterprise England led in 2019 to a project to bring White-tailed Eagles back to the south of England. They were once widespread from Cornwall to Kent, and northward. The project is a partnership between Roy Dennis Wildlife Foundation (2021) and Forestry England with additional support from conservation organisations and other key stakeholders and organisations based on both the Isle of Wight and mainland who form the project steering group.

The *Anglo-Saxon Chronicles* report birds that were almost certainly White-tailed Eagles as feasting on the bodies of dead warriors during the period that what is now England was composed of several separate kingdoms, at times fighting between themselves and also with Viking invaders. However, dead human flesh is not an essential habitat requirement. The eagles were driven to extinction by relentless persecution that began in the Middle Ages. The last pair bred on Culver Cliff on the Isle of Wight in 1780. Many parts of southern England remain highly suitable for the species.

In addition to the conservation benefits, the project is expected to give a significant boost to the Isle of Wight economy, including in winter. In Scotland, eagle tourism is extremely popular and recent reports have shown White-tailed Eagles generate up to £5 million to the economy of the Isle of Mull each year, and £2.4 million to the Isle of Skye.

Juvenile White-tailed Eagles are collected under licence, issued by Scottish Natural Heritage, from nests in Scotland and translocated to the Isle of Wight in late June. In the months after release, the dispersing eagles have been seen widely, including over parts of London by October 2020.

Osprey – natural recolonization Scotland; reintroduction to England
Ospreys became extinct as breeding birds in England in 1840 and in Scotland in 1916, though they continued to occur as passage migrants. A long-distance seasonal migrant (they winter in west Africa) perhaps has more likelihood of re-establishing naturally and, indeed, a pair returned naturally to nest at Loch Garten in Scotland in 1954. The population very slowly increased, with help from nest protection and public engagement initiatives, including "Operation Osprey" led by George Waterson, the then Director of RSPB Scotland, at Loch Garten. Despite these positive steps, populations remained low as egg-collection was still prevalent, especially as the Osprey eggs now had increased rarity. The population growth was further slowed through pesticide use, including DDT, which affected the quality of the eggs laid by the Ospreys. Only after harsher consequences for egg-collection and the ban on DDT in 1972, did the Osprey population in Scotland properly make a comeback from two pairs in 1967, and by the 1990s there were over 60 pairs. There was a then steady increase in breeding numbers in Scotland to 150 pairs in 2000, and approximately 250 in 2018. There are also many juvenile birds around each year but the total population is probably less than 1,500 birds (Dennis 1995; Anon. 2021b; Scottish Wildlife Trust, undated).

Following the success of the Experimental Red Kite project and using similar techniques, Ospreys were transported from Scotland to England, at Rutland Water in the East

Midlands. In partnership with the Leicestershire & Rutland Wildlife Trust, as well as Anglian Water, the project started in 1996. Five years after the project began, Ospreys returned as a breeding bird to England, with a nest both at Rutland and another in the Lake District in the north of England, by natural spread. The Lake District pair raised a chick at their lakeside nest in 2001, 2 in 2002 and another in 2003. The natural spread in northernmost England has continued. For example, for many years, Ospreys were seen passing through Kielder in Northumberland, without stopping, on the way north to more long-standing nesting sites in Scotland. As more of the best nesting spots were taken, it was perhaps just a matter of time before they stayed south of the border. To encourage this, Forestry England installed a number of platforms around Kielder Forest. This paid off as, following an absence of about 200 years in Northumberland, Ospreys returned to nest successfully at Kielder in 2009 (Northumberland Wildlife Trust, undated). The spread in Northumbria has continued.

Osprey brings branch to nest platform. [MP]

The Rutland translocation was successful. The project reached a milestone in 2001 when male tagged 03, which had been translocated to Rutland Water in 1997, raised a single chick with an un-ringed female close to the reservoir. Over 150 young ospreys have fledged from nests in the Rutland Water area since the first chick in 2001 (Leicester & Rutland Wildlife Trust, undated). There is now a self-sustaining population, with some fledged individuals even spreading to breed in other parts of England and Wales.

After years of attempting to restore a breeding population to the English south coast naturally, the Poole Harbour Osprey Translocation Project was initiated to help spread their population further, with the hope of eventually linking the populations between Rutland, Wales and France (Anon. 2021b). Poole Harbour already hosts high numbers of Ospreys passing through from northern nests on migration in spring and autumn. They spend anywhere between a few hours and a few weeks in the harbour, stopping off to make the most of the abundant fishing opportunities. Historically, Ospreys were locally referred to as "Mullet Hawks" due to the high number of Grey Mullet, an ideal meal for the birds, in the harbour. Since 2017, which marked the start of the Poole Harbour Osprey Translocation Project, there had been a resident female, ringed CJ7, which returned to the area each summer until 2019. CJ7 had fledged from a nesting site in Rutland in 2015, but was seemingly attracted to Poole Harbour by the young birds released through the project. In 2019, when a young translocated male, LS7, returned for the first time, CJ7 bonded with him over the summer, creating potential for nesting the following year. However, LS7 did not return again in 2020, and so the hope for a returning male to breed with CJ7 continued.

There are now close to 300 breeding pairs in the UK – the majority are in Scotland, while numbers in England and Wales are on the up thanks to the efforts of Wildlife Trusts and others.

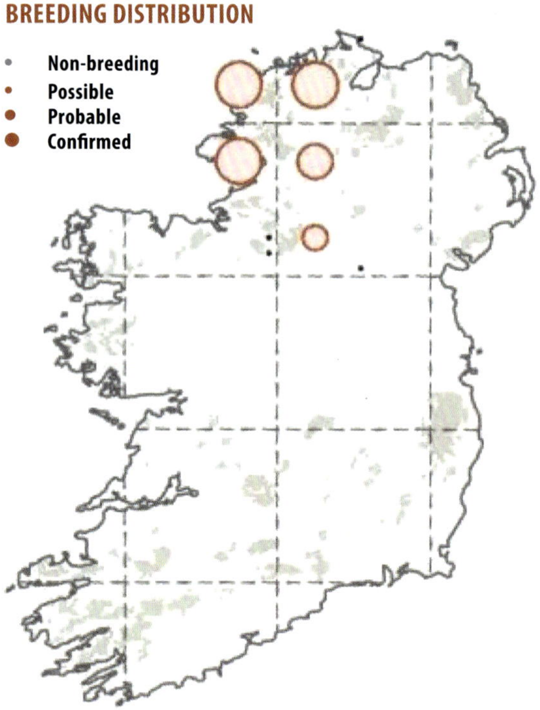

BREEDING DISTRIBUTION

- Non-breeding
- Possible
- Probable
- Confirmed

Figure 12.13. Breeding distribution of re-established Golden Eagles in Ireland. Reproduced with the approval of BirdWatch Ireland and BTO from Bird Atlas 2007–11 (Balmer *et al.* 2013), which was a joint project between BTO, BirdWatch Ireland and the Scottish Ornithologists' Club

Golden Eagle in Ireland

Golden Eagles *Aquila chrysaetos* were once widespread in Ireland but, by the early 20th century, the birds of prey were no longer seen soaring in Irish skies. The population decline and subsequent extinction in Ireland was largely due to persecution, in the form of shootings and poisoning.

Following the success of Red Kites and, eventually, White-tailed Eagles in Britain, and the resulting surge in conservationist interest in ecosystem and species restoration work, Ireland too took up such issues, including Red Kites and White-tailed Eagles (see above) and also Golden Eagles. This last project was first envisioned over 30 years ago, in 1989 by the Golden Eagle Trust, a charity dedicated to the conservation and restoration of Ireland's native birds and their habitats.

After many years of preparation, suitable habitat for Golden Eagles was approved in Glenveagh National Park, Co. Donegal. In 2001, twelve eaglets arrived from Scotland. A total of 60 Golden Eagles were released and, since breeding began in 2007, twenty Irish-born Golden Eagle chicks have fledged in Donegal. Wandering birds from this project have been observed in upland areas throughout Ireland.

The Highland Foundation for Wildlife assisted the Irish Golden Eagle Project from its inception by assisting with feasibility studies and then later on by helping with the collection of 6-week old chicks in the Scottish Highlands. Irish project manager Lorcan O'Toole previously worked for the Red Kite project (National Museum of Ireland 2020; BirdWatch Ireland 2021).

Lorcan O'Toole said: "Ireland appears to have lost six species of birds of prey in recent centuries, including some of our most striking and charismatic birds such as Osprey, Red Kite and Golden Eagle. We hope this imbalance and loss can be redressed in the new millennium."

White Stork

White Storks *Ciconia ciconia* were once a breeding bird of Britain, with an archaeological record stretching back 360,000 years, and many references in historical documents. Knepp (2020), who are attempting a restoration project for this and other species, point out that White Storks are well associated with their county of Sussex. The Saxon name for the village of Storrington, near Worthing, was originally "Estorchestone", meaning "the village of the storks". A pair of White Storks still features on the village emblem. Other place names in the area, such as Storwood and Storgelond, evoke the stork's historical presence here.

White Stork last bred in Britain on St Giles Cathedral, Edinburgh, Scotland in 1416. To put this in another time framework, this was within a year of the Battle of Agincourt between England and France on 25 October 1415 – Saint Crispin's Day, famed in Shakespeare's (1600) even then historical play *Henry V*.

Together with a number of private landowners in West Sussex, East Sussex and Surrey, and in partnership with the Roy Dennis Wildlife Foundation, Warsaw Zoo and Cotswold Wildlife Park, Knepp Estate is helping to establish a breeding population of free-living White Storks in Britain once again. Successful reintroductions in France, Sweden, Poland, the Netherlands, Belgium and Switzerland have demonstrated how this can be done, by building up a number of colonies in close proximity in a given region. This creates a kind of critical mass that makes the population viable.

At Knepp, a fox-proof, mink-proof pen covering about six and a half acres was built, and a number of White Storks imported from Warsaw Zoo, from 2016 for 5 years. Using techniques from the successful Alsace reintroduction programme, the flight feathers of the juveniles were clipped for the first three years to allow the birds to become loyal to the region and lose the urge to migrate. Every year more birds were added to each of the pens. When they reached maturity, at around three or four years old, the young White Storks are allowed to fly freely and forage in the surrounding landscape where, it was hoped, they would begin to build nests and successfully rear their young. As soon as a breeding population is established, first-year birds will also be released in order to enhance the expanding colony. In time this may result in the population becoming migratory, but evidence from Alsace and other parts of Europe suggests that Sussex and the wider landscape in southern England is well capable of supporting a wintering population of storks.

White Storks work on further building of nest on tall pole and catch small prey item in shallow pool. [MP]

White Storks like living in close proximity to people, building their large shaggy nests on roofs and church towers. In continental Europe they are so beloved, and ubiquitously considered a sign of good luck, that people erect horizontal cartwheels on their roofs as platforms to attract them. Their nests provide opportunities for colonies of other birds such as Tree and House Sparrows *Passer montanus* & *domesticus*.

The first pair of wild White Storks flying over Hammer Pond towards the holding pen were seen in early January 2017, and then a single stork in February 2017, just months after the captive storks had arrived. This was an encouraging sign that the reared birds would, once they reach maturity, be joined by continental birds. With several first-year birds free-flying, one bird was recorded in Brittany, having flown across the Channel from the Isle of Wight.

In early April 2020, it was confirmed that there were five eggs in a nest at the Knepp project and, in the following weeks, the birds were regularly observed taking great care to incubate the eggs. The nest was in a large Oak tree, making viewing difficult but despite this, the Project Officer watched as eggshell was removed from the nest and the parents were seen regurgitating food for the chicks to eat. The chicks, when grown, were large enough to be seen by distant television cameras. The chicks, once fledged, flew down to the ground to feed on grasshoppers under the watchful eye of their parents and roosted in nearby trees at night.

It is believed that the parents are the same pair that attempted to nest at Knepp the previous year, when the eggs failed to hatch. The female is a ringed bird from the project, which came to Knepp in 2016 from Poland. The male, however, has no identifying ring, so this is likely to be one of the twenty or so vagrant storks which visit the UK each year.

Draining of wetlands, habitat for amphibians and small fish the birds eat, and pesticide-driven absences of insects that supplement their diet, combined with fatalities from collisions with power lines, have led to declines in many parts of Europe. These losses in part have been offset by reintroductions in France, Italy, Spain, the Netherlands, Switzerland, Poland, and Sweden.

Isabella Tree, of the project, said *"In the UK – one of the most nature-depleted countries in the world, ranked 189th out of 218 countries, according to a Biodiversity Intactness Index run by the Predicts project – more than two-fifths of mammals, insects, birds, and other wildlife have seen significant declines since the 1970s. White Storks are emblematic of a wider movement to repair nature in the country, of which Knepp Estate – run by my husband, Charlie Burrell, and me – is a pioneer. To kickstart natural processes, in 2000 we began rewilding our 3,500 acres of depleted, loss-making farmland. This hinged on restoring the river, ponds, and wetlands, allowing thorny scrub and trees to regenerate, and introducing free-roaming herbivores such as old English longhorn cattle, Exmoor ponies, and Tamworth pigs as proxies of extinct aurochs* [Bos primigenius], *tarpans* [Equus ferus], *and wild boars* [Sus scrofa]. *Then we stood back and allowed nature to take over."*

This underlines the close overlap of reintroduction, re-wilding, and farming extensification as closely overlapping aspects of restoration work.

Mammals: Beavers

I was slightly surprised to realise that our Red Kite project was being cited as a precedent for some mammal projects too. Partly, this is related to the increasing integrated rewilding programme, such as that at Knepp. Much of the work done at Knepp to restore watercourses, including returning a stretch of the River Adur to its floodplain, could have been done more efficiently and at no expense, by a family of Beavers *Castor fiber* (Knepp, undated).

Beavers were once part of the British landscape. Place names echo their presence – from Beverley in Yorkshire to Beverston in Gloucestershire and Beverley Brook running through Richmond Park to the Thames. They were hunted to the verge of extinction during the reign of King Henry VIII, prized for their silky fur and castoreum – the secretion from the scent

Beaver and its lodge [MP]

sacs close to the tail, used for making perfume and medicines. The last known British Beaver was killed in 1789 in Bolton Percy, Yorkshire.

Research in America, Canada and Europe has identified Beavers as a 'keystone species' whose activities result in a huge maintenance or restoration of biodiversity. Their coppicing of trees along the riverbanks – for food and to build dams and lodges – lets in sunlight which encourages oxygen-producing aquatic plants. Native trees such as Willow *Salix* spp. and Alder *Alnus glutinosa* evolved alongside Beavers for millions of years. When gnawed on by Beavers, they quickly regrow from felled stems or cuttings. This process thins trees and allows space for other plants to grow in the area, creating a rich and diverse ecosystem. Woody debris dragged into the water by the Beavers provides a jungle of substrate for micro-organisms to grow on – fuel for populations of invertebrates which, in turn, provide food for fish and aquatic birds. As hydrological engineers, Beavers are also hugely effective at creating water-systems that are able to purify water, store it, and protect against devastating floods.

Rather than increase resilience to floods, human activity has too often done the opposite. One aspect of this is by converting wetlands – which could have soaked up much of the water – to farmland, housing and industrial land, as well as straightening and canalising rivers, with the effect of rapidly concentrating floodwaters in downstream areas, rather than dispersing it in less damaging ways. One of the appalling examples of profoundly stupid and irresponsible failures of statutory responsibilities in recent decades – despite widespread warnings of the potential consequences – has been the approval and, indeed, encouragement by national and regional governments in UK for building of homes and industry on former water-meadows, the very locations used in former years to store floodwaters until they can lower. Not only does this put these new constructions at high risk, but it also reduces the area into which water can be stored safely, thereby putting other areas at risk also. Sadly, ministers and senior officials are rarely held accountable for their errors and neglect.

Macdonald *et al*. (1995) reviewed positively the case for reintroductions of European Beavers to UK. Begum (2021) summarised the progress in reintroduction projects since. In 2001, a group of up to 200 wild Beavers were discovered on the River Tay, Scotland's longest river. Several wildlife organisations worked together and established the Scottish Beaver Trial in 2009, to introduce and monitor a wild Beaver family for five years. Following the results, the Scottish government confirmed Beavers as a native species and gave them a European Protected Species status.

In March 2011, a pair of juveniles were released into a three-hectare fenced enclosure on private land in northern Devon. This was so they could restore a nationally important wet grassland area. In 2013, three wild Beavers were spotted on the River Otter in Devon – the first time in England in over 400 years. However, due to their lengthy absence, Beavers were not considered a native species in England, and the government planned to capture and place them in a zoo or wildlife park. This was met with passionate resistance from local residents and campaign groups which made the government reconsider. This led to a five-year monitoring programme called the River Otter Beaver Trial. A couple of years later, Natural England announced the Beavers could stay as long as they were of Eurasian descent and disease-free, which they were. There have since been many research projects involving controlled releases in various locations in Britain to find out how Beavers will impact the environment.

The return of Beavers has been a mixture of unauthorised or accidental releases followed by review and carefully monitored experimental releases. However, the eventual results, boosted by an increasing recognition of their role in mitigating increasingly frequent and severe flooding events, seem to have great positive potential.

Pine Marten

By 1800, due to loss of woodland cover, Pine Martens *Martes martes* were rare in many lowland areas of Great Britain and Ireland; hunting and trapping by gamekeepers reduced numbers further through the 19th and early 20th centuries, and today they are still very rare. Pine Martens are agile, cat-sized mammals, solitary and secretive, and are mostly nocturnal. They are skilful climbers and spend much of their time in trees, but hunt also on the ground. During the day, they rest on branches or in birds' nests, or in burrows, amongst rocks. Now, they are locally common in parts of Scotland but very rare in England and Wales. Numbers were estimated for Scotland as 3,500, with fewer than 100 in either England or Wales (PTES undated). There is strong evidence that the presence of Pine Martens depresses the numbers of invasive Grey Squirrels and increases native Red Squirrels (Spencer *et al*. 2018).

Andrew Buncombe (2000) summarised in *The Independent* newspaper:

Prized for their fur by medieval royalty, despised by Victorian gamekeepers, the rare and elusive pine martens may be set for a comeback. By the early 1900s the shy, largely nocturnal hunter had been trapped almost to extinction and pushed to a last refuge in the north of Scotland. But it could be returned to habitats in England and Wales, a wildlife charity said yesterday. A report by the People's Trust for Endangered Species and English Nature said

Pine Marten [RC]

changes in both the environment and the law could give the pine marten a chance of being reintroduced.

The report, based on research by Royal Holloway College, University of London, says: "As there is now more woodland, and pine martens are protected, there is no reason why they could not be reintroduced to the English countryside." The research by Dr Paul Bright surveyed six woodland areas in Devon, Somerset, Dorset, Avon, East Sussex and Cumbria. The researchers polled local people, including farmers and gamekeepers, on attitudes towards the animal, which is often blamed for killing game birds. They found most were in favour of reintroduction. Dr Bright said: "Reintroduction of species such as the red kite shows what can be done to help pine martens. Conservation efforts for such a rare species are long overdue." …

The plan by English Nature and the Trust would involve taking about 30 animals from Scotland from areas where they are relatively numerous, allowing them to acclimatise to their new surroundings in prerelease cages, and then releasing them into woodlands. The progress of each animal would be monitored by fitting them with radio collars.

In fact, doubts about whether all the requirements for reintroduction were met delayed matters while these were investigated (*e.g.* Birks & Messenger 2000). With these matters eventually resolved, both the prominent debating bodies, Vincent Wildlife Trust (VWT) and the People's Trust for Endangered Species (PTES), collaborated with Chester Zoo and the Woodland Trust, with VWT reintroducing a total of 51 Pine Martens to Mid-Wales between 2015 and 2017.

Meanwhile, in Scotland, their distribution mostly in the northwest was expanding into Grampian, Tayside, Central and Strathclyde regions. There has been spread, some human-assisted, in southern Scotland and northernmost England. In England and Wales, records are concentrated to the northwest of the Humber-Severn axis, and the population seems to be being maintained by breeding rather than new releases or escapes of captive individuals. However, the new reintroduction and recovery project in Wales will boost numbers and distribution.

The Wildlife Trusts (2019) announced that 18 pine martens had been moved from Scotland to the Forest of Dean in Gloucestershire, the first reintroduction of this species to England following near extinction. Gloucestershire Wildlife Trust led this first formal reintroduction of a once familiar feature of English woodlands – but which had been reduced to a population of fewer than 20.

Rebecca Wilson, Forestry England's Planning and Environment Manager in West England, said *"We are delighted be involved with the return of the Pine Marten, a charming, but highly elusive mammal that was once widespread throughout England. As native omnivores, Pine Martens play a vital role in the delicate balance of woodland ecosystems. Living at low densities in the landscape, they forage on fruit, fungi and a range of prey including the Grey Squirrel, a non-native species which is having a detrimental impact on broadleaf woodland throughout England. We are looking forward to working with volunteers, local communities and partner organisations to monitor how the Pine Martens are moving throughout the Forest of Dean and the wider landscape."*

Wild Boar

Wild Boar, a native species, was originally hunted to extinction during the Middle Ages. In the 1990s, sightings of free-living boar became relatively common. These animals are thought to have escaped or been released illegally from farms where they were raised for meat. The genetic make-up of these animals is uncertain, with many likely to have interbred with domestic pigs (of which Wild Boars are the ancestors) in captivity. An estimated 2,600 animals are now living wild in several breeding populations. The largest of these is in the Forest of Dean, but Wild Boars are present also in parts of south-east and south-west

Wild Boars [flickr CC BY 2.0]

England, south-east Wales and north-west Scotland. Wild boars are common on mainland Europe, with an estimated population of several million.

This is a difficult case to assess, simply because there was no overall plan or comparison with guidelines and little information collected. Defra's (2008) review, following its public consultation of 2006, came to very few substantive conclusions, except for the need for more information, and the need for decisions to be taken locally.

There is no doubt that Wild Boar could be beneficial ecologically in some situations. For example, Rewilding Britain (2021) note "Wild boar is the quintessential soil ecosystem engineer. It ploughs through woodland leaf litter, upturning clods in its search for tasty tubers and grubs. By breaking up the sward, the seeds of annual wildflowers, shrubs and trees are given space to germinate. Disturbed ground provides warm basking spots for grasshoppers and burrowing opportunities for myriad species of bees and beetles. By exposing buried seeds, boar provide access to food for hungry birds during the leanest months. Wild boar need cooling mud baths to regulate their body temperature in summer months, and they create their own wallows. This, in turn, creates small seasonal wetlands much loved by amphibians and dragonflies. These wetlands also attract myriad birds in need of a bath or a drink, and even feeding egrets and storks. Boar will happily wallow in larger ponds and lakes, and also love Beaver pools."

However, the lack of a plan or mechanism by which other interests can be understood and addressed seriously undermines this approach, despite the potential benefits. The fact that aggressive adult males or sows with young surprised by humans may reverse their usual avoidance of people and attack to defend themselves is just one of many features that are not necessarily impracticable to overcome – but only with proper consultative planning. People on continental Europe live in areas of high wild boar density – so there are solutions.

Lynx

Lynxes were extirpated on the island of Great Britain by the Middle Ages and, since the extinction of the Wolf, the island contains no natural apex predator mammals. Since then, deer populations have increased dramatically due to having no natural predators, with excessive deer foraging leading to prevention of forest regeneration, the stripping of tree vegetation, and removing of the forest shrub layer, which provides a habitat for birds such as Nightingales *Luscinia megarhynchos* and Willow Warblers *Phylloscopus trochilus*. Reintroducing medium or large predators, such as the Lynx, are seen by some rewilding conservationists as ways to restore balance in the ecosystem and keep deer numbers under control.

Lynx Trust UK is a registered charity campaigning for the reintroduction of Lynxes to the Kielder Forest in Northumberland. In 2018, a proposal to release six animals was turned down by then Environment Secretary Michael Gove, due to findings that the proposal did not "meet the necessary standards set out in the IUCN (International Union for Conservation of Nature) guidelines and fails to give confidence that the project could be completed in practical terms or that the outputs would meet the stated aims". In 2020, the Trust began preparing a second proposal to be submitted, with three animals proposed, considering that it had addressed the points raised earlier. The Wild East Project has proposed Lynx reintroduction to areas of East Anglia. Tony Juniper, Chairman of Natural England, voiced his support for the "inspiring" proposal in 2020, the year of his commendation of the Red Kite project, stating that it could help to cut deer numbers.

Lynx reintroduction into the Scottish Highlands has been proposed since 2008 (*e.g.* Hetherington *et al.* 2008). In 2020, Lynx Trust UK began a consultation into releasing Lynxes into the Queen Elizabeth Forest Park north of Glasgow. The proposals have met opposition from sheep farmers, citing threats the Lynxes would pose to their flocks – despite research indicating that, because Lynxes also predate on foxes, the number of lambs killed would reduce. Scottish rewilding charity Trees for Life supports lynx reintroduction, claiming it would "restore ecological processes that have been missing for centuries, and provide a free and efficient deer management service", although political views are strong (sources in Anon. 2021c).

Young Eurasian Lynx [Tambako The Jaguar "Walking and looking at me" flickr CC BY-ND 2.0]

There appears to be a momentum, including from high-level personnel, building behind this proposal and the case made for reintroducing this medium-sized cat, which is rather shy of humans, and I expect that permission for a trial is likely in the fairly near future.

Wolf

Anon. (2021d) gives a useful and readable summary the history of Wolves *Canis lupus* in Great Britain, with supporting references, from which the following is extracted. Roman and later Saxon chronicles indicate that Wolves appear to have been extraordinarily numerous in Great Britain. The species was exterminated from Britain through a combination of deforestation and active hunting through bounty systems.

According to some historians, in AD 950, King Athelstan (the first king to unite the previous several English kingdoms and, for a while, adding Wales and Scotland too) imposed an annual tribute of 300 Wolf skins on Welsh king Hywel Dda, while William of Malmesbury states that Athelstan requested gold and silver, and that it was his nephew Edgar the Peaceful who gave up that fine and instead demanded a tribute of Wolf skins on King Constantine of Wales. Wolves at that time were especially numerous in the districts bordering Wales, which were heavily forested.

Wolves are generally thought to have become extinct, or at least very rare, in England during the reign of Henry VII (AD 1485–1509). By this time, Wolves had become limited to the Lancashire forests of Blackburnshire and Bowland, the wilder parts of the Derbyshire Peak District, and the Yorkshire Wolds. Indeed, Wolf bounties were still maintained, in theory at least, in the East Riding of Yorkshire until the early 19th century.

Wolves probably became extinct in the Scottish Lowlands during the thirteenth to fifteenth centuries, when immense tracts of forest were cleared. Official records indicate that the last Scottish Wolf was killed by Sir Ewen Cameron in 1680 in Killiecrankie, Perthshire,

It is strange and somewhat disturbing that those wolf descendants which are dogs are so loved by many humans but those which are still wolves are so loathed by many. After centuries of persecution by humans, wolf distribution and numbers are vastly reduced and the survivors avoid humans, by becoming nocturnal and secretive. This wolf and its companion, in eastern Finland, in late May, cannot hide in darkness because there is not any. However, they are active in the lowest levels of light and stay in the forest, hurrying past more open areas like this and staying constantly wary. [MP]

but there are reports that Wolves survived in Scotland up until the 18th century, and a tale even exists of one being seen as late as 1888.

Although there are many folk stories about Wolves attacking humans in Europe, these are mainly narrative and, when investigated, most seem unlikely. In a comprehensive study (Linnell *et al.* 2002; see also Anon. 2017), those very few that were assessed as likely (9 in Europe in the 20th century) all related to cases of children in poor areas, most of whom had been left, without adults, to guard livestock (which the Wolves treat as prey). Also, a substantial number of these deaths were due to rabies (which was essentially untreatable and invariably deadly until the 1950s) – and that does not occur in UK. Wolves tend not to be a reservoir of rabies, and the cases of deaths via rabies appear to have been due to the Wolves involved being infected by dogs or other wildlife species.

The incidence of attacks appears to have dropped dramatically during the 20th century. The authors say that a fair summary of their results would be "in those extremely rare cases where Wolves have killed people, most attacks have been by rabid Wolves, predatory attacks are aimed mainly at children, attacks in general are unusual but episodic, and humans are not part of their normal prey". They continue: "When the frequency of Wolf attacks on people is compared to that from other large carnivores or wildlife in general, it is obvious that Wolves are among the least dangerous species for their size and predatory potential. Given the fact that Wolves have posed a threat to human safety [historically], it is easy to understand why we have a 'cultural fear' of Wolves, which is reinforced through stories and mythology."

I know this too from personal experience; my father was born in what was then eastern Poland in 1914, growing up during the First World War, the continuing war of Polish independence and the 1920s. In his mature years, he passed on to me stories of people being pulled from their winter sledges by Wolves as almost commonplace. What we hear as children lasts long. Although a high-scoring graduate scientist (albeit in the physical, rather than biological, sciences) and generally rather critical, he clearly believed these stories. (His further career was interrupted by national service in the Polish Air Force, the 1939 invasion from the west by Nazi Germany followed shortly, when UK and France failed to implement the prior agreement to invade Germany from the west, the cynical invasion of Poland by the Soviet Union from the east. Dad managed to find his way across Europe to join the Polish arm of the French Air Force and then the Royal Air Force. After the war, having served in the Western forces, married an English woman (Mum), and coming from that large area of eastern Poland which had been "ethnically cleansed" of Poles and was now part of the Soviet Union, a return would have been foolhardy, so he stayed in UK.) I did not choose to argue pointlessly the Wolf case with someone who had had a much harder life than me and who worked endlessly for the benefit of his family – but I have to say that, in this particular case, unusually the evidence is against Dad's view!

Linnell *et al.* (2002) conclude also that risks of Wolf attacks in Europe, including Scandinavia, (and also North America) today appear to be very low, with only 4 records of people being killed in Europe during the 50 years to 2000. Cars are substantially more lethal, as are domestic cattle, killing 12 people in UK alone in the 7 years 2008 to 2014. There has been, of course, immense selection pressure for many years against any Wolf with a tendency to attack humans (as it will almost certainly be hunted down and killed), leading to increasing tendency of Wolves to avoid humans.

In 1999, Dr Martyn Gorman, senior lecturer in zoology at Aberdeen University and vice chairman of the UK Mammal Society, called for a reintroduction of Wolves to the Scottish Highlands and English countryside in order to deal with the then 350,000 Red Deer damaging young trees in commercial forests. Scottish National Heritage considered re-establishing carefully controlled colonies of Wolves, but shelved the idea following an outcry from sheep farmers.

In 2002, Paul van Vlissingen, a landowner at Letterewe, Achnasheen, Ross-shire, in the western Highlands, proposed the reintroduction of both Wolves and Lynxes to Scotland and England, stating that current deer-culling methods were inadequate, and that Wolves would boost the Scottish tourist industry.

In 2007, British and Norwegian researchers, including from Imperial College London, concluded that Wolf reintroduction into the Scottish Highlands and English countryside would aid in the re-establishment of plants and birds currently hampered by the deer population. Their study also assessed people's attitudes towards the idea of releasing Wolves into the wild. While the public were generally positive, people living in rural areas were more sensitive, though they were open to the idea provided that they would be reimbursed for livestock losses.

Although the prospect of reintroducing Wolves and other large carnivores in the Highlands of Scotland remains highly controversial, there are some who are already making plans for reintroductions. Paul Lister, the laird of Alladale Estate in the Caledonian Forest of North Scotland, has plans to reintroduce large carnivores into his wildlife reserve, such as Wolves, Lynxes, and Bears. Many of the arguments against this kind of reintroduction are due to the potential impacts these animals could have on farming, but Lister argues that this would not be a problem in Alladale as there is very little farming in the area that could be affected. This type of reintroduction could be beneficial for the economy and ecology of the UK, just as it has in the US. In 1995, Wolves were reintroduced into Yellowstone National Park, which transformed the ecology of the area, allowing forests to regenerate and biodiversity to increase. Wolf-related tourism also brings $35.5 million annually to Wyoming.

Will it happen? This is difficult to predict, because of the folk myths noted earlier, but also the real concerns of sheep farmers, with whom a sensible deal would need negotiating. I suspect that it may happen within a few years, probably within one or more extensive and fenced estates initially. The economics of farming are ever changing and, provided a mechanism can be devised so that farmers receive some of the tourism income from viewing Wolves, as well as other science-based and publicly accepted management plans, a wider distribution may come earlier than some may think.

Outcome: public attitudes and perceptions

Chapters 6, 8, 9 and particularly 10 looked at public awareness during the Experimental Reintroduction phase, and Chapter 11 made some mention of this continuing approach. There were also many third-party initiatives as the idea became more widespread. Here are just a few examples.

In 1997, a children's book (Burgess 1997) featured the fortunes of a pair of Red Kites and explored the dangers to them in an adventure story.

In February 1998, I was amazed to find my credit card statement from the Royal Bank of Scotland printed over a background of a Red Kite picture, with a note at the bottom of the page: "Red Kite. Recently re-introduced to Scotland, it is easy to identify when seen hanging motionless above some wooded ridge with its distinctive red and grey markings. A spectacular sight in midwinter."

The scientific civil service union IPMS (now Prospect) used the Red Kite story as its front page lead in its March 2000 newsletter criticising cuts in the conservation budget.

I received holiday cottage brochures in a mail shot, advertising wildlife features, amongst which were kites at some of the conservation project areas.

Awareness in the wider public has become very widespread. A few months ago (in 2020), a specialist electrical engineer needed to call at my house. Pictures of kites on the wall generated questions, so that I outlined the project. To my amazement, he turned out to come from the general vicinity of our first English release site and expressed profound gratitude

A June day at Wormsley: Red Kite family life: (above) kites take advantage of scarifying a grass field to capture invertebrates disturbed; (below left top) kite carries items in bill and talons to nest; (below left bottom) kite carries nestling bird prey to nest; (below right) two views of kite carrying to nest parts of a bird in its bill and both talons. [MP]

for "providing" the now large numbers of kites in the area. Like many of the public with only a passing interest in nature, he found the kites an inspiring element of their surroundings.

Several drama broadcasts on radio and television have indicated a changing perception of the assumption of continuity of the countryside. I first noticed this in a drama on BBC Radio 4 (the national public service network for news, drama, discussion *etc.*) in the first decade of the 2000s. The play was set in the North-East of England in the mid-20th century, a time when there was no possibility of Red Kites being present in the area, yet watching of Red Kites formed an important sub-plot.

A more visual example is in Netflix's leading series, *The Crown*. In Series 1 Episode 6, Princess Margaret is depicted riding at Windsor in 1950s to meet Group Captain Peter Townsend, the man whom she loved but was not allowed to marry. As she rides, a Red Kite is visible thermalling overhead. So, the kite is either 100 years too late for the scene or 40 years too early – but *The Crown* is not a documentary; it is a drama, based with varying degree of looseness on a true story, and the kites have now found their way to Windsor Great Park regardless.

This gives me certain mixed feelings. Is it better that people consider reintroduced wildlife as inherent parts of the ecosystem which they previously inhabited, or to be aware of the major efforts to restore them after earlier losses due to human failings – in the hope that this will help avoid future errors?

My answer is both. I do want people to see these as part of the earlier and present-day natural ecosystems and their own human environments. But I also want them to be aware how easy it is to lose these wonderful things through human action, ignorance or unawareness – and how much work it takes to bring them back, if we still can, recognising that we will not be able to restore all.

Red Kite at Wormsley in February 2022 [MP]

A June day at Wormsley: Red Kite family life (continued): (top) parent kite gives alarm call while flying near nest, and later perches near nest; (middle) nearly fully grown chick (alone in nest as no longer needs brooding) calls to parent overhead, and peers out of nest; (bottom) nest in tree, and the well-grown chick tries "branching", feeling its way along branches near the nest. [MP]

Recognition that even the much changed bodies responsible for this work have imperfect corporate memories is why I started writing this book – and resumed it many years later. In doing so, I have tried to make it readable, but accurate. For someone trained in scientific writing at a time when everything had to be in the third party, and a passive rather than active style (and therefore very unreadable!), this was not always easy. However, I have done a lot of writing in different styles since – and I hope that this works. If you have got this far (and even if not), thanks for reading it. And may luck and success follow your own conservation challenges as you rise to them like soaring kites.

Red Kite in north Northamptonshire August 2022 [MP]

References

Aldasoro, J.E. (1985) *Navarra. Atlas de aves nidificantes (1982–1984)*. Caja de Ahorros de Navarra, Pamplona, Spain.

Anon. (1995) *Red kite monitoring report 1995*.

Anon. (1997) *Red kite newsletter (England) Summer 1997 – Issue 1*.

Anon. (2000) *The state of the UK's birds 2000*. BTO, WWT & RSPB, Sandy, UK.

Anon. (2017) *Are large carnivores dangerous?* The Wolves and Humans Foundation. https://www.wolvesandhumans.org/articles/are_large_carnivores_dangerous.html Accessed 19/07/2021.

Anon. (2021a) *White-tailed Eagles arrive in Munster as part of reintroduction project*. https://www.gov.ie/en/press-release/22531-white-tailed-eagles-arrive-in-munster-as-part-of-reintroduction-project/ Accessed 18/07/2021.

Anon. (2021b) *Poole Harbour Ospreys*. https://www.birdsofpooleharbour.co.uk/osprey/history/ Accessed 18/07/2021.

Anon. (2021c) *Lynx reintroduction in Great Britain*. Wikipedia. https://en.wikipedia.org/wiki/Lynx_reintroduction_in_Great_Britain Accessed 19/07/2021.

Anon. (2021d) *Wolves in Great Britain*. https://en.wikipedia.org/wiki/Wolves_in_Great_Britain Accessed 20/07/2021.

Arcà, G. (1989) Il nibbio reale *Milvus milvus* nei monti della Tolfa (Lazio settentrionale). *Avocetta*, 13: 1–7.

Ballou, J. (1995) An overview of small population biology. In: R.C. Lacy, K.A. Hughes & P.S. Miller (Eds), *VORTEX: A stochastic simulation of the extinction process. Version 7 User's Manual*. IUCN/SSC Conservation Breeding Specialist Group, Apple Valley, pp. 53–62.

Balmer, D., Gillings, S., Caffrey, B., Swann, B., Downie, I. & Fuller, R. (2013) *Bird Atlas 2007–11: the breeding and wintering birds of Britain and Ireland*. BTO Books, Thetford, UK. 2013.

Burns, F., Eaton, M.A., Balmer, D.E., Banks, A., Caldow, R., Donelan, J.L., Douse, A., Duigan, C., Foster, S., Frost, T., Grice, P.V., Hall, C., Hanmer, H.J., Harris, S.J., Johnstone, I., Lindley, P., McCulloch, N., Noble, D.G., Risely, K., Robinson, R.A., Wotton, S. (2020) *The state of the UK's birds 2020*. RSPB, BTO, WWT, DAERA, JNCC, NatureScot, NE and NRW, Sandy, Bedfordshire.

Bourne, W.R.P. (1955). The birds of the Cape Verde Islands. *Ibis*, 97: 508–556.

Beaman, M. & Galea, C. (1974) The Visible Migration of Raptors over the Maltese Islands. *Ibis*, 116: 419–431.

Begum, T. (2021) *Record numbers of Beavers are being introduced to the UK*. https://www.nhm.ac.uk/discover/news/2021/april/record-numbers-of-Beavers-are-being-introduced-to-the-uk.html Accessed 19/07/2021.

Bergier, P. (1987). Les rapaces diunes du Maroc. *Annales du C.E.E.P.*, 3, Aix en Provence.

Bignal, E.M., & Curtis, D.J. (Eds) (1989) *Choughs and land-use in Europe*. Scottish Chough Study Group, Tarbert, Argyll, UK.

Birds on the Edge (undated) *Restoration of the red-billed chough in Jersey*. http://www.birdsontheedge.org/projects/choughs/ Accessed 23/07/2021.

BirdWatch Ireland (2021) Golden Eagle. https://birdwatchireland.ie/birds/golden-eagle/ Accessed 18/07/2021.

Birks, J. & Messenger, J. (2000) *A Response from The Vincent Wildlife Trust to 'Return of the Pine Marten to England' public consultation by the People's Trust for Endangered Species*. Vincent Wildlife Trust.

Blaker, G.B. (1934) *The Barn Owl in England and Wales*. RSPB, London.
Blanco, J.C., Hiraldo, F., Heredia, B. & García, L. (1987) Alimentación inveral del Milano Real *Milvus milvus* en El Parque Nacional de Doñana. *Bol. Estac. Central Ecol.*, 16: 93–97.
Buncombe, A. (2000) *The Independent*, Saturday 9 September 2000.
Bunn, D.S., Warburton, A.B. & Wilson, R.D.S. (1982) *The Barn Owl*. Poyser, Calton, UK.
Burgess, M. 1997. *Kite*. Anderson Press, London.
Burns, F., Eaton, M.A., Balmer, D.E., Banks, A., Caldow, R., Donelan, J.L., Douse, A., Duigan, C., Foster, S., Frost, T., Grice, P.V., Hall, C., Hanmer, H.J., Harris, S.J., Johnstone, I., Lindley, P., McCulloch, N., Noble, D.G., Risely, K., Robinson, R.A. & Wotton, S. (2020) *The state of the UK's birds 2020*. RSPB, BTO, WWT, DAERA, JNCC, NatureScot, NE and NRW, Sandy, Bedfordshire.
Cadbury, J. (1992) This illegal killing must stop: a review of bird of prey persecution and poison abuse. *RSPB Conservation Review*, 6: 28–35.
Cade, T.J. (1985) Peregrine recovery in the United States. In: I. Newton & R.D. Chancellor (Eds) *Conservation Studies on Raptors*, ICBP Technical Publication No. 5, International Council for Bird Preservation, Cambridge, UK, pp. 331–342.
Cade, T.J. & Jones, C.G. (1993) Progress in restoration of the Mauritius Kestrel. *Conserv. Biol.*, 7: 169–175.
Carson, R. (1962) *Silent Spring*. Houghton Mifflin, Boston.
Carter, I. (2001). *The Red Kite*. Arlequin Press, Chelmsford, UK.
Carter, I. & Ivens, K. (1998) *Red kite newsletter, English Midlands re-introduction project*. Issue 3.
Carter, I. & Whitlow, G. (2005) *Red Kites in the Chilterns*. English Nature & The Chilterns Conservation Board.
Collar, N. J. & Andrew, P. (1988) *Birds to Watch: the ICBP world checklist of threatened birds*. ICBP, Cambridge.
Cordero, P.J., Evans, L.M., Parkin, D.T., & Galbraith, C.A. (1997) Studies of the genetics of a naturalised population of Red Kites *Milvus milvus* in England established by translocation. In: T.J. Crawford, J. Spencer, D. Stevens, M.B. Usher, T.E. Tew & J. Warren (Eds) *The role of genetics in Conserving Small Populations, Proc. Br. Ecol. Soc. Symp., 18–19 Sept. 1995, York*. JNCC, Peterborough. pp. 87–96.
Cramp, S. & Simmons, K.E.L. (Eds) (1980) *The Birds of the Western Palearctic, Vol 2*. Oxford University Press.
Cross, A.V. & Davis, P.E. (2005) *The Red Kites of Wales*. Welsh Kite Trust.
Darwin, C. (1859) *On the Origin of Species*. John Murray, London.
Darwin, C. & Wallace, A.R. (1858). On the Tendency of Species to form Varieties; and on the Perpetuation of Varieties and Species by Natural Means of Selection. *Zoological Journal of the Linnean Society*, 3 (9): 46–62.
Davis, P. (1993) The Red Kite in Wales: setting the record straight. *Br. Birds*, 86: 295–298.
Davis, P.E. & Davis, J.E. (1981) The food of the Red Kite in Wales. *Bird Study*, 28: 33–40.
Davis, P.E. & Davis, J.E. (1992) Dispersal and age of first breeding of Buzzards in Central Wales. *Br. Birds*, 85: 578–587.
Davis, P.E. & Newton, I. (1981) Population and Breeding of Red Kites in Wales over 30-year Period. *Journal of Animal Ecology*, 50: 759–772.
Deacon, B. (2020) *Cornish studies resources: The Cornish chough*. https://bernarddeacon.com/2020/07/28/the-cornish-chough/ Accessed 23/07/2021.
Defra (2008) *Feral wild boar in England: An action plan*. Department for Environment, Food and Rural Affairs, London.
Dennis, R.H. (1968) Sea eagles. *Fair Isle Bird Obs. Rep.*, 21: 17–21.
Dennis, R.H. (1969) Sea eagles. *Fair Isle Bird Obs. Rep.*, 22: 23–29.

Dennis, R. (1995) Ospreys *Pandion haliaetus* in Scotland – a study of recolonization. *Vogelwelt*, 116: 193–195.

Donázar, J.A., Naveso, M.A., Tella, J.L. & Campión, D. (1997) Extensive grazing and raptors in Spain. In: D.J. Pain & M.W. Pienkowski (Eds) *Farming and Birds in Europe*. Academic Press, London, pp. 117–149.

Elliot, G.D. & Avery, M.I. (1991) A review of reports of Buzzard persecution 1975–1989. *Bird Study*, 38: 52–56.

Evans, I. (1994) *Red Kite Reintroduction Project: future plan 1994–1997*. Internal Report JNCC.

Evans, I.M. (1995) *Translocation as an aid to conserving birds in the United Kingdom*. Report to Red Kite Project Team.

Evans, I. & Pienkowski, M. (1989) The Red Kite Project *Progress Report no 1, November 1989*. Nature Conservancy Council & Royal Society for the Protection of Birds, Peterborough, UK.

Evans, I.M. & Pienkowski, M.W. (1991) World status of the red kite: a background to the experimental re-introduction to England and Scotland. *Br. Birds*, 84: 171–187.

Evans, I.M., Pienkowski, M.W. & Dennis, R.H. (1990) *Experimental re-introduction of red kites: report to 1990: a joint project by NCC and RSPB*. NCC Chief Scientist Directorate report no 1224, Peterborough, UK.

Evans, I.M., Love, J.A., Galbraith, C.A. & Pienkowski, M.W. (1994) Population and range restoration of threatened raptors in the United Kingdom. In: B.-U. Meyburg & R.D. Chancellor (Eds) *Raptor Conservation Today*. WWGBP/Pica Press, Berlin, pp. 447–457.

Evans, I.M., Dennis, R.H., Orr-Ewing, D.C., Kjellen, N., Andersson, P.-O., Sylven, M., Senosiain, A. & Compaired Carbo, F. (1997) The re-establishment of Red Kite breeding populations in Scotland and England. *British Birds*, 90: 123–138.

Evans, I.M., Cordero, P.J. & Parkin, D.T. (1998) Successful breeding at one year of age by Red Kites *Milvus milvus* in southern England. *Ibis*, 140: 53–57.

Evans, I.M., Summers, R.W., Orr-Ewing, D., O'Toole, L., Evans, R. & Snell, N. (1999) Evaluating the success of translocation of red kites *Milvus milvus* into the UK. *Bird Study*, 46: 129–144.

Fletcher, M.R., Hunter, K., Quick, M.P., Thompson, H.M. & Greig-Smith, P.W. (1991) *Pesticide poisoning of animals 1990: investigations of suspected incidents in Great Britain*. MAFF report, London.

Fletcher, M.R., Hunter, K., Quick, M.P. & Grave, R.C. (1992) *Pesticide poisoning of animals 1991: investigations of suspected incidents in Great Britain*. MAFF report, London.

Friends of Red Kites 2021. https://friendsofredkites.org.uk/latest-news Accessed 08/08/2021.

Galea, C. & Massa, B. (1985) Notes on the Raptor Migration across the Central Mediterranean. In: I. Newton & R.D. Chancellor (Eds) *Conservation Studies on Raptors*, ICBP Technical Publication 5: 257–261.

Game Conservancy Advisory Service (1992) *Wild Partridge Management*. The Game Conservancy Trust, Fordingbridge, UK.

Gibbons, D.W., Reid, J.B. & Chapman, R.A. (1993) *The New Atlas of Breeding Birds in Britain and Ireland: 1988–1991*. T. & A.D. Poyser, London.

Golden Eagle Trust (2010) *The Red Kite Project*. https://web.archive.org/web/20120305215209/http://www.goldeneagle.ie/news_viewnews.php?x=3&z=44&news_id=9&article=277 Archived from the original on 5 March 2012. Accessed 17/08/2021.

Goriup, P.D. & Collar, N.J. (1980). Bringing back bustards. *Ecos*, 2: 24–25.

Green, B.H. (1979). *Wildlife Introductions to Great Britain*. Report by the Working Group on Introductions of the UK Committee for International Nature Conservation. Nature Conservancy Council, London. Unpublished.

Green, R.E., Pienkowski, M.W. & Love, J.A. (1996) Long-term viability of the re-introduced population of the white-tailed eagle *Haliaeetus albicilla* in Scotland. *Journal of Applied Ecology*, 33: 357–368.

Hagemeijer, E.J.M. & Blair, M.J (Eds) (1997) *The EBCC Atlas of European Breeding Birds: Their Distribution and Abundance.* T & A.D Poyser, London.

Hales, R. (2021) *Operation Chough.* https://chough.org/the-red-billed-chough/return-of-the-cornish-chough, Paradise Park, Cornwall, UK.

Harvey, R.J. (1939) Buzzards in the Home Counties: A Surrey Experiment. *The Times*, 10 August.

Harvey-Brown, J.A. (1879). *The Capercaillie in Scotland.* David Douglas, Edinburgh, UK.

Heredia, B., Alonso, J.A. & Hiraldo, F. (1991). Space and habitat use by Red Kites *Milvus milvus* during winter in the Guadalquivir marshes: A comparison between resident and wintering populations. *Ibis*, 133: 374–381.

Hetherington, D.A., Miller, D.R., Macleod, C.D. & Gorman, M.L. (2008) A potential habitat network for the Eurasian lynx *Lynx lynx* in Scotland. *Mammal Rev.*, 38 (4): 285–303.

Hiraldo, F., Heredia, B. & Alonso, J.C. (1993) Communal roosting of wintering Red Kites *Milvus milvus* (Aves, Accipitridae): Social feeding strategies for the exploitation of food resources. *Ethology*, 93: 117–124.

Holmes, J.S., Jones, A. & Batten, L.A. (1994) The campaign to stop illegal poisoning of our wildlife. In: S.P. Carter (Ed.) *Britain's Birds in 1991–92: the conservation and monitoring review.* BTO/JNCC, Thetford, UK, pp. 10–12.

Iapichino, C. & Massa, B. (1989) *The birds of Sicily. B.O.U. check list, 11.* British Ornithologists' Union, London.

Illner, H. (1992) Road deaths of Westphalian owls: methodological problems, influence of road type and possible effects on population levels. In: C.A. Galbraith, I.R. Taylor and S. Percival (Eds) *The ecology and conservation of European owls.* JNCC, Peterborough, UK, pp. 94–100.

International Union for the Conservation of Nature and Natural Resources. (1987) *Translocation of living organisms: introductions, re-introductions, and re-stocking.* IUCN position statement. Gland, Switzerland.

Johnson, J.A., Watson, R.T. & Mindell, D.P. (2005) Prioritizing species conservation: does the Cape Verde kite exist? *Proc. Biol. Sci.*, 272: 1365–1371. doi: 10.1098/rspb.2005.3098

Jørgensen, H.E. (1989). *Danmarks Rovfugle.* Frederikshus, Copenhagen, Denmark.

Joveniaux et al. (1993) *Atlas des oiseaux nicheurs du Jura.* Groupe Ornithologique du Jura, France.

Kenward, R.E, Marquiss, M. & Newton, I. (1981) What happens to goshawks trained for falconry. *Journal of Wildlife Management*, 45(3): 802–806.

Kjellén, N. (1994) Gladan: En Rovfågel på Frammarsch i Sverige. *Vår Fågelv.*, 6: 6–19.

Kjellén, N. (1995) Projekt Glada . Årsrapport 1994. *Anser*, 34: 11–16.

Kjellén, N. (1996) Projekt Glada - Årsrapport 1995. *Anser*, 35: 17–25.

Knepp (2020) *White Storks.* https://knepp.co.uk/white-storks Accessed 18/07/2021.

Knepp (undated) *Beavers.* https://knepp.co.uk/Beavers Accessed 19/07/2021.

Lack, D. & Southern, H.N. (1949) Birds of Tenerife. *Ibis*, 91: 607–626.

Lambert, A. (1957). Birds of Greece. *Ibis*, 99: 43–68.

Ledant, J.P., Jacod, J.P., Jacobs, P., Malher, F., Ochando, B. & Roche, J. (1981) Mise a jour de l'avifaune algerienne. *Le Gerfaut*, 71: 295–398.

Leicester & Rutland Wildlife Trust (undated) *About the Rutland Ospreys.* Leicestershire and Rutland Wildlife Trust. https://www.lrwt.org.uk/rutlandospreys/about-rutland-ospreys Accessed 18/07/2021.

Lindsay, R.A., Charman, D.J., Everingham, F., O'Reilly, R.M., Palmer, M.A., Rowell, T.A. & Stroud, D.A. (1988) *The Flow Country: The Peatlands of Caithness and Sutherland.* 121 pp. Nature Conservancy Council, Peterborough, UK.

Linnell, J.O.C., Andersen, R., Andersone, Z., Balciauskas, L., Blanco, J.C., Boitani, L., Brainerd, S., Breitenmoser, U., Kojola, I., Liberg, O., Løe, J., Okarma, H., Pedersen, H.C., Promberger, C., Sand, H., Solberg, E.J., Valdmann, H. & Wabakken, P. (2002) The fear of wolves: A review of wolf attacks on humans. *NINA Oppdragsmeldrng*, 731: 1–65.

Lloyd, C., Tasker, M.L. & Partridge, K. (1991) *The Status of Seabirds in Britain and Ireland*. 355 pp. T. & A.D. Poyser, London.

Lloyd, D.E.B. (1976) *Avian Predation of Reared Pheasants*. Joint Publication: BFSS, G.C., RSPB & WAGBI.

Long, J.L. (1981) *Introduced birds of the world: the worldwide history, distribution and influence of birds introduced to new environments*. Universe Books, New York.

Love, J. (1983) *The return of the sea eagle*. Cambridge University Press.

Love, J.A. (1988) *The reintroduction of the white-tailed sea eagle to Scotland: 1975–1987. Research & Survey in Nature Conservation no 12*. NCC, Peterborough. 48 pp.

Lovegrove, R. (1990) *The Kite's Tale: The Story of the Red Kite in Wales*. RSPB, Sandy.

Lovegrove, R., Williams, I. & Fuller, C. (1990) *Kite Newsletter 1990*. Wales Kite Committee.

Macdonald, D.W., Tattersall, F.H., Brown E.D. & Balharry D. (1995) Reintroducing the European Beaver to Britain: nostalgic meddling or restoring biodiversity? *Mammal Rev,*. 25(4): 161–200.

Massa, B. (1980) Ricerche sui rapaci in un'area campione della Sicilia. *Naturalista sicilia*, S IV, IV (3–4): 59–72.

May, C.A., Wetton, J.H., Davis, P.E., Brookfield, J.F.Y. & Parkin, D.T. (1993) Single-locus profiling reveals loss of variation in inbred populations of the red kite (*Milvus milvus*). *Proceedings of the Royal Society of London series B*, 251: 165–170.

Meyburg, B.U. & Mayburg, C. (1987) Present status of diurnal birds of prey in various countries bordering the Mediterranean. *Istuto Nazionale di Biologia della Selvagina*. XII. Bologne.

Morris, F.O. (1904) *A History of British Birds, Vol 1, 5th Ed*. John C. Nimmo, London.

Mosimann, P. & Juillard, M. (1988) Brutbestand und Winterverbreitung des Rotmilans *Milvus milvus* in der Schweiz. *Der Ornithologishe Beobachter*, 85: 199–206.

Mullie, W.C. & Meininger, P.L. (1985) The Decline of Bird of Prey Populations in Egypt. In: I. Newton & R.D. Chancellor (Eds) *Conservation Studies on Raptors, ICBP Technical Publication 5*: 61–82.

Muntaner, J. (1981) Le statut des rapaces diurnes des Baleares. In: *Rapaces Mediteraneens. Annales du CROP*, 1, 62–65. Aix.

Muntaner, J. (1985) The Status of Diurnal Birds of Prey in Catalonia Northeastern. In: I. Newton & R.D. Chancellor (Eds) *Conservation Studies on Raptors, ICBP Technical Publication 5*: 29–43.

National Audit Office (1986) *Review of Forestry Commission Objectives and Achievements*. HC 75, HMSO, London.

National Museum of Ireland (2020) *Golden Eagle*. https://www.museum.ie/en-IE/Collections-Research/Collection/Resilience/Artefact/Golden-Eagle/2a344480-a23c-446b-9f6d-442a1dd05655 Accessed 18/07/2021.

Natural England (2020) *30-year anniversary of landmark release of red kites in the Chiltern Hills*. Press Release 20 July 2020. Natural England. https://www.gov.uk/government/news/30-year-anniversary-of-landmark-release-of-red-kites-in-the-chiltern-hills Accessed 18/08/2021.

NCC (1985) *The sea eagle*. Nature Conservancy Council, Peterborough, UK. 12 pp.

Newton, I. (1979) *Population ecology of raptors*. T. & A.D. Poyser, Berkhampsted, UK.

Newton, I. (1986) *The Sparrowhawk*. T. & A.D. Poyser, Berkhampsted, UK.

Newton, I. (1988) Reintroduction, and its relation to the management of raptor populations. In *Proc. of the international symposium on raptor reintroduction, 1985*. 1–15. Institute for Wildlife Studies, Arcata, California.

Newton, I. (1989) *Lifetime Reproduction in Birds*. Academic Press, London.

Newton, I. (2015) Pesticides and birds of prey – the breakthrough. In: D. Thompson, H. Birks & J. Birks (Eds) *Nature's Conscience: The life and legacy of Derek Ratcliffe*. Langford Press, Kings Lynn, Norfolk, UK, pp. 281–299.

Newton, I. & Wyllie, I. (1992) Effects of new rodenticides on owls. In: C.A. Galbraith, I.R. Taylor, S. Percival and S.M. Davies (Eds) *The ecology and conservation of European owls (UK Nature Conservation No. 5)*. Joint Nature Conservation Committee, Peterborough, UK, pp. 49–54.

Newton, I., Davis, P.E. & Davis, J.E. (1989) Age of first breeding, dispersal and survival of Red Kites *Milvus milvus* in Wales. *Ibis*, 131: 16–21.

Newton, I., Davis, P.E. & Moss, D. (1994) Philopatry and population growth of Red Kites, *Milvus milvus*, in Wales. *Proc. R. Soc. Lond. Ser. B*, 257: 317–323.

Newton, I., Davis, P.E. & Moss, D. (1996) Distribution and breeding of Red Kites *Milvus milvus* in relation to afforestation and other land-use in Wales. *J. Appl. Ecol.*, 33: 210–224.

Nisbet, I.C.T. (1959) The kites of sixteenth-century London. *British Birds*, 52: 239–240.

Northumberland Wildlife Trust (undated) *Kielder Ospreys*. https://www.nwt.org.uk/what-we-do/projects/kielder-ospreys Accessed 18/07/2021.

Orr-Ewing, D. (undated) *Monitoring and conserving Scotland's birds of prey*. Scottish Raptor Study Group. https://www.scottishraptorstudygroup.org/raptors/red-kite/ Accessed 08/08/2021.

Ortlieb, R. (1980) *Ser Rotmilan*. Wittenberg Lutherstadt, Germany.

O'Toole, L., Etheridge, B., Crooke, C. & Walton, P. (1998) *Scottish Red Kite Newsletter 9 – spring 1998*.

Pain, D.J. & Pienkowski, M.W. (Eds) (1997) *Farming and Birds in Europe: Common Agricultural Policy and its implications for bird conservation*. Academic Press.

Palma, L. (1985) The Present Situation of Birds of Prey in Portugal. In: I. Newton & R.D. Chancellor (Eds) *Conservation Studies on Raptors, ICBP Technical Publication 5*: 3–14.

Patrimonio, O. (1990) *Le Milan Royal (Milvus milvus) en Corse: Repartition et Reproduction*. Travaux Scientifiques du Parc Naturel Regional et des Reserves Naturelles de Corse.

Percival, S.M. (1991) Population trends in British Barn Owls - a review of some possible causes. *British Wildlife*, 2: 131–140.

Percival, S.M., Evans, I.M, Davies, S., Galbraith, C.A. & Pienkowski, M.W. (1992) *Conservation of the Barn Owl Tyto alba in the United Kingdom*. Ornithology Notes, JNCC, Peterborough, UK.

Peterson, R.T. & Mountfort, G. & Hollom, P.A.D. (1974) *A field guide to the birds of Britain and Europe*. London.

Pienkowki, M.W. (1989–1990). *Red Kite Project Team Update Notes* (8 April 1989, 21 May 1989, 3 May 1990). Nature Conservancy Council, Peterborough, UK.

Pienkowski, M.W. (1989). *Bird reintroduction schemes in Britain. Ornithology Note no. 14, Version 1*. Nature Conservancy Council, Peterborough, UK.

Pienkowski, M.W. & Love, J.A. (1989) *Current work in ornithology: the reintroduction of the white-tailed sea-eagle. Ornithology Note no. 5, Version 1*. Nature Conservancy Council, Peterborough, UK.

Poole, A.F. (1989) *Ospreys: A Natural and Unnatural History*. Cambridge University Press, Cambridge.

PTES (undated) *Pine Marten*. https://ptes.org/get-informed/facts-figures/pine-marten/ Accessed 10/07/2021.

Radler, K. (1992) Genetic differentiation in a released population of Eagle Owl *Bubo bubo*. In: C.A. Galbraith, I.R. Taylor & S. Percival (Eds) *The Ecology and Conservation of European Owls. UK Nature Conservation No. 5*. JNCC, Peterborough, pp. 22–27.

Ratcliffe, D. (1980) *The Peregrine Falcon*. T. & A.D. Poyser, London.
Rewilding Britain (2021) *Wild boar (pig)*. https://www.rewildingbritain.org.uk/explore-rewilding/reintroductions-key-species/rewilding-superstars/wild-boar-pig Accessed 19/07/2021.
Rheinwald, G. (1982) Brutvogelatlas der Bundesrepublik Deutschland-Kartierung 1980. *Schriftenreihe des Dachverbands Deutscher Avifaunisten*, 6: 128.
Roy Dennis Wildlife Foundation (2021) *White-tailed Eagle Reintroduction on the Isle of Wight*. https://www.roydennis.org/isleofwight/ Accessed 17/07/2021.
RSPB (undated1) *Corncrake*. https://www.rspb.org.uk/birds-and-wildlife/wildlife-guides/bird-a-z/corncrake/ Accessed 19/07/2021.
RSPB (undated2) *Northern Ireland red kites*. https://www.rspb.org.uk/our-work/conservation/projects/northern-ireland-red-kites/ Accessed 17/08/2021.
RSPB (undated3) *Red kites in the UK*. https://www.rspb.org.uk/our-work/conservation/conservation-and-sustainability/safeguarding-species/case-studies/red-kite/ Accessed 17/07/2021.
Rufino, R., Araujo, A. & Abreu, M. (1985) Breeding Raptors in Portugal: Distribution and Population Estimates. In: I. Newton & R.D. Chancellor (Eds) *Conservation Studies on Raptors, ICBP Technical Publication 5*: 15–28.
Sandeman, P. (1965) Attempted reintroduction of white-tailed eagle to Scotland. *Scot. Birds*, 3: 411–412.
Scharringa, C.J.G. (1978) European news. *British Birds*, 71: 255.
Schenk, H. (1981) *Lista Rossa degli Ucelli della Sardegna*. Lega Italiana Protezione Ucelli ed., Parma.
Scottish Wildlife Trust (undated) *Osprey Fact File*. https://scottishwildlifetrust.org.uk/scotlands-wildlife/osprey-fact-file/ Accessed 18/07/2021.
Shakespeare, W. (1600) *The Cronicle History of Henry the fift*. [sic] Millington & Busby, London.
Shakespeare, W. (1608) *The True Chronicle History of the Life and Death of King Leir and his Three Daughters*. Nathaniel Butter, London.
Shakespeare, W. (1623). *The Winter's Tale*. Edward Blount and William and Isaac Jaggard, London.
Sharrock, J.T.R. (1976) *The Atlas of Breeding Birds in Britain and Ireland*. British Trust for Ornithology/Irish Wild Bird Conservancy. T. & A.D. Poyser, London.
Shaw, G. & Dowell, A. (1990) *Barn Owl Conservation in Forests*. Forestry Commission Bulletin 90. HMSO, London.
Shawyer, C. (1987) *The Barn Owl in the British Isles; its past, present and future*. Hawk Trust, London.
Shirihai, H. (1996) *Birds of Israel*. Academic Press, London.
Smart, J., Amar, A., Sim, I.M.W., Etheridge, B., Cameron, D., Christie, G. & Wilson, J.D. (2010) Illegal killing slows population recovery of a reintroduced raptor of high conservation concern – The red kite *Milvus milvus*. *Biological Conservation*, 143: 1278–1286.
Smith, G. (1997) £13,000 fine for killing rare bird: farmer 87, had poison-kit of syringes. *Oxford Mail*, Saturday, 24 May.
Spencer, J., Striner, A. & Sheehy, E. (2018) Martens, Squirrels & Forestry. *Quarterly Journal of Forestry*, 112: 257–261.
Stevens, P. (2012) Red Kite *Milvus milvus*. In: D. Ferguson. *Birds of Buckinghamshire, 2nd edition*. Buckinghamshire Bird Club, pp. 119–122.
Stevens, P. (2017) *Report to UK Steering Group*.
Stroud, D.A., Reed, T.M., Pienkowski, M.W. & Lindsay, R.A. (1987) *Birds, Bogs and forestry: The Peatlands of Caithness and Sutherland*. 121pp. Nature Conservancy Council, Peterborough, UK.

Stroud, D.A., Reed, T.M., Pienkowski, M.W. & Lindsay, R.A. (2015) The Flow Country: battles fought, war won, organisation lost. In: D. Thompson, H. Birks & J. Birks (Eds) *Nature's Conscience: The life and legacy of Derek Ratcliffe*. Langford Press, Kings Lynn, Norfolk, UK, pp. 401–439.

Stubbe, M. & Gedeon, K. (1989) *Jahresbericht zum Monitoring Greifvogel und Eulen der DDR 1*, Martin-Luther-Universitat Halle/Saale.

Swann, R.L. & Etheridge, B. (1995) A comparison of breeding success and prey of the common buzzard *Buteo buteo* in two areas of northern Scotland. *Bird Study*. 42: 37–43.

Sylvén, M. (1984) Verksamheten inom project glada under 1983. *Vår Fågelv.*, 43: 363–365.

Sylvén, M. (1987). Verksomheten inom Projekt Glada 1986. *Var Fagelvarld*, 46: 137–143.

Tasker, M.L. & Pienkowski, M.W. (1987) *Vulnerable Concentrations of birds in the North Sea*. 39 pp. Nature Conservancy Council, Peterborough, UK.

Tasker, M.L., Webb, A., Hall, A.J., Pienkowski, M.W. & Langslow, D.R. (1987) *Seabirds in the North Sea*. 336 pp. Nature Conservancy Council, Peterborough, UK.

Taylor, I.R. (1989) *The Barn Owl*. Shire Publications, Aylesbury, UK.

Taylor, I. (1992) An assessment of the significance of annual variations in snow cover in determining short-term population changes in Field Voles *Microtus agrestis* and Barn Owls *Tyto alba* in Britain. In: C.A. Galbraith, I.R. Taylor, S. Percival & S.M. Davies (Eds) *The ecology and conservation of European owls, UK Nature Conservation, No 5*. Joint Nature Conservation Committee, Peterborough, pp. 28–32.

Taylor, I.R. (1993) *Barn Owls: An action plan and practical guide for their conservation in Scotland*. University of Edinburgh, Edinburgh.

Taylor, I.R., Dowell, A., Irving, T., Langford, I.K. & Shaw, G. (1988). The distribution and abundance of the Barn Owl in south-west Scotland. *Scottish Birds*, 15: 40–43.

Taylor, K., Hudson, R. & Horne, G. (1988) Buzzard breeding distribution and abundance in Britain and Northern Ireland in 1983. *Bird Study*, 35: 109–118.

Terrasse, M., Bagnoli, C., Bonnet, J., Pinna, J-L. & Sarrazin, F. (1994) Reintroduction of the Griffon Vulture *Gyps fulvus* in the Massif Central, France. In: *Raptor Conservation Today* (eds B.-U. Meyburg & R.D. Chancellor), pp. 479–491. WWGBP/Pica Press, Berlin.

Thévenot, M., Bergier, P. & Beaubrun, P. (1985). Present Distribution and Status of Raptors in Morocco. In: I. Newton & R.D. Chancellor (Eds) *Conservation Studies on Raptors, ICBP Technical Publication 5*: 83–101.

Thiollay, J.M. & Terrasse, J.F., ed. (1984) *Estimation des effectifs de rapaces nicheurs diurnes et non rupestres en France*. Fonds d'intervention pour les rapaces, La Garenne-Colombes, France.

Ticehurst, N.F. (1930) On the former abundance of the kite, buzzard and raven in Kent. *British Birds*, 24: 34–37.

Tubbs, C.R. (1974) *The Buzzard*. David & Charles, London.

UK Committee for International Nature Conservation (1979) *Wildlife introductions to Great Britain*. Report by the Working Group on Introductions.

Vasić, V., Grubac, B., Susic, G. & Marinkovic, S. (1985) The Status of Birds of Prey in Yugoslavia, with Particular Reference to Macedonia. In: I. Newton & R.D. Chancellor (Eds) *Conservation Studies on Raptors, ICBP Technical Publication 5*: 45–54.

Village, A. (1990) *The Kestrel*. T. & A.D. Poyser, London.

Walls, S.S. & Kenward, R.E. (1994a) *Experimental release of buzzards in 1994*. Unpublished report.

Walls, S.S. & Kenward, R.E. (1994b) The systematic study of radio-tagged raptors: II. Sociality and dispersal. In: Meyburg, B.-U. & Chancellor (Eds), *Raptor Conservation Today*. WWGBP/Pica Press, pp. 317–324.

Walls, S.S. & Kenward, R.E. (1995) Movements of radio-tagged Common Buzzard *Buteo buteo* in their first year. *Ibis*, 137: 177–182.

Walters Davies, P. & Davis, P.E. (1973). The ecology and conservation of the Red Kite in Wales. *British Birds*, 66: 183–224, 241–270.

Watson, J. (1991) The Golden Eagle and pastoralism across Europe. In: D.J. Curtis, E.M. Bignal & M.A. Curtis (Eds), *Birds and Pastoralism in Europe. Proceedings of the Second European Forum on Birds and Pastoralism, Port Erin, Isle of Man, 26–30 October 1990.* Scottish Chough Study Group/ Joint Nature Conservation Committee, pp. 56–67.

Welsh Kite Trust (2011) *Boda Wennol* Issue 26, Autumn 2011.

The Wildlife Trusts (2019) *Pine martens reintroduced to England.* https://www.wildlifetrusts.org/news/pine-martens-reintroduced-england Accessed 19/07/2021.

Wilkinson, W. (1989) Chairman's review. Pp. 7–10 in *Nature Conservancy Council 15th Report, 1 April 1988–31 March 1989.* Nature Conservancy Council, Peterborough.

Witherby, H.F. (1909) The present status of the British kite. *British Birds* 2: 84–85.

Yorkshire Red Kites (2020) *History/ Red Kite Reintroduction Programme.* http://www.yorkshireredkites.net/general/history-red-kite-reintroduction-programme Accessed 08/08/2021.

Annexes

Annex 1: Chronology

Up to around 1600 Red Kites in Britain abundant, valued and, in many situations, protected for their service in scavenging to clean towns and villages.

From 1450 Start to change in attitude in some areas to regard predatory birds (or those perceived to be predatory) as competitors or vermin.

1450–early 1900s Persecution of birds of prey intensified to industrial scales throughout UK (then including all of Ireland). As they became rare in the 1800s, egg-collecting became additional threat.

1859 Last sighting of Red Kite over London.

1880s Extinction of Red Kites as breeding birds in England and Scotland.

1916 Last pair of White-tailed Eagles bred in UK.

Early 1900s Remnant Red Kite population in Wales reduced to about 5–20 pairs; intensive protection measures introduced.

1975–1985 Nature Conservancy Council (NCC) imported from Norway White-tailed Eagle chicks to rear and release in W Scotland.

Late 1984 Author joined NCC as Head of Ornithology, and started review of bird conservation work and needs, including consultation with some other organisations.

1985–1988 First Sea-eagle reared in Scotland by released birds in 1986, but still only 2 or 3 per year in following years; 1987 review of further needs started.

1985–1986 Author discussed status and potential for Red Kite with colleagues in NCC and RSPB, including the joint Wales Red Kite Committee.

August 1986 Initial investigations warranted formal assessment, so we arranged for RSPB to write to NCC to raise the issue.

Late 1986 to 1987 Author consulted confidentially key senior stake-holders in NCC, and RSPB colleagues did similarly internally. Review of status of Red Kites across Europe started and potential source populations identified.

July 1987 On behalf of NCC's governing Council, NCC's Advisory Committee on Birds considered and supported author's paper on potential joint NCC/RSPB reintroduction project and authorised author to set in motion more formal consideration and potentially action.

20 October 1987 Following preparations with RSPB colleagues, including developing evidence-based criteria for selecting potential release areas, author convened at NCC HQ in Peterborough the 1st meeting of what became the Red Kite Project Team. On the basis of the criteria, one area in southern England identified as the most promising release area, followed by one in northern Scotland. We would work with regional colleagues to identify potential sites within these areas. Joint NCC/RSPB funding agreed, with RSPB taking the lead in Scotland and NCC in England. Agreed to approach Sweden and East Germany as source of birds. Licencing needs to be reviewed.

8 February 1988 2nd Project Team meeting. Funding from both partners had been confirmed. Permission had been secured from suitable estates in both release areas. We agreed to proceed with both areas provided enough kites could be secured. A public relations plan would be developed, balancing as much open-ness as possible with security for the birds and the helpful estates.

1988 We contracted a start to work on genetic analysis of Red Kites, which eventually indicated that 83% of the very inbred Welsh kites were descended from 1 female, and the other 17% from a continental female which must have arrived about 20 years earlier.

6 October 1988 3rd Project Team meeting, held in the vicinity of the proposed English release area. Positive reply received from Sweden, so author would make formal request. A plan for release of information was agreed.

October–December 1988 Local NCC colleagues and author discovered a major problem with the management of the English site and decided that the safest option was to change site. Within 2 months we had found and agreed an even better site.

24 January 1989 4th Project Team meeting, in Inverness with visit to proposed Scottish release site. Deadline agreed as 15th March to have all arrangements in place; otherwise postpone to 1990. Licencing arrangements had been investigated, ready for the final details. Indications that RAF might provide transport were being followed up.

8 April 1989 Project Team Update Note reported appointment of Dr Ian Evans as Project Officer in England. Welsh team agreed that "surplus" rescued kites could go to the new sites. Licences had been secured for all necessary aspects.

21 May 1989 Project Team Update Note reported appointment of Dee Doody as first of the Project Officers in Scotland. Appalling levels of illegal poisoning in Wales (see below) meant that only one chick from there reached the new sites. RAF had agreed to transport the Swedish kites.

13 June 1989 First Red Kite chicks imported from Sweden to RAF Kinloss, Scotland, where press event held. 6 moved to quarantine at Scottish site, while 4 driven to English quarantine site to join one rescued Welsh chick.

11 July 1989 UK Government announces its break-up of NCC.

20 & 23 July 1989 Kites at Scottish site released.

1 August 1989 Kites at English site released.

12 August 1989 First Scottish kite leaves release area; this and others were tracked or re-found across Scotland.

20 August 1989 First kites left English release area; these and others were tracked or re-found over long distances within England.

20 November 1989 One of the English released kites found dead in Shropshire; a successful prosecution for illegal poisoning followed.

27 November 1989 5th Project Team meeting, at RSPB HQ, Sandy. On the basis of a range of contacts, decided to approach Sweden and Spain for kites in future years. Future veterinary arrangements agreed on the basis of those trialled at the English site.

1 December 1989 One Scottish kite found killed by illegal poisoning.

1989–90 winter Hurricane-force winds destroyed one of the English cages; at both sites, more cages built.

1989–1990 Welsh population creeps up to 62 pairs but, in 1989, at least 11 Red Kites poisoned in Wales. In 1990, eggs stolen from at least 8 nests. Little sign of a spread in distribution.

February–March 1990 3, or possibly all 4, surviving English kites back in the general vicinity of the English release area.

March–May 1990 3 to 5 1-year-old kites present in the general vicinity of the Scottish release area.

3 May 1990 Project Team Update Note confirmed that both sources seemed to be in order.

24–31 May 1990 Author, with colleagues from NCC and Spain, collected 11 young kites in Navarra, with British Airways Assisting Nature Conservation providing transportation. These, and 2 rescued Welsh young, delivered to the English quarantine site.

11–15 June 1990 Roy Dennis and Swedish colleagues collected 20 young kites and RAF flew them to Scotland; then driven to the Scottish quarantine site.

July 1990 By arrangement, first press presence at releases at English site, under conditions of site-confidentiality.

September 1990 One of the 1989 released kites associating with the 1990 releases at the English site.

25 October 1990 6th Project Team meeting, at NCC HQ Peterborough, assessed that all actions set at its previous meeting had been met, and confirmed continuing similar arrangements for the following year. Improvements in radio-tracking discussed.

1991–1995 Similar collection and transportation arrangements continued until the end of releases at the first 2 sites, 1993 for Scotland and 1994 for England.

March–June 1991 1st two pairs of Red Kites (all 1-year-old) nested in England, but the eggs did not survive.

1 April 1991 Successor bodies (3 country agencies and the Joint Nature Conservation Committee, JNCC) replaced NCC.

3 December 1991 7th Project Team meeting, held at NCC for Scotland Regional Office in Inverness, noted continuing satisfactory progress and reviewed future plans, taking account of first tentative population modelling.

Spring 1992 4 pairs in England bred successfully, rearing 8 chicks. The 1st pair on territory in Scotland reared 1 chick.

14 December 1992 8th Project Team meeting, at JNCC offices in Peterborough, brought in new personnel from the new agencies. Improvements in tag-fitting were agreed. It was agreed that routine nest-protection was not needed. The needs for continuing the experimental project with UK coordination was stressed, including when to end releases at the first two sites and possibly start others.

1993 BBC TV Countryfile provided with facilities at English site, with broadcast resulting.

1993 For the first time in well over a century, more than 100 pairs of kites nested in Wales.

12 April 1994 9th Project Team meeting, at JNCC Peterborough. There would be no releases in Scotland that year, but a further release was planned for England, to bring the total numbers released to about (actually, it turned out, exactly) the same as in Scotland. The need for a plan for kite operations after the end of the successful experimental project agreed. The author and JNCC colleagues prepared this, consulting with the other partners.

1994 In England, for the first time that century, wild-bred Red Kites themselves fledged young.

July 1994 Government Minister and wide press coverage at the last release at the first English site, launching major anti-poisoning campaign.

10 November 1994 10th (and last) Project Team meeting, at JNCC Peterborough. There were estimated to be 120–130 Red Kites in southern England and around 40 in Scotland. Both areas were now thought to be self-supporting. Our paper on moving from experimental to operational phases of the Red Kite work was accepted, and set the structure for the next 2 decades.

1995 At least 26, and probably 30, breeding pairs located in England and 17 in Scotland.

1995 JNCC handed the lead to country agencies, but continued to advise and help.

1995–1998 Kites released at a new site in Northamptonshire, in the first two years with birds from Spain and a few from Wales, and in 1997 10 from Spain and 10 from the first English site in the Chilterns, which also provided all the young in the final year. The first of these reared young themselves in 1997.

1996–2001 Kites released at a second Scottish site, the source being Germany.

1999–2003 Kites from the Chilterns released in Yorkshire, with 16 breeding pairs established by the final year of releases.

2001–2005 Red Kite chicks from the Chilterns and the Black Isle (the first two release sites) released in Dumfries & Galloway

2004–2006 Young kites from the Chilterns released in NE England.

2007–2009 Young kites from the Chilterns and central Scotland released near Aberdeen.

2006–2011 Young kites from Wales released in Co. Wicklow & Co. Dublin, Republic of Ireland.

2008–2010 Young kites from Wales released in Co. Down, Northern Ireland.

2010–2012 Young kites from central England released in the Lake District.

2020 Estimated 1800 pairs of Red Kites breeding in the UK, with kites regularly seen throughout Britain and much of Ireland. UK now a stronghold of the world Red Kite population.

Annex 2: Extracts from the note for the file, prepared by the Wales kite leaders, following the [Wales] Kite Meeting of 13 March 1987

A meeting of NCC officers was held at Dyfed Powys regional office to consider the future involvement of NCC in kite matters. Those attending were: Mr D A White (chair), Dr R P Bray, Mr P E Davis [PED], Dr M Pienkowski, Dr D Ratcliffe and Mr P Walters Davies [PWD].

The meeting arose from a paper circulated by PWD in September 1986. A review of NCC involvement with kites was clearly desirable; the last one was in 1970. The recent retirement of PWD and the impending retirement of PED in 1988 made it imperative to look at the situation now. … A proposal to try to establish a new kite population outside Wales would need detailed appraisal in the near future.

The main conclusions and recommendations of the meeting were as follows:

1 The Kite Committee
This was created by the 1970 kite conference, to advise NCC and RSPB on kite matters. Each organisation had two representatives and each body held the Chair in alternate years. PWD and PED represented NCC, and Messrs Lovegrove and Porter represented RSPB. … The Committee should be represented … in any steering group set up to oversee a reintroduction in Scotland or England.

2 Population Monitoring and Recording
… Full monitoring of an increasing population could not be maintained indefinitely, but was very valuable, and should be continued for the immediate future. The outcome of the egg manipulation programme would need to be carefully monitored. If a reintroduction took place, both the new and the old populations would need to be fully recorded also; an interchange of birds was not improbable.

3 Nest Protection
… Only selected nests were protected by wardens. The question of cost-effectiveness perhaps needs to be looked at, since physical protection seems to produce few additional young…

4 Law Enforcement
RSPB have always made the running in this field…

5 Research and Development
NCC had led the way in the past, but RSPB was increasingly wanting to put resources into new developments rather than maintaining the *status quo*. The egg manipulation programme starting in 1987 (and planned to continue for several seasons if successful) could obviously have implications for a reintroduction scheme. NCC gives 'cautious encouragement' to appropriate reintroductions, with adequate safeguards. NCC should be involved in a kite reintroduction programme. The area of release needed to be carefully chosen and prepared. A further look at some of the Welsh data could help in this. A first step would be to obtain the views of ACB [NCC's high-level Advisory Committee on Birds]. RSPB was unlikely to go ahead without NCC approval…

6 Public relations/publicity
No early changes were envisaged…

7 Manpower and resources requirement
Suggested timing and programme as follows:

1987–88: continue along existing lines, plus a contract worker to help with the egg manipulation scheme. PWD's contract to act as NCC joint chairman of the Kite Committee and to advise/assist in other kite matters, to continue. There is no likelihood of any increase in the regional commitment to kites, and perhaps less time may be available, due to pressures of work upon a static warden establishment…

1989–90: aim to retain the services of PWD and PED on contract, with the addition of field worker contracts as needed…

1991–93: aim to maintain the whole existing programme to the end of the five-year period, but with a review of the situation in 1991, in good time for the 1993–94 forward planning.

CSD [NCC's Chief Scientist Directorate] (Dr Pienkowski) will discuss with RSPB and aim to convene a higher level joint RSPB/NCC meeting on kite affairs. Other interested parties such as Dr I Newton may be involved. Decisions on timing, etc of this meeting should be taken by summer 1987. The meeting would look ahead and plan a conservation programme for the following period of five or more years.

Annex 3: NCC's Ornithology Note no. 5. Current work in ornithology: the reintroduction of the White-tailed Eagle (Project Bi3) (Pienkowski & Love 1989)

Words in square parentheses are explanatory insertions. Photographs have been added.

Why is the work needed?
The White-tailed Eagle *Haliaeetus albicilla* is the fourth largest eagle in the world. With a wingspan of nearly 3 metres, it is an imposing spectacle in flight, not unlike a huge vulture, or, less respectfully, a flying barn-door. More poetically, the Gaelic name *Iolaire suil na grein*, means the eagle with the sunlit eye. In fact, the eyes and large, hooked bill are all bright yellow. These features, its larger size and greater attachment to the coast distinguish this species from the golden eagle.

Once common throughout the north and west of Britain (and, indeed, occurring throughout the country at earlier times), the sea eagle suffered drastically from persecution last century [1800s]. Its predominantly coastal distribution made the whole population relatively accessible to humans, whereas golden eagles managed to survive in the remote inland mountains. The last pair [of sea-eagles] in Britain bred on the Isle of Skye in 1916.

In recent times, populations throughout the species' range, except those in Norway and Greenland, have been much reduced by habitat loss and, especially, by pesticides. Any species whose healthy population is limited to a small part of its range is very vulnerable to extinction. However, birds of this species are very sedentary, and unlikely to recolonise areas now again suitable. The coasts of north and west Britain are again suitable for this species due to a more enlightened view of birds of prey. There were thus good international, as well as national, reasons for reintroducing the species.

Both NCC and RSPB (as well as international bodies) have guidelines as to when reintroductions may be appropriate…

Since 1975, the Nature Conservancy Council has co-operated with the Royal Society for the Protection of Birds (RSPB), the Institute of Terrestrial Ecology (ITE), and the Scottish Wildlife Trust (SWT) in a programme to reintroduce the sea-eagle to Britain.

How are we doing the work?
Each year between 1975 and 1985, the Norwegian government granted licences to take up to 10 eaglets from eyries in northern Norway. They were transported to Scotland by 120 Nimrod Squadron of the Royal Air Force, Kinloss, and in one year by the Royal Norwegian Air Force [in 1982, when RAF capacity was concentrated on freeing the Falkland Islands from foreign military invaders]. The eaglets were about 8 to 10 weeks old and not yet fledged. They were retained in captivity but in as near natural conditions as possible on the Isle of

White-tailed Eagle chicks in nest in Norway [JL]

White-tailed Eagle chicks arrive at RAF Kinloss, and feeding chick at Rum. [JL]

Rhum [as then normally spelt, an affectation of a previous owner of the island; now restored to 'Rum'], a National Nature Reserve (owned by NCC) in the Hebrides. The young eagles were set free in late summer, after marking with coloured leg-rings and/or wing-tags.

Food in the form of fish and carrion was provided until the eagles were able to hunt and to fend for themselves. From Rhum, most spread out while immature to other suitable localities in the west of Scotland – from Shetland to Kintyre – and even Northern Ireland. Their diet consists of fish, seabirds, rabbits and hares, supplemented in the winter months with carrion.

In addition to the work in reintroducing the birds, largely handled by NCC, there was an increasing need to co-ordinate sightings and investigate how the birds fitted into their new environment. As the birds matured and started to nest, protection was required, much of this being undertaken by RSPB.

In common with all other birds of prey, sea-eagles are fully protected by law. Nonetheless, two of the birds reared and released on Rhum have died at poisoned baits illegally laid out for foxes and crows. Six other eagles have died from natural causes. However, the survival rate is very high: between 50% and 70% of the 82 eagles released are thought to be thriving in the wild.

Table: Number of White-tailed Eagles released on Rum in 1975–1985

No. released:	1975	1976	1977	1978	1979	1980	1981	1982	1983	1984	1985	Total
males	0	5	2	4	3	5	3	3	3	6	5	39
females	3	4	2	3	3	3	2	7	7	4	5	43
Total	3	9	4	7	6	8	5	10	10	10	10	82

Sea-eagles take at least 5 years to reach adulthood, and in 1982 the first courtship and nest-building were seen. In 1983, the first eggs recorded were laid – by a pair of birds 3–4 years old and by a trio of 2 females and a male. The young pair laid again in 1984 but again no eggs hatched. In 1985 this pair (now fully adult) successfully hatched and reared one chick – the first to have been bred in Britain for 70 years. They repeated their success with two more chicks the following year, by which time several other pairs were laying eggs. They reared another two chicks in 1987, when another pair (part of the earlier trio) also fledged one chick. Both these pairs failed in 1988 (the previously very successful pair losing their nest in a storm); but a third pair succeeded in fledging two eaglets: particularly noteworthy since this pair (6 years old) had never bred before.

A total of 10 or 11 pairs had established territories by 1988, and 6 or 7 of them produced eggs. So far, any failures to breed successfully seem due to age and inexperience, and

2-year-old male White-tailed Eagle and nest in captive breeding at Rum [JL]

sometimes to bad weather. Nest sites are protected by RSPB and NCC and, of course, the localities are kept secret to give the eagles every chance of success.

What have we done so far?

As can be seen from the above, the project has been extremely successful. Several major targets have been achieved:
1. The sea eaglets were successfully collected, imported, reared and released.
2. The released sea eagles survived well and became self-supporting.
3. These birds are now reaching maturity and breeding successfully. Our fourth main target remains:
4. That the birds breed sufficiently successfully for the population to maintain itself and spread throughout the sea eagle's former haunts. This is the reason for the continuing work (see below).

Table: Number of White-tailed Eagles bred in the wild

Fledged:	1985	1986	1987	1988	Total
males	1	0	1	0	2
females	0	2	2	2	6
Total	1	2	3	2	8
Known deaths:			1 female		

How are the results being used?

This is a project in which the research and application proceed alongside each other, in an interactive way. The project is well on the way to restoring a nationally extinct species to the British fauna, and in the process enhancing the prospects for its world survival. The viability of the reintroduction technique has been established, and the maintained suitability of western Scotland for sea eagles confirmed. In addition, the project has proven extremely effective in gaining wider support for nature conservation and NCC. The project has become well-known among the general public, and drawn their imagination and support.

What are we doing next?

In the next few years, we need to monitor numbers, distribution, survival and productivity of the birds and investigate any problems, while ensuring the well-being of the nesting birds. In particular we need to decide whether a further supply of eaglets is required: importations were suspended in 1985 for a trial period of about 5 years. Analysing the need is difficult because of the problems in analysing the dynamics of a small, remote, population in a situation when most of the birds are only just reaching breeding age. Efforts are being made in 1989 to establish more precisely the survival and recruitment, by special surveys and analyses of earlier sightings.

Who is doing the work?
NCC's Nominated Officer for this project is Dr Mike Pienkowski. NCC retain Mr John Love to co-ordinate work on a day-to-day basis. The joint project team consists of Dr M W Pienkowski (Chairman; NCC), M E Ball, J A Love (both NCC), Dr I Newton (ITE), R H Dennis, R A Broad, G D Elliott (all RSPB), and Dr A J Watson (SWT). A very large number of people have helped in the project and these are more fully acknowledged by Love (1988) – see below.

Where can more information be obtained?
Love, J.1983. *The return of-the sea eagle.* Cambridge University Press.
NCC 1985. *The sea eagle.* 12pp (Colour booklet outlining the past and history and status of sea-eagles in Britain up until 1985).
Love, J. A.1988. *The reintroduction of the white-tailed sea eagle to Scotland: 1975–1987.* Research & Survey in Nature Conservation no. 12. NCC, Peterborough. 48pp.

How can readers help?
Disturbance causes breeding failures in eagles. Do not go looking for nest sites. If you are in the area in the breeding season and see an eagle frequenting one area, please move away from it if you can.

Sightings of sea eagles at any season are useful in helping us to assess the present position, and therefore further needs. Details of colours and positions of any wing-tags are very helpful, but simple sightings of the birds are also useful. Please send any records (present or past) to: …

Annex 4: Extracts from Ornithology Note: Conservation of the Barn Owl *Tyto alba* in the United Kingdom (revised edition, Percival *et al*. 1992)

Words in square parentheses are explanatory insertions.

1. Introduction

This note outlines the ecology of the barn owl, its current population status, reasons for its decline and appropriate measures which can be taken to effectively conserve the species.

The barn owl *Tyto alba* is one of many species of British birds that has suffered a major decline in numbers and range contraction during the last few decades. As one of our most attractive birds its plight has attracted much attention from conservationists and the general public, alike. It was once a common and widespread species on farmland pastures and field margins but is now in need of urgent conservation action to assure its survival…

2. Population Trends and Distribution

The barn owl is found in many other parts of the world; however, nowhere else does it occur at such northerly latitudes as in Britain. Most European countries have reported population declines, including France, the Netherlands and Sweden (Cramp & Simmons 1980), and numbers have fallen in many parts of the United States.

The barn owl was one of the first British bird species for which a national survey was attempted. In 1932 Blaker (1934) gathered information on breeding sites throughout England and Wales, and estimated a total of 12,000 pairs. A total for the British Isles of 4,500–9,000 pairs was estimated in the Breeding Bird Atlas in 1968–72 (Sharrock 1976) and the Hawk Trust survey estimated that there were 4,400 pairs between 1982–85 (Shawyer 1987). The UK now supports around one third of the barn owls that it did sixty years ago.

The barn owl is still widespread across the country, but more restricted than sixty years ago. The change in distribution can be seen by comparing the BTO *Breeding Bird Atlas* map for 1968–72 (Sharrock 1976) with the BTO New Breeding Bird Atlas map for 1988–1991 (Gibbons *et al*. 1993). The *New Breeding Bird Atlas* map shows that the population is now restricted to a number of concentrations with barn owls absent from much of the intervening land. There are few clear patterns in the distribution of these high density areas, with several along the west coast of Britain but also some southwards along the east coast from Yorkshire.

Mortality rates can be high in periods of freezing temperatures and snow (Percival 1991), as might be expected for a species on the northern fringe of its range and therefore perhaps susceptible to such severe weather conditions.

3. Ecology of the Barn Owl

The ecology of the barn owl has been well described across much of its world range. Its breeding success is generally high in comparison with many other owl species. In Britain, however, a large proportion of the chicks perish before fledging, almost always as a result of starvation. Their lifestyle therefore is adapted to exploit suitable conditions when they can raise large numbers of young and enjoy a high chance of survival.

3.1 Feeding

Their diet in Britain is almost exclusively comprised of small mammals, over half of the food the field vole *Microtus agrestis* (Taylor, I. *et al*. 1988). The barn owl not only requires an abundance of suitable prey species to ensure its survival, but that prey most also be 'available' to the owls. This point is best illustrated by the effect of winter snow cover. Although snow does not reduce the small mammal populations, it makes them 'unavailable' to the owls. Several days of deep snow cover often means that the owls cannot get at their food supply and starvation occurs.

3.2 Nesting
They require a generally dark spacious cavity, with enough room to hold up to 6 chicks for a period of seven weeks at which point the chicks fledge. Barn owls are also intolerant of repeated disturbance, so this too will influence their choice of where to nest. Amongst natural sites, three tree species are particularly preferred: oak *Quercus* sp., elm *Ulmus* sp. and ash *Fraxinus* sp. (Shawyer 1987). This probably reflects the fact the cavities ideally suited to the owls are naturally and regularly formed in these species. Barn owls will however also readily take to artificial sites and a large proportion are now found in nest boxes.

4. Possible reasons for the decline of the Barn Owl in Great Britain
Many reasons have been suggested as a way of explaining the decline in the barn owl in Britain…

4.1 Reduction in the availability of suitable feeding habitat
Barn owl distributions in Britain closely match the distribution of their main prey species, the field vole *Microtus agrestis* (Taylor *et al.* 1988). Any factor that reduces the numbers of field voles would therefore be expected also to reduce the number of barn owls. Many of the practices associated with the intensification of agriculture have certainly had such an effect, including hedgerow removal, loss of permanent grassland, and the change over to autumn-sown cereals. Several authors have also suggested that the mechanisation of harvesting techniques with the associated loss of the traditional stack-yards, must have led to a further decline in farmland small mammal populations.
This loss of feeding habitat is likely to have been an important contributor to the overall decline but it is not the whole story. It cannot, for instance, explain the recent improvement in barn owl breeding success and survival rates as there has not been a simultaneous increase in small mammals.

4.2 Reduction in the availability of nesting sites
Barn owls have quite specific requirements for their nest site. Loss of old buildings through both dereliction and conversion to residences, and old trees, through felling and Dutch Elm Disease, have reduced the number of sites available to owls, such that in some areas suitable nest sites have become a scarce resource. Though this may limit barn owl populations at a local scale (which can be addressed directly by provision of nest boxes), it is generally agreed that it is unlikely to have been a major contributor to the overall decline. There are many areas where there are ample nest sites in existence, but barn owl numbers have still fallen.

4.3 Climate change
Both Bunn *et al.* (1982) and Shawyer (1987) concluded that increasing winter severity, and in particular more snow lie (by reducing food availability), have caused substantial barn owl mortality. Other more detailed studies (Taylor 1989, Taylor 1992) have however shown that weather has a relatively small effect on owl numbers. Further examination of the BTO ringing data tended to support the latter hypothesis; adult mortality rates were slightly higher in winters with more rainfall (which reduces hunting time for the owls), and more juvenile owls died in colder winters, the weather conditions explained only part of the variation in mortality rates. The logical conclusion is that the weather has some effect on owl populations, but not sufficient to explain all the changes in numbers that have occurred.

4.4 Pesticides - (organochlorines DDT & dieldrin, and rodenticides)
Organochlorine pesticides have been strongly implicated in the decline of many British raptors during the 1950s and 60s. Two chemicals of particular note are (i) DDT that is now known to cause breeding failure by reducing the thickness of the egg shells and hence their viability, and (ii) the dieldrin/aldrin group, which is more toxic and has a more direct effect by causing adult

mortality. Birds and mammals at the top of the food chain were at particular risk because these chemicals become increasingly concentrated in the body tissues. The timing of the barn owl decline, and particularly its subsequent recovery, suggests that these pesticides had a major impact on barn owl populations too. The pattern of decline through the 1950s and 60s, then recovery from 1970s onwards was the same as that found in both the sparrowhawk and the peregrine populations. Post-mortem analyses showed that barn owls from the 1960s and early 1970s were often heavily contaminated, particularly with dieldrin/aldrin residues. By the 1980s these residue levels had fallen dramatically and no barn owl deaths due to organochlorine poisoning were recorded. The high contamination of owls in the earlier samples, together with the observed population changes, suggest that direct poisoning of owls by dieldrin/aldrin may have been the key factor in reducing barn owl populations.

A second, more recent, group of pesticides may pose a threat to current barn owl populations. These are the 'second generation' rodenticides, developed as highly toxic compounds to poison rats in areas where they had become resistant to the older (and much less toxic) warfarin-based products. There are two potential routes by which these new chemicals might affect barn owls: (i) indirectly, by reducing their food supply, (ii) directly, by poisoning owls feeding on contaminated small mammals. These 'second generation' chemicals also persist in the bodies of animals which are exposed but not killed and therefore represent an additional source of residues to the barn owl long after initial exposure (Newton & Wyllie 1992). None of these should happen if the pesticides are used correctly but, when used in contravention of the product guidelines in fields and hedgerows, they can be a serious problem for barn owls. During 1983–89 some 145 barn owl carcasses were received from various parts of Britain and chemically analysed for 'second generation' rodenticides. 10% of all the birds examined contained one of these chemicals at the time of their death (Newton & Wyllie 1992).

4.5 Competition for resources

It has been suggested that the barn owl and the larger, more aggressive tawny owl *Strix aluco* may compete for scarce resources in some circumstances (*e.g.* Shawyer 1987). Competition for nest sites is probably most likely especially where large cavities, in trees or buildings, are in short supply. There is however, no evidence published to support this idea and indeed many examples have been cited of the two species co-existing in close proximity, even occupying adjacent nest boxes (Shaw & Dowell 1990). The two species have slightly different site requirements, tawny owls preferring smaller and more enclosed cavities, so under usual circumstances the chance of any such competition is slight. There is however another potential source of competition for wild barn owls: captive bred birds which are released into the wild. Many such individuals have been released into areas where wild birds are scarce in an attempt to boost the local populations. In such areas, however, where resources for the owls are likely to be limited, these introduced birds could add further pressure to the wild population. The very poor survival of released birds means that competition is fairly limited but, at a local level, could be an important factor. Releases of captive-bred barn owls are of course now subject to licence controls by DoE [Department of the Environment, predecessor of Defra]. Any release without a licence, or [allowing] escape into the wild, is illegal.

4.6 Increasing road mortality

Recoveries of ringed birds and birds found dead by the public generally suggest that a high proportion of Britain's barn owls are killed on the roads. Increasing road traffic and the speed at which it travels may have played a contributory role to the birds' decline, but it is important that the impact of road deaths on populations is not over-emphasised. These findings are highly biased as birds dying on roads are much more likely to be found by the public. A recent study in Germany by Illner (1992) has shown that such results can over exaggerate the importance of roads as a mortality factor by as much as 400%. Roads, and indeed railways, may have been locally important factors influencing barn owl populations, but it is unlikely that they have had a major effect at the national level…

5. Advice on the conservation of the Barn Owl

When thinking about our overall objective for barn owl conservation, there are two underlying principles that must be considered:
1. Consolidation and promotion of barn owl populations in core areas.
2. Facilitation of the expansion of the population into areas from which they have disappeared in the 1960s and 70s, both through the provision of suitable habitat and links to enhance population movement.

5.1. Farmers and landowners

A primary objective of barn owl conservation action is to improve their food supply, *i.e.* habitat management to promote small mammal populations. The provision of grassland with reduced grazing levels is essential. One practical application of this idea is to develop strips around fields, in a similar way to conservation headlands to promote the value of field margins. Such grassland strips are already used by barn owls in some areas of the country that have lost traditional owl habitat, *e.g.* the Fens of East Anglia where considerable numbers of owls are dependent on grass strips, fringing ditches and drains, for their feeding habitat.

Farmers are also the group which makes the most use of the pesticides that may affect barn owls. Conservation management should aim to minimise any risk of poisoning to owls. The organochlorine compounds that caused problems to barn owls in the past are no longer widely used and therefore unlikely to be a problem. The most likely current threats to barn owls now come from second generation rodenticides. It is essential that the product guidelines are strictly followed and that these poisons are not allowed to find their way into the barn owl's food chain. It would be prudent to use products known to be less toxic to barn owls. Whilst the control of rats around farm buildings may be essential, care must be taken to ensure that populations of other small mammals are not destroyed unnecessarily, with consequent impact on the barn owl feeding success.

Farmers and landowners can also ensure that barn owls on their land have adequate and safe nest sites. If there is a shortage of sites, perhaps through the felling of trees after Dutch elm disease or the clearing of old buildings, and there is suitable barn owl feeding habitat in the vicinity, then the provision of artificial sites could be considered.

By considering the ecology of the whole landscape, providing grassland edges and corridors across many areas of farmland rather than just in isolated pockets, it may be possible to ensure that there is suitable habitat to allow barn owls to recolonise their old haunts as quickly as possible. This will not only benefit barn owls but might also improve the general wildlife value of our countryside at the same time.

5.2 Planners and building constructors
1. Ensure that any demolition or conversion work in sites currently used by barn owls is done outside the breeding season (*i.e.* between October and February). Indeed, such action is a legal obligation as nesting barn owls are protected under Schedule 1 of the Wildlife and Countryside Act 1981. Any disturbance of nesting birds will be liable to prosecution.
2. Where barn owl sites are unavoidably lost, this reduction in nest-availability should be compensated by the provision of alternative sites, ideally the erection of a specifically designed nest box.

5.3 Land use and policy makers

Perhaps the best way forward may be to incorporate management for barn owls into a national scheme to promote conservation management, as an active use of farmland that would otherwise be producing unwanted surplus crops. Such an approach would not only benefit barn owl conservation but would improve the overall richness of all our farmland communities. Within the field of agriculture, grant-aided schemes to improve, for example, barn owl feeding habitats could become part of an integrated strategy for farmland conservation. The provision of nest sites also could become part of such 'farming for wildlife' schemes…

Recent success in barn owl conservation in [forestry plantations] (*e.g.* Shaw & Dowell 1990) has been attributed to planning forests with conservation in mind. As the design of the forest rotation has been modified in the last thirty years to provide a more varied environment with native tree species and open feeding habitat available to owls throughout the cycle of the rotation, barn owls have responded by using these areas in ever-increasing numbers…

5.4 Release of captive-reared and rehabilitated barn owls into the wild

Many of the birds released in the past have been ringed as a part of the BTO national ringing scheme, enabling their fate to be monitored. Comparison of their survival rate with that of wild birds has shown these released birds suffer much greater mortality. Only 15% of adults released and 10% of juveniles survived to the end of their first year (compared with 71% and 21% in wild birds). In other words, they are more than twice as likely to die than wild birds; in most instances they are simply being released to an early death. There are several reasons why this is happening: many are released into unsuitable habitat, and almost all are coming into an environment of which they have no experience. This fact is further emphasised by examination of looking at the ways in which released birds have died. Many more have been found starved than wild ones, and more become victims of road accidents, again probably because of their weakened state.

The question of releasing captive-bred barn owls into the wild is not simply allowing them to come to a rapid demise. The introduction of different genes into the population may often not be a healthy process for the conservation of the local wild birds. Birds are generally closely adapted to their local conditions. The viability of wild genetic stock could be reduced if they interbreed with introductions from other regions or in some cases other countries. Introductions of disease to local birds could also be a potential problem. These released birds could also compete with the wild birds in areas where resources (*e.g.* food supply, nest sites) are limited, again harming rather than benefiting local wild populations.

For these reasons, JNCC and a number of conservation organisations advised government, through a Department of the Environment (DoE) working group, that the barn owl should be given further statutory protection under the Wildlife and Countryside Act, 1981. Following advice to government from the JNCC, the barn owl was added to Part 1, Schedule 9 of the Wildlife and Countryside Act, 1981 on 25 November 1992. This Schedule applies throughout Great Britain and lists species which may not be released, except under licence from DoE, or allowed to escape into the wild. This addition to Schedule 9 was a welcome step towards the adoption of appropriate conservation measures for this species. Habitat management issues, amongst others, must be addressed as a priority if the population decline of the barn owl is to be arrested and the population successfully conserved.

Releasing captive bred barn owls makes people feel good, but is often cruel to the released bird and could harm the wild population also. The simple advice to people wishing to release barn owls is DON'T DO IT.

5.5 Watching barn owls; advice to bird watchers and the general public

The barn own is such an attractive and appealing species. We need to be careful that, in promoting its conservation, we do not increase the level of disturbance to which it is subjected… Known roosts or nest-sites should never be disturbed at any time of the year but instead watched from a distance…

Annex 5: The options and consequences of manipulating Red Kite broods in Wales
Internal note for kite workers in Wales by Dr Ian Evans, 1989

Introduction
Thanks to the efforts of kite workers in Wales over the years, the population of Red Kites breeding in Wales has now increased to around 50 pairs. However, the breeding success of Welsh birds is low and the increase is sustained only by the continued high survival rate of fully grown birds. In recent years, two initiatives have been taken to improve the prospects for red kites in Britain; the manipulation of the clutches of Welsh birds to improve the overall productivity, and the establishment of new breeding populations elsewhere using released birds. This paper sets out to review the options for the future.

The manipulation programme has been in operation for three years with variable success. The ground rules have been that only vulnerable or abandoned clutches have been taken. The success rate has been variable but this has depended to some extent on the circumstances surrounding the collection of eggs. One unexpected problem has been the difficulty in finding foster homes for the extra birds. In general, it has been found that Welsh birds are not capable of rearing an extra adopted chick successfully. The RSPB research work with video cameras also indicates that the loss of chicks, either when very young or as a result of aggression between siblings, is one of the major causes of the low productivity in Wales. Thus all this work points to food supply to chicks being a problem.

In order to safeguard the future of Red Kites in Britain and internationally, a programme to reintroduce the birds to Scotland and England was started in 1989. Ten chicks were obtained from Sweden and one from Wales. It is still too early to draw firm conclusions, but so far the project is extremely encouraging with the released birds surviving well. There has been considerable dispersal from both the release sites, but it will be one or two years before we know if birds return to their release area to breed. In the meantime, it is essential that the release programmes continue.

To model the impact of the manipulation programme on the Welsh population, an analysis has been done using the published breeding and survival parameters. This indicates that, with no intervention, 100 egg-laying pairs will be reached in 2005. If 10 birds are added per year as a result of manipulations (a figure rather difficult to achieve), this year will come forward to 2002. The reason why the effect is so small is that the Welsh population is already so large that 10 extra birds is not all that significant to it. It would therefore become increasingly difficult to justify the effort and expenditure on the manipulations on the basis of their impact on the Welsh population alone. In contrast, a small number of birds from Wales would have a major impact on the reintroduction programmes where there is currently a shortfall of about ten birds per year.

Possible sources of birds for range extension in Britain
The first experimental year of reintroductions, aimed at safeguarding the long-term future of the population in Britain and internationally, has been successful to date. We therefore need to look at ways of providing the essential small concentrations of birds to allow them to become self supporting. We undertook a detailed review of all the options, and this is summarised below.
1. Obtaining 4–6 week-old chicks from overseas. This was done and we will propose it continues. There are, however, practical difficulties in obtaining all required from this source. There is also the moral point as to how appropriate it is to seek to obtain all the birds from overseas if some could be obtained from within Britain without damaging the British population. This has bearing too on the attitude of foreign authorities.
2. Obtaining 4–6 week-old chicks from Welsh nests. The consequences of this have not been investigated as it would be considered inappropriate in the Welsh situation.

3. Artificially incubating some eggs from first-time breeders. Whilst superficially attractive, an examination of the data is unable to establish that first-time breeders are less successful than older birds. There are some indications that this is because the productivity of older birds in the centre of the range may be suffering some density-dependent reduction. However, this option is not recommended.
4. Artificially incubating eggs from home-ranges which are almost always unsuccessful. There are 8 such home-ranges but each is irregularly used. It would be appropriate here to rescue all but 2 eggs from each clutch.
5. Artificially incubating eggs from nests close to Raven nests. The work by Davis, Davies and Newton suggests that it would be appropriate to remove whole clutches in such situations, which could also encourage the birds to renest in a better situation. The difficulty, however, is defining "close".
6. Artificially incubating eggs laid after a certain date. Whilst later clutches are less successful, the difference is not great enough to recommend this option.
7. Artificially incubating clutches that are habitually robbed or vulnerable to robbery. 3 nests are habitually robbed and it would be appropriate to continue to remove clutches from these. Identifying other nests "vulnerable" to robbing is more difficult and is not recommended at present.
8. Artificially incubating deserted clutches. Whilst this is worthwhile if an incubating facility exists, it should not be regarded as a prime source because of both the unpredictability and the very slim chance that eggs will still be viable when rescued.
9. Artificially incubating some eggs from 3- or 4-egg clutches. Except in Area IV, 3-egg clutches rarely (and 4-egg clutches never) produce 3 fledged young. Indeed, there are some indications that smaller clutches may produce more young than large ones because of the feeding problems. It would therefore be appropriate to rescue 1 egg from 3-egg clutches (and 2 from any 4-egg clutches) except in Area IV (where 1 should be removed from any 4-egg clutches. This would have either no or an extremely small impact on the Welsh population. Taking the most pessimistic (and unlikely assumptions), it could delay the reaching of 100 egg-laying pairs by 1 or 2 years.
10. Artificially incubating one egg from 2-egg clutches. Outside Area IV, at least 40% of such clutches fail and less than 14% fledge two chicks. Early removal of one might even increase the proportion rearing the other. In area V, over 50% of such clutches fail and none rear 2 chicks. It would therefore be appropriate to try this option (removal of 1 egg from 2-egg clutches and a second from 3-egg clutches) initially just in that area.
11. Artificially rearing the youngest chick from nests with 3 chicks. This was successfully done in 2 cases in 1989. However, option 9 is preferable because that would save the lives of far more chicks, as demonstrated by this analysis and the video work. The present option would be sensible as a back-up to option 9.
12. Artificially rearing chicks unlikely to survive due to sibling rivalry. This relates to option 10 in the same way as 11 relates to 9. The same comments apply.
13. Captive breeding. This is a potential option if planning further work at least 2 years ahead. However, it could not help in the present situation.

Conclusions and recommendations

Based on the scientific information analysed in detail and summarised here, the following recommendations have been drafted as a basis for discussion. The goal throughout has been to recommend what is best for the conservation of kites, rather than giving priority to bird-watching, the ambitions of individuals, or more narrow views.
1. The RSPB/NCC Welsh Kite Committee supports the NCC/RSPB Experimental Kite Re-introduction Project as the most practicable way of contributing to the long-term survival of the British population and internationally the species as a whole.

2. The manipulation experiments in Wales have been successful in the aim of establishing the viability of this technique so that it is available when required.
3. Because of the difficulties in returning chicks to nests and the very marginal effect on increasing the rate of population increase, further returns of chicks to Welsh nests should not be continued at present.
4. A large loss of kites occurs in Wales in the late egg/early chick stage due to generally poor food supply, except in the southern areas.
5. The detailed studies have shown that eggs likely to fail can be identified and reared artificially without affecting the size or rate of increase of the population in Wales.
6. To aid the spread of the population in Wales, and contribute to the international survival of this endangered species, such eggs and young will be rescued, reared and released into other parts of Britain.
7. A set of guidelines are necessary to decide which eggs or chicks to rescue. This is essential to maximising the chance of survival of these kites. The following guidelines are based on the scientific analysis to examine which could be removed without adversely affecting (but possibly assisting) the numbers in Wales.
    a) All but 1 egg from each of 8 irregularly occupied home ranges which are almost always unsuccessful. (… [On] average …, the maximum number of eggs which would be rescued by this means would result in 1.2 [per year] if all could be found.)
    b) All eggs from 3 nests habitually robbed. (Maximum on average 6.0 eggs.)
    c) 1 egg from 3–egg clutches (and a second egg from 3–egg clutches in Area V.) (Maximum on average 7.5 eggs.)
    d) 1 chick from 2–egg clutches (and a second egg from 3–egg clutches in Area V.) (Maximum on average 2.4 eggs.)
    e) 1 chick from any broods of 3 except in the southern area.
    f) Broods to be inspected at 7–10 days and younger chick to be rescued if any indications of low weight or related problems. (After allowing for earlier components the maximum on average would be 3.6 chicks, but there is more uncertainty about this than other figures.)
    g) Removing all eggs from nests close to Ravens, if "close" can be defined (Maximum on average 2–4 chicks.)

Additionally, any deserted clutches should be added to the group, but the chances of viable young are low.

Annex 6: Some of the points we made to landowners and their staff, when arranging rearing/release sites, in relation to kite/gamebird interactions

We should make clear that some pheasant mortality from kites may occur. Addressing the main potential problem areas individually:

Release pens – poult predation

The Red Kite is essentially a bird of open habitats and this is where it does most of its feeding. It is unlikely that it would exhibit a swoop response in a woodland release pen and one would not envisage this as a major problem. Avian predation of reared pheasants was the subject of a major study in 1976 which considered Buzzard, Sparrowhawk and Tawny Owl (Lloyd 1976). All three species, in particular the latter two, have a strong association with woodlands and would be expected to account for a much higher percentage than, for instance, a kite. However, despite this, predation by these species only accounts for between 1–3% of pheasant poult deaths in the study (and between 0.7–1.7% if dubious cases are discounted). Sparrowhawks are, of course, far more abundant in the area than kites would ever be expected to be, but the shooting is still good.

We have talked to Dr Peter Robertson, head of the Game Conservancy *Pheasants in Woodlands* project, and he was able to suggest a relatively successful method for deterring even those birds of prey of woodland from large release pens. The most effective technique is to criss-cross strings over the top of the pen, perhaps with (thin metal foil) milk bottle tops threaded on to them. This seems to deter predators at least until poults reach a size when they are seldom killed. Some estates release birds into a small covered pen within the release pen to acclimatize them to their new area and harden them off. As far as avian predation is concerned this has the same effect as keeping them in the rearing pen a little bit longer.

Release pens – disturbance

This was clearly the second major potential issue, it being likely that adult birds and poults over 10 or 11 weeks would be reasonably safe from predation. It might be useful to quote directly from the Lloyd (1976) report mentioned above:

"Many keepers claim that the disturbance caused by birds of prey is more serious than the actual killing of pheasant poults. These complaints fall into three categories.
a) Tawny owls attacking poults at roost causing them to fly to the ground where, if they are outside the pen, they are susceptible to mammalian predators, chiefly foxes. Repeated attacks and even the presence of owls is reported to make poults loath to go up to roost at all, with similar effects.
b) The presence of sparrowhawks and buzzards at a pen or feeding site causing the birds to desert the area and straying over the shoot boundary or going to parts of the shoot where they are not wanted, for instance areas where it is difficult to present them over the guns well.
c) Disturbance by sparrowhawks and buzzards in release pens causing poults to be frightened to come out of cover to feed, resulting in depressed growth and poor condition.

"Disturbance is of course extremely difficult to quantify, but almost all the reports of it were anecdotal, and none were reported to me while the study was in progress, so none were investigated first hand.

"In only one case is quantitative information available on disturbance related to the dispersal of pheasants from a release pen and feed ride. Prior to the visit of a buzzard about 100 pheasants were regularly feeding at a particular site. The buzzard remained around this area for about five days and, although during that time no kills were found, the number of pheasants declined to between 20 and 30. Subsequently some birds returned until there were about 50 birds there. The keeper thus blamed the buzzard for the loss of 50% of his pheasants from this particular wood, which provided one of his best stands. However, this occurred when the poults were about 12 weeks old and would have begun to disperse anyway and many of the 50 missing birds were probably elsewhere on the shoot. So, once again, it is impossible to quantify this effect accurately. My impression from discussion with keepers was that this effect was more marked where a vagrant buzzard appeared outside the normal breeding range, than in areas on the Welsh border or in the south-west where these birds were widespread, as the poults could avoid the presence of a buzzard in the former area by moving, but could not do so in the latter.

"On three occasions I watched a sparrowhawk fly through a release pen and on all these occasions the effect on the poults was minimal. They froze for a moment then continued feeding etc when the bird of prey disappeared. The reaction to the presence of a falconer's buzzard near the pen was similar; the birds were initially alarmed and moved to the far side of the pen, but soon began to feed again though they remained wary. They began to behave normally almost as soon as the bird was removed. On none of these occasions did an attack take place.

"These last observations do not seem consistent with the last of the three categories of disturbance, causing impaired growth rate and loss of condition. In these cases, birds of prey may be a convenient scapegoat when poults do not do well due to disease or unsuitable food."

Effect on adult birds

We should consider this briefly in relation to the effect on breeding birds. If we assume that, from 10–11 weeks onwards, they are relatively safe from predation (according to the experts) we must still be aware of the possibility of disturbance to territorial cocks and adult birds feeding in open ground. Inexperienced young Kites might be tempted to swoop at pheasants larger than they could kill and eat and their presence in the sky as 'predator silhouettes' may provide a further distraction. Again this should not present a major problem but it should be monitored.

When they are released next June, the Kites – which will have been imported from Sweden – will have to spend at least 5 weeks in their cages (under quarantine regulations). By the time they are flying free the danger to poults should, therefore, have passed.

Having consulted the Game Conservancy and the relevant literature, it appears that the following methods are appropriate when dealing with avian predators. If we assume that effective measures are already taken to deter mammalian predators (*e.g.* foxes) changes in release techniques that may help to reduce losses are as follows.

If it is possible to keep poults on the rearing field without feather pecking, they should be released at 7 or, preferably, 8 weeks. If only one release is planned, then it is recommended that older birds be released in August if this does not affect the shooting programme. Release groups should be kept to less than 500 birds where possible, and if poults are released in larger groups their density shall not exceed one bird to half a yard of the release pen perimeter.

Release pens should have at least 20% shrub cover and 60% ground cover of herbs and brambles. It is suggested that attempts are made to modify vegetation in existing pens to achieve this pattern, by clearing trees and coppicing, planting temporary or permanent ground cover where practical, or creating cover with brashings. It is inadvisable to have a release pen sticking out of the edge of a wood unless there is adequate cover in the part outside the wood. If a choice exists, then releases should be made in woods smaller than 50 acres rather than larger woods.

If avian predation starts, deterrents should be tried. Though probably temporary, their effect may be sufficient to protect poults until they are no longer susceptible to predation. Silvered balls, criss-cross tape or the more easily obtained 'Glitterbang' tin-foil bird scarers could be hung around or across the pen, particularly across any obvious line of access such as a ride; moving their positions will probably enhance their effect.

It is quite likely that the keepers already employ some of these practices.

About the author

Mike Pienkowski has been involved in research and conservation for over 50 years. Early work was on waders (shorebirds). As an undergraduate, he organised and led an Iceland Expedition in 1970, and the University of East Anglia (UEA) Expeditions to Morocco 1971 & 1972, to study migration systems and conservation requirements of coastal birds. He was joint organiser, scientific co-ordinator and leader of advance party for Joint Biological Expedition to NE Greenland 1974. He was one of the founders in 1970 of the International Wader Study Group and, as Chairman, coordinated its international conference in Ukraine in 1992, resulting in the Odessa Protocol on international co-operation on migratory flyway research and conservation. He obtained his doctorate at Durham University in 1980 on the ecology and behaviour of plovers, and stayed there as a post-doc, first to research Shelduck behaviour and population dynamics and then to coordinate a European Union study of migration patterns of shorebirds around western Europe.

Mike with his wife, Ann

In 1984, he became Head of Ornithology at the Nature Conservancy Council where, amongst other initiatives including negotiating and managing the contract providing most of the British Trust for Ornithology's funding, he initiated, jointly with others, the Experimental Reintroduction of Red Kites to England and Scotland, chairing the joint NCC/RSPB project team from 1987 to 1995. He became Assistant Chief Scientist of the Nature Conservancy Council 1990–91, and Head of the Implementation Team (1990–1) and first Director of the Joint Nature Conservation Committee (1991–5). In these roles, he also Co-Chaired the international conference on lead-poisoning in wetlands (Brussels 1991), and Chaired UK Government's group to end the use of gunshot lead in wetlands. He served as Senior Editor of the *Journal of Applied Ecology* 1994–9.

After leaving JNCC, he was Head of International Legislation & Funding Department at the Royal Society for the Protection of Birds (1995–1997), then Director of the European Forum on Nature Conservation & Pastoralism (1998–2001), with voluntary roles on the Council of Wetlands International (1988–1998), Vice-President & Council Member of the British Ornithologists' Union (1991–2003), the Programme Committee of WWF-UK (1992–2002), Council of the British Ecological Society (1993–1999), Environment Committee of the Institute of Petroleum (1994–5), Vice-President, Advisory Committee on Agriculture & Environment to Directorate-General Agriculture of the European Commission (1999–2001), Ramsar Advisory Mission for the Ramsar Convention on Wetlands of International Importance (2001–2), reviewer for UK Department of Environment, Food and Rural Affairs of actual and potential Ramsar Wetlands of International Importance in UK Overseas Territories and Crown Dependencies (2004–5), UK Executive Committee of the International Union for the Conservation of Nature (2006–2022), Expert Panel advising the Minister in the UK Department of Culture, Media & Sport on UK's Tentative List of World Heritage Sites (2010–11), External Examiner for the University of Durham (1995–1999), and PhD examiner for universities in UK, Canada and South Africa.

Since 1995, he has donated his time as Chairman of the UK Overseas Territories Conservation Forum, and managed conservation projects across the territories. In this role, he leads the Secretariat of the UK Overseas Territories & Crown Dependencies Environment Ministers' Council.